Anglophone Poetry
in Colonial India,
1780–1913

Anglophone Poetry in Colonial India, 1780–1913

a critical anthology

edited by

Mary Ellis Gibson

OHIO UNIVERSITY PRESS

Athens

Ohio University Press, Athens, Ohio 45701
www.ohioswallow.com
© 2011 by Ohio University Press

To obtain permission to quote, reprint, or otherwise reproduce or distribute material
from Ohio University Press publications, please contact our rights and permissions
department at (740) 593-1154 or (740) 593-4536 (fax).

Printed in the United States of America
Ohio University Press books are printed on acid-free paper ⊚ ™

First paperback printing in 2013
Paperback ISBN 978-0-8214-2078-2

hardcover 18 17 16 15 14 13 12 11   5 4 3 2 1
paperback 20 19 18 17 16 15 14 13   5 4 3 2 1

Library of Congress Cataloging-in-Publication Data

Anglophone poetry in colonial India, 1780–1913 : a critical anthology / edited by Mary
Ellis Gibson.
     p. cm.
Includes bibliographical references and indexes.
ISBN 978-0-8214-1942-7 (hardcover : alk. paper) — ISBN 978-0-8214-4357-6
(electronic)
1. Indic poetry (English) 2. Indic poetry (English)—19th century. 3. Indic poetry
(English)—18th century. 4. India—Poetry. 5. Indic poetry (English)—History and
criticism. I. Gibson, Mary Ellis, 1952–
PR9495.25.A64 2011
821'.914080954—dc22

                          2010053684

For Charlie and Emily Orzech

and for Julia Kimmel

Contents

Acknowledgments

This book has accrued many debts, personal and professional, to friends and family, to scholars whom I know well, and to those whom I scarcely know at all. I want to express here my gratitude to several scholars who are pioneering new ways of understanding English language literature in India. I owe more than I can acknowledge to Priya Joshi, Rimi Chatterjee, Tricia Lootens, Ghulam Murshid, Michael J. Franklin, and especially to Rosinka Chaudhuri, whose wonderful edition of Derozio appeared just as I was revising my work and whose monograph and essays had already guided my thinking.

Without substantial material support at crucial times, I would not have been able to research this book, and for this I am grateful to my home institution, the University of North Carolina, Greensboro, which provided travel funding and research assignments on more than one occasion. I am especially grateful to Anne Wallace, chair of the English Department and fellow scholar of nineteenth-century literature, to Timothy Johnston, dean of the College of Arts and Sciences, and to former provost Edward Uprichard for their willingness to support an extended research assignment. Another form of support, no less important, came from Carole Lindsey-Potter, whose exemplary patience, energy, and creativity allowed me to continue work on this project even during my administrative assignment as director of the Women's and Gender Studies Program.

For the financial assistance that made this research possible, I am grateful to the Fulbright Commission, and for assistance in India, to the wonderful staff at the U.S. Educational Foundation office in Kolkata, including Sunrit Mullick and Shevanti Narayan. They did much to make my stay in Kolkata pleasant and to connect me with scholars in Kolkata and North Bengal.

I received crucial support from the National Endowment for the Humanities, whose research fellowship allowed me to complete this project. At the National Humanities Center, help went well beyond the financial. The John Sawyer Fellowship at the Humanities Center had more impact on this anthology than any other form of assistance I have received, for the Humanities Center provided exactly the kind of cross-disciplinary exchange that fed my thinking—and it fed me in body and spirit as well. The staff of the NHC and its director, Geoffrey Harpham, created an atmosphere of congenial exchange and intellectual excitement. I am grateful to Kent Mullikin for being master of arrangements and raconteur par excellence; to Lois Whittington for providing photocopying, scheduling, and encouragement to enable a year-long seminar; to Pat Shreiber and James Getkin for keeping me fit and wonderfully fed; to Joel Elliott for technical support; to

Marie Brubaker; to Marianne Wason for teaching me to create effective Power-Point presentations; to Sarah Payne for biscuit baking; and to all the staff for much good conversation.

My colleagues at the Humanities Center shaped this work in more ways than I can say. Amelie Rorty, Judith Farquhar, Kate Flint, Roger Gilbert, Alexandra Wettlaufer, John Wilkinson, Terry Smith, and Maud Ellman provided ideas, argument, lunch companionship, and personal encouragement. To the members of the Master Languages and Vernaculars Seminar, I am especially grateful. Nigel Smith and Timothy Kircher provided organizational energy, and they and other members of the seminar—Catherine Chin, Su Fang Ng, Stephen Rupp, Alison Keith, and David Samuels—made wonderful suggestions that profoundly shaped my thinking. A thousand thanks. And finally, I cannot express adequate thanks to Elizabeth Helsinger, a fellow at the Humanities Center but much more to me—both my mentor and my example over many years and at last, for a year, a colleague.

Nor could this book have been made without ongoing assistance from many librarians. The librarians at the National Humanities Center were indispensable to this project: Eliza Robertson provided important ideas and database assistance, Jean Houston provided books of all sorts, and Josiah Drewery managed to find in distant libraries obscure texts in languages he did not read. To the librarians at the University of North Carolina, Greensboro, I am equally grateful—they supplied books from storage and remained patient when the dog ate the ones made with horsehair glue. To Gaylor Callahan, head of interlibrary loan, and to Nancy Fogarty, emerita head of the Reference Department, I owe a major debt. In Kolkata, I am grateful to M. Mukherjee of reader services at the National Library, who saved me from despair. I am also grateful to Fr. Dr. Felix Raj, director of the Goethals Library, St. Xavier's College, Kolkata, and to the staff of the library, especially former head of staff Warren Brown, who provided kind assistance and searched the collection in aid of my project. Similarly, the staff of the Carey Library, Serampore, allowed me access to their valuable collection of English language books and pamphlets. The staff of the Asian and African Studies Reading Room of the British Library were unfailingly helpful; to all of them I am grateful, as I am to special collections librarians at Harvard University, the University of Virginia, the University of Delaware, the University of North Carolina, and Duke University.

For research assistance, I thank Thera Webb, fine poet and patient bibliographer; Hao Nguyen; and especially Julia Kimmel, who rescued me. To Charles Orzech, who can find anything on the Web, I am very grateful; in Kolkata, I am especially thankful for Hena Basu of Basu Research and Documentation Services, who provided me with invaluable aid of all sorts.

I also thank my colleagues in Kolkata, especially Jharna Sanyal, who made my affiliation with Calcutta University particularly delightful. I thank as well Geraldine Forbes, colleague extraordinaire, and I remember, with sadness and gratitude, the late Lucinda Peach, my Fulbright companion in 2004. To Mousumi Mukherjee, I owe what I know of Bangla and how to direct a cab driver in Kolkata; I am vastly appreciative of her help in myriad ways during my stay in Kolkata, for her ongoing encouragement, and for the hospitality of her family.

This book began with suggestions from Paul Courtright of Emory University, who got me started and lately shared my enthusiasm for the satires of William Combe. I owe many thanks to Tony Stewart, who encouraged me, provided advice about matters obscure and diacritical, and shared his friends in Kolkata. And to our mutual friends in Kolkata—Ajoy and Trina Roy and the late Anna Roy; Rukshana and Nasheed Moiz, and the late Jaweed—I owe many happy hours, much laughter, and delicious jazz and biryani.

Nancy Basmajian at Ohio University Press has provided ongoing support and unfailing attention to detail. To her and to copyeditor Sally Bennett, I am most grateful.

Finally, I thank Sanjukta Dasgupta, professor of English and now Dean of Humanities at Calcutta University. She argued with me about mother tongues, took me to poetry readings, fed me, and encouraged me. The best of landladies, the best of colleagues, the best of friends. To her and to Anjan Dasgupta I am most grateful.

To my husband, Charles Orzech—fine historian and theorist, enthusiastic and patient traveling companion, and general encourager—and to my daughter, Emily Orzech, I owe so much. They have tolerated my obsessions, supported my work, and put up with file boxes piled on many square feet of floor space. Their encouragement, suggestions, and laughter cheered the way. To Pauline Orzech, Ed Gibson, Pam Bruce, and David and Jacqueline Hagler, I owe many thanks—for their patience, understanding, and encouragement.

And for the greatest patience of all, I am deeply grateful to David Sanders of Ohio University Press, most understanding editor—who maintained his own sense of humor, so that I could survive with mine.

A Note on Names

Aside from the acknowledgments and mentions of contemporary cities where I follow current usage, I have followed the nineteenth-century convention in naming Indian cities. Thus, instead of Kolkata, Mumbai, and Chennai, I refer—as the poets I discuss do—to Calcutta, Bombay, and Madras, respectively.

In referring to persons with Indian names, I follow the conventions of Anglicization that they adopted, so rather than Torulata Datta or Rabindranath Thakur, I use Toru Dutt and Rabindranath Tagore. Similarly, though Ghosh (Kasiprasad Ghosh) can be transliterated as Ghose, I follow the writer's own practice. A more complex case is Michael Madhusudan Datta, who at the end of his life preferred Datta to Dutt. His translator Clinton Seely follows his wishes and always transliterates his name as Datta; because I am discussing primarily his early English work, published under the name Dutt, I use the poet's earlier transliteration.

Many writers in Bengal share surnames—for example, Toru, Aru, Girish (Greece) Chunder, and Michael Madhusudan Dutt—and it is conventional to refer to them by given name as well as surname. I follow this practice for writers with Indian names. When discussing writers with European names, however, I follow the common scholarly practice of referring to them by surname. For example, I generally speak of Toru when referring to Toru Dutt but to Carshore when speaking of Mary Seyers Carshore.

A second issue of transliteration—the use of diacritics—arises with respect to words from Indian languages. When I quote texts directly, I always reproduce diacritics, if any, as given in the text. When I refer to terms now commonly used as English words, I follow common English practice, omitting the diacritics.

Abbreviations

Hobson-Jobson   *Hobson-Jobson: A Glossary of Colloquial Anglo-Indian Words and Phrases, and of Kindred Terms, Etymological, Historical, Geographical and Discursive,* Henry Yule, A. C. Burnell, and William Crooke (Delhi: Munshiram Manoharlal, 1968). A virtually identical edition of *Hobson-Jobson* may be accessed through Digital Dictionaries of South Asia at http://dsal.uchicago.edu/dictionaries/hobsonjobson.

ODNB   *Oxford Dictionary of National Biography,* ed. H. C. G. Matthew and Brian Harrison (Oxford: Oxford University Press, 2004); on-line edition, ed. Lawrence Goldman, May 2006. http://www.oxforddnb.com/view/article. Reference is made through this link to the current online edition of the *ODNB,* to the archived original print edition of the *ODNB,* and to individually revised entries. Authors and titles of articles are specified in the sources, as are references to the archived print edition.

Anglophone Poetry
in Colonial India,
1780–1913

Introduction

IN 1799, a British officer took it upon himself to catalog and celebrate "the most distinguished men of the Asiatic Society" of Calcutta. The society, then just fifteen years old, had already changed the landscape of European literature, giving impetus to a new kind of orientalism in British poetry. British verse, imbued with orientalist tropes and themes, in its turn was shaping English language poetry written in India. At the beginning of this complex formation of literary culture, that same English officer—one John Horsford, former fellow of St. Johns, Oxford—commemorated Sir William Jones, the founder of the Asiatic Society. Jones, Horsford wrote, had been commissioned by Britannia herself to explore the "mystic mines of Asiatic Lore."[1]

Horsford's panegyric captured an important moment in the creation of English language letters, for Jones's excursions into "Asiatic Lore" brought Europeans and North Americans access to Persian and Sanskrit verse. Jones's translations influenced the English romantic poets and inspired Goethe and Schiller, Emerson and Thoreau. In the decades following Jones's death in 1794, poets born in India, in turn, made poems shaped by Persian, Sanskrit, and vernacular poetry as well as by the poetic practices of British romanticism. Over the course of the nineteenth century, the range of English language poetic production in India widened, drawing poets from varied backgrounds and moving into realms domestic, religious, and political.

Anglophone Poetry in Colonial India, 1780–1913 traces these arcs of cultural exchange from the beginnings of English language literature in India through the long nineteenth century. It begins with Jones, along with various members of his circle, and concludes with poems written in the early twentieth century, taking as its end point Rabindranath Tagore's Nobel Prize in Literature. The trajectory of these poems moves from Indian and British romanticism to the poetry of the fin de siècle and early modernism, yet these poems complicate traditional narratives of literary history. The poets whose works are presented here engaged in intricate networks of affiliation and disaffiliation, and their poems challenge simple periodization and nationalist narratives.

---

1. John Horsford, *Poems in Three Parts* (Calcutta: Thomas Hollingbery, Hircarrah Press, 1800), 51.

Nationalist parameters have, to date, shaped most attempts to collect English language writing in India. With the exception of Elleke Boehmer's wide-ranging collection, *Empire Writing* (1870–1918), which is global in scope, English language poetry written by British poets has languished, the last collection of any note being T. O. D. Dunn's *Poets of John Company* (1921). Dunn treated Indian poets separately from British ones, also assembling a useful collection (though biased entirely toward Bengal, as the title suggests) in *The Bengali Book of English Verse*. In the many years since Dunn's work, British and North American scholars have tended to ignore most English language poetry in India, focusing instead on prose fiction and nonfiction.

Indian scholars, for their part, have until recently focused only on those poets who can be claimed for an Indian nationalist canon. Since about 1920, anthologies of Indian English language poets have omitted all British- and American-born poets.[2] In India, Indian English language poetry has typically been understood to begin with Henry Louis Vivian Derozio, unfolding in a genealogical continuum from his verse to the modernist experiments of the Calcutta Writers' Workshop and beyond.

But literary exchange is never simply a respecter of persons or political boundaries. Derozio's life attests to the complexity of genealogical narratives—both familial and literary—for his mother was born in Hampshire and his father came from Portuguese and Indian ancestors. Derozio's literary antecedents, colleagues, and successors were similarly various.[3] Building the premise of a shared literary culture, in this anthology I bring together a full selection of the poets who were writing in English in colonial India in the long nineteenth century.

Instead of assembling the poetic canon along nationalist lines, I work here to reconstruct the conversations among poets that constituted early Indian English language literature. At the same time, I bring back to visibility poets whose work has long been ignored—poets such as Mary Carshore and Mary Leslie, who were born and died in India, and Henry Page, a radical Baptist of obscure origin, who identified himself as a friend of Derozio's and an Indian patriot. Their texts, along with those of better-known poets such as Rabindranath Tagore and Aurobindo Ghose, are organized chronologically by authors' dates of birth.

The first generation of poets presented here was born in Britain. With the exception of the anonymous Anna Maria, they were men who went to India in

---

2. Such anthologies include, most notably, Eunice De Souza, *Early Indian Poetry in English: An Anthology, 1829–1947* (New Delhi: Oxford University Press, 2005); and Vinayak Krishna Gokak, *The Golden Treasury of Indo-Anglian Poetry, 1828–1965* (New Delhi: Sahitya Akademi, 1970). T. O. D. Dunn's collections include *The Bengali Book of English Verse* (Calcutta: Longmans, Green, 1918) and *Poets of John Company* (Calcutta: Thacker, 1921). See also A. N. Diwedi, *Indian Poetry in English: A Literary History and Anthology* (Atlantic Highlands, NJ: Humanities Press, 1980); and V. N. Bhushan, *The Peacock Lute* (Bombay: Padma Publications, 1945).

3. I have relied here and elsewhere on Rosinka Chaudhuri's pioneering work: *Derozio, Poet of India: The Definitive Edition* (New Delhi: Oxford University Press, 2008) and *Gentlemen Poets of Colonial Bengal* (Calcutta: Seagull, 2002).

the late eighteenth century to make their fortunes. The first English language poets born in India, Kasiprasad Ghosh and Derozio, were a generation younger, but they, like their British-born counterparts, participated in a complex web of influence and acknowledgment. Kasiprasad Ghosh, for example, dedicated verses to the British civil servant and orientalist Horace Hayman Wilson, while the anonymous American poet E.L. dedicated poems to Kasiprasad. Henry Derozio acknowledged Wilson along with the poet and civil servant Henry Meredith Parker. In turn, Emma Roberts, the first woman journalist in India, dedicated her volume of verse, published in Calcutta in 1830, to Derozio, many of whose political views she shared. Derozio called himself "East Indian," and his defense of India was acknowledged and echoed two decades later by another Indian-born poet, Henry Page. The biographical sketches through which I introduce these poets trace the contours of their exchanges with each other, with British poets whose work they read, and with classical and vernacular Indian and European literatures.

A detailed exploration of the social, political, and material contexts of English language poetry in India is provided in the monograph that accompanies this volume, *Indian Angles: English Verse in Colonial India from Jones to Tagore*. Here I wish, in brief compass, to place English language poets' intellectual and personal exchanges in their historical contexts. I focus first on the sociolinguistic context for reading and writing, providing an overview of the cosmopolitan and polyglot culture that gave rise to English language verse. I then sketch the changes in the circumstances of publishing and reading over the long nineteenth century, as they were shaped by the rise of print culture, by shifts in publishing practices, and by political events. In focusing on the poems, I supply the reader new to these poems a survey of the dominant tropes and important modes of English language poetry in India in this period—from the satire to devotional verse, from the tropes of bardic nationalism to the reiterated discourses of exile. Finally, I lay out the editorial principles that shaped the selection and presentation of these English language poems, poems that emerged from the overlapping contact zones of multiple languages.

English Language Poetry in a Polyglot Culture

Many American and British readers of poetry are now being educated in a monolingual way—though this limitation is being challenged on many fronts. Education in Britain and India in the long nineteenth century, by contrast, made much higher linguistic demands on its students. Educated men in Britain and India were expected to have facility in more than one classical and modern language. Moreover, in India, even ordinary men and women, though they had limited access to education and literacy, learned (at least in urban centers) to operate in a multilingual context. The polyglot environment of urban India in the long nineteenth century proved fertile ground for a new kind of poetry.

Though for brevity's sake the title of this anthology relies on the word *Anglophone* to establish its linguistic contours, my preference is to speak of the verse included here as *English language poetry*. This awkward phrase makes space for the wide variety of speakers and readers and for the extraordinary variety of dialects and social locations that formed the cultural ground in India for English language writing. The phrase *English language poetry* evades the postcolonial ambiance and monolingual implications often attaching to the word *Anglophone*, even as it points to the variety of poets who made verse in English.

Poets writing English in India emerged in a thoroughly multilingual space. English itself comprised multiple regional and class dialects, and these dialects were in turn situated in a context of multiple vernacular Indian languages and dialects. Writers such as Michael Madhusudan Dutt and Sarojini Naidu were multilingual and, with respect to language preference, were actively bilingual or trilingual, code shifting and moving between or among languages at will. For instance, Michael Madhusudan and his best friend Gour Bysack no doubt spoke Bangla (often anglicized as Bengali) with many members of their families, especially the women, but their letters to each other were written in English. From these letters, one can readily imagine that their spoken language shifted from Bangla to English to Bangla at will. Sarojini Naidu, to take a second example, was something of a linguistic prodigy, early on learning Persian to a high level and becoming fluent in Urdu, among other languages. Although she became a nationalist leader and eventually president of the Congress Party, Sarojini nonetheless insisted that her children write to her in English. Even for Rabindranath Tagore, who wrote primarily in Bangla and staunchly defended writing in Bangla on nationalist and aesthetic terms, English served more than a utilitarian purpose. Though as a boy he famously resisted English lessons, Tagore also spoke enthusiastically in his letters and essays of transcreating his Bengali poems into English. He wrote to his niece about his famous English language volume *Gitanjali*, "I simply felt an urge to recapture, through the medium of another language, the feelings and sentiments which had created such a feast of joy within me in past days." Evoking the traditional language of inspiration, elsewhere he declared, "I was possessed by the pleasure of receiving anew my feelings as expressed in a foreign tongue. I was making fresh acquaintance with my own heart by dressing it in other clothes."[4] Tagore and other poets—including Derozio, Manmohan Ghose, and Sarojini Naidu (who read Persian and spoke Urdu, Tamil, Telugu, Bangla, and English)—could scarcely be said to have experienced English as more foreign than other languages. Though Tagore refers to English as a foreign language in the essay quoted here, the very notion of the "mother" tongue underlying this characterization of English-as-foreign was by the end of the nineteenth century ideologically fraught. Finding your mother can be com-

---

4. The first statement, in a letter by Rabindranath to his niece Indira Devi, is quoted by Sisir Kumar Das in his preface to *The English Writings of Rabindranath Tagore* (New Delhi: Sahitya Akademi, 1994), 1:10; the second is quoted by M. K. Naik in *Perspectives on Indian Poetry in English* (New Delhi: Abhinav Publications, 1984), 59–60.

plicated if, like Kipling, you learned to speak in India or if, like Manmohan Ghose and his brother Aurobindo, you spent your childhood and young manhood in England. In many cases, code switching occurred in both oral and written language, and poets operated in a variety of languages, dialects, and registers of dialects, which impinged directly or indirectly on their verse.

Although few people on the subcontinent were even literate, those who did write English language poetry operated among multiple classical languages (Persian, Arabic, Greek, Latin, and sometimes Hebrew) and vernaculars (Hindustani [as it was formerly known, now divided into Hindi and Urdu] and Bangla principally, though also in South Indian and European languages [especially French and Italian and sometimes German]). Literary creation emerged from a shifting array of literacies and from shifting dynamics of the classical and the vernacular. English language *poetry* in particular could be understood as a kind of cosmopolitan polyglossia, for poetry is, of all genres, the most dependent on allusion and various forms of intertextual citation. This poetic polyglossia emerged from a complex sociolinguistic scene.

In the long nineteenth century, English in India was a minority language—as it still is—and a high level of literacy in any language was reserved almost entirely for elite European women and for elite men. But the spoken word was rich with mingled languages and dialects, especially in the larger cities, where one might also find access to printing. Calcutta, for example, in the late 1830s was home to a rich mix of people speaking Bangla, Hindustani (Hindi/Urdu), Chinese, French, Portuguese, Arabic, Persian, Burmese, Armenian, and Tamil, in addition to languages spoken by Parsis and Jews or read by those classically trained in Sanskrit, Persian, Hebrew, Greek, or Latin.[5] Spoken language was further enriched—and complicated—by local dialects of many of these languages.

To further complicate the scene, the poets collected here spoke various dialects of English—with Scottish and Irish variations being the most prominent vectors of differentiation. We can presume that Mary Carshore spoke some version of an Irish dialect, a dialect no doubt modulated by her birth in India and the language she learned from her Indian nursemaid, while Honoria Lawrence's speech would have been inflected more thoroughly by her upbringing in Ireland. Both of these poets wrote in a version of the received or standard educated English of their time, but it is useful to remember that their ear would have been attuned differently from those poets born in London or in Scotland. The dominant nonstandard dialect of English in Calcutta—aside from the working-class

---

5. See Tithi Bhattacharya, *The Sentinels of Culture: Class, Education, and the Colonial Intellectual in Bengal, 1848–85* (New Delhi: Oxford University Press, 2005) and especially Bhattacharya, "A World of Learning: The Material Culture of Education and Class in Nineteenth-century Bengal" in *Beyond Representation,* ed. Crispin Bates (New Delhi: Oxford University Press, 2006), 177–209. See also S. N. Mukherjee, "Class, Caste and Politics, 1814–38," in *Elites in South Asia,* ed. Edmund Leach and S. N. Mukherjee (Cambridge: Cambridge University Press, 1975), 33–78.

dialects and regional dialects of common soldiers—would have been a variety of lowland Scots. John Leyden, for example, wrote poetry in English, but his speech was another matter. He protested to his mentor—another Scotsman, John Malcolm—that learning English had "spoilt [his] Scotch." However many odes he might compose in Oxbridge English, Leyden considered his speech—his Borders "Scotch"—too precious to lose.[6] Leyden was by no means alone in cultivating his Scots. One need only imagine the conversation at the monthly meetings of the St. Andrews Society, a refuge in Calcutta for educated Scotsmen like Leyden. Given the superior nature of technical and scientific education in Scotland and the broad literacy among men educated in local schools, Scots medical men, divines, and schoolmasters exercised a disproportionate influence on institutions of publishing and English-medium education in India. Their Indian students could not but be exposed alike to the poetry of Robert Burns and to the Scottish burr.

Poets going from Great Britain to India in the late eighteenth and nineteenth centuries entered an already lively field of literary production, one in which poets negotiated the shifting domains of orality and print. Before the advent of print technology in eighteenth-century India, multiple rich poetic traditions were created through manuscript transmission and oral performance. In what C. A. Bayly calls the Indian ecumene—roughly, northern India in the ambit of Hindustani (Hindi/Urdu)—a vibrant literary culture relied on a variety of means of transmission, both oral and written; it depended upon what Bayly calls "linguistic plurality running through the whole society."[7] Bayly, Anindita Ghosh, and Robert Darnton, along with Graham Shaw, have provided a detailed picture of this linguistic plurality, describing a complex array of written texts, oral performances of written texts, and oral texts—many of them poetic texts.[8]

Educated elites in colonial India were multilingual and had been so well before the arrival of the British. For literate male elites, as Ruth Vanita has argued, English was simply added to the languages that "the educated were required to know, but not displacing Persian, Sanskrit or the modern Indian languages."[9]

6. John Malcolm, "To the Editor of the Bombay Courier," quoted in "Supplementary Memoir," which prefaces John Leyden, *Poems and Ballads*, ed. Walter Scott (Kelso, Scotland: J. and J. H. Rutherford, 1858), xli.

7. C. A. Bayly, "The Indian Ecumene," in *The Book History Reader*, ed. David Finkelstein and Alistair McCleery (London: Routledge, 2002), 174–88; quotation from 175.

8. See Robert Darnton, "Literary Surveillance in the British Raj: The Contradictions of Liberal Imperialism," *Book History* 2 (2005): 133–76; Anindita Ghosh, "Identities Made in Print: Literary Bengali and Its 'Others,' c. 1800–1905," in *Beyond Representation*, ed. Crispin Bates (New Delhi: Oxford University Press, 2006), 210–31; Anindita Ghosh, "An Uncertain Coming of the Book: Early Print Cultures in Colonial India," *Book History* 6 (2003): 23–55; *Power in Print: Popular Publishing and the Politics of Language and Culture in a Colonial Society, 1778–1905* (New Delhi: Oxford University Press, 2006); Graham Shaw, "Printing at Mangalore and Tellicherry by the Basel Mission," *Libri* 27 (June 1977): 154–64, and Graham Shaw, *Printing in Calcutta to 1800: A Description and Checklist of Printing in Late 18th-Century Calcutta* (London: Bibliographical Society, 1976).

9. Ruth Vanita, "Gandhi's Tiger: Multilingual Elites, the Battle for Minds, and English Romantic Literature in Colonial India," *Postcolonial Studies* 5 (2002): 95–110: quotation from 97.

For male elites, Vanita argues, "oral translation was part of everyday life in cities such as Delhi, Lucknow, Hyderabad, [and] Varanasi, with cosmopolitan, polyglot cultures, and there were also sophisticated written traditions of translation between various Indian languages in pre-colonial India" (98).

At the same time, poetic traditions went well beyond the elite, as did polyglot cultures, as Bayly has argued in detail. His examples show how "the learned reached down to incorporate these more localized language cultures in order to broaden cultural community" (176). Literary biography, aristocratic and personal libraries or book houses large and small, and a variety of forms of oral and written communication, Bayly argues, made for a rapid transmission of news and information. Poetry remained a central genre of both elite and popular cultures.

With the coming of print technology in the late eighteenth century—largely the work of European missionaries—the transmission of news and poetry took additional forms. Anindita Ghosh describes, for example, the expansion of the book market in mid-nineteenth-century Bengal. Beginning with missionary type founders in the eighteenth century, print culture by the middle of the nineteenth century had expanded enormously—although the rapid growth of print culture did not simply displace oral traditions, which continued to thrive. Literacy expanded rapidly (though for women, as always, later than for men). Though literacy never reached a majority of people in the eighteenth or indeed in the nineteenth century, those who did read, as in Britain in similar circumstances, expanded the reach of print culture by reading to others. Ghosh argues that the "rapid spread of literacy and the availability of cheap print technology bred enormous popular markets for ephemeral genres that encapsulated the desires of a reading public still geared to preprint tastes" ("Uncertain Coming," 25). Elites in Bengal—Vanita's focus—lamented the state of Bengali literate culture in much the same way that their British counterparts might have done, but they participated by the middle of the century in an explosion of vernacular print. Meanwhile, European missionary literature in vernacular languages was also produced apace; the Serampore Press in the first third of the century produced almost a quarter of a million books in forty languages ("Uncertain Coming," 27).

In entering this multilingual space, poets choosing to write in English had widely different access to language depending on their place of birth, the languages spoken by their parents, and their education, religion, gender, and social class or caste. Religion, class, and gender were crucial markers of access to literacy, to belletristic writing, and to participation in constructions of nation and nationalism. Access to education, and hence to literacy and languages, varied widely. For example, Mary Eliza Leslie (daughter and granddaughter of missionaries) managed to acquire Greek, Italian, and German. Given her active work in Indian girls' education, we can deduce that she probably also spoke and wrote Bangla and perhaps Hindustani (Hindi/Urdu). Leslie's contemporary Mary Carshore was less fortunate in her education and seems to have acquired only some spoken Hindustani but no classical languages and perhaps no written Indian language. In contrast to Carshore's limited education, William Jones, John Leyden, Horace Hayman Wilson, Michael Madhusudan Dutt, Toru Dutt, and Sarojini Naidu all attained facility in a variety of modern and classical languages—with Jones, Leyden, Wilson, and Naidu, like Manmohan Ghose, becoming accomplished linguists.

From one point of view, English language poetry in India was only the preoccupation of a small set of British and Indian elites, mere froth on the waters of the Ganges as it flowed into the Bay of Bengal. English speakers in India—whether they were from Britain or were educated in English on the subcontinent—were generally intent on professional and pecuniary advancement. In India, as elsewhere, poetry was seldom a successful commercial enterprise. By the middle of the nineteenth century, moreover, there was a lively debate about the legitimacy of writing English poetry rather than poetry in Indian vernaculars. Yet in the same period, English (along with Hindi) came to serve as a lingua franca of political, commercial, and intellectual elites, and poets from a variety of social locations composed lyric and narrative verse and published their work by subscription, in newspapers, in literary annuals, and in volumes printed both in India and in London. In the first half of the period, poetry was by far the most important genre of English language belletristic writing, and it formed a common, if not always harmonious, bond among writers from varied backgrounds.

Print, Reading, and the Politics of Poetry

The long nineteenth century, as I have been calling it here, can for the purposes of thinking about poetry be roughly divided into the period between the 1780s and about 1835; the midcentury; and finally the period from the 1880s to 1913. While some things remain constant over this long period—a polyglot culture, for example—many historians have noted cultural, political, and material shifts that influenced literature written in English and in Indian vernaculars. Poetry, however, remained an important genre (in fact, the central belletristic genre) on the subcontinent. Although, as Priya Joshi has shown, fiction gradually came to dominate the English-reading market, poetry remained central in English-language school curricula and was by numbers of volumes produced extremely important in the growing market for vernacular literature as well as in persisting oral literary cultures.[10] Between 1780 and the midcentury, poetry was not only the most prestigious but also the dominant English language genre, as measured by texts printed in India. It remained crucial in book imports as well.

As I have shown in detail in *Indian Angles: English Verse in Colonial India from Jones to Tagore*, poetry maintained an important place in Indian publishing and in imported books, in private libraries, and in new lending libraries both private and

---

10. Priya Joshi, *In Another Country: Colonialism, Culture, and the English Novel in India* (New York: Columbia University Press, 2002).

public that were established in the three presidencies—Calcutta, Madras, and Bombay.[11] Reformers also encouraged the British military to substitute reading for drunkenness and supported the establishment of regimental libraries and book clubs, which ordered books from urban booksellers.[12] In the period when the press was largely uncensored, a variety of English language newspapers flourished, publishing locally written poetry along with reviews and poems reprinted from British periodicals. Even as control of the press by the East India Company tightened and even as writers lamented the small size of the English-speaking audience, a surprisingly large number of periodicals continued to appear. The English press in the early part of this period exhibited a much wider variety of opinion than is commonly recognized, with radical and republican sentiment vying with East India Company politics and commerce. Early collections of poetry emphasized orientalist learning, while newspaper verse consisted of occasional verse, translation, and traditional lyric topics given a global turn.

An examination of the Indian press in the period 1780–1820 also reveals a remarkable ability on the part of its editors to remain au courant with the London literary scene; particularly powerful British influences were Burns, Moore, Byron, Keats, and L.E.L. (Letitia Landon), while Wordsworth, Coleridge, Southey, and Charlotte Smith were acknowledged but less frequently praised. Discussion of contemporary British poetry (a good bit of it orientalist in nature) mingled with discussion and translations of the Persian poets Ḥāfiz, Firdausī, and Saʿdī and with translations from Sanskrit texts (not to mention the occasional translations from modern European languages). Political dissent, religious skepticism, and intense interest in commerce were hallmarks of the literary scene, along with the more unexceptionable patriotic and sentimental emotions. Orientalist learning made its way into the periodical press, well beyond the publications of the Asiatic Society, through translations and brief essays. At the beginnings of English education for the colonized and of orientalist education for the colonizers, literary discourse in English was marked by a vigorous dialogue touching on politics, religion, and the relative merits of British writers.

With the coming of missionaries after the renewal of the East India Company's charter in 1813, the press began to take on a somewhat different tone. English belletristic writing owed much to William Carey's Serampore Press (established in 1800) and later to the Baptist Mission Press in Calcutta. The Baptist Mission Press published a wide array of texts, many of them having little explicit Christian content, for it served as one of the principal printing establishments in English and in Bangla (not to mention its work and that of the Serampore Press in designing and casting type for translations of the Bible into numerous South Asian languages).

---

11. The three principal administrative centers of British India.

12. For details, see Gibson, *Indian Angles: English Verse in India from Jones to Tagore* (Athens: Ohio University Press, 2011), chapter 3.

The period from about 1820 through the 1840s was marked, as many scholars have noted, by the entry into the field of English publishing by Indian and East Indian (sometimes called "Eurasian") poets, including notably Kasiprasad Ghose and H. L. V. Derozio. The continuing work of Scottish and English poets in India and the new contributions of Indian poets arose with the further development of institutions and informal networks that fostered literary sociality. By the 1830s, the literary annual (in imitation of the London literary annuals that combined engravings and poetry) had become popular. To this day, English language newspapers in Kolkata print a substantial annual literary supplement.

By the 1850s, printing had spread beyond Bengal. And in Bengal itself, print had exceeded the purview of missionaries and the British government. Hence, despite Sir Charles Metcalfe's lifting of censorship in Bengal in 1835, the authorities soon reverted to surveillance and control of the press. In 1857, the Reverend James Long was charged with surveying vernacular Bangla publications, with the result that, for Bengal, unlike the rest of British India at this period, we have a fairly accurate sense of literary production. Long recorded 571,670 books printed for sale in Calcutta in 1857—a significant increase over the number in 1853 (Ghosh, "Uncertain Coming," 28). Vernacular publications and smaller numbers of English language publications vied for the public's attention, literary genres being outnumbered by schoolbooks, almanacs, and tracts. Nonetheless, poetry from the first had an important place in the vernacular press. With respect to the English press, from the beginning of the century through at least midcentury, poetry was the predominant literary genre in periodicals and English language books published on the subcontinent.

Between about 1840 and 1870, English language poetry was marked by a diversity of perspectives and the rise of other centers of publishing, particularly Bombay and Madras. The number of volumes written by Indian men, educated British women, and British working-class men rose significantly, and this growth in publishing was more than matched by an outpouring of print in the vernacular languages.[13] Poems reflecting the perspectives of the ordinary soldier appeared and, along with various satirical volumes throughout the century, gave rise later in the century to Kipling's satirical and demotic verse.

In this period, political developments also had an immediate and palpable impact on poets, especially the Afghan campaigns of the 1840s and the revolt of 1857. English language poetry in India always included a considerable amount of topical political poetry, particularly satire, but political stresses at midcentury either were elided in favor of sentiment or led to verse meditation on political events. In 1842, for example, Honoria Lawrence wrote multiple drafts of an elegy for her brother, who had been sent to India in her care—he had proven a difficult

---

13. For details, see Ghosh, "An Uncertain 'Coming of the Book.'"

young man but was found a commission in the army. After his death at the disastrous end of the first Afghan campaign, Lawrence drafted, but did not publish, a poem in which she attempted to come to terms with his loss. At about the same time, T. W. Smyth, who had come to India as an assistant to the Church Missionary Society, wrote a diatribe titled "On the Late Assassination of the Queen" after Victoria escaped two attempts on her life in 1842. Smyth compared his sovereign to a worm, declaring that she should grovel for her political and religious sins before the throne of God. Happily, he argued, God had spared the queen so that she might amend her ways. According to Smyth, the Afghan disaster, like the failed assassination attempts, was a warning:

> See India groaning under countless ills,
>   Cathay well drug'd with opium and with blood,
> The heathen martyr'd, while the Christian kills,
>   With war and havoc roaring in a flood;
> Oh! sin out-sinning persecution's sin!
>   The brand of double infamy burnt in!
>
> Look on Cabool!—and in Victoria's reign?—
>   Shall this be told posterity, ev'n this?
> Oh sov'reign sacred! lov'd and honor'd Queen!
>   Be not thy name a mark for history's hiss!—
> Think too, what He might think—thy Maker!—King!
> Before whom summon'd, what art thou?
>   —a thing
>
> Of dust,—a worm, a something, nothing now,
>   Then, less than nothingness—a shadow flown—
> A phantom pale with her undiadem'd brow
>   Thy breath a bubble; and thy glory gone—
> Thy scepter broken—shot to dust thy throne
>   Thy stewardship demanded now and done![14]

A less apocalyptic view than Smyth's pervaded Mary Leslie's conflicted sonnet sequence on the revolt of 1857. Born and reared in India, with neither prospect nor evident intention of leaving, Leslie was torn by the sensational reports of violence during the revolt (known as the Mutiny or the Sepoy Rebellion). Her long sonnet sequence printed in *Sorrows, Aspirations and Legends from India* reveals her conflicted response to the violence. On the one hand, she surprises herself by

---

14. T. W. Smyth, *Ella, or A Tale of the Waldensian Martyrs, and Other Poems* (Calcutta: W. Thacker, 1843), 153.

praying for divine vengeance on the rebels, and on the other she concludes that the rebellion marks a sorrowful centenary of empire, ending in "deep griefs" (see Leslie in this volume).

The decades after 1857 Rosinka Chaudhuri has characterized—at least for Bengali elite poets—as the "loyal hours." Taking the phrase from the title of a collection edited by Greece Chunder Dutt on the visit of the Prince of Wales to India, Chaudhuri argues that the decades after the rebellion of 1857 saw both a renaissance in vernacular publishing, especially in Bengal, and the efforts of Indian poets writing in English to accommodate their verse to their professional positions, which often depended on the British bureaucracy directly or indirectly (*Gentlemen Poets*). Govin Chunder Dutt, for example, praised Charles, Lord Canning (then governor-general), for his conduct during the rebellion of 1857; reflecting a Bengali distrust of the rebellion, Govin Chunder also defended Canning for his refusal to exact summary vengeance on the mutineers—a refusal that had earned the governor-general the nickname "Clemency Canning" among the most bloody-minded Britishers. Thus, Govin both opposed British jingoist hysteria and accommodated British lawful authority (see Govin Dutt, "To Lord Canning," in this volume).

Even as it was articulated, Govin Chunder's temporizing seemed ineffectual or old-fashioned to those among his peers whom we might call protonationalist. One could say that Govin Chunder's edited volume, *The Dutt Family Album* (1870), was bookended on one side by Michael Madhusudan Dutt's protonationalism and on the other by the more overtly nationalist poetry of Sarojini Naidu and Aurobindo Ghose, along with the subtle lyrics of Govin's daughter Toru. At mid-century, Michael Madhusudan Dutt had turned from English poetry to writing a highly stylized (even deliberately Miltonic) Bangla. He had begun the 1840s by sighing "for Albion's distant shore." But his conventional—though fascinating—volume *The Captive Ladie* earned him little praise; it brought instead a reprimand from the Calcutta educationist John Drinkwater Bethune, who urged Michael Madhusudan to write in Bangla. Bethune opined, in the double-edged way characteristic of midcentury, that Bengal wanted its own poet: "[W]hat we lack is a Byron or a Shelley in Bengali literature."[15] Michael's turn to writing in Bangla anticipated the nationalist politics of language in the late nineteenth century, which suggested that to adopt literary English was in some measure to adulterate the nationalist cause. Govin Chunder Dutt's and Greece Chunder Dutt's work seemed, by the end of the century, to have missed the main current of the time—the nationalist current.

After the generation of the elder Dutts, many Indian poets writing in English searched for ways to identify with or to imagine a nation, even if they did not

---

15. Bethune's advice is quoted in Clinton B. Seely, introduction to Michael Madhusudan Dutt, *The Slaying of Meghanada: A Ramayana from Colonial Bengal*, trans. Seely (New York: Oxford University Press, 2004), 26–27. Michael Madhusudan Dutt was no relation to Govin Chunder Dutt's family.

turn to the vernacular. We can see a subtle version of such nationalism in Toru Dutt's English language poems. Toru's poems implied their nationalist themes, extolling the lotus, for example, over the conventional flowers of English poetry. By the time Sarojini Naidu came to publish her first volume in 1905, her fin-de-siècle musings were accompanied by explicitly nationalist verse. And though his poems of 1905 are flavored with the British fin de siècle, Aurobindo Ghose likewise struck an implicitly political note, writing several poems on Irish subjects that relied on comparisons between Ireland and India. Aurobindo turned from the "Hellenic" muses to the Indian goddess of poetry and learning, Sarasvatī, thus cementing his nationalist loyalties, but he clearly bid a reluctant (and temporary) farewell to the classical European languages he so loved. Although these turn-of-the-century volumes of verse have their own linguistic and political timbre, they emerged from a literary marketplace in which the dissemination of poetry took place mostly through residual forms.

The middle of the nineteenth century had seen a greater diversity of voices entering the literary dialogue and a shift in the forms of literary sociality and literary markets. In the eighteenth century and early nineteenth century (and later in India than in Britain), poetry was often published by subscription. Through references in periodicals, dedications of volumes, and subscription lists, we can trace for the earlier periods complex networks of education and employment, access to publishing, and social networks. Male-only (and British-only) organizations such as the St. Andrews Society, the Irish Harp Society, and the Masons also contributed to these literary social networks. By the middle of the nineteenth century, publishing in India was coming to resemble that in the United States and in Britain, transforming itself from a patronage to a market economy. Poetry remained more or less tied to the gift economy, however, as it still for the most part is. Poets, then and now, have not often made a living by their art. Moreover, Indian poets writing in English continued to be understood with reference to British tradition; the famed Derozio, for example, was routinely referred to in the decades after his death as the Indian Keats. Madhusudan Dutt was exhorted to become an Indian Byron, though he chose to become, rather, something of an Indian Milton. Publishers and reviewers similarly appropriated other Indian writers to the British canon, and this trend continued well into the twentieth century. A key player in the effort to encourage literary publishing and in attempting to market verse was David Lester Richardson, whose thirty-year career as editor, poet, and educator had a profound effect on the development of the English language literary canon in India. Beyond Richardson's efforts, we can trace the pattern of Indian reading in school and college syllabi and in the beginnings of public and subscription libraries after 1850. While libraries stocked numerous novels, as detailed in Priya Joshi's *In Another Country,* school syllabi and examination questions remained ruthlessly tied to poetry for many decades, as I have shown in detail in *Indian Angles.*

The last quarter of the nineteenth century saw both a new spate of satirical poems and a turn to aestheticism; it reflected the impact of British spiritualism and British and American fascination with Asian religions. Edwin Arnold with his long poem *The Light of Asia* had a significant impact on the British reception of these poems, as did Edmund Gosse, who in London sponsored the work of any number of young Indian poets and introduced them to the poets of British fin-de-siècle aestheticism. As a very young woman, for example, Sarojini Naidu was introduced by Gosse to W. B. Yeats and Arthur Symons, as well as to Alice Meynell and Mathilde Blinde; she found Gosse's at-homes distinctly more congenial than the athleticism of Girton College, where she was supposed to be studying. Greater access to international education meant that, like Sarojini, more Indian poets resided abroad for prolonged periods, and this led to the penetration of Indian writers into the newly developing British market for small press books produced along aesthetic lines. In this historical context, we can see how phenomena as different as Kipling's early success and the Tagore phenomenon in Britain and America participated in larger trends. The shift from patronage and publishing of English language poetry by subscription to initial publication by private printing and small press books was a change in detail rather than in kind. Tagore's *Gitanjali* was in its first edition (1912), published privately by the members of the India Society, while the second edition by the commercial press Macmillan appealed to Euro-American audiences who viewed the poet as a spiritual teacher. Over the course of the long nineteenth century, then, English language poetry retained its salience, modulating its dominant tropes and themes but continuing to speak to its small but significant audience.

Satire and Devotion, Bards and Exiles: The Transperipheral in the Tropes of English Language Poetry

Even as the forms of publishing shifted, the modes and tropes of English poetry in India likewise developed over the long nineteenth century. Yet the dominant tropes of this poetry and its modes—satire, verse narrative, the loco-descriptive lyric, and expressive lyric—also evidence continuity. For instance, though Kipling's idiom in his dialect poems is quite different from, say, Thomas Medwin's or John Leyden's, his early narrative verse betrays a common debt to orientalist tropes and plots. Moreover, across the long nineteenth century the tropes of bardic nationalism persisted, relying as they did on transperipheral as well as metropole/colonial relations. British-born poets continued to think of themselves as exiles, although this trope and its entailments were differently activated by poets born in India. Religious and devotional poetry, similarly, had a continuing importance, though the nature of religiosity shifted across the period. And finally, the cliché of Britain as the home of freedom, which was given force in newspaper verse in the late eighteenth century, persisted but was transformed in the climate of Indian nationalism.

A remarkable number of the English language poets in India in the long nineteenth century identified with the peripheries of British internal colonialism—Scotland, Ireland, and Wales. Like some of their Indian peers, these poets took up the tropes of bardic nationalism—most notably the silent harp hung upon the willow. The legacies of Britain's internal colonialism—the ambivalent constitution of regional loyalties by the Scots, the Irish, and the Welsh—often provided the foundation for poetic efforts. Transperipheral relations among Britain's internal colonies, her former colonies in North America, and India shaped the idea of the bard, the experience of "exile," and the definition of home and its freedoms.

Many of the poets included in this volume came from Scotland; a smaller number owed complex allegiances to Ireland, Wales, or the United States. The Scotsmen celebrated or longed for Teviotdale, for the banks of the Esk, for the drawing rooms of Edinburgh, or for Highland glens. Among the Scots included here are John Leyden, James Ross Hutchinson, and George Anderson Vetch. Mary Leslie, who was born and died in India, was the daughter of another Scot, Andrew Leslie, who had come to India after training as a Baptist missionary. As for Wales, both Sir William Jones and Emma Roberts were of Welsh ancestry. Before coming to India, Jones served by choice as a judge on the Welsh circuit, becoming fascinated with Welsh poetic traditions and increasingly impatient with English-speaking monoglot magistrates. The Irish too have their place in this complex transperipheral conversation, with Honoria Marshall Lawrence coming from an Anglo-Irish family and Mary Carshore, who was born and died in India, from an Irish Catholic one. Carshore's "Lines to a Withered Shamrock" casts a fascinating light on a young poet's understanding of her father's nostalgia for an Ireland he was never again to see. Carshore presents a poetic dialogue between the shamrock and the poem's speaker, in which the shamrock describes how it became detached from its "parent stem" to bring a message to a much missed brother:

> "I've told the exile's heart a tale
> "Of childhood's fields and flowers;
> "I've told him of his native vale,
> "And of his boyhood's hours.
>
> "The music of the lark and thrush,
> "His own loved Island tongue,
> "Have in one wild melodious gush
> "Fond memory's echoes rung."[16]

The representatives of poetry—the lark and the thrush—of the dialect of Ireland have rushed back into the exile's heart, but of course the poet, though she shares

---

16. Mary Carshore, "Lines to a Withered Shamrock," in *Songs of the East: By Mrs. W. S. Carshore*, 2nd ed. (Calcutta: Englishman Press, 1871), 164.

her father's "loved Island tongue," is not herself an exile; unlike the shamrock, she has not been detached from her "parent stem." To the contrary, Carshore sees herself as very much the native of India, setting to rights the misperceptions of those born elsewhere. Nonetheless, even a second-generation emigrant such as Mary Carshore thought of poetic music in the context of a transperipheral poetics—she re-created the lark and the tongue of Ireland, mutatis mutandis, in the English language poetry of India.

Not all transperipheral relationships were between Britain's internal colonies (that is, Scotland, Ireland, and Wales) and India. Several of the poets here found their lives triangulated by Britain, the United States, and India. John Lawson is often considered an early American poet, for en route to India he spent two years in Philadelphia, where he published his first volume of poetry. Maria Skinner Nugent was born in North America, where her father was advocate-general of New Jersey; he remained a loyalist and at the end of the American War of Independence took his family to England. Maria, however, spent much time in Ireland, with her mother's family; in Dublin, she met and married George Nugent, an army officer with family ties to Cornwall, and she followed him first to Jamaica and then to India. The anonymous E.L. seems to have had no important familial connections to Britain; E.L. appears to have grown up in the United States and to have lived for many years in India. Her love for her adopted country and its people is palpable.

In many cases—including John Lawson, whose affiliations were with Baptists around the world; John Leyden, who refused to give up speaking Scots; James Atkinson, who studied medicine in Edinburgh and owed his success to a common bond of nostalgia for Scotland, shared with Lord Minto, the governor-general of India; and Mary Carshore, for whom Ireland was a distant dream—the peripheries of empire competed with metropolitan power in the poetic imagination.

A census of the poets included here who sometimes identified as Scottish, Irish, or Welsh only begins to indicate how important transperipheral relations were in the creation of English language literary culture in India, for the tropes of what Katie Trumpener has called bardic nationalism early on permeated the poems of British, "East Indian," and Indian poets alike.[17] Although in matters of trade and conquest cultural differences among the Irish, the Scots, and the English were subsumed in commercial and military institutions understood as British, in matters of culture—especially poetry—such differences continued to matter. The early volumes by Indian (or East Indian poets) published in India were permeated with the early-nineteenth-century forms of bardic nationalism. Derozio's first volume included a poem called "Here's a Health to Thee, Lassie!" written in imitation of the Scots verse of his teacher

---

17. For the most complete exploration of "bardic nationalism" and its accompanying trope of the harp hung upon the willow, see Katie Trumpener, *Bardic Nationalism: The Romantic Novel and the British Empire* (Princeton, NJ: Princeton University Press, 1997).

David Drummond.[18] In addition to alluding to his mentor's Scots poetry, Derozio adopted the bardic trope, quoting most immediately from Thomas Moore's *Irish Melodies*. Like his peer Kasiprasad Ghosh, Derozio took up the trope of the harp hung upon the willow. The silent harp, which is based on the persecution of Welsh bards at the time of the English conquest of Wales, appears repeatedly in Scottish and Irish poetry as a signal of cultural nationalism, although English poets adopted it as a form of nostalgia. For Derozio, the untuned harp represented the cultural power of an imaginary future India, and it was assimilated into Enlightenment antislavery discourse, for the poet implicitly compared his countrymen to the Jews taken captive into Babylon (see Psalm 137). Kasiprasad similarly acknowledged multiple influences; over the course of his one volume of English verse the tragic bard—clearly influenced by Thomas Moore, Letitia Landon, and James Beattie—gives place to poems on Hindu festivals. The harp hung upon the willow is transformed into a vina, an Indian lute, which becomes a synecdoche for the volume as a whole. Yet beneath Kasiprasad's Indian and explicitly Hindu reconstruction still lies the narrative structure of the doomed bard and the metaphor of the silent harp. Years later Henry Page took up the bardic harp again, lamenting Derozio's death and imagining a triumphant and free India in his "Land of Poesy." Mary Carshore, for her part, lamented the common lot of the peripheral colonial in her elegy for Letitia Landon, "The Ivied Harp."

In the course of the long nineteenth century, the bardic trope declined in importance, though transperipheral vectors retained their impact. At the end of the century, both Sarojini Naidu and Manmohan Ghose were influenced by racialized notions of the passionate and poetic Celtic soul, which had been common in various forms at least since Matthew Arnold's *On the Study of Celtic Literature*. Sarojini understood her relationship with Arthur Symons in these terms—he was from Cornwall and she from India, she reasoned, and thus they shared an implicitly non-English passion for life and for verse. Manmohan Ghose wrote numerous poems arising from his vacations in Wales, and his brother Aurobindo is represented in this volume by early—and explicitly political—poems on Charles Stuart Parnell and the condition of Ireland. Even Rabindranath Tagore was not exempt from the longevity of the bardic harp. How else to account for Ezra Pound's improbable comparison of Tagore to the troubadours of twelfth-century Provence or Yeats's declaration that Tagore's work bespoke the days of Tristan, the days of oral poetry even preceding Chaucer?[19] Tagore became in Pound's hands nothing less than a modern survival of the Anglo-Saxon bard.

---

18. Derozio wrote a memorable poem for his brother, who had been sent to study medicine in Scotland, and he owed his first publications to the enthusiasm of John Grant, a Scottish newspaper editor in Calcutta.

19. See W. B. Yeats, introduction to Rabindranath Tagore, *Gitanjali* (London: Macmillan, 1913); and Ezra Pound, "Troubadours: Their Sorts and Conditions," *Quarterly Review* (London) 219 (October 1913): 426–40.

Although bardic nationalism provided poets such as Derozio, Kasiprasad, and Henry Page with a way to meld English language verse conventions and their own sense of place and language, many poets born in the British Isles insisted—sometimes despite strong evidence to the contrary—on writing of themselves as poetic exiles. Particularly between 1800 and 1880, they reconstructed the romantic lyric as a poem of exile. Not surprisingly, significant themes included separation from children, lovers, or parents. Indeed, so many poems were written on these themes that one could say exile became a defensive trope. From the perspectives of cultural and postcolonial studies, one can argue that the very notion of exile itself formed a poetic stance that balanced the contradictions implicit in "British" identity. Paradoxically, this identity in exile was flexible enough to include a nostalgic longing for Scotland or Ireland and, often, to recuperate the critique of empire that was implicit in Irish or Scottish nationalism. *The Asiatic Journal* in 1816, for example, printed a song written for the "Celebration of the Feast of St Andrew at Calcutta, November 30 1815." This homage to Burns, though not quite metrical, neatly captures the exchange of oatcakes for rupees:

> Though far we've left the land we loo,
>   The land o' cakes behind,
> Our hearts are there this day I trow
>   'Mang scenes o' lang syne.
>   *   *   *
> What cheers us 'mid the sultry toils
>   O' India's scorch'in clime?
> It's nae the rupees' witchin smiles,
>   It's thoughts o' lang syne.[20]

While for some poets the process of internal colonialism, as Michael Hechter calls it, motivated criticism of all British imperial endeavors, for other poets ethnic differences primarily provided opportunities for affiliative association and attendant patronage.[21] The Irish Harp Society of Calcutta supported a blind harper in Dublin; the Burns monument in Edinburgh was largely built with contributions from India. As for poets in India, however deep one's nationalism might run, one's brother Masons or Scots could provide a ready list of subscribers.

Presenting themselves through a lyric subjectivity defined by exile, many British poets avoided writing about the very work of empire that had brought them to India. Such poets never tired of evoking the absent mother's grave. The daisy in India became a cliché, a trope for deracination, a memento mori for absent friends and climes. Whether "exile" served as a defense against daily re-

---

20. *Asiatic Journal* 2 (1816): 364.

21. Michael Hechter, *Internal Colonialism: The Celtic Fringe in British National Development, 1536–1966,* International Library of Sociology (London: Taylor and Francis, 1975).

alities or a link to British romantic attachment to place or a connection to a Scottish homeland, male British-born poets almost obsessively adopted the exile's stance. David Lester Richardson was among the most insistent in lamenting his lost home, and although many of his laments scarcely rose above the conventional, his poems on his absent children (living with their mother in England) do have a certain immediacy, for all their Wordsworthian imitativeness. Take these lines from "Consolations of Exile," for example:

> Fair children! still, like phantoms of delight,
>   Ye haunt my soul on this strange distant shore,
> As the same stars shine through the tropic night
>   That charmed me at my own sweet cottage door.
> Though I have left ye long, I love not less;
>   Though ye are far away, I watch ye still;
> Though I can ne'er embrace ye, I may bless,
>   And e'en though absent, guard ye from each ill![22]

Home for Richardson is always rural England—always constructed as the pleasant cottage and the verdant field. Yet Richardson's homesick poems are balanced by his book on Indian flower gardening, a text that remained the most popular of his productions. Clearly, he made a home in India and enjoyed doing it. Although Richardson resisted the recognition that Britain would perforce be strange to him should he return permanently, other poets realized that the returned exile might feel displaced in the place he had nostalgically considered home. The ambivalences of empire often emerged most strongly when a poet imagined the prospect of returning to Britain.

From time to time, moreover, even poets of British parentage resisted the trope of exile altogether. Missionaries and women appear to have been most resistant to the seductions of exile. John Lawson, for example, proved in a long poem to his wife that India was for them the best choice of a new life, and not an exile at all—though in other poems collected in *Orient Harping,* he drew a painful and nostalgic contrast between the British sabbath and a hot and noisy Calcutta Sunday. Drawing on different religious parameters but a similar sense of religious vocation, other British-born poets likewise avoided the trope of exile in favor of responding to the beauties of India. Perhaps the most famous Indian topographical poem in English at the beginning of the century was Reginald Heber's "Evening Walk in Bengal." If a British-born poet could escape the notion of exile through religious vocation and topographical meditation, others, not unlike their so-called Eurasian counterparts, were unlikely to imagine themselves

---

22. David Lester Richardson, "Consolations of Exile," in *Literary Leaves,* 2nd ed. (London: W. H. Allen, 1840), 37.

as exiles. Mary Carshore, for example, lived all her life in India and never expected to travel to England; the trope of exile scarcely entered her poetic vocabulary except, as we have seen, as a survival of a preceding generation's cultural moment. Carshore's poetry draws on sources as various as Indian folk song traditions and the urbane diction of a poem like Shelley's "To Jane: An Invitation." Rather than exile, Carshore claimed connection to the land and the people she encountered in daily life. The topography and the social networks of her poetry owe nothing to any posited "home" outside of India. Ironically, both Carshore and her family were murdered in the rebellion of 1857.

Gender as well as place of birth and social location, then, might shape one's view of one's circumstances. British-born women poets and common soldiers were sometimes not so fully able as men to position themselves as exiles, for they lacked the sense of British entitlement common to their male counterparts. Emma Roberts's poems at once construct and deconstruct the position of exile. In "Indian Graves," for example, she seems to take the typical position. For the European in India, life is exile and death is more poignant because it occurs far from home:

> How many thoughts oppress the heart,
>   Where early doomed, an exiled band
> From their paternal homes apart
>   Lie buried in a heathen land,
> Unwept, unhonoured, and unknown?[23]

In Roberts's "Stanzas Written in a Pavilion of the Rambaugh," by contrast, something more interesting happens to the topographical poem and to the trope of exile. The poem begins with an a description of natural Indian beauties, moves on to a conventional nostalgic lament for a distant British landscape, but then shows us a person in Britain looking at pictures of India and longing to be there. Roberts's poem finally cannot cohere around the nostalgic trope of exile. Honoria Lawrence, likewise, did not simply cultivate exilic nostalgia. At the beginning of her life in India, she created an enthusiastic journal/letter/poem that was anything but nostalgic. "A Day in the District," Lawrence's remarkable poem, recounts her delight with the flora and fauna, employment, and even the hardships of daily life as she followed and assisted her husband in his surveying tasks. Exile was the furthest thing from her mind—though she missed family and friends at home—for as a woman of a certain age and as the impecunious daughter of a highly respectable but large family, Honoria Marshall was no doubt delighted to find in Henry Lawrence a compatible husband, the prospect of adventure, and

---

23. Emma Roberts, "Indian Graves," in *Oriental Scenes, Sketches and Tales,* 2nd ed. (London: Edward Bull, 1832), 116.

the security of his substantial income. Never mind illness, elephants, and living in tents.

Like British-born poets, Indian and Eurasian poets in India also wrote satiric, narrative, lyric, and topographical poetry, and they too translated Indian and European languages. But their paths diverged from their counterparts' in important ways. Exile, for example, took on a variety of very different meanings. Praise of the Indian rural landscape in the topographical poem and urban satire alike developed outside the ambit of exile/nostalgia that was common in much British Indian poetry in the period. Late in the century, for example, Manmohan Ghose spoke of his return to India as an estrangement from England, where he had been sent to school at age ten. But at the same time, in an early poem titled "Myvanwy," addressed to a fictitious Welsh "maiden" of that name, he lamented,

> How shall I picture to her all the strangeness,
>   All the enchantment,
>
> In that enchanted land of noon? My heart faints
> And my tongue falters: For long ago, Myvanwy,
> Deep in the east where now but evening gathers,
>   Lost is my country.
>
> Long ago hither in passionate boyhood,
> Lightly an exile, lightly leagues I wandered
> Over the bitter foam; so far Fate led me
>   Only to love thee.
>
> Lost is that country, and all-but forgotten
> Mid these chill breezes, yet still, oh, believe me,
> All her meridian suns and ardent summers
>   Burn in my bosom.[24]

Thus, Manmohan felt a double exile—exile from India during his youth and from England in his middle age.

Other ways to resist the trope of exile were provided to British-born poets through formal choices. Satirical poems, many owing a great deal to Samuel Butler's *Hudibras* and also to Byron's verse appeared regularly throughout the period. *The Grand Master; or, Adventures of Qui Hi* by the anonymous "Quiz" was published in London in 1816 by Thomas Tegg and circulated widely in English-speaking India. Quiz engaged in a broad satire against British pretension, and although

---

24. Manmohan Ghose, "Myvanwy," in *Songs of Love and Death,* ed. Laurence Binyon (Oxford: Basil Blackwell, 1926), 27. A different poem with the same title appeared in Ghose's *Love Songs and Elegies* (London: Elkin Mathews, 1898) and is reproduced in this volume.

he is sometimes critical of things Indian, he vigorously defends Indian knowledge. The young East India Company writer whose career the poem chronicles naively presumes that India's "natives" are in need of Western scientific and mathematical knowledge. But the young man's pundit corrects him:

> The learned Bramins well could see
> The wonders of astronomy:
> If master ever went so far as
> The famous city of Benares,
> He'd see some magnifying glasses
> That Herschel's telescope surpasses.
> For English pundits condescend
> Th' observatory to ascend;
> And sometimes are surprised to find
> *Comets* of a malignant kind.[25]

There follows a brief allegory on the British ascendancy, which, like a passing comet or a mere "Jack-a-lanthorn," is soon to be eclipsed. Other satirists later in the century are more sanguine about British hegemony than was Quiz but are still critical of the British. The satiric types depicted in *Qui Hi* reappear in various comic guises over the century. Satire allowed British poets in India to avoid the clichés of exile and, often, the pathos or jingoism of patriotic verse.

Nearly as common as satire, religious poetry took a variety of tones and exhibited a broad range of politics. The poetry of conversion and poems by converts reflected the influence of missionaries on education and publishing. John Lawson exhorted his readers on various topics but always with evangelical ends. Less evangelical than Lawson but equally pious, Govin Chunder Dutt, a Christian convert, wrote poems reflecting both the comforts of Christianity and the strains that his conversion had caused in his domestic circle. Michael Madhusudan Dutt's conversion gave rise to a poem of pious conventionality but also lent a Miltonic flavor to his Bangla epic, *The Slaying of Meghanada*. Kasiprasad Ghosh's poems on Hindu festivals absorbed the influence of Christian evangelicalism and of British orientalism in quite another way—one could say that both the Hindu reaction to Christian missionary zeal and the British orientalist project shaped his English poems. Sir William Jones's hymns to Indian deities had been taken for translations, and Jones's notes and other apparatus made frequent comparison of Indian gods to the gods of Greece and Rome. This latter strategy was adopted and revised by Kasiprasad. Kasiprasad upended the orientalist equation by implying, with a subtle jab at Christian missionizing, that Krishna

---

25. Quiz [William Combe], *The Grand Master, or The Adventures of Qui Hi* (London: Thomas Tegg, 1816), 72–73.

was the Indian Jesus. A few years later, T. W. Smyth forwarded a different critique of British culture and policies; his radical Christian politics issued in an eschatological vision of the end of empire. The complexities of religious affiliation were felt much more acutely, of course, by Indian and "Eurasian" poets than by poets of British or American parentage. As Bruce King has shown for the twentieth century, in the nineteenth century many Indians writing in English were agnostic, were Christian converts, or came from families that had converted to Christianity.[26]

Devotional poetry, more properly speaking, also had a place in English language verse in India, yet of course the subjects of devotion varied widely. The most striking Christian devotional poet during the century was Mary E. Leslie, the best of whose work can be justly compared to John Keble's and to Christina Rossetti's. Poems reflecting other traditions were produced in English to serve the purposes of devotional poetry for British and American audiences. Though it was not often the case that Sanskrit poetry, as translated over the course of the century, affected its non-Hindu readers as devotional verse, nonetheless, people of a transcendentalist frame of mind found inspiration in Indian sacred texts (witness, in America, for example, Emerson and Thoreau). Later in the century, Sir Edwin Arnold's long poem on the life of the Buddha, *The Light of Asia,* met a ready audience in Britain and America; it went on to a long life in India as well. Orientalist translation, Arnold's life of the Buddha, and Euro-American spiritualism and Theosophy prepared the way for the British and American reception of Tagore's *Gitanjali* as a sacred text and for the construction of the poet as something of a guru. In their turn, the English poems of *Gitanjali* circulated widely in India outside of Bengal.

Much more common than devotional poetry were verse narratives modeled principally on Scott or Byron. For both Indian and British poets in India, the Oriental tale or lay often owed its genesis to early antiquarian researches or to James Tod's *Annals and Antiquities of Rajasthan* (1829). Other sources were mined as well, and translation of Sanskrit and Persian classics provided not only a lyric vocabulary but also sources for narrative. Derozio's "Fakeer of Jungheera," Michael Madhusudan Dutt's "Captive Ladie," and Thomas Medwin's *Oswald and Edwin* are among the most notable poems in this genre, but most poets working in India in the nineteenth century, whatever their origins, tried their hands at

---

26. Both of the principals of Hindu College in Calcutta, David Hare and David Lester Richardson, were confirmed agnostics. Between them, they directed for many years the training of many of the most important Bengali intellectuals of the century. A Scotsman, Hare had strong allegiance to radical democratic sentiments; he began as a watchmaker and found significant opportunity in India as a schoolmaster and a leader in English education. Though not a poet, he oversaw a curriculum dominated by thinkers of the Scottish Enlightenment and by a canon of English language poetry and classical prose. The legacy of the Scottish Enlightenment, though attenuated, lingered for decades. See also Bruce King, *Modern Indian Poetry in English* (New Delhi: Oxford University Press, 2002).

ballads and legends. James Hutchinson's *Sunyassee, an Eastern Tale, and Other Poems* (1838) is a typical example, though his elegy for his brother who died in the East India Company's army in 1825 is by far the outstanding poem of the volume. Narrative verse, especially verse treating historical or pseudo historical themes, allowed significant scope both for romance and for politics by way of narration. In shaping their narratives, both British-born and Indian poets engaged in a discourse of nation and freedom, though with differing valences.

In a cliché oft repeated by those imprisoned in the tropes of exile, England or Britain was praised as the home of freedom, especially freedom for the common man. Be he ever so humble, these poets argued, the poor man in Britain was, at the least, free. The rural British cottage became a magnet for the exile's home-sickness and a symbol of the independence of the average British man. By impli-cation, then, the poor in India were anything but free, and the reforming job of empire, by extension, was to replace despotism with the rule of law. The poets of exile longed for a nostalgically constructed Britain in which the humble cottage represented both domesticity and an androcentric but compelling picture of freedom from caste and aristocratic tyranny. Never mind that the cottage seldom seemed to entail hard manual labor. In yet another version, the notion of free-dom was linked to the Oriental tale, which was often premised on a historiogra-phy that claimed that the Muslim conquest of northern India had enslaved the virtuous (and free) Hindu, who might, in turn, be freed via British rule.

These notions of freedom, particularly as expressed through Scottish or Irish sentiment, however, resonated uncomfortably with the structure of empire it-self. The sight of the company extracting revenue or the pageantry of a viceregal durbar was hardly calculated to enforce a notion of freedom for the humble. Consequently, the reflexive association of Britain and freedom was subject to modulation, critique, or use in a more radical historical project. Radical poets in India (including Henry Page, T. W. Smyth, Derozio, and Aurobindo) readily turned the traditional praise of British freedom into an explicit critique of British hegemony. In contrast, evangelical poets were prone to equating Christianity with freedom—freedom from sin, which is implicitly a peculiarly British freedom.

The one sort of freedom, or rather the one sort of slavery seldom mentioned except in satirical poems, was the principal end of empire: commerce. Though one might read David Lester Richardson's sonnet on the beauties of the Calcutta harbor as a paean to free trade and the beauties of commerce, few poems directly treated the commercial bases of empire. A dimmer note was sounded by two Scotsmen: James Atkinson and John Leyden. Interestingly, their poems—Atkin-son's "City of Palaces" and Leyden's "Ode to an Indian Gold Coin"—remained popular throughout the century. Though it was mostly satirical and took its epi-graph from Diogenes the cynic, Atkinson's poem contributed a nickname to Calcutta, which it wears to this day. Leyden's poem was often reprinted in the nineteenth century, for it captured that moment of regret common to those who had emigrated to India to seek their fortunes. Though he was raised in relative poverty, Leyden contrasted the childhood freedom of Scotland with the commercial slavery of his Indian interests. He apostrophizes the Indian gold coin as a slave, clearly feeling that he himself has become a slave to the slave.

> Slave of the dark and dirty mine!
>   What vanity has brought thee here?
> How can I love to see thee shine
>   So bright, whom I have bought so dear?—
>   The tent-ropes flapping lone I hear
> For twilight-converse, arm in arm;
>   The jackal's shriek bursts on mine ear,
> When mirth and music wont to charm.
>
> By Cherical's dark wandering streams,
>   Where cane-tufts shadow all the wild,
> Sweet visions haunt my waking dreams
>   Of Teviot loved while still a child,
>   Of castled rocks stupendous piled
> By Esk or Eden's classic wave,
>   Where loves of youth and friendships smiled,
> Uncursed by thee, vile yellow slave![27]

So John Leyden directs his ire at the yellow slave—all the while suffering a liver complaint that would have made his face a twin to the slave's.

As they extended the scope and concerns of English language verse across the long nineteenth century, poets from John Leyden and Emma Roberts to Rabindranath Tagore and Rudyard Kipling created an English language literary culture that still has resonance among English speakers in India. Their English language poems also inflected verse written in both Britain and the United States.

Theoretical Premises and Editorial Principles

In the metropolitan centers of Britain and the United States, the nuances of Indian English poetry were easily missed, and after their first publication the poems themselves were often lost to view. My effort here is bring forgotten poems back to view and to re-create the complex conversation among poets that shaped them. I hope to make these poems both literally and culturally legible to American and British readers. Given the explosion of print in nineteenth-century

---

27. John Leyden, "Ode to an Indian Gold Coin," in *Poems and Ballads*, ed. Walter Scott (Kelso, Scotland: J. and J. H. Rutherfurd, 1858), 312.

India and the expansion of English-medium education, I have found it impossible in one volume to represent all the significant English language poems written in India during this period. Nor would I claim enduring aesthetic merit for every poem included here—some are well-made poems, while some are so ugly that they are interesting. I have made these texts available not because every one is a "masterpiece" but because, taken together, they establish the contours of a significant field of literary production.

These poems allow us to ask how writing in English, writing verse in English, in nineteenth-century India was legitimated and what it legitimated. They allow us further to understand the complex processes by which languages and the people who speak, learn, and teach them encounter each other. Though some of these poems were written by British or Indian officials, these poems move us away from official discourse and into the drawing rooms and school rooms, clubs and booksellers' establishments of India and Britain. They arose from a global circulation of texts, tropes, ideas, and arguments. And if we look at them not merely through the dyad of metropolis/colony (or, say, London/Calcutta) but transperipherally, we can identify the complex relations of developed and nascent nationalisms that now patrol the boundaries of literary canons. I hope that reading these poems side by side—Kipling with Aurobindo, Kasiprasad Ghosh with Jones, Emma Roberts with Derozio—will make visible and call into question the nationalist biases of canon formation as we still experience it. These texts taken together allow us to ask what they *once meant* and how those meanings continue to shape literary endeavor.[28]

My theoretical premises and editorial practices here require thinking about canons outside of nationalism. Even the globalization attendant on mercantile imperialism in the eighteenth century evidenced what David Harvey has characterized, for the twentieth century, as space-time compression.[29] The poems collected here emerged in a fundamentally heterogeneous space. Geographical gaps between texts and readers, between literary conventions and local circumstances, and between technologies available in the metropole and on the peripheries were the facts of empire most salient to writers, publishers, editors, and readers. The interchange between peripheries and metropole was neither one way nor two way but multiple, with metropolitan forms and tropes constituting themselves through complex exchanges with the peripheries and vice versa. The editorial apparatus supporting these poems—footnotes and critical biographical introductions to each poet—is designed to trace the arcs of exchange as well as to elucidate particular verses.

---

28. I take the terms of this question from David Shields, who discusses colonial poetry in much the same way. See Shields, *Civil Tongues and Polite Letters in British America* (Chapel Hill: University of North Carolina Press, 1997).

29. David Harvey, *Justice, Nature and the Geography of Difference* (Oxford: Blackwell, 1996).

Despite the fact that many of these poems—those written by Tagore and Kipling excepted—are virtually unknown to most readers in Britain and North America, the profusion of verse collected here represents only a small part of the English language verse written in India in the long nineteenth century. My principles of selection shifted somewhat as the project grew, but for the most part I have included here only poets who published a volume of English language verse in the period, and I have favored volumes that were published in India or were initially published in India. Thus, I have ignored many writers whose poetry appeared *only* in the English language press in Britain. Privileging whole volumes of poetry allowed me both a wide selection and the ability to fairly represent a poet's work. Both of these rules, however, have their exceptions. I have included manuscript poems of Horace Hayman Wilson, who, although he published many volumes of translation and history, never brought out a volume of his own verse. His manuscript poems appear here along with his published translations. A second exception to this rule is Honoria Marshall Lawrence. Lawrence's diaries were published in the twentieth century, but the editors of that publication chose to omit her poems; in her own time, most of her published poems appeared as epigraphs to the chapters of a novel she jointly authored with her husband, Henry Lawrence, or in periodicals. In both cases, I think their manuscript or periodical poetry adds a fullness to our understanding of the literary scene, emphasizing in Wilson's case the importance of the early nineteenth-century manuscript book as a form of literary circulation and emphasizing in Honoria Lawrence's case the importance of poetic circulation within small groups of family and friends. The second rule of selection here—my decision to favor poems published on the subcontinent—I have more frequently violated. I found that some texts published first in Britain had a lasting impact on the literary scene, as in the case of Edwin Arnold's work, or represented new technologies of publishing and distribution, as in volumes by Manmohan Ghose, Sarojini Naidu, and Rabindranath Tagore.

Any anthology, of course, has a certain arbitrariness—omissions occasioned by its commissions. In addition to being weighted toward the book rather than the periodical as a form of distribution, this collection is weighted toward northern India. In part, this bias simply reflects publishing realities; more books of English language poems appeared from Calcutta than from any other location, as Calcutta was the seat of imperial government. At the same time, my desire to fully represent the interconnections among poets and across generations caused me to include writers who most fully participated in these networks.

Finally, I have made a special effort to represent poets from a wide range of social locations, as understood by gender, class, and access to education. Hence, I have included Maria Nugent and Honoria Lawrence, though they did not publish books of verse but instead wrote voluminous diaries, and I have included

John Horsford and John Denning, both of whom began their careers in India as common soldiers, though Horsford, unlike Denning, came originally from the gentry. I have restricted the poems of Aurobindo Ghose to his early English verse, which falls within the limits of the period I am examining, thus ignoring his later religious verse. Despite its inevitable omissions, then, I hope this compilation of Indian English language poems will enable readers in Britain and North America access to a rich array of work and will provide Indian readers with the other half of the conversation that constituted nineteenth-century English language poetics.

The copy text for the poems included here has been, in most cases, provided by the last edition of a volume of verse that was at least nominally supervised by its author. Many of the texts reproduced here are available only in a single edition. In the rare cases where the author made revisions in a later edition, editorial notes indicate important changes. Indian copyediting was often poor during the period when these texts were published, and where necessary I have silently amended spelling and, sometimes, punctuation. In all but a few cases I have chosen to follow the spelling of the original wherever there is no evidence of typographical error. The bibliography for these copy texts is included in a paragraph immediately following each critical biographical introduction. The copy texts for the poems reprinted here are listed first in the bibliographical paragraph, followed by other useful editions and the sources for the biographical information used in the headnotes to each poet. In addition, the texts are fully annotated. Although overlooking annotations and relying on them only for information is sometimes tempting, the footnotes to these poems are crucial. The footnotes here include two kinds of materials: those originally provided by the poets themselves and the editor's explanatory notes.

The footnote was an important feature in orientalist verse and in early to midcentury Indian English poems generally. In their footnotes, poets carried on political arguments and literary controversies and legitimated themselves as experts on Indian intellectual and historical matters. The practices of annotation developed in India were widely adopted in Britain for orientalist subjects. In India, poets such as H. L. V. Derozio and Emma Roberts used footnotes to provide a running commentary and framework for reading. In addition, the learned footnote cataloging the flora and fauna of India was endemic to poems that the authors imagined might be read in Britain. Footnotes to the poems, like the other paratexts to volumes of verse published in India, are a crucial part of the reading experience. Without exception, the author's footnotes have been retained here and are marked in brackets with the author's initials. All other notes are the responsibility of the editor. In only two cases have I abridged a poet's footnotes, shortening Horace Hayman Wilson's disquisitions on flora, fauna, and literature and abridging Derozio's political notes. Derozio's extensive footnotes included whole articles reprinted from his journalistic writings on sati and other topics. They have been abridged here because they are unwieldy, but enough has been retained to suggest the nature of Derozio's political arguments.

Even as I have preserved the poets' footnotes, so too have I followed their practices with respect to diacritical markings of foreign, usually Sanskrit or Persian, words. At the beginning of this period, there was no common practice in English print for transliterating foreign words, and poets engaged in different practices in this regard. By the end of the century, possibly because fewer of them were learned in Sanskrit and Persian, poets tended to use no diacritical markings in transliteration of either classical or vernacular languages. It is interesting, for example, that in the 1830s Kasiprasad used diacritics in his English verse, while Derozio did not—as in the matter of matching religious meanings, so too in transliterating Sanskrit, Kasiprasad chose to exhibit a high degree of learning. In most cases, poets chose not to use diacritical markings, and I have followed their practice in their texts. For myself, in notes and biographical introductions, I have omitted diacritical markings for words that have become common in English.

The poems selected here represent a mix of narrative, lyric, and satiric modes and are, in most cases, complete. A few long narrative poems and translations have been abridged. The length of Oriental tales has limited both their number and the length of passages selected from them. This collection, consequently, is a fair representation of lyric poems from the period, but it underrepresents the long narrative poem. Very recently, many volumes from which these long poems have been excerpted have become available in digital form, and I urge readers to seek them out.

The poems in the volume range from William Jones's witty poem to his wife, "Plassey-Plain"—in which the animals speak multiple languages to warn her of lurking dangers—to Sarojini Naidu's sad meditation "At Twilight," in which the poet meditates on communal strife in India dividing the nationalist movement. Jones found a global audience for his more serious hymns to Indian deities and a local Calcutta audience for his witty satirical verses. Naidu claimed a London audience for much of her personal poetry, but her nationalist verse was recited in English at Congress Party rallies across India. The poems in this volume continue their long history of migration. I hope that an understanding of what they once meant will tune our ears differently to the migratory poetics of our own time.

Sir William Jones

WHEN he stepped from the *Crocodile* onto a Calcutta ghat in 1783, Sir William Jones was thirty-seven years old and already a distinguished jurist and scholar of classical languages. Jones (1746–1794) was to live in India for only a dozen years, but he had a profound effect on the European understanding of oriental languages, on British imperial law, on English language poetry, and on European orientalism. He also made significant contributions to Western understandings of comparative linguistics, Indian music, numismatics, and botany.

Although his father, a brilliant mathematician, died when he was only three, Jones's gifted mother quickly recognized her son's talents and provided him with an unusual and flexible early education. His precocity quickly led to a scholarship at Harrow, an elite boarding school, followed by a scholarship at University College, Oxford, where he distinguished himself in classical languages. With the help of his private tutor, a Syrian named Mirza, he studied Arabic and then, inspired by the poetry of Sa'dī, began to study Persian as well. Financial need led him to combine study with employment, and he became private tutor to Lord Althrop, son of the first Earl Spencer. This connection to Althrop, then just a boy, resulted in a lasting friendship, access to one of England's great private libraries, and numerous opportunities to travel on the Continent; it cemented Jones's connection with the great Whig families.

Jones soon realized that the scholar's life was an impecunious one, and modeling himself on his hero Cicero, he planned a career in law, which he hoped to follow with retirement to the country, where he could then pursue the literary and scholarly life. Accordingly, Jones resigned his Oxford fellowship and studied for the bar at the Middle Temple. Following a short stint in London, he chose to practice on the Welsh circuit, thereby connecting himself to his Welsh roots and also developing an interest in Welsh bardic traditions.

From this point, the three principal threads in Jones's life continually intertwined—law, public service, and poetry. Jones found himself in sympathy with freethinking religious notions and with radical Whig politics. On the Welsh circuit he defended poor clients pro bono, and as Michael J. Franklin succinctly puts it, he opposed "the arbitrary and discretionary power exercised by the largely Anglicized landowners, a rack-renting squirearchy, and English-speaking monoglot magistrates and judges" (*ODNB*). Moreover, Jones's sympathy with the American Revolution led him to travel to Paris and to a lasting friendship with Benjamin Franklin and his compatriots. He even contemplated emigrating to North America. Jones made no secret of his pro-independence sentiments. These views, along with the authoring of a radical pamphlet widely reprinted in England and Wales, made for a substantial delay in a desired post in India.

Finally, in 1783, he was appointed to a judicial post in India, where he experienced the tension between his radical ideals and his role as a colonial administrator. The nature of Jones's freethinking meant an unusual kind of sympathy with Indian thought and poetry, even as the poet had to compartmentalize his dislike for political tyranny and monarchism of all sorts. Jones believed in the utility of linguistic study to further what he understood as British interests. To this end, he translated significant works of Muslim and Hindu law, believing that he was contributing to a restoration of legal systems built on Indian principles. Jones brought to bear on his study of Arabic, Persian, and Sanskrit, an Enlightenment belief in the power of knowledge to create understanding among cultures and religions. He had an unusual respect for what he saw as ancient traditions of Indian knowledge, believing them to be even more valuable than the traditions of Greece and Rome. Within weeks of his arrival in Bengal, he had founded the Asiatic Society to promote research of all kinds, though he was unable to persuade its British members to admit Indian scholars to their number.

On the banks of the Hooghly in Bengal, Jones believed he was making discoveries as important as those made by the humanists who encountered classical learning in the early modern period. Jones, writing to Richard Johnson, stated that the Sanskrit *Māhābhrata*'s heroes appeared "greater in [his] eyes than Agamemnon, and Ajax, and Achilles appeared, when [he] first read the *Iliad*" (*Letters*, 2:652). Jones's work in comparative religion, astronomy, and botany all argue that he was highly self-conscious about his role as a translator of knowledge. Perhaps the most important indication of this open-mindedness was his willingness to acknowledge Nadia as the third university at which he had studied, after Oxford and the Temple—third in the chronology of his life but not in its importance.

Jones thus saw himself as a cultural translator—both literally and figuratively. His willingness to see the "University of the Brahmans" as a source of significant knowledge exemplifies the open-mindedness that allowed him to postulate a common ancestor for all Indo-European languages. In his famous hypothesis of a common source for classical and modern European languages, Sanskrit, and modern northern Indian languages, Jones virtually invented the field of comparative linguistics (comparative philology). He argued that Indian culture was by no means inferior to European culture but was in fact its cousin.

Jones's poems derive from his devotion to cultural translation. The selections here cannot fully represent the scope of his poetical works, his translations from

Latin, Sanskrit, Italian, and French among them. I include here two of Jones's translations, though at least one of them was written—as an example in his *Grammar of the Persian Language*—before his time in India. These poems from the Persian represent three approaches to translation: the first is Jones's paraphrase of a poem by the famous poet Hāfiz; the second, Jones's rendering of the same in English verse; and the third, a unique (but, I think, particularly effective) effort to re-create the meter and form of the Persian ghazal, a very difficult form to render in a rhyme-poor language like English. This trio of translations suggests Jones's awareness of the difficulty of his task. His care as translator and the unique access his work provided to Persian and Sanskrit texts made his poems highly influential among British, American, and European writers, from the British romantic poets to Emerson and Tennyson and beyond. Still more influential than his translations of Persian lyrics was Jones's translation from the Sanskrit of Kālidāsa's play *Śakuntalā*, which went into six editions between 1790 and 1807. Jones's version was further translated into many European languages, inspiring Friedrich Schiller and Johann Wolfgang von Goethe, among many others.

The last two poems reproduced here represent translations of a different kind. "Plassey-Plain" is something of a jeu d'esprit, rewriting the eighteenth-century topographical poem on the spot where in 1757 Robert Clive had defeated the Nawab of Bengal, Sirj Ud Daulah, thus consolidating the East India Company's control of Bengal. "Plassey-Plain" recalls an occasion when Jones believed his beloved wife, Anna Maria, a gifted botanist, was endangered on a walk. Jones used the moment as a metaphor for her negotiation with the welter of classical and vernacular languages in India. She had not yet learned her "moors" (that is, Hindustani [Hindi/Urdu]), but the beasts of Bengal vainly attempted to communicate her danger. In the end all is well, and the heroic gives way to the domestic or mock heroic.

Jones's odes or hymns to Indian deities, in contrast to "Plassey-Plain," are elevated expressions of philosophical and moral ideas much in the vein of his acknowledged antecedents, the classical odes of Pindar and the eighteenth-century odes of Thomas Gray. Of all the British-born poets of eighteenth-century India, Jones had the most intellectual curiosity and was the most linguistically gifted. Arguably, this gave rise to his poetry's significant impact in Europe. His talents allowed him to study his interests in detail: the movement between the vernacular and the classical, the movement among languages in the contact zone, and the re-creation of English as a contact language for mediating European, classical, and Indian languages.

Jones saw himself as a person to whom the responsibility of contact, of translation both literal and figurative, and of cultural mediation was entrusted by historical circumstance. Unsurprisingly, Jones's hymns to Indian deities were mistaken by many readers for translations, a misapprehension encouraged by the title page to the first London edition of the hymns. Not until 1796, two years after the author's death, did the *Monthly Review* clarify the provenance of Jones's hymns (Franklin, *Selected Works*, 98). In the hymns, Jones abandoned learned footnotes—much loved by him and by other orientalists—and replaced them with sometimes-lengthy headnotes. Nonetheless, as Martin Priestman has accurately observed, Jones's poetry appeared to be "encrusted" with words and allusions unfamiliar to the European reader. The hymns often come close to suggesting that the poet is a devotee of the addressed deity. The "Hymn to Náráyena" describes a philosophy the poet finds to be "no less pious than sublime." Jones's evocation of the sublime argues for his belief that Hindu religious traditions provided a potential path to spiritual and philosophical truths.

Sources

The Works of Sir William Jones, with the Life of the Author by Lord Teignmouth, ed. Anna Maria Jones (London: J. Stockdale and J. Walker, 1807). See also Michael J. Franklin, "Jones, Sir William (1746–1794)," in *ODNB*; Michael J. Franklin, ed., *Sir William Jones: Selected Poetical and Prose Works* (Cardiff: University of Wales Press, 1995); Garland Cannon, ed., *The Letters of Sir William Jones* (Oxford: Clarendon Press, 1970); and Martin Priestman, *Romantic Atheism: Poetry and Freethought, 1780–1830* (Cambridge: Cambridge University Press, 1999).

from *A Grammar of the Persian Language*
[*a ghazal of Hāfiz*]

If that lovely maid of Shiraz would accept my heart, I would
give for the mole on her cheek the cities of Samarcand and Bokhara.[1]
Boy, bring me the wine that remains, for them wilt not find in paradise the
    sweet banks of our Rocnabad,[2] or the rosy bowers of our Mosella.[3]
Alas! these wanton nymphs, these fair deceivers, whose beauty raises a tumult
    in our city, rob my heart of rest and patience, like the Turks that are
    seizing their plunder.

---

1. Samarcand and Bokhara: cities of legendary wealth and culture often invoked in Persian poetry. Samarkand is now in Uzbekistan, in the valley of the Zarafshan River; along with Bokhara it remains an important Uzbek center. Both cities lay on the ancient Silk Road and were important centers of trade.

2. Rocnabad: the spring of Shiraz, associated by Jones with the source of Hāfiz's inspiration.

3. Mosella, or Moselláy: the gardens of Shiraz, celebrated in Persian poetry as a place of nearly legendary beauty. Shiraz is still a center of Iranian learning and culture; home to the poet Hāfiz, it was famed for its gardens, wine, and flowers.

Yet the charms of our darlings have no need of our imperfect love; what occasion
    has a face naturally lovely for perfumes, paint, and artificial ornaments?

Talk to me of the fingers, and of wine, and seek not to disclose the secrets of
    futurity; for no one, however wise, ever has discovered, or ever will
    discover them.

I can easily conceive how the enchanting beauties of Joseph affected Zoleikha[4]
    so deeply, that her love tore the veil of her chastity.

Attend, O my soul! to prudent counsels; for youths of a good disposition love
    the advice of the aged better than their own souls.

Thou hast spoken ill of me; yet I am not offended; may Heaven forgive thee!
    thou hast spoken well: but do bitter words become a lip like a ruby, which
    ought to shed nothing but sweetness?

O Hāfiz! when thou composest verses, thou seemest to make a string of pearls:
    come, sing them sweetly: for Heaven seems to have shed on thy poetry the
    clearness and beauty of the Pleïads.[5]

A Persian Song

Sweet maid, if thou wouldst charm my sight,
And bid these arms thy neck enfold
That rosy cheek, that lily hand
Would give thy poet more delight
Than all Bokhára's vaunted gold,   5
Than all the gems of Samarcand.

Boy, let yon liquid ruby[6] flow,
And bid thy pensive heart be glad,
Whate'er the frowning zealots say:
Tell them their Eden cannot show   10
A stream so clear as Rocnabad,
A bow'r so sweet as Mosellày.

Oh! when these fair, perfidious maids,
Whose eyes our secret haunts infest,

---

4. Joseph and Zoleikha: Zoleika was married to the Egyptian pharoah's grand vizier Potiphar,
following a vision about a man whom she was to love. After arriving in Egypt, she discovered that it
was not Potiphar but the pharoah's slave Joseph whom she loved. Joseph resisted her advances, and
Zoleika turned to God.

5. Pleïads: the Pleiades.

6. Jones gives the Persian characters for the phrase he translates as "liquid ruby": he notes that
"melted ruby is a common periphrasis for wine in the Persian poetry. See Hafiz, ode 22." [WJ]

Their dear destructive charms display,   15
Each glance my tender breast invades,
And robs my wounded soul of rest,
As Tartars seize their destin'd prey.

In vain with love our bosoms glow;
Can all our tears, can all our sighs   20
New lustre to those charms impart?
Can cheeks where living roses blow,
Where nature spreads her richest dyes,
Require the borrow'd gloss of art?

Speak not of fate—ah! change the theme,   25
And talk of odours, talk of wine,
Talk of the flow'rs that round us bloom:
'Tis all a cloud, 'tis all a dream;
To love and joy thy thoughts confine
Nor hope to pierce the sacred gloom.   30

Beauty has such resistless pow'r
That ev'n the chaste Egyptian dame[7]
Sigh'd for the blooming Hebrew boy:
For her how fatal was the hour,
When to the banks of Nilus came   35
A youth so lovely and so coy.[8]

But ah! sweet maid, my counsel hear
(Youth should attend when those advise
Whom long experience renders sage.):
While music charms the ravag'd ear,   40
While sparkling cups delight our eyes.
Be gay and scorn the frowns of age.

What cruel answer have I heard!
And yet, by heav'n, I love thee still:
Can aught be cruel from thy lip?   45
Yet say, how fell that bitter word
From lips which streams of sweetness fill,
Which nought but drops of honey sip?

---

7. Zuleikha, Potiphar's wife. [WJ] (See note 4 above.)
8. Joseph, called by the Persians and the Arabians Jusuf. [WJ] (See note 4 above.)

Go boldly forth, my simple lay,
Whose accents flow with artless ease,   50
Like orient pearls at random strung;
Thy notes are sweet, the damsels say,
But, oh, far sweeter, if they please
The nymph for whom these notes are sung!

An Ode of Jami

In the Persian form and measure

How sweet the gale of morning breathes! Sweet news of my *delight* he brings;
News, that the rose will soon approach the tuneful bird of *night*, he brings.
Soon will a thousand parted souls be led, his captives, through the sky,
Since tidings, which in every heart must ardent flames *excite*, he brings.
Late near my charmer's flowing robe he pass'd, and kiss'd the fragrant hem;   5
Thence, odour to the rose bud's veil, and jasmine's mantle *white*, he brings.
Painful is absence, and that pain to some base rival oft is ow'd;
Thou know'st, dear maid! when to thine ear false tales, contriv'd in *spite*, he brings.
Why should I trace love's mazy path, since destiny my bliss forbids?
Black destiny! my lot is woe, to me no ray of *light* he brings.   10
In vain, a friend his mind disturbs, in vain a childish trouble gives,
When sage physician to the couch, of heartsick love-lorn *wight*, he brings.
A roving stranger in thy town no guidance can sad JAMI find,[9]
'Till this his name, and rambling lay to thine all-piercing *sight* he brings.

---

9. Jāmī, or Nur ad-Din Abd ar-Rahman Jāmī (1414–1492), was one of the greatest Persian poets. Like Hāfiz he was a Sufi.

Plassey-Plain

A Ballad, addressed to Lady Jones, by her Husband[10]

AUG. 3, 1784[11]

'Tis not of Jâfer, nor of Clive,
    On Plassey's glorious field I sing;
'Tis of the best good girl alive,
    Which most will deem a prettier thing.

The Sun, in gaudy palanqueen,[12]   5
    Curtain'd with purple, fring'd with gold,
Firing no more heav'n's vault serene,
    Retir'd to sup with Ganges old.

When Anna, to her bard long dear,
    (Who lov'd not Anna on the banks   10
Of Elwy swift, or Testa clear?)[13]
    Tripp'd thro' the palm grove's verdant ranks.

Where thou, blood-thirsty Subahdar,
    Wast wont thy kindred beasts to chase,
Till Britain's vengeful hounds of war,   15
    Chas'd thee to that well-destin'd place.

She knew what monsters ring'd the brake,
    Stain'd like thyself with human gore,
The hooded and the necklac'd snake,
    The tiger huge, and tusked boar.   20

To worth, and innocence approv'd,
    E'en monsters of the brake are friends:
Thus o'er the plain at ease she mov'd:—
    Who fears offence that ne'er offends:

---

10. It can scarcely be necessary to recall to the recollection of the reader, the victory gained by Lord Clive, over Seraj'uddoula, Subahdar, or Viceroy of Bengal, on Plassey-Plain. [WJ]

11. John Shore, Lord Teignmouth, first published this poem in London, as part of his preface to Jones's collected works, edited by Lady Jones. His headnote to this poem reads, "Lady Jones having been exposed to some danger in an evening walk over the plains of Plassey, Sir William almost immediately wrote the following stanzas."

12. Palanqueen, or palanquin: a litter or curtained sedan chair.

13. Elwy, a river in northern Wales; Testa, a river on the border of West Bengal and Sikkim.

Wild perroquets first silence broke,   25
　　Eager of dangers near to prate;
But they in English never spoke,
　　And she began her moors[14] of late.

Next, patient dromedaries stalk'd,
　　And wish'd her speech to understand;   30
But Arabic was all they talk'd;—
　　Oh, had her Arab been at hand!

A serpent dire, of size minute,
　　With necklace brown, and freckled side,
Then hasten'd from her path to shoot,   35
　　And o'er the narrow causey glide.

Three elephants, to warn her, call,
　　But they no western tongue could speak;
Though once, at Philobiblian[15] stall,
　　Fame says, a brother jabber'd Greek.   40

Superfluous was their friendly zeal;
　　For what has conscious truth to fear?
Fierce boars her pow'rful influence feel,
　　Mad buffaloes, or furious deer.

E'en tigers, never aw'd before,   45
　　And panting for so rare a food,
She dauntless heard around her roar,
　　While they the jackals vile pursued.

No wonder since, on Elfin Land,
　　Prais'd in sweet verse by bards adept,   50
A lion vast was known to stand,
　　Fair virtue's guard, while Una slept.[16]

---

14. A common expression for the Hindustanee, or vernacular language of India. [WJ]

15. Philobiblian: an allusion to John Gay's "Fable X," "The Elephant and the Bookseller," which in turn alludes to Pliny's tale of an elephant reading Greek. *Philobiblian* literally means lover of books.

16. Jones alludes to Edmund Spenser's *Faerie Queene*. The poem compares Lady Jones to Spenser's Una, protected by her own virtue while strolling on Plassey Plain. Like Spenser's Redcrosse knight, William is missing in action while the damsel is in distress.

Yet oh! had ONE her perils known,
(Tho' all the lions in all space
Made her security their own)
He ne'er had found a resting place.

55

A Hymn to Náráyena

The Argument

A complete introduction to the following Ode would be no less than a full comment on the Vayds and Pura'ns of the Hindus, the remains of *Egyptian* and *Persian* Theology, and the tenets of the Ionick and Italick Schools;[17] but this is not the place for so vast a disquisition.[18] It will be sufficient here to premise, that the inextricable difficulties attending *the vulgar notion of material substances,* concerning which

"We know this only, that we nothing know,"[19]

induced many of the wisest among the Ancients, and some of the most enlightened among the Moderns, to believe, that the whole Creation was rather an *energy* than a *work,* by which the Infinite Being, who is present at all times in all places, exhibits to the minds of his creatures a set of perceptions, like a wonderful picture or piece of musick, always varied, yet always uniform; so that all bodies and their qualities exist, indeed, to every wise and useful purpose, but exist only as far they are *perceived;* a theory no less pious than sublime, and as different from any principle of Atheism, as the brightest sunshine differs from the blackest midnight. This *illusive operation* of the Deity the Hindu philosophers call, Máyá, or *Deception;* and the word occurs in this sense more than once in the commentary on the *Rig Vayd,* by the great Vasishtha, of which Mr. Halhed[20] has given us an admirable specimen.

The *first* stanza of the Hymn represents the sublimest attributes of the Supreme Being, and the three forms, in which they most clearly appear to us, *Power, Wisdom,* and *Goodness,* or, in the language of Orpheus and his disciples, *Love:* the second comprises the *Indian* and *Egyptian* doctrine of the Divine Essence and Archetypal *Ideas;* for a distinct account of which the reader must be referred

17. Vayds: Vedas. Ionick and Italick Schools: Greek and Roman gods.
18. Jones's "Argument" provides the equivalent of notes to the poem, as he hopes to explain Indian deities and his own rhetorical and poetic practices.
19. Alexander Pope, *Essay on Man,* IV:260–61.
20. Nathaniel Brassy Halhed: Jones's friend Halhed wrote *A Code of Gentoo Laws,* which included a translation of Vasistha's commentary on the *Rig Veda.*

Sir William Jones ☞ 39

to a noble description in the sixth book of Plato's *Republick;* and the fine expla-
nation of that passage in an elegant discourse by the author of Cyrus,[21] from
whose learned work a hint has been borrowed for the conclusion of this piece.
The *third* and *fourth* are taken from the Institutes of Menu, and the eighteenth
Puran of Vyásá, entitled *Srey Bhagawat,* part of which has been translated into
Persian, not without elegance, but rather too paraphrastically. From Brehme, or
the *Great Being,* in the neuter gender, is formed Brehmá, in the *masculine;* and the
second word is appropriated to the *creative power* of the Divinity.[22]

The spirit of God, call'd Náráyena, or *moving on the water,* has a multiplicity
of other epithets in Sanscrit, the principal of which are introduced, expressly
or by allusion, in the *fifth* stanza; and two of them contain the names of the *evil
beings,* who are feigned to have sprung from the ears of Vishnu; for thus the
divine spirit is entitled, when considered as the *preserving power:* the *sixth* ascribes
the perception of *secondary* qualities by our senses to the immediate influence of
Máyá; and the *seventh* imputes to her operation the *primary* qualities of *extension*
and *solidity.*

The Hymn

Spirit of Spirits, who, through ev'ry part
    Of space expanded and of endless time,
    Beyond the stretch of lab'ring thought sublime,
    Badst uproar into beauteous order start,
      Before Heav'n was, Thou art: 5
Ere spheres beneath us roll'd or spheres above,
    Ere earth in firmamental ether hung,
    Thou satst alone; till, through thy mystick Love,
    Things unexisting to existence sprung,
      And grateful descant sung.   10
What first impell'd thee to exert thy might?
    Goodness unlimited. What glorious light
    Thy pow'r directed? Wisdom without bound.
    What prov'd it first? Oh! guide my fancy right;
      Oh! raise from cumbrous ground   15
      My soul in rapture drown'd,

---

21. Michael Franklin in *Selected Works* identifies the author of Cyrus as John Hoole, whose play
on the founder of the Persian Empire was first performed in 1768. Hoole also translated Tasso, the
Italian poet much loved by William and Anna Maria Jones.

22. All these transliterations are now normally rendered as Brahma.

That fearless it may soar on wings of fire;
For Thou, who only knowst, Thou only canst inspire.

Wrapt in eternal solitary shade,
    Th' impenetrable gloom of light intense,   20
    Impervious, inaccessible, immense,
    Ere spirits were infus'd or forms display'd,
        BREHM his own Mind survey'd,
As mortal eyes (thus finite we compare
    With infinite) in smoothest mirrors gaze: 25
    Swift, at his look, a shape supremely fair
    Leap'd into being with a boundless blaze,
        That fifty suns might daze.
Primeval MAYA was the Goddess nam'd,
    Who to her sire, with Love divine inflam'd,   30
    A casket gave with rich *Ideas* fill'd,
From which this gorgeous Universe he fram'd;
        For, when th' Almighty will'd,
        Unnumber'd worlds to build,
    From Unity diversified he sprang,   35
While gay Creation laugh'd, and procreant Nature rang.

First an all-potent all-pervading sound
    Bade flow the waters—and the waters flow'd,
    Exulting in their measureless abode,
    Diffusive, multitudinous, profound,   40
        Above, beneath, around;
Then o'er the vast expanse primordial wind
    Breath'd gently, till a lucid bubble rose,
    Which grew in perfect shape an Egg refin'd:
    Created substance no such lustre shows,   45
        Earth no such beauty knows.
Above the warring waves it danc'd elate,
    Till from its bursting shell with lovely state
    A form cerulean flutter'd o'er the deep,
    Brightest of beings, greatest of the great: 50
        Who, not as mortals steep,
        Their eyes in dewy sleep,
    But heav'nly-pensive on the Lotos lay,
That blossom'd at his touch and shed a golden ray.

Hail, primal blossom! hail empyreal gem!　　　　　　　　55
   KEMEL, or PEDMA, or whate'er high name[23]
   Delight thee, say, what four-form'd Godhead came,
   With graceful stole and beamy diadem,
      Forth from thy verdant stem?
Full-gifted BREHMA! Rapt in solemn thought　　　　　　　60
   He stood, and round his eyes fire-darting threw;
   But, whilst his viewless origin he sought,
   One plain he saw of living waters blue,
      Their spring nor saw nor knew.
Then, in his parent stalk again retir'd,　　　　　　　　　65
   With restless pain for ages he inquir'd
   What were his pow'rs, by whom, and why conferr'd:
   With doubts perplex'd, with keen impatience fir'd
      He rose, and rising heard
      Th' unknown all-knowing Word,—.　　　　　70
   "BREHMA! no more in vain research persist:
My veil thou canst not move—Go; bid all worlds exist."

Hail, self-existent, in celestial speech
   NARAYEN, from thy wat'ry cradle, nam'd;
   Or VENAMALY[24] may I sing unblam'd,　　　　　　　75
   With flow'ry braids, that to thy sandals reach,
      Whose beauties, who can teach?
Or high PEITAMBER[25] clad in yellow robes
   Than sunbeams brighter in meridian glow,
   That weave their heav'n-spun light o'er circling globes?　　80
   Unwearied, lotos-eyed, with dreadful bow,
      Dire Evil's constant foe!
Great PEDMANABHA,[26] o'er thy cherish'd world
   The pointed *Checra*,[27] by thy fingers whirl'd,
   Fierce KYTABH shall destroy and MEDHU grim　　　　85
      To black despair and deep destruction hurl'd.[28]

---

23. Kemel and Pedma: the goddess Lakshmi is often addressed as Kamalā or Padmā (lotus).

24. Venemaly, or Vana-malā (garland of the forest): garland worn by Vishnu and his various incarnations, including Krishna.

25. Peitamber, or Pītāmbara: glossed by Franklin as "the golden yellow veil or robe worn by Vishnu and his incarnations. It is woven of three threads representing the letters of the sacred syllable AUM" (*Selected Works*, 111).

26. Pedmanabha: Jones's transliteration of Padma-nābha, or Vishnu, whose navel gives rise to the lotus that supports the world.

27. Checra, or cakra: Vishnu's weapon.

28. Kytabh and Medhu: Kaitabh and Madhu were two asuras, or demons, who were to annihilate either Brahma or the Vedas. Vishnu slew them, hence his name Madhusudana (killer of Madhu).

Such views my senses dim,
My eyes in darkness swim:
What eye can bear thy blaze, what utt'rance tell
Thy deeds with silver trump or many-wreathed shell?

90

Omniscient Spirit, whose all-ruling pow'r
Bids from each sense bright emanations beam;
Glows in the rainbow, sparkles in the stream,
Smiles in the bud, and glistens in the flow'r
That crowns each vernal bow'r;

95

Sighs in the gale, and warbles in the throat
Of ev'ry bird, that hails the bloomy spring,
Or tells his love in many a liquid note,
Whilst envious artists touch the rival string,
Till rocks and forests ring;

100

Breathes in rich fragrance from the sandal grove,
Or where the precious musk-deer playful rove;
In dulcet juice from clust'ring fruit distills,
And burns salubrious in the tasteful clove:
Soft banks and verd'rous hills

105

Thy present influence fills;
In air, in floods, in caverns, woods, and plains;
Thy will inspirits all, thy sov'reign MAYA reigns.

Blue crystal vault, and elemental fires,
That in th' ethereal fluid blaze and breathe;

110

Thou, tossing main, whose snaky branches wreathe
This pensile orb with intertwisted gyres;
Mountains, whose radiant spires
Presumptuous rear their summits to the skies,
And blend their em'rald hue with sapphire light;

115

Smooth meads and lawns, that glow with varying dyes
Of dew-bespangled leaves and blossoms bright,
Hence! vanish from my sight:

Delusive Pictures! unsubstantial shows!
My soul absorb'd One only Being knows,

120

Of all perceptions One abundant source,
Whence ev'ry object ev'ry moment flows:
Suns hence derive their force,
Hence planets learn their course;
But suns and fading worlds I view no more:

125

GOD only I perceive; GOD only I adore.

Sir John Horsford

WHEN he was twenty years old, John Horsford (1751–1817) abruptly gave up a fellowship at Oxford and enlisted as "John Rover" in the Bengal Artillery. Within weeks he was aboard the *Duke of Grafton,* bound for India. Why Horsford abandoned Oxford is not entirely clear, though he did claim that the pursuit of poetry "ruined" him. His biographer H. M. Chichester reported that he was disinclined to "enter the church as his friends desired" (*DNB* Archive, *ODNB*). I take this to mean that his family expected him to take holy orders.

Whatever the case, Horsford arrived in India in an anomalous position. Educated men of good family were expected to find, or to have purchased for them, commissions in the army. Most common soldiers were scarcely literate, much less educated, as Horsford had been, at two of the most prominent educational institutions in England: the Merchant Taylor's School and St. John's College, Oxford. Despite his assumed name, his disguise could scarcely have been complete, but Horsford served for six years as an enlisted man in the artillery, a position that at that time was highly unusual for a gentleman. The story goes that his commanding officer, alerted by inquiries after him, discovered his true identity when Horsford corrected a Greek quotation in some papers he was copying. The colonel called him by name, and the soldier answered to his true identity. Following this episode, Horsford was appointed a cadet in the commissioned corps. Appointments from the enlisted ranks to the commissioned corps were extremely rare, but Horsford's appointment reflected his family's status, his education, and his exemplary service in the enlisted ranks.

Horsford's service as an enlisted man made him an effective officer, and over a long career he rose through the ranks. At his death of heart failure in 1817, he was a major general on the staff of the Grand Army, having served forty-five years with distinction. Francis Stubbs, in a history of the Bengal Artillery, praised Horsford as a man whose "habits of system and application" and whose "perfect integrity" allied with temperance made him an ideal officer. In addition to poetry and contributions to the Asiatic Society, Horsford wrote extensively about military matters, and his memoranda led, after his death, to the successful reorganization of the Bengal Artillery.

Despite a long career on active duty, Horsford published two books of poetry in Calcutta: *A Collection of Poems, Written in the East Indies* (1797) and *Poems in Three Parts*

(1800). His poems were flanked by a considerable subscriber list, as Horsford managed to pre-sell 170 copies of his first volume and 196 of the second. *Poems in Three Parts* is cataloged in Worldcat and in the Eighteenth-Century Collections Online database as written by three authors: Sir William Jones, John Hawkesworth, and John Horsford. This attribution, however, is misleading, for part one, as I detail below, consists of facing page translations into English of Jones's Latin poems by an author writing after Jones's death; the author of the translations is anonymous, but his style is coherent with Horsford's, as is the esteem in which the translator holds Sir William. The second section of the volume is attributed by bibliographers to Hawkesworth, but I can find no warrant for this claim, and indeed the poem "Literary Characteristicks of the Most Distinguished Members of the Asiatic Society" was published under a different pseudonym, "John Collegins Esq.," in the *Asiatic Annual Register, 1801* (London, 1802): 118. The conclusion of the poem includes a paean to the Howrah Orphanage, from which the author claims to have taken two daughters, a claim identical to that made by J— H— [John Horsford] in the third section of *Poems in Three Parts*, which is signed with his own initials. Internal evidence, then, these examples among others, makes for a strong claim that Horsford was the author of all three parts of this volume, modestly saving the expanded collection of his own verse for the end of the volume. The many fulsome dedications of his poems, the occasional nature of his verse, his frequent address to his superiors, and his footnotes were efforts to establish a context for belles lettres among officers and East India Company servants in Calcutta and the Bengal Presidency. Many of these company employees and officers would have shared his education in the Greek and Latin classics; a very few would closely approximate Sir William Jones's learning in Persian and Arabic if not Sanskrit.

Horsford was at Oxford at the same time as Jones, preceding him in India by several years. One of Horsford's more interesting poems is a verse paean commemorating the members of the Asiatic Society, beginning with Jones, its founder. His admiration for Jones led him to translate several of Jones's Latin poems as the entire first section of *Poems in Three Parts*. Jones's poems were themselves largely translations or imitations from Persian, Arabic, and Greek; his Latin and Horsford's English—translations of translations—appear on facing pages.

In addition to his translations of Jones's poems and his commemoration of the Asiatic Society, Horsford often undertook occasional verse, and he appended to his first volume of poetry various brief sententious essays. Horsford dedicated this prose to his brother, hoping that the young man would "Court Virtue and shun the depravities which I have fallen into" (*Collection of Poems*, 69). The poems, likewise, provide clues to Horsford's abrupt departure from England; in his youth, he says, he was led astray by poetry. Horsford recounts his admiration for the poet William Hayley and recalls that he left home as a young man with the sole desire of meeting Hayley. His hero being abroad, Horsford was disappointed and things went from bad to worse. He says (speaking of himself in third person) that "this extraordinary journey among strangers, led him into innumerable extravagant irregularities, which hastened his ruin, as being then too young to guard against the allurements of folly; it also drew upon him the frowns of maternal displeasure" (*Collection of Poems*, 3).

Horsford the officer was as respected as Horsford the youth was dissipated, but he defined respectability quite differently from later nineteenth-century notions. He entered into a long-term relationship with an Indian woman, Sahib Juan, with whom he had several children. His anxiety for his daughters, particularly, led him to deplore the discrimination against "Eurasians" or "East Indians," as persons of mixed ethnicity were called. In the selection here from his poem on the Asiatic Society, Horsford defends relationships that were, in later decades, viewed with increasing negativity. His praise for Colonel Kirkpatrick as a promoter of the Bengal Orphan Institution, moreover, includes language implying that Horsford adopted two children from this institution or at least became in some way the legal guardian of such infants. In another poem, a satire called "The Art of Living in India," published in his second book, Horsford addressed the biracial children in the Howrah orphanage as "my auburn beauties" and counseled young British men in India to marry them. Though he hoped that nobler bards would sing their praises, he dedicated "The Art of Living in India" finally to the young women of the orphanage:

> Ye shapely Nymphs, who form my pleasing theme!
> Ye, born where Ganga rolls her hallow'd stream,
> Accept the numbers, written with spirit free,
> I love your India and your India me!

> (*Three Parts*, 119)

Though he deplored discrimination against Eurasian children, Horsford's poems as a whole defend the British conquest of India. He praises, among others, Lord Cornwallis and the Marquis of Hastings. Nonetheless, he critiques English prejudices in the prose of his first volume, criticizing the traditional mockery of the Scots and the Irish and arguing that both countries have produced the very soldiers upon whom the English rely. In his own experience and that of the soldiers in his charge, Horsford no doubt had ample opportunity to confront the human consequences of the British presence in India. Officers were typically in charge of collecting mandatory contributions to the military orphan societies and placing children in the care of orphanages—a child of a British father and an Indian mother was often considered, on the father's death, to be an orphan in the care of the regiment. In Horsford, then, are mixed the habitus of a soldier, the prejudices of a man tied directly to imperial conquest, and the sentiments of a father defending his children.

Sources

John Horsford, *A Collection of Poems, Written in the East Indies with Miscellaneous Remarks, in Real Life, by J—H—* (Calcutta: Joseph Cooper, Telegraph Press, 1797); Horsford, *Poems in Three Parts* (Calcutta: Thomas Hollingbery, Hircarrah Press, 1800). See also H. M. Chichester, "Horsford, Sir John (1751–1817), major-general H.E.I.C. Bengal artillery," *DNB* Archive (1891), accessed via H. M. Chichester, "Horsford, Sir John (1751–1817)," *ODNB*; Francis W. Stubbs, *History of the Organization, Equipment, and War Services of the Regiment of Bengal Artillery: Compiled from Published Works, Official Records, and Various Private Sources* (London: Henry S. King and Co., 1877).

Epistle to Sir William Jones
Written to Him during the Late War with Tippoo

1790

Tho' haughty pow'rs against us turn their rage,[1]
Let not the fate of war your mind engage,
Be from your bosom such ideas far,
To vet'ran Meadows[2] leave the cares of war:
But ah! to Persian lore devote the hour,   5
You Lord in Poesy's inspiring bow'r;
Khakani's[3] thought t'admiring ears express,
Or your lov'd Hafiz bring in English dress:
With Khoosru sing how gentle pangs t'assuage,
And trace pure Sadi thro' his moral page;   10
But if fatigu'd in this too tender field,
Then seek the joys Gillaliden can yield,

---

1. Tippoo: Tipu Sultan (Sultan Fateh Ali Tipu) was the ruler of Mysore—scholar, soldier, and poet—who allied himself with the French against the English. He was defeated in the Third and Fourth Anglo-Mysore wars and died defending his capital, Srirangapattana (Seringapatnam), in 1799. Known as the "Tiger of Mysore," Tipu became a symbol to the British of Indian ferocity; ten years after this poem was written, in his defeat, he became an affirmation of British power.

2. Meadows: British general who on May 26, 1790, began the campaign that is now called the Third Mysore War.

3. Khakani, Hafiz, Khoosru, Sa'di, Gillaliden [Rūmī], and Attar: classical Persian poets. Horsford praises Jones's translations from the Persian, many of which were published in Jones's *Grammar of the Persian Language*. Jones had studied Persian initially for his own pleasure, though perhaps also with an eye to an Indian preferment; Persian was until 1830 the legal language in northern India.

With Attar join in philosophic taste,
Th' enlighten'd Rochfoucalt[4] of half the East:
Their daring works to justly understand,   15
I'd give thy wealth, O golden Samarcand![5]

Let some with study'd grace allure the fair,
Some in glit palanquins to routs repair,
Let some, more proud, spread Folly's painted wings,
And ape the bright magnificence of kings;   20
Let some with slaves the public walks parade,
In Asia's shewy pageantry array'd,
While you with noblest thought improve the heart,
And your reflections to the world impart;
Of the Sun's bards unfold the lofty rhyme,   25
Which swells the bosom with divine sublime.
The high expression of whose mighty verse,
Wou'd best the glories of the God rehearse.

Or sing the rosy bow'rs of Mosellay,[6]
Where Persia's youths pass'd tender hours away;   30
Ah! sweetly social make the fragrant shade,
With a mild beautiful Circassian[7] maid,
For whom the birds of wondrous plumage sing,
For whom sits Nature in eternal spring,
For whom the mango comes of luscious taste,   35
Our fav'rite fruit in the luxurious East:
Let Love's pure care her ev'ry hour employ—
Let her heart heave with plenitude of joy—
Let such an angel cause the soft alarm
And then no tales of Cassimere[8] can charm.   40
Let the sweet maid in your fair page appear,
And tune the polish'd note to Beauty's ear.

---

4. Rochfoucalt: François, duc de la Rochefoucauld, prince de Marcillac (1613–1680), known for his *Memoirs* and especially for his *Maxims*; he is compared here to the Persian poet Attar, author of *The Conference of the Birds*.

5. Samarcand [Samarkand]: city of legendary wealth and culture often invoked in Persian poetry. On the ancient Silk Road, it was an important center of trade and remains an important Uzbek center.

6. Mosellay: the gardens of Shiraz, celebrated in Persian poetry as a place of nearly legendary beauty.

7. Circassian maid: by the late eighteenth century, the "Circassian" beauty had come to represent the apex of female loveliness. Circassian women from the northern Caucasus had a reputation for beauty and refinement in the harems of the Ottoman court, and allusions to them were taken to evoke exemplary beauty.

8. Cassimere: Kashmir.

Or, if your soul to soft-ey'd Pity giv'n,
Melts with th' affection of your kindred Heav'n,
Since of each orphan child you stop the cry,   45
Wipe the big tear from Magdalena's eye.

To you what joy can jarring armies yield,
Or levell'd cities, or th'ensanguined field,
Or sack'd Pagodas, or the plunder'd fanes,
Or Indians gasping on their native plains,   50
Or pillag'd wealth from Hyder's lov'd abodes,[9]
Or ransack'd ornaments from idol gods?
The spoils of war no real joys can give,
Tis Poetry's soothing voice that makes us live.
With her I left my home in hapless hour,   55
And felt of diff'rent climes th' unequal pow'r:
With her thro' either tropic have I gone,
And burnt beneath the equinoctial sun;
Refin'd Europa's fatal pomp she's shewn;
And Afric's sooty race to me made known;   60
With her I rov'd the sunny wilds among,
When brown-hair'd Ganga only heard my song;
Retir'd to contemplate at her command,
With your immortal tablets in my hand.
Th' enthusiast I, of that enchanting art,   65
Which charms and steals away the human heart.

from *"Literary Characteristicks of the Most Distinguished Members of the Asiatic Society, 1799"*

Who are yon Maids array'd in heavenly white,
Whose beauteous aspect shines divinely bright?
Yes!—tis the lovely VIRTUES I behold
(I know their tresses of loose floating gold)
In sweet assemblage seated to proclaim,   5
How much they reverence their KIRKPATRICK's name!
But first see CHASTITY—that blushing fair—
The doves of INNOCENCE for him prepare.
In ready concord all the sisters join,
To celebrate the man in songs divine   10

---

9. Hyder Ali (1722–1782): father of Tipu Sultan and ruler of Mysore.

Whose genius plan'd the charitable dome—
Who bad th'unguarded houseless Orphan come.[10]
Eternal Echoes shall his name repeat,
In yon green groves round Howrah's sacred seat!
Oh man of sense refin'd!—how justly due,   15
The thanks of rising Virgins given to you!
Sweet blooming black ey'd girls, of shapely forms,
Whose speaking looks my melting bosom warms.
To Virtue form'd by your paternal care,
And more preserved from the Seducer's snare.   20
Could Mortals trace whence every matter springs,
And penetrate the secret source of things,
Or dive into Futurity's dark womb—
Or prophesy of people yet to come—
Hence, ASIAN's born, may rise of deathless fame,   25
To make States tremble at the BRITISH name!
Perhaps I owe from hence (in chaste embrace)
Two smiling Infants now before my face.
From lower origin and meaner birth,
Sprang the proud Romans—Rulers of the Earth!   30
KIRKPATRICK GONE TO CLIMES OUR ARMS SUBDU'D,[11]
WILL TEACH ANOTHER PEOPLE TO BE GOOD.
Then shall his God in holy radiance shed,
Perpetual blessings on his honour'd head,
Give him to slumber each revolving night,   35
Entranc'd in pleasing dreams of soft delight;
Then shall his years unknown to care be spent,
In one eternal round of true content.
And when the awful messenger of death,
Shall wave the flaming sword and snatch his breath,   40
On silver wings shall vigil angels fly,
And singly bear him to the Realms of Joy.[12]

---

10. Colonel Kirkpatrick was one of the most active promoters of the Bengal Orphan Institution. His example in India was followed by Lady Campbell, under whose patronage the Female Asylum at Madras was erected in 1787. Posterity will place their names on the list with that most humane and best of Women, the Lady ARABELLA DENNY, the Foundress of the Magdalen Asylum in Dublin. [JH]

11. When this part of the Poem was written, Colonel Kirkpatrick was one of the Commissioners for managing the affairs of Mysore. [JH]

12. I might equally have celebrated Colonel Kirkpatrick as a great Orientalist, but I show this more splendid part of his Character. [JH]

Ode to My Infant Daughter, Eliza Howrah

Come Smiler! in my lap repose,
Child of the Lily and the Rose,
Come to me from thy mother's arms,
I'll gaze upon thy opening charms;
Come, Love! and see me flowers prepare,　　　　5
To tangle round thy flaxen hair;
Or playful strew before thy feet,
Champac,[13] the golden and the sweet,
Or if more pleasing to thy sight,
Bela,[14] the delicate and white.　　　　10

Come and I'll tune a tender lay
for that, to me, auspicious day,
I got thee from Connubial Love,
In Howrah's Whampee-scented grove,[15]
Bestow'd me near the opening glade　　　　15
Of yon tall spreading almost shade,
Eliza born—the wood nymphs smil'd,
And Hougly stop'd to kiss the child.[16]

The Virtues all came to behold,
Their ringlets shone in circling gold,　　　　20
Modesty in sky blue array,
And innocence as fair as day!
Th' attendant girls danc'd at the sight,
Apparel'd in the purest white,
Each silver slipper'd virgin smil'd　　　　25
Bestowing kisses on the child.

Kiss, little Smiler, and go then
To thy fond mother's arms again:
Go, in her bosom find repose,
Child of the Lily and the Rose.　　　　30

---

13. Michelia Champaca. [JH] Now *Magnolia champaca,* magnolia tree.

14. Nyctanthes Multiflora. [JH] Now *Jasminum multiflorum* (Burm. f.), Andrews star jasmine.

15. Whampee, or wampee (*huang pi* in Chinese; *Clausena lansium*): a strongly scented evergreen tree native to Southeast Asia, with white flowers and fruit resembling grapes that is popular for both culinary and medicinal uses.

16. Hougly: the river Hooghly [Hugli], which flows through Calcutta to the Bay of Bengal.

Anna Maria

To this early poet of British India we can attach no definite name, no parentage, no dates of birth and death. Of all the English language poets in eighteenth-century India, Anna Maria remains the most resistant to identification. We can specify her probable social class, her education in Latin and modern European languages, and her literary tastes, and we can identify many people among her circle of friends and acquaintances. It is probable that Anna Maria was born in Britain around 1770 and not unlikely that she died there sometime after 1793. If her poems are to be trusted, she lived in Calcutta between 1790 and 1793.

A persistent—but surely erroneous—theory identifies this first woman writer of English language poetry in India as Anna Maria Shipley Jones, the wife of the famous linguist and jurist Sir William Jones. Anna Maria provided clues, however, suggesting that this identification is improbable. She attached datelines—a place and date—to nearly all the poems in the slim volume printed by Thomas and Ferris in Calcutta in 1793. Among them, the earliest poem is datelined London, 1790, presumably before the poet's departure for India. The last dated poem, "Adieu to India," is labeled "Gardens, November 24, 1793." All the rest are datelined from either Calcutta or "Gardens," that is, Garden Reach, the elegant suburb along the river where Sir William and Anna Maria Jones and Sir John Shore (governor-general of Bengal) also lived. This common residence has given rise to the theory that Anna Maria Jones and "Anna Maria" might be the same person. The poet, however, lists among the subscribers to her volume both Sir William and his wife. Typically, a poet would not list herself or her husband among her subscribers. Nor did Sir William Jones in his correspondence attribute any poems to his wife, though he discusses her botanizing and letter writing in some detail. Although the poet and Anna Maria Jones appear to have left India about the same time in late 1793, the poet dated her earliest verse from London in 1790, when Lady Jones was already resident in India. These facts, and the fact that most newspaper publication of poetry was pseudonymous in Calcutta at this time, suggest that we must look elsewhere for Anna Maria's identity.

Perhaps "Anna Maria" chose a pseudonym in honor of Anna Maria Jones or Anna Maria Hastings, the second wife of Warren Hastings, former governor-general of Bengal, but it is much more likely that she chose her poetic name in hopes of attaching herself to the Della Cruscan poets of late eighteenth-century Florence and London. In her poems published in the *Asiatic Mirror* and the *Calcutta Morning Post,* Anna Maria connected her work to the London scene, where Robert Merry as "Della Crusca" and Hannah Cowley as "Anna Matilda" had conducted a sensational poetic affair, publishing numerous poems in lowbrow newspapers; theirs was verse in costume, verse as melodrama, an epistolary courtship productively prolonged. Like Anna Maria in Calcutta, many women poets in England took up their pens in pursuit of Della Cruscan fame; their poetry depended for its pleasures not on tranquil reflection but on immediate emotion expressed immediately. For Anna Maria, whose name echoed Anna Matilda's, the distance between London and Calcutta proved a nearly insuperable obstacle to composing successful Della Cruscan verse, which depended for its effect on immediacy and convivial exchange. A letter or newspaper from London could take six months to arrive in Calcutta, sometimes with awkward consequences. Anna Maria, for instance, composed an elegy for Robert Merry on hearing a false report of his death. Despite the gaffe, she published both the elegy and its retraction in her collected volume. As her verse makes clear, she was painfully attuned to the latest literary developments in London but uncomfortably distant from them.

Such embarrassment as well as ill health seem to have induced Anna Maria to return to London after only a few years. Her slim volume of verse allows us to measure the social uses of art even within a culture whose main concerns were undoubtedly martial and commercial. I conjecture that while Anna Maria was genteel and well educated for a woman of her time, she was in relatively straitened circumstances. Most of her poems were written over a period of a few months, and the long list of subscribers and high price of the slim volume (priced at one gold mohur) suggest that book publication was a socially acceptable way for the poet to raise some ready cash for a return to England.

Source

The Poems of Anna Maria (Calcutta: Thomas and Ferris, 1793).

Ode

INSCRIBED TO DELLA CRUSCA.

The Propriety of the following ODE *to* DELLA CRUSCA, *it is presumed, will be readily admitted.—An Elegiac Poem to that distinguished Writer's Memory was written, in consequence of the Intelligence of his Death, and is inserted in Page 23:—*ANNA MARIA *has the pleasure of knowing Mr.* MERRY *still lives.*[1]

TRIUMPHANT Bard, my Verse inspire,
With bright APOLLO's sparkling Fire;
To THEE, the wild Delirium runs,
Like Comets to their Centre Suns;
I feel the proud impassion'd Glow   5
Thro' every trilling Fibre flow;
My Muse, on Rapture's rosy Wings,
Her Harmony o'er Passion flings:
For THEE, the vivid Fancies dare,
To range the lustrous Orbs of Air;   10
From Star to Star their Glories trace,
And with them DELLA CRUSCA grace.
Thou liv'st!—my fetter'd Senses seem,
Deluded by some motley Dream,
That on the doubtful Slumbers plays,   15
Like Fairies in the pale Moon's Rays:—
Ah!—let me taste thy purer Song,
Where Imagery's Beauties throng;
And as I scan the polish'd Line,
Steal the rich Fervor from thy Soul divine.—   20

Induct me through the hallow'd Glade,
Where Learning's mould'ring Sons are laid;
Where VIRGIL's ancient Bust appears,
Gemm'd with mild Ev'ning's brilliant Tears,
Those Tears, by blue Olympus shed   25
O'er *Rome's* immortal sainted Dead:—

---

1. Robert Merry took his pseudonym from the Accademia della Crusca, founded in Florence in 1582 to purify the Tuscan language; no doubt Merry was bowing to the Tuscan academicians' admiration for Petrarch (best known for his love sonnets to Laura) and for Boccaccio's vernacular vigor. I follow Anna Maria's eighteenth-century style of capitalization here to give a full sense of her exclamatory poetics.

Or where by Midnight's sparry Gloom,
FAIR SAPPHO bends o'er PHAON's Tomb;[2]
Or PETRARCH's Shade still loiters nigh,
To lisp his cruel LAURA's Sigh:—   30
There lead me, thou delightful Muse,
To drink the chaste Olympian Dews;
With *Thee* to tread the classic Ground,
Where GENIUS first the LAUREL found;
To view the sacred tufted Bow'rs,   35
Adorn'd with gay ambrosial Flow'rs;
Derive from *Thee* the lucid Ray,
That dignifies the modern Lay;
My Muse with wild Ambition fire,
And bid the burning Thought to Fame aspire.   40

Or, I will stray by Night's pale Orb;
Whose Beams the lesser Lights absorb:
Where INDIA's GOD in secret roves,
Through the rich consecrated Groves;
Where BRAHMA pours his pious Pray'r,   45
To the religious, list'ning Air;
And from the Fervor of his Lays,
I'll weave a Wreath of magic Praise;
Shall circle round thy crescent Brows,
Proud Token of far distant Vows!—   50
And should'st *Thou* e'er my hapless Verse peruse,
Pause on the Line, and own the simple Muse;
Say, that in Regions far from laurel'd Fame,
MARIA wept o'er DELLA CRUSCA's Name;
Say, as thy Death upon the Ev'ning hung,   55
Unnerv'd the Sense, and petrified the Tongue,
MARIA bound her Lyre with Sprigs of Yew,
And bath'd the Chords in Nightshade's weeping Dew;
While, as the muffled Sounds attun'd her Ear,
On its bright Threshold stood the GENUINE Tear!—   60

GARDENS, OCTOBER 29, 1793.

---

2. In legend, the Greek lyric poet Sappho was said to have leaped to her death from the Leuca-
dian rock for unrequited love of Phaon, a ferryman who had been made beautiful by the gods.

Elegiac Ode

INSCRIBED TO SIR JOHN SHORE,
BARONET, ON THE DEATH OF HIS TWO
INFANT CHILDREN, IN ENGLAND.

Remorseless Tyrant, Savage brave,[3]
Lord of the silent, mould'ring Grave,
Unsated DEATH!—whose Glance severe
Levels the scorpion-pointed Spear;
Oh!—quit the Charnel's loathsome Gloom,   5
The baleful Vault—the fretted Tomb;—
One Moment leave thy shrouded Throne,
Where Night's lorn Birds their Anguish moan:
I charge *Thee* to the garish Day,
To eke thy venom'd Spleen away!   10
Ah!—could'st thou not the Shaft recede,
Nor pause upon the barb'rous Deed;
Had blushing Innocence no Pow'r
To lure thee—for a longer Hour!
A Mother's Storm of Grief no Sway,   15
To lengthen yet their little Day,
Nor One thine Avarice supply,
But *two bright Cherubins* must die?
Unfeeling *Death*—thy Triumph's great,
Yet *Thou*, proud Fiend, shall yield to Time and Fate.   20

Beneath yon aged Yew-tree's Shade,
The loit'ring *Genius* of the Glade,
O'er the fresh Sod his wild Gaze throws,
That Gaze impierc'd with sharpest Woes;

---

3. John Shore later became governor-general of Bengal, but when these lines were written he was on the staff of Lord Cornwallis (the governor-general at that time), and he had become a devout evangelical Anglican. His son's memoir records his receipt on September 15, 1793, of news that two of his children left behind in England had died of measles. In a letter to Charles Grant, he described his habitual resignation to divine providence and went on to say, "These are the habitual sentiments of my heart. But in the first agonies of sorrow, their usual impression was suspended. Our Religion requires submission, but does not demand insensibility. I felt as a man, as a husband, and a parent; but I murmured not against the Hand that had inflicted my wounds. The offences of my life have been too many, not to acknowledge the justice of Divine punishment. How little indeed have I suffered, in proportion to my demerits! But the justice of the Almighty is inseparable from His benevolence." Charles John Shore, *Memoir of the Life and Correspondence of John, Lord Teignmouth* (London: Hatchard, 1843), 243.

By Grief subdued, his Eyes refuse   25
To shed their pure consoling Dews;
And thus in soft pathetic Strains,
To the *lone Mansions* he complains:
"Ah me!—whose solitary Breath
"Dwells on the faint chill Ear of Death;   30
"In vain does rosy Morning bring,
"The Perfumes of the blooming Spring;

"In vain do Nature's Charms appear,
"Drest in the Pride of vernal Year;
"Alas!—to me, the ruby Light,   35
"*Is but the Shadow of the Night!*—
"Those Joys I fondly strove to keep,
"In their cold Cell forever sleep:—
"Then Hope no more my Feelings mock,
"By thy Delusions tam'd I'll bear the Shock!—"   40

PHILOSOPHY, thou Saint Divine,
Around each quiv'ring Fibre twine;
The *Muse* with temper'd Lustre skill,
And calm the Pulse of Passion's Trill;
O'er *Sorrow's* fainting fev'rish Sense   45
Thy mental Solaces dispense.—
Lo, meek eyed *Pity*, Virgin bright,
As to her GOD she wings her Flight,
Drops from her Eye the sacred Tear,
And with it gems the *Infant Bier*;   50
To meet her, the celestial Band,
On the VIA LACTEA[4] stand;

The *little Cherubs* lead the Maid,
Through the transparent brilliant Glade;
Where Stars on Stars the Concave grace,   55
The Diamonds of ethereal Space:
And thus the lovely Seraphs sing,
"Return to Earth on Glory's Wing,
"Our SIRE this fond Assurance give
"That We in Heaven's fair Realms for ever live!"   60

---

4. Via Lactea: the Milky Way.

Adieu to India

Et vix sustinuit dicere Lingua—vale![5]

OCEAN, I call thee from the sapphire Deep,
Where the young Billows on their pearl-beds sleep;
And the fair Beauties of the boist'rous Main,
Far from the jarring Elements complain:
Where in the coral Groves transparent Court,   5
The green-hair'd Tritons and their Nymphs resort:
Haste and subdue the Turbulence that laves
The long-drawn Shadows of the mountain Waves;
Still the proud Tempest, whose impetuous Sway,
Heaves into monstrous Forms the watry Way.   10
MARIA asks—nor thou the Boon refuse,
Urg'd by the pensive melancholy Muse!
Who oft to *Thee*, when keen Despair hath spread
Her awful Terrors o'er her timid Head,
Has pour'd with fervid Lay the suppliant Pray'r,   15
And twin'd her Sorrows in thy sedgy Hair:
While *Thou* attentive to the weeping Tale,
Dispers'd her Fears, and quell'd the ruthless Gale.
     Adieu to INDIA'S fertile Plains,
     Where *Brahma's* holy Doctrine reigns;   20
     Whose virt'ous Principles still bind
     The *Hindoo's* meek untainted Mind;
     Far other Scenes my Thoughts employ,
     Source of Anguish, Hope and Joy;
     I hasten to my NATIVE SHORE,   25
     Where *Art* and *Science* blend their Lore;
     There *Learning* keeps her chosen Seat—
     A million Vot'ries at her Feet,

---

5. The epigraph for Anna Maria's "Adieu" is from Ovid's *Heroides,* the "Oenone Paride," and translates as "Your tongue was scarcely able to utter a last farewell." It is unclear here whether the poet adopts the persona of Oenone, who in this epistle laments the desertion of Paris, or whether the poet herself, like Paris, is deserting Calcutta, her own Oenone. R. Ehwald translates the longer Ovidian passage in Oenone's voice: "You clasped your arms round my neck, more closely than the curling vines embrace the towering elm. How did your companions smile, when you complained of the unfriendly winds! They favored; but love detained you. How often at parting did you repeat the ardent kisses; while your tongue was scarcely able to utter a last farewell!" See Ovid, *The Epistles,* ed. and trans. R. Ehwald, http://www.perseus.tufts.edu/cgi-bin/ptext?doc=Perseus%3Atext %3A1999.02.0085.

Ambitious of the LAUREL BOUGH,
To wind about their honor'd Brow.   30
Yet ere I go—a grateful Pain
Involves the Muse's parting Strain;
The sad Regret my Mind imbues,
And fills with Grief—*my last Adieus!*
For I have felt the subtle Praise,   35
That cheer'd the *Minstrel's* doubtful Lays;
That fed the infant lambent Flame,
And bade me hope for FUTURE FAME.

Farewell, ye sacred Haunts, where oft I've stray'd
With mild REFLECTION—solitary Maid!—   40
Ye Streams that swell the winding *Hougly's* tide, [6]
The Seat of Commerce and the Muse's Pride,
FAREWELL!—the Mariners unfurl the Sails,
Eager to meet the Pressure of the Gales;
And now the lofty Vessel cleaves the Way,   45
Dashing th' impelling Waves with silver Spray.—
Why springs my Heart with many an aching Sigh,
Why stands impearl'd the *Trembler* on mine eye?—
Alas!—fond Mem'ry weeps the Vision past,
"For ever fled, like yonder sweeping Blast:"   50
Those Hours of Bliss, those Scenes of soft Delight,
Vanish like Mists before the Rays of Light;
But still Remembrance holds the Objects dear,
And bathes their *Shadows* with Regret's pure Tear;
Nor shall th' oblivious Pow'r of TIME subdue,   55
The painful Feelings of the last—ADIEU!

GARDENS, NOVEMBER 24, 1793.

---

6. Hougly: the Hooghly [Hugli] River, a distributary of the Ganges in West Bengal. Flowing through Calcutta the river helped to create the city's strategic and commercial importance. The port was very active in the eighteenth and nineteenth centuries in Calcutta proper, but commerce has since moved downstream to Haldia, owing to silting. The Hooghly and the Ganges are often referred to interchangeably by Calcutta poets.

Lady Maria Nugent

ADY Maria Nugent (1770/1–1834) became after her marriage a prolific
diarist. Although she was born in America, where her father was the advocate
general of New Jersey, Maria Skinner soon accompanied her family to
England. Her father, who had been the speaker of the New Jersey Assembly, had
declined an offer to remain in office at independence. Although the American
patriots confiscated his considerable estates at the end of the War of Indepen-
dence, the British parliament compensated Skinner, and he retired with his
family to Bristol, England. Maria Skinner spent her youth in England and in
Ireland, earning a reputation as a vivacious and fashionable young woman. At
the age of twenty-six or twenty-seven, she married George Nugent, an army
officer who had served in the war in the American colonies and had by then be-
come brigadier general on the staff in Ireland and the captain and keeper of St.
Mawes Castle, Cornwall.

In 1801, the British army posted George Nugent to Jamaica as lieutenant
governor and commander in chief. Maria accompanied her husband and bore
two children there. Much of her diary concerns itself with daily life in the col-
ony. In the beginning of her life in Jamaica, Nugent saw the African inhabitants
as innocents and deplored their enslavement, particularly the sexual exploita-
tion of the female slaves. After experiencing a slave rebellion, however, Nugent
changed her mind, quickly growing to fear the people she had once pitied, now
seeing them as "savage" and "brutal."

In 1806, the family returned to England, where they spent several happy years
at their country house and had two more surviving children. George Nugent was
posted to India in 1811, and the couple decided to leave their children with En-
glish relatives and to embark together for Calcutta. The poem below records Maria
Nugent's grief at leaving her children, including a daughter eighteen months old
and a son born just weeks before his parents' departure. Once in India, Maria
Nugent traveled widely, including the trip to Delhi and Agra recorded in her
poem on the Taj Mahal. Her diaries reveal a combination of keen social observa-
tion, evangelical piety, and a motherly concern for the young officers on her
husband's staff.

In 1815, the family was reunited in England, where George embarked on a
political career. Maria Nugent continued her diaries. They were published post-
humously for the family in 1839.

Sources

Maria Nugent, *Journal from the Year 1811 till the Year 1815, Including a Voyage to and Residence in India*, 2 vols. (London: T. and W. Boone, 1839). See also Rosemary Cargill Raza, "Nugent, Maria, Lady Nugent (1770/71–1834)," in *ODNB*; and Raza, *In Their Own Words: British Women Writers and India, 1740–1857* (New Delhi: Oxford University Press, 2006).

from the *Journal of Maria Nugent*

The hour is past—Oh hour of woe![1]
Children beloved, a long adieu!
But, though to distant climes I go,
    A mother's heart remains with you.

Nor shall that heart know rest or peace,   5
    Nor shall that heart forget its care,
Nor shall, while absent, ever cease
    Thy tender mother's fervent prayer.

And may that God who sits on high,
    Who every thought and wish can see,   10
The secret sob, the smothered sigh,
    The bitter tears oft shed for thee;

In mercy may He grant me this,
    The only blessing I implore,
The dear delight, the heartfelt bliss,   15
    To see my darling babes once more;

---

1. Nugent's diary records her grief at this moment: "Saturday July 6. From this time till the 20th watching the winds, but they continued adverse to our sailing. My feelings mixed and various—sometimes quite happy with my children, and seeing the dear baby thriving so well—then again, almost in despair, at the idea of parting with them. . . . On Saturday the 20th we embarked on board the Baring East Indiaman—but I wish to forget all I felt on that day. . . . Passed a wretched night, and on Sunday, the 21st, the wind came round to its old point, and we returned once more to our dear ones, with whom we spent another happy week—it seemed to me as if the spell were broken, and this return was a delightful omen of our getting safe back in some five or six years;— but what a space of time! we must try and not think of it. . . . I see my dear Nugent suffers as much as I do but he does not indulge his grief, and I must endeavour to follow his example.—My greatest, my only consolation is in prayer, and I find myself able to put on a calm appearance often, when my heart is nearly breaking" (353–54).

Once more in Westhorpe's[2] shades to roam,
 The dear ones sporting by my side,
And never more I'll quit my home,
 For India's glory, India's pride.   20

And oh! may he, whose manly care
 Chases my grief in accents sweet,
My happiness be doomed to share,
 And make that happiness complete!

Lines Written on Seeing the Taaje, at Agra

Here all conspires to charm the ravish'd sight,
 And fill with wonder the admiring eye,
Here splendid gems and marble spotless white,
 That with the sunbeam and the snow might vie,
Their various beauties so commix and blend,   5
As nature did to art her best assistance lend.

The stately rising dome, the burnish'd spire,
 The casement, that their soften'd light impart,
Each in its turn, and all alike, conspire
 To strike the wondering eye, and touch the heart;   10
And while, rapt in delight, I silent gaze,
My heart to wedded love its well earn'd tribute pays.

For not alone this pile presents to me
 Proportions fair of architectural pride,
In every polish'd stone and gem I see   15
 All that's to love or sentiment allied;
And to the mental vision here appear,
All the affections that the feeling mind holds dear.

The basis, formed of marble white and pure,
 Portrays the groundwork of a well-placed love,   20
Which firm through life unshaken shall endure,
 Nor shall the hand of death that love remove—
For true affection, in the tender heart,
Stands unsubdued by time, or death's unerring dart.

---

2. Westhorpe was the Nugents' country seat in Buckinghamshire.

The pale ferosah, modest azure blue,[3]   25
  Emblem of truth and love the most sincere,
The brilliant sapphire's deeper regal hue,
  Tells how above all other love doth peer;
The love which, under Hymen's blest control,
Exalts the human mind, and dignifies the soul.   30

The yellow topaz speaks the anxious cares,
  That ever on affection's steps attend,
And the rich diamond, as it brightly glares,
  Shews the high value of a real friend:
But far beyond the brightest gems are found   35
Friendship and faithful love, in one soft union bound.

These pearls, the tears that fond affection shed
  O'er the pale corse of her he loved alone,[4]
These rubies, precious drops that heart has bled
  For her alas! for ever, ever gone!—   40
And pity's eye the tribute pearl bestows,
While faintly through the heart the ruby current flowers.—

But see, the emerald glads the tearful eye,
  And offers balsam to the troubled breast,
Pointing to regions far beyond the sky,   45
  Regions of peace, the mansions of the blest—
For Hope is e'er arrayed in brightest green,
All nature too in Hope's attire is seen!—

Sweet smiling Hope, thou soother of our cares,
  Thou first, best boon, to hapless mortals given—   50
Thou, who, when miserable man despairs,
  Bid'st him to look for happiness in heaven—
What e'er of wretchedness be still my lot,
Oh! let thy cheering ray, thy smile forsake me not.

And ye, blest pair! so fond, so true of heart,   55
  Who underneath this marble mouldering lie,
Ye who have known the agony to part,
  Are now rewarded with eternal joy;
So may fond love and truth for ever rest,
And like Jehan and Taaje eternally be blest.   60

---

3. Ferosah: turquoise.
4. Corse: corpse.

John Leyden

JOHN LEYDEN (1775–1811) set out to be a minister in the Church of Scotland, but his voice from the pulpit was so unpleasant, his person so unprepossessing, and his spirit of adventure so strong that he went to India instead. His Indian appointment meant that despite his divinity degrees and his years as a tutor in Scotland, Leyden needed to complete a rapid course of study for a medical license. This he accomplished in only six months, passing the examinations that allowed him to take up a position as assistant surgeon to the East India Company in Madras.

Like many another Scotsman of humble background, Leyden owed his success to the willingness of the Scottish church to assist poor young men toward an education, to his native genius, and to much hard work. Leyden's literary talents and intellectual energy led him from a poor cottage in the Scottish borders to acquaintance in the best society of Edinburgh.

Growing up on a small farm in Teviotdale, Leyden was taught to read by his grandmother and attended school when opportunity permitted from the age of ten. He was tutored by a local clergyman and finally was able to go up to Edinburgh to study divinity. There he completed B.A. and M.A. degrees in divinity, studied much on his own, and began to write, mainly on historical and literary subjects. When a position in the church was not forthcoming, he conceived the notion of going to Africa to make his fortune, for he was a great admirer of the Scots explorer Mungo Park. His friends, however, were alarmed at the prospect; with the help of the influential William Dundas, Leyden was appointed to a position at Madras in 1802.

As Walter Scott wrote in a memoir of his fellow poet, it was understood that Leyden's medical appointment was pro forma and that his great facility with languages would be called into service upon his arrival in India. During his years in Edinburgh, Leyden had studied Latin and Greek, as well as French, Italian, Spanish, and German. According to Scott, he was also familiar with ancient Icelandic and had studied Arabic, Persian, and Hebrew. Leyden's ambition, once he was set on a course toward India, was to equal the linguistic knowledge of Sir William Jones.

Early in his service in Madras, Leyden fell ill. Despite his doctor's orders, he used his period of recuperation to undertake a significant academic project. Recommended to take a sea voyage and recover his health, he traveled to Kerala in

South India and onward to Malaysia, but instead of relaxing, he conducted research in the various places he visited. On his return, he was posted to Calcutta, publishing there in 1808 his *Dissertation on the Languages and Literature of the Indo-Chinese Nations*. Leyden surveyed in this work fourteen different languages and literatures, including those of Malaysia, Java, the Philippines, Burma, Thailand, Cambodia, and Bali, and assessed the current European scholarship on these languages.

As the ambition of his linguistic studies attests, Leyden threw himself fervently into all his undertakings, his passions for poetry and Scottish antiquities among them. Before his departure for India, he published a learned discourse on fairies, authored a journal of Highland travel, edited the early modern *Complaynt of Scotland*, and assisted Scott with *The Minstrelsy of the Scottish Borders*. Of this last undertaking, Scott recalled an instance when he and Leyden were unable to locate the whole of a ballad they especially wished to include, whereupon Leyden walked forty or fifty miles to visit "an old person who possessed this precious remnant of antiquity." Two days later, Scott was sitting with friends after dinner when they heard a sound like the "whistling of a tempest through the torn rigging of a vessel." It was Leyden singing in his "saw-tones" the whole of the ballad they had sought (Leyden, *Poems and Ballads*, 29).

As Leyden's friends predicted, his work in India was more linguistic than medical. Lord Minto appointed Leyden to judgeships in rural Bengal and then in Calcutta, following which he became assay master of the Calcutta mint. In 1811, he enthusiastically accompanied his patron to Java, where he was needed primarily for his linguistic skills. His personal object was to acquire manuscripts for his own study of languages, but Java (particularly the Dutch settlement of Batavia, which had been ceded to the British) had a deadly reputation for disease. After a very short time, Leyden fell ill of a fever and died at Cornelis on August 28, 1811. In later years, rumor had it that he had died from ransacking an ill-ventilated library.

Among his poems, Leyden is primarily known for a volume that was published at the time of his departure from Britain—*Scenes of Infancy, Descriptive of Teviotdale* (1803). This long poem provides an appreciative description of a countryside the poet knew well, from his childhood as a shepherd and from his later collecting of ballads. It also anticipates his emigration and—most unusually—laments the fact that poor Scots, unable to survive in their own country, would become agents of depriving others (notably, native North Americans) of their lands. A similar skepticism is evident in Leyden's most famous Indian poem, "Ode to an Indian Gold Coin," which takes an unblinking view of the imperial enterprise. Though Leyden, a Scots divine to his core, could be appalled at Indian religions, he was also nearly as appalled at British materialism.

Leyden lived the contradictions of English internal colonialism and British imperialism, just as he lived the contradictions between learning for its own delights and learning as an arm of imperial conquest. He kept his strong Borders accent yet wrote accomplished English—not Scots—verse. He was passionate about learning multiple languages, but he died "translating" the British conquest of Java.

Sources

John Leyden, *Poems and Ballads, with a Memoir of the Author by Sir Walter Scott, Bart.* (Kelso, Scotland: J. and J. H. Rutherfurd, 1858). See also Leyden, *Scenes of Infancy, Descriptive of Teviotdale* (London: T. N. Longman and O. Rees, 1803).

Ode to an Indian Gold Coin

WRITTEN IN CHERICAL, MALABAR[1]

Slave of the dark and dirty mine!
    What vanity has brought thee here?
How can I love to see thee shine
    So bright, whom I have bought so dear?—
    The tent-ropes flapping lone I hear   5
For twilight-converse, arm in arm;
    The jackal's shriek bursts on mine ear,
When mirth and music wont to charm.

By Cherical's dark wandering streams,
    Where cane-tufts shadow all the wild,   10
Sweet visions haunt my waking dreams
    Of Teviot loved while still a child,
    Of castled rocks stupendous piled
By Esk or Eden's classic wave,[2]

---

1. The Malabar coast ordinarily refers to India's southwest coast, lying between the Western Ghats and the Arabian Sea and running from the south of Goa to Cape Comorin on the subcontinent's southern tip. Walter Scott added this headnote to the poem: "This is one of Leyden's most beautiful pieces, breathing the spirit of poetry from beginning to end. It would seem he had moments of regret that he left home with all its endearments for the chance of acquiring something like an independence in an eastern land; and on one of these occasions, being awakened to a sense of his position by the sight of a gold coin, he gave vent to his feelings in these impassioned lines" (Leyden, *Poems and Ballads,* 312).

2. The River Teviot flows through the Scottish Borders, rising on the border of Dumfries and Galloway. The Esk, also a Border river, flows through Dumfries and Galloway in Scotland and through Cumbria (the Lake District) in northwestern England. The Esk enters Solway Firth near the mouth of the River Eden.

Where loves of youth and friendships smiled,   15
Uncursed by thee, vile yellow slave!

Fade, day-dreams sweet, from memory fade!—
    The perish'd bliss of youth's first prime,
That once so bright on fancy play'd,
      Revives no more in after-time.   20
      Far from my sacred natal clime,
I haste to an untimely grave;
    The daring thoughts that soar'd sublime
Are sunk in ocean's southern wave.

Slave of the mine! Thy yellow light   25
    Gleams baleful as the tomb-fire drear,—
A gentle vision comes by night
      My lonely widow'd heart to cheer;
      Her eyes are dim with many a tear,
That once were guiding stars to mine: 30
    Her fond heart throbs with many a fear!—
I cannot bear to see thee shine.

For thee, for thee, vile yellow slave,
    I left a heart that loved me true!
I cross'd the tedious ocean-wave,   35
      To roam in climes unkind and new.
      The cold wind of the stranger blew
Chill on my wither'd heart:—the grave
    Dark and untimely met my view—
And all for thee, vile yellow slave!   40

Ha! comest thou now so late to mock
    A wanderer's banish'd heart forlorn,
Now that his frame the lightning shock
      Of sun-rays tipt with death has borne?
      From love, from friendship, country, torn,   45
To memory's fond regrets the prey,
    Vile slave, thy yellow dross I scorn!—
Go mix thee with thy kindred clay!

Ode

To the Scenes of Infancy

WRITTEN IN 1801.

My native stream, my native vale,
And you, green meads of Teviotdale,
    That after absence long I view!
Your bleakest scenes, that rise around,
Assume the tints of fairy ground,   5
    And infancy revive anew.

Thrice blest the days I here have seen,
When light I traced that margin green,
    Blithe as the linnet[3] on the spray;
And thought the days would ever last   10
As gay and cheerful as the past;—
    The sunshine of a summer's day.

Fair visions, innocently sweet!
Though soon you pass'd on viewless feet,
    And vanish'd to return no more;   15
Still, when this anxious breast shall grieve,
You shall my pensive heart relieve,
    And every former joy restore.

When first around mine infant head
Delusive dreams their visions shed,   20
    To soften or to soothe the soul;
In every scene, with glad surprise,
I saw my native groves arise,
    And Teviot's crystal waters roll.

And when religion raised my view   25
Beyond this concave's azure blue,
    Where flowers of fairer lustre blow,
Where Eden's groves again shall bloom,
Beyond the desert of the tomb,
    And living streams for ever flow,—   30

---

3. Linnet: *Carduelis cannabina*, a species of finch that used to be very common in the British Isles.

The groves of soft celestial dye
Where such as oft had met mine eye,
 Expanding green on Teviot's side;
The living stream, whose pearly wave
In fancy's eye appear'd to lave,   35
 Resembled Teviot's limpid tide.

When first each joy that childhood yields
I left, and saw my native fields
 At distance fading dark and blue,
As if my feet had gone astray   40
In some lone desart's pathless way,
 I turn'd, my distant home to view.

Now tired of folly's fluttering breed,
And scenes where oft the heart must bleed,
 Where every joy is mix'd with pain; 45
Back to this lonely green retreat,
Which Infancy has render'd sweet,
 I guide my wandering steps again.

And now, when rosy sun-beams lie
In thin streaks o'er the eastern sky, 50
 Beside my native stream I rove;
When the gray sea of fading light
Ebbs gradual down the western height,
 I softly trace my native grove.

When forth at morn the heifers go, 55
And fill the fields with plaintive low,
 Re-echoed by their young confined;
When sun-beams wake the slumbering breeze,
And light the dew-drops on the trees,
 Beside the stream I lie reclined, 60

And view the water-spiders glide
Along the smooth and level tide,
 Which, printless, yields not as they pass;
While still their slender frisky feet
Scarce seem with tiny step to meet 65
 The surface blue and clear as glass.

Beside the twisted hazel bush
I love to sit, and hear the thrush,
　　　Where clustered nuts around me spring;
While from a thousand mellow throats　　　　　　　　70
High thrill the gently-trembling notes,
　　　And winding woodland echoes ring.

The shadow of my native grove,
And wavy streaks of light I love,
　　　When brightest glows the eye of day;　　　　　75
And shelter'd from the noon-tide beam,
I pensive muse beside the stream,
　　　Or by the pebbled channel stray.

Where little playful eddies wind,
The banks with silvery foam are lined,　　　　　　　80
　　　Untainted as the mountain snow;
And round the rock, incrusted white,
The rippling waves in murmurs light
　　　Reply to gales that whispering blow.

I love the riv'let's stilly chime,　　　　　　　　　　　85
That marks the ceaseless lapse of time,
　　　And seems in fancy's ear to say—
"A few short suns, and thou no more
Shalt linger on thy parent shore,
　　　But like the foam-streak pass away."—　　　　90

Dear fields, in vivid green array'd!
When every tint at last shall fade
　　　In death's funereal cheerless hue,
As sinks the latest fainting beam
Of light that on mine eyes shall gleam,　　　　　　95
　　　Still shall I turn your scenes to view.

James Atkinson

J AMES ATKINSON (1780–1852) was a man of many trades. By turns a portrait painter, medical doctor, chemist (as assay master of the Calcutta mint), scholar of Persian, poet, and travel writer, he lived in India for more than thirty-five years. Born in Darlington in the north of England, he studied medicine at Edinburgh and afterward in London. At the age of twenty-five, he sailed as a medical officer on board an East Indiaman and, after landing in Calcutta, was appointed assistant surgeon (or physician) in the Bengal Medical Service. In his posting near Dhaka, he undertook the study of Persian and began collecting Persian manuscripts. In 1813, he was invited to Calcutta by Lord Minto, the governor-general of India, and assumed the office of assistant assay master at the mint, an employment he continued until 1828. After Minto's death, Atkinson commemorated him in an elegy appreciative of Minto's longing for the Scotland of his youth.

Evidently a person of considerable energy, Atkinson combined his work in the mint with myriad other activities. In part, one surmises, these multifarious occupations reflected his wide-ranging interests and talents; in addition, they may have contributed to a more stable income, for medical officers in the 1820s were disgruntled about their pensions, comparing them unfavorably to those of military officers (see *Oriental Herald,* January 1, 1827). Whatever his motivations, during his sixteen years at the mint, Atkinson continued his medical practice, edited the *Government Gazette* and ran the government press, translated Persian, wrote original poetry, and served for a year as a professor of Persian at Fort William College.

After an extended leave in London, Atkinson returned to India in 1833 as surgeon to the 55th Regiment of the Bengal Native Infantry, and five years later he became superintending surgeon to the Army of the Indus on its first Afghan campaign. Fortunately for Atkinson, he was posted back to Calcutta before the massacre of the British forces in the winter of 1842, but his time in Afghanistan served him well, as he brought back with him a sketchbook and a journal that were the foundation for his best-known works. His edited journal was published immediately in London as *The Expedition into Afghanistan; Notes and Sketches Descriptive of the Country, Contained in a Personal Narrative during the Campaign of 1839 & 1840, up to the Surrender of Dost Mahomed Khan,* and his drawings were reproduced in a separate volume,

Sketches in Afghanistan, which is still much sought by collectors. The popularity of Atkinson's sketches is unsurprising, as they constituted scenes of travel and news of a conflict both distant and, eventually, disastrous. But Atkinson's drawings in Afghanistan were also skillful—probably because, though an amateur, Atkinson had considerable experience as a painter. His son recorded in a memoir that Atkinson had "early exhibited a remarkable talent for portrait-painting"; several of these portraits, including a self-portrait, are in the National Portrait Gallery in London. The British Library holds two of Atkinson's paintings on popular—if sensational—Indian subjects: a painting of a double sati and a painting of "hook-swinging," a religious ritual practiced in Bengal and south India that involved a man being swung from a hook and pulley. While Atkinson's paintings are competent, particularly the market scene in the latter work, they were clearly designed to portray popular and controversial subjects.

Atkinson was equally well known for his poems and translations. His earliest works included translations from the Italian; *Hatim Tye* (1818), a translation of a popular Persian romance; and *Soohrab* (1814), which rendered into English verse portions of Firdausi's epic the *Shāh Nāmeh.* Atkinson returned to Firdausi in 1832, publishing a translated abridgement of the *Shāh Nāmeh,* or "great book of kings," and appending his earlier translation. This work was sponsored by the Oriental Translation Fund, which awarded it a gold medal. Atkinson's next translation—excerpted here—rendered into English Nizāmī's *Lailī and Majnún,* the most popular of Persian romances.

In addition to translations from the Persian, Atkinson wrote original verses. Among these, the poem that lingers into the twenty-first century is the often-satirical one that lent its title to his volume *The City of Palaces* (Calcutta, 1824). It might surprise North American readers, entranced with the image of Mother Teresa in Calcutta slums, that the City of Palaces even now remains a common nickname for the capital of West Bengal. Atkinson's characterization of Calcutta—and its British and Indian inhabitants—creates a skeptical view of what was then a thriving and often beautiful city, replete with slums but also with green public spaces, impressive public buildings, a bustling port, and a "white town" characterized by elegant mansions. Like his fellow Britons, Atkinson sought his fortune in the East, but he was willing to admit that India, in more ways than one, "gave a new complexion." Calcutta may have been a city of palaces for Atkinson, but he characterized it equally as "nurse of opulence and vice" (*City of Palaces,* 14). He was willing to describe Hindu rituals as "orgies" yet declared that the people of India should be free to worship as they pleased, for after all, "They did not come to us, but conquering we to them" (18). No wonder Atkinson dedicated his poem to Diogenes, the Cynic.

The physician, realizing perhaps that he could cure neither the army nor its empire, returned to Britain in retirement in 1847, dying five years later in London at the age of seventy-two.

Sources

James Atkinson, *The City of Palaces, and Other Poems* (Calcutta: Government Gazette Press, 1824); Atkinson, *Lailí and Majnún* (London: Oriental Translation Fund, 1836); Atkinson, "Monody on the Death of the Earl of Minto," *Calcutta Annual Register for the Year 1821* (1823): 37–39. See also Stanley Lane-Poole, "Atkinson, James (1780–1852)," rev. Parvin Loloi, *ODNB*.

from *The City of Palaces: A Fragment*

Philomenes. Then begin thy Diogenes strain
In the true moralizing vein.
Mask of the Cynics.

I

Empires rise from the dust, extend, decay,
Slow in their growth, oft rapid in their fall;
Babylon, Carthage, Rome; these had their day,
Their centuries of glory,—proud to call
The conquered world their own, holding in thrall   5
Millions of subjects. But we here behold
A prodigy of power, transcending all
The conquests, and the governments, of old,
An empire of the Sun, a gorgeous realm of gold.

II

For us, in half a century, India blooms   10
The garden of Hesperides, and we
Placed in its porch, CALCUTTA, with its tombs
And dazzling splendors, towering peerlessly,
May taste its sweets, yet bitters too there be
Under attractive seeming. Drink again   15
The frothy draught, and revel joyously;
From the gay round of pleasure why refrain!
Thou'rt on the brink of death, luxuriate on thy bane.

III

When first I stood upon the landing place,
Of the proud City of the gorgeous East,   20
I saw a swarthy turban-covered race,
Whose noise and tumult momently increased;
They looked as if from Bedlam just released;
A Babel of strange tongues encompassed me,
Fawning for service, so I thought at least,   25
And I, a thing of nought, a worm, to be
Thus hailed upon the shore, like Knight of high degree.

IV

I stood a wondering stranger at the *Ghaut*,[1]
And, gazing round, beheld the pomp of spires
And palaces, to view like magic brought;   30
All glittering in the sun-beam. Man's desires
Are here superbly pampered, yet he tires—
No wish ungratified, yet he complains;
And miracles to please himself requires;
An idle, splendid, household he maintains;   35
A petty tyrant here, in lordly state he reigns.

V

The Hooghly[2] flowed majestic at my feet,
Bearing upon its bosom many a bark,
(Wanderers o'er every sea) a numerous fleet,
Thick as a winter forest, tall and dark,   40
But on the ebbing waters I could mark
Dead bodies floating in the face of day,—
Aweful mementos, with corruption stark,—
I turned my sight from the revolting prey
Of Vultures, festering fast, and rolling to the Bay.   45

---

1. Ghaut (Ghat): a set of broad steps that lead down into a river.
2. Hooghly: the Hooghly [Hugli] River flows through Calcutta and formerly gave the city its strategic and commercial importance.

VI

The bustling clang of Commerce struck my ear,—
Mortality's terrific wreck was there,
Amidst the busy scene to tell how near
Life is to Death and Desolation—where,
Where am I now—Is this the tyger's lair? 50
Has the world lost its pity and its pride,
That human corpses thus infect the air,
Rudely like worn out garments thrown aside,
To rot in public view, upon the loitering tide?

VII

But years have passed since that momentous day 55
Which gave a new complexion to my fate;
How many here in avarice waste away
The summer of existence; when too late,
They hurry home, or haply lingering wait
Till their bones rest beneath a sculptured tomb, 60
In that Necropolis, of mournful state,
Where structures rise, not in sepulchral gloom,
But as gay temple, tower, light obelisk, or dome.

VIII

From scenes of brightest fortune, brightest joy,
Where pomp and power ensnare us, how we turn 65
Instinctively to England, and employ
Our mind in retrospection, till we burn,
With feverish impatience;—here we learn
To value that which Time can not allay,
The cherished love of home: our bosoms yearn 70
For that sweet close of life, for that we pray,
To roam o'er sunny fields, where Childhood loved to stray.

from *Lailí and Majnún*

Alone, unseen; his vassals keep remote
Curious intruders from that sacred spot;
Alone, with wasted form and sombre eyes,
Groaning in anguish he exhausted lies;
No more life's joys or miseries will he meet, 5
Nothing to rouse him from this last retreat;
Upon a sinking gravestone he is laid,
The gates already opening for the dead!
 Selim, the generous, who had twice before
Sought his romantic refuge, to implore 10
The wanderer to renounce the life he led,
And shun the ruin bursting o'er his head,
Again explored the wilderness, again
Cross'd craggy rock, deep glen, and dusty plain,
To find his new abode. A month had pass'd 15
'Mid mountain wild, when, turning back, at last
He spied the wretched sufferer alone,
Stretch'd on the ground, his head upon a stone
Majnún, up-gazing, recognised his face,
And bade his growling followers give him place; 20
Then said,—"Why art thou here again, since thou
Left me in wrath? What are thy wishes now?
I am a wretch bow'd down with bitterest woe,
Doom'd the extremes of misery to know,
Whilst thou, in affluence born, in pleasure nursed, 25
Stranger to ills the direst and the worst,
Can never join, unless in mockery,
With one so lost to all the world as me!"
Selim replied:—"Fain would I change thy will,
And bear thee hence,—be thy companion still: 30
Wealth shall be thine, and peace and social joy,
And tranquil days, no sorrow to annoy;
And she for whom thy soul has yearn'd so long
May yet be gain'd, and none shall do thee wrong."
—Deeply he groan'd, and wept:—"No more, no more! 35
Speak not of her whose memory I adore;
She whom I loved, than life itself more dear,
My friend, my angel-bride, is buried here!
Dead!—but her spirit is now in heaven, whilst I

Live, and am dead with grief—yet do not die.   40
This is the fatal spot, my Lailí's tomb,—
This the lamented place of martyrdom.
Here lies my life's sole treasure, life's sole trust;
All that was bright in beauty gone to dust!"

    Selim before him in amazement stood,   45
Stricken with anguish, weeping tears of blood;
And consolation blandly tried to give.
What consolation? Make his Lailí live?
His gentle words and looks were only found
To aggravate the agonising wound;   50
And weeks in fruitless sympathy had pass'd,
But, patient still, he linger'd to the last;
Then, with an anxious heart, of hope bereft,
The melancholy spot, reluctant, left.
The life of Majnún had received its blight;   55
His troubled day was closing fast in night.
Still weeping, bitter, bitter tears he shed,
As grovelling in the dust his hands he spread
In holy prayer. "O God! thy servant hear
    And in thy gracious mercy set him free   60
From the afflictions which oppress him here,
    That, in the Prophet's name, he may return to Thee!"
Thus murmuring, on the tomb he laid his head,
And with a sigh his wearied spirit fled.

And he, too, has perform'd his pilgrimage.   65
And who, existing on this earthly stage,
But follows the same path? whate'er his claim
To virtue, honour,—worthy praise, or blame;
So will he answer at the judgment-throne,
Where secrets are unveil'd, and all things known;   70
Where felon-deeds of darkness meet the light,
And goodness wears its crown with glory bright.
Majnún, removed from this tumultuous scene,
Which had to him unceasing misery been,
At length slept on the couch his bride possess'd,   75
And, wakening, saw her mingled with the bless'd.
There still lay stretch'd his body many a day,
Protected by his faithful beasts of prey;
Whose presence fill'd with terror all around,
Who sought to know where Majnún might be found: 80

Listening they heard low murmurs on the breeze,
Now loud and mournful, like the hum of bees;
But still supposed him seated in his place,
Watch'd by those sentinels of the savage race.
—A year had pass'd, and still their watch they kept,   85
As if their sovereign was not dead, but slept;
Some had been call'd away, and some had died—
At last the mouldering relics were descried;
And when the truth had caught the breath of fame,
Assembled friends from every quarter came;   90
Weeping, they wash'd his bones, now silvery white,
With ceaseless tears perform'd the funeral rite,
And, opening the incumbent tablet wide,
Mournfully laid him by his Lailí's side.
One promise bound their faithful hearts—one bed   95
Of cold, cold earth united them when dead.
Sever'd in life, how cruel was their doom!
Ne'er to be join'd but in the silent tomb!

Monody on the Death of the Earl of Minto

THUS MAN decays, thus earthly visions fade,
And life's bright scenes dissolve in empty shade;
Day after day the mortal chain is riven,
No stay unfragile but the HOPE OF HEAVEN.

Yet though unceasing is the fate we find,   5
And DEATH still holds the mirror to the mind,
Scarcely we feel the universal doom,
Which hurries MAN unthinking to the tomb;
Till friends fall off, and those at length depart,
Whom fond AFFECTION binds around the heart;   10
Then bursts the sigh—the tears unbidden flow,
And all the soul is desolate with woe.

The mournful strain now echoing from the shore,
Breathes the sad tale that MINTO IS NO MORE!

How oft, ere India vanished from his sight,   15
Had FANCY painted scenes of proud delight,

When native bowers should open to his view,
And AGE be solaced 'midst the kindred few:
There, when the toils of public life were o'er,
Enjoy the calm of leisure yet in store!   20

   Those crags which raise their summits to the sky,
Still loved, still seen in FANCY'S roving eye,
Were wont to yield to his untravelled heart,
That rapturous joy which scenes of home impart;
The magic charm which soothes the exile's woe,   25
With strongest feelings bade his bosom glow;
Years had not dimmed the prospect, but more bright,
The well-known woodlands struck his mental sight;
The copse, the dell, and all which childhood knew,
In fair array his kindled memory drew.   30
Full of the thought, how oft his eye retraced,
The pictured rock³ by foliage dark embraced;
And fondly marked the rugged path which led,
To Barnhill's rude traditionary bed;
These to survey near Teviot's wandering tide,   35
Compassed by friends had been his dearest pride:
But HEAVEN forbade, relentless to destroy,⁴
And snatched away the boon of promised joy.

   Now all is past; in vain he sought to close,
A well-spent life in dignified repose;   40

---

3. *The pictured rock.* Atkinson's extensive note reads, "this was a view of Minto crags, painted by the
author, which his Lordship always contemplated with delight. WALTER SCOTT, in the *Lay of the Last
Minstrel*, has thus described the subject of the picture:

> On Minto crags the moon-beams glint,
> Where *Barnhill* hewed his bed of flint;
> Who flung his outlawed arms to rest,
> Where falcons hang their giddy nest,
> Mid cliffs, from whence his eagle eye,
> For many a league his prey could spy.

To these lines the following note is affixed. 'A romantic assemblage of cliffs, which rise sud-
denly above the vale of Teviot, in the immediate vicinity of the family seat, from which LORD
MINTO takes his title. A small platform, on a projecting crag, commanding a most beautiful pros-
pect, is termed *Barnhill's bed.* This Barnhill is said to have been a robber, and an outlaw. There are
remains of a strong tower beneath the rocks, where he is supposed to have dwelt, and from which
he is said to have derived his name.'" [JA]

4. *But heaven forbade.* LORD MINTO died suddenly, on the 21st of June, 1814, at Stevenage, about a
month after his return to England from India. He was on his way to Scotland, and had left London in
a bad state of health. In the course of his illness, he had no presentiment of approaching dissolution,
and seemed only anxious to proceed on his journey and to reach MINTO as early as possible. [JA]

Fled is that soul where honor sate enthroned,
Inspired with thoughts which every Virtue owned;
Firm, wise, and just; with patriot-zeal imprest,
His country's glory ever warmed his breast.
Whence sprung that high-wrought energy which gave,   45
The glittering spoils of JAVA to the brave?
And placed, unhurt by power, another gem,
Richer than all, in England's diadem?
Bold and intrepid in the sacred cause,
He nobly gained a nation's just applause!   50

    Yet while resplendent shone his public fame,
The gentler virtues[5] more endeared his name,
Mild, though exalted, generous and serene,
Pure social love illumed his placid mien;
The lively temper still unknown to strife,   55
The soft enchantments of domestic life,
Cherished by him, a magic influence threw,
O'er all the circle which his friendship knew;
And who but felt, within that envied range,
His heart still ardent, still unprone to change?   60
A Poet's mind,[6] endued with heavenly fire,
Marked the sweet warblings of his rustic lyre;
The Sage's grasp of intellect supplied,
A firm, resistless, and unerring guide;
But classic Lore in modest garb arrayed,   65
No boast in him, nor idle pomp displayed.

    And thou bright structure,[7] sacred to the brave,
Glittering with pride o'er Gunga's rolling wave,
Long as thy walls of JAVA's fate shall tell,
How many heroes crowned with glory fell;   70
Even when thy record, faithless to its trust,
Sinks with decay and crumbles in the dust.
His name, revered through India's distant clime,
Shall live triumphant o'er the wrecks of time.

CALCUTTA; DECEMBER, 1814.

---

5. *The gentler virtues.* In his domestic circle no man ever displayed a kinder heart, or was ever more affectionately beloved. [JA]

6. *A Poet's mind.* LORD MINTO is the author of a number of beautiful little poems. The MINTO VISION, descriptive of the romantic seat of his ancestors, is a production of high merit. [JA]

7. *And thou bright structure.* The Cenotaph at Barrackpore, erected by his Lordship to the memory of those brave officers and men who fell at the conquest of Bourbon, Mauritius, and Java. [JA]

Reginald Heber

≈) (≈

REGINALD HEBER'S legacy lingers in Calcutta in the shape of Bishop's College and in Britain and North America through his hymns, which to this day are sung in Anglican and Protestant churches. Born of an old Yorkshire family, Heber (1783–1826) is principally remembered for his work as the bishop of Calcutta, a diocese that then included all of India, Ceylon (Sri Lanka), and Australasia.

From his early days at Oxford, Heber pursued an avocation as a poet, winning the Newdigate Prize for "Palestine" in 1803 and reciting it to an enthusiastic crowd in the Sheldonian Theatre. Legend has it that his father was so overcome with delight at his son's resounding success that, in his weakened state from a long illness, he "may be said to have died of the joy dearest to a parent's heart" (*Poetical Works* [1885], 43). This legend, though an exaggeration, nonetheless indicates Heber's powers of recitation and portends his later success as a preacher. In India, as at Oxford, Heber combined his intellectual gifts with an unassuming and loving character. By all accounts, he succeeded in bridging chasms of race, religion, and education wherever he found himself.

Receiving his B.A. from Brasenose, Heber was elected a fellow of All Souls, Oxford, but he resigned his fellowship to succeed his father in 1807 as the rector of Hodnet, the family living in Shropshire. This post allowed him to marry Amelia Shipley, the daughter of Sir William Jones's brother-in-law and friend William Shipley. In one of those striking coincidences common to Anglo-Indian history, Amelia Shipley Heber and her aunt Anna Maria Shipley Jones both were widowed early and spent their first years back in England editing the writings of their famous husbands. During her married life, Amelia served unofficially as Heber's private secretary. Heber's enduring devotion to Amelia is reflected in the poem below, which he wrote while he was on his visitation to Anglican churches in India, having left his family behind in Calcutta.

At Hodnet, Heber found himself both a parson and a squire, taking responsibility for the family's Shropshire manor as well as for his congregation. He proved assiduous in his duties, and in Shropshire, as in Calcutta, he earned the love and affection of his colleagues and parishioners. Through William Shipley's influence, he became a prebendary of the Cathedral of St. Aspah, where Shipley was dean, and subsequently he was appointed preacher to Lincoln's Inn in London. The latter appointment allowed him to foster his literary connections.

Heber continued to write poetry and also hymns; he edited the works of Jeremy Taylor and served as an editor of the *Quarterly Review*. Owing partly to a youthful trip to Russia and the Caucasus and partly to his early interest in India, Heber maintained a strong interest in Asia during the years at Hodnet.

In England, as later in India, Heber combined his evangelical leanings with a dedication to bringing together various factions in the Church of England. He was sympathetic to both "High Church" clergy, who emphasized liturgy and tradition, and "Low Church" evangelicals, who emphasized personal religious feeling and missionary zeal. Even during his time at Hodnet, he actively supported the work of the Society for the Propagation of the Gospel and of the Church Missionary Society, both organizations associated with Low Church evangelical zeal. His famous hymn "From Greenland's Icy Mountains" was written at the request of his father-in-law for a special missionary offering. Though hymns were not officially approved for use in Anglican churches at the time, Heber wrote more than fifty-seven, because he sensed their increasing popularity outside the Church of England. He believed that Anglican services could usefully incorporate theologically and artistically superior hymns. No doubt his Welsh connections strengthened this conviction, for hymn singing was especially popular in Wales. "From Greenland's Icy Mountains" became the standard nineteenth-century missionary hymn. Among Heber's other hymns, the best known are "The Son of God Goes Forth to War," "Brightest and Best the Sons of the Morning," and "Holy, Holy, Holy."

Though he wrote one of the best-known early Anglo-Indian poems, "An Evening Walk in Bengal," Heber had little leisure for poetry during his years as the bishop of Calcutta (1823–26). Arriving in India, he faced a huge backlog of episcopal work and had to bring to bear all his diplomatic skills on the various controversies left unresolved at the death of his predecessor. As the first bishop allowed to ordain native priests, he put the Bishop's College on a sound financial footing to provide an education to young men of European, Indian, and Anglo-Indian descent, and he even attended to schools for Indian girls. His principal writing was a journal of his travels to the scattered Anglican congregations of India and Ceylon. After his sudden death, at the age of forty-two, at Trichinopoly (Trichi, Tamil Nadu), Amelia Heber edited his journals and letters, publishing them in 1828 as *A Narrative of a Journey through the Upper Provinces of India, from Calcutta to Bombay, 1824–1825 (with Notes upon Ceylon)*. A collection of his poems was also issued in 1830. Both volumes went into several editions in the course of the nineteenth century.

Sources

Reginald Heber, *Poems* (Hingham, England: C. and E. B. Gill, 1830). See also M. A. DeWolfe, ed. *The Poetical Works of Reginald Heber* (New York: Worthington, 1885); Amelia

Heber, *The Life of Reginald Heber, D.D., Lord Bishop of Calcutta, with Selections from his Correspondence* (London: John Murray, 1830); Derrick Hughes, *Bishop Sahib: A Life of Reginald Heber* (Worthing, UK: Churchman, 1986); and Michael Laird, "Heber, Reginald (1783–1826)," *ODNB*.

Intended to Be Sung on Occasion of His Preaching a Sermon for the Church Missionary Society, in April 1820

From Greenland's icy mountains,
From India's coral strand,
Where Afric's sunny fountains
Roll down their golden sand;
From many an ancient river,   5
From many a palmy plain,
They call us to deliver
Their land from error's chain.

What though the spicy breezes
Blow soft o'er Ceylon's isle,   10
Though every prospect pleases,
And only man is vile:
In vain with lavish kindness
The gifts of God are strown,
The heathen, in his blindness,   15
Bows down to wood and stone.

Can we, whose souls are lighted
With wisdom from on high,
Can we to men benighted
The lamp of life deny?   20
Salvation, O salvation!
The joyful sound proclaim,
Till each remotest nation
Has learned Messiah's name.

Waft, waft, ye winds, his story,   25
And you, ye waters, roll,

Till, like a sea of glory,
It spreads from pole to pole;
Till o'er our ransomed nature,
The Lamb for sinners slain, 30
Redeemer, King, Creator,
In bliss returns to reign.

The Outward-Bound Ship

As borne along with favouring gale
    And streamers waving bright,
How gaily sweeps the glancing sail
    O'er yonder sea of light!

With painted sides the vessel glides, 5
    In seeming revelry;
And still we hear the sailor's cheer
    Around the capstan tree.

Is sorrow there where all is fair,
    Where all is outward glee? 10
Go, fool, to yonder mariner,
    And he shall lesson thee!

Upon that deck walks tyrant sway
    Wild as his conquer'd wave,
And murmuring hate that must obey; 15
    The captain and his slave.

And pinching care is lurking there,
    And dark ambition's swell,
And some that part with bursting heart
    From objects loved too well; 20

And many a grief with gazing fed
    On yonder distant shore,
And many a tear in secret shed
    For friends beheld no more;

Yet sails the ship with streamers drest   25
    And shouts of seeming glee:
Oh God! how loves mortal breast
    To hide its misery!

Lines Addressed to Mrs. Heber

If thou wert by my side, my love,
    How fast would evening fail
In green Bengala's palmy grove
    Listening the nightingale!

If thou, my love, wert by my side,   5
    My babies at me knee,
How gaily would our pinnace glide
    O'er Gunga's[1] mimic sea!

I miss thee at the dawning gray
    When, on our deck reclined,   10
In careless ease my limbs I lay
    And woo the cooler wind.

I miss thee when by Gunga's stream
    My twilight steps I guide,
But most beneath the lamp's pale beam   15
    I miss thee from my side.

I spread my books, my pencil try
    The lingering noon to cheer,
But miss thy kind approving eye,
    Thy meek attentive ear.   20

But when of morn and eve the star
    Beholds me on my knee,
I feel, though thou art distant far,
    Thy prayers ascend for me.

---

1. Gunga's mimic sea: a reference to the Ganges River as it empties into the Bay of Bengal.

Then on! then on! where duty leads,   25
 My course be onward still,
O'er broad Hindostan's sultry mead,
 O'er bleak Almorah's[2] hill.

That course, nor Delhi's kingly gates,
 Nor wild Malwah[3] detain;   30
For sweet the bliss us both awaits
 By yonder western main.

Thy towers, Bombay, gleam bright they say,
 Across the dark blue sea,
But ne'er were hearts so light and gay   35
 As then shall meet in thee

An Evening Walk in Bengal

Our task is done! on Gunga's breast
The sun is sinking down to rest;
And, moored beneath the tamarind bough,
Our bark has found its harbour now.
With furled sail and painted side   5
Behold the tiny frigate ride.
Upon her deck, 'mid charcoal gleams,
The Moslem's savoury supper steams;
While all apart, beneath the wood,
The Hindoo cooks his simpler food.   10
 Come walk with me the jungle through.
If yonder hunter told us true,
Far off, in desert dank and rude,
The tiger holds its solitude;
Nor (taught by recent harm to shun   15
The thunders of the English gun)
A dreadful guest but rarely seen,
Returns to scare the village green.
Come boldly on! no venom'd snake

---

2. Almorah (Almora): a town atop a ridge in the Kumaon foothills of the Himalayas.

3. Malwah (Malwa): a region in central India, which in the eighteenth century was subject to fighting between opposing Maratha rulers and in the early nineteenth century was at least partially controlled by the Pindaris, until they were expelled by Lord Hastings in 1818.

Can shelter in so cool a brake. 20
Child of the Sun! he loves to lie
'Midst Nature's embers, parch'd and dry,
Where o'er some tower in ruin laid,
The peepul[4] spreads its haunted shade;
Or round a tomb his scales to wreathe 25
Fit warder in the gate of Death.
Come on! yet pause! Behold us now
Beneath the bamboo's arched bough,
Where, gemming oft that sacred gloom
Glows the geranium's scarlet bloom,[5] 30
And winds our path through many a bower
Of fragrant tree and giant flower;
The ceiba's[6] crimson pomp displayed
O'er the broad plantain's humbler shade,
And dusk anana's[7] prickly glade; 35
While o'er the brake, so wild and fair
The betel[8] waves his crest in air.
With pendant train and rushing wings
Aloft the gorgeous peacock springs;
And he, the bird of hundred dyes,[9] 40
Whose plumes the dames of Ava[10] prize.
So rich a shade, so green a sod
Our English Fairies never trod!
Yet who in Indian bowers has stood,
But thought on England's "good green wood!" 45

---

4. Peepul: more commonly spelled "pipal"; an indigenous name for the sacred fig, *Ficus religiosa*.

5. A shrub whose deep scarlet flowers very much resemble the geranium, and thence called the Indian geranium. [RH]

6. Ceiba: probably *Bombax ceiba*, commonly known as the cotton tree, or semal tree (also spelled seemul or simmul), a tall tree that blooms with red flowers.

7. Anana: pineapple.

8. Betel: the acerca palm, from which comes the acerca nut, commonly (though mistakenly) called the betel nut.

9. The Mucharunga. [RH]

The *Quarterly Oriental Magazine, Review and Register* (8 [1827]: 178–252, see especially 184) published a review of Heber's journals and concluded that he had intended to refer here to the bird of paradise but by a "curious mistake" (184) used the word for kingfisher, *mucharunga*, in the prose below his poem. In his notes, Heber writes that *mucharunga* means "many colored" (*Narrative*, 181), but the reviewer explains that Heber has made a linguistic error, as the word actually translates literally as "the bird that is fond of fish" (184). In fact, Heber mentions "the mucharunga, a kind of kingfisher" earlier in his journal (*Narrative*, 116), so it seems that he did indeed make a curious mistake. The plumes of the bird of paradise, not the kingfisher, were popular adornments among wealthy ladies of the time.

10. Until 1841, Ava was the capital of Burma.

And bless'd, beneath the palmy shade,
Her hazel and her hawthorn glade,
And breath'd a prayer, (how oft in vain!)
To gaze upon her oaks again?
    A truce to thought,—the jackall's cry   50
Resounds like sylvan revelry;
And through the trees yon failing ray
Will scantly serve to guide our way.
Yet mark, as fade the upper skies
Each thicket opes ten thousand eyes.   55
Before, beside us, and above,
The fire-fly lights his lamp of love,
Retreating, chasing, sinking, soaring
The darkness of the copse exploring,
While to this cooler air confest,   60
The broad Dhatura[11] bares her breast,
Of fragrant scent and virgin white,
A pearl around the locks of night!
Still as we pass, in softened hum
Along the breezy alleys come   65
The village song, the horn, the drum.
Still as we pass, from bush and briar,
The shrill Cigali[12] strikes his lyre;
And, what is she whose liquid strain
Trills through yon copse of sugar-cane?   70
I know that soul-entrancing swell,
It is—it must be—Philomel![13]
    Enough, enough, the rustling trees
Announce a shower upon the breeze,
The flashes of the summer sky   75
Assume a deeper, ruddier dye;
Yon lamp that trembles on the stream,
From forth our cabin sheds its beam;
And we must early sleep, to find
Betimes the morning's healthy wind.   80

---

11. Dhatura: *Datura* (common name, jimsonweed or thorn apple), a genus of herbs with a white flower and a pungent smell.

12. Cigali: cicada.

13. Philomel: nightingale. Philomela, in Greek and Roman mythology, was raped by her brother-in-law, who cut out her tongue. She was then turned into a nightingale. (The bird was a swallow in the original Greek, but in Roman mythology and in the later works of English poets, she is the nightingale.)

But oh! with thankful hearts confess
E'en here there may be happiness;
And He, the bounteous Sire, has given
His peace on earth,—his hope of Heaven!

From the Gulistan

Who the silent man can prize,[14]
If a fool he be or wise?
Yet, though lonely seem the wood,
Therein may lurk the beast of blood.
Often bashful looks conceal   5
Tongue of fire and heart of steel.
And deem not thou, in forest gray,
Every dappled skin thy prey;
Lest thou rouse, with luckless spear,
The tiger for the fallow deer!   10

---

14. The Gulistan: a famous and often quoted collection of poems and stories by the Persian poet Sa'dī.

George Anderson Vetch

≈⁾ ⁽≈

G EORGE ANDERSON VETCH (1785–1873) left his home in Scotland for India in 1807. As a lieutenant in the Bengal Native Infantry, Vetch fought in the Anglo-Nepalese War (1814–16) and was wounded at the siege of Kamaoun. He retired from the army as a lieutenant colonel in 1836.

Vetch's book *Sultry Hours,* a volume of poems and "metrical sketches," was published in 1820, while he was still in the army. But his first effort was dismissed scathingly in the *Asiatic Journal and Monthly Miscellany,* whose reviewer declared, "[W]e have no doubt of his military merits; and among his circle of private acquaintance, he may possibly pass for a very pretty poet. . . . [B]ut we would earnestly advise the young gentleman to return again to his place, and rest his pretensions to fame on his sword, or his canary birds, or any thing he pleases rather than his pen . . . we would recommend to this young gentleman, when a sentimental or scribbling fit comes upon him again, to divert his mind, if possible, by fondling his baby, or sit down quietly and take a moderate cup of tea with its nurse" (12 [1821]: 452–540).

Undeterred by such advice, Vetch published at least three other book-length poems or collections: *Songs of the Exile* in 1820 under the anonymous designation "a Bengal Officer"; *Dara, or, the Minstrel Prince: An Indian History* (1850); and *Milton at Rome, a Dramatic Piece* (1851), under the name "Major Vetch." His 1852 book, *The Gong; or, Reminiscences of India* (sometimes referred to as *Gregory's Gong*), is an account of a fictional Scot's life in India. The *Calcutta Review* took a favorable view of his prose, saying, "[H]is subject is the trite one, a Cadet going to, in, and returning from India, but he throws a new charm over the old story. . . . That Major Vetch is a true son of Fingal, imaginative as the fleecy clouds on his own hills, and filled with all the superstitions of lone Highland glens" (24 [1855]: 90–120).

In fact, Vetch seems to have found the charms of poetry in attaching himself to a poetic tradition he identified as uniquely Scottish. One of the stronger poems in his first collection lamented the death of John Leyden (who appears in this volume) in precisely these terms:

> But thou, lov'd minstrel of my native land!
> Sound is thy sleep on Java's blazing shore;
> First of the sons of song who graced our strand,
> And shall we hear thy thrilling lyre no more?

'Tis said, in ancient times, that still before
Its master's death, his harp, untouch'd, would swell;
But ne'er aerial lyre, in days of yore.
Did breathe so sweet, so sad a passing knell,
As that in anguish pour'd from thy prophetic shell.

The *Edinburgh Magazine,* not sharing entirely the skepticism of the *Asiatic Journal,* poured measured praise on Vetch's Scottish lyre as it commemorated the verse of his fellow poet, the "first of the sons of song who graced" an Indian strand.

Sources

George Anderson Vetch, *Sultry Hours: Containing Metrical Sketches of India, and Other Poems* (Calcutta: n.p., 1820); Vetch, *The Gong; or, Reminiscences of India* (Edinburgh: J. Hogg, 1852); and Vetch, "The Exile's Tribute," in *Burns Centenary Poems: A Collection of Fifty of the Best Written on the Occasion of the Centenary Celebration,* ed. George Anderson and John Finlay (Glasgow: T. Murray, 1859). See also *Edinburgh Magazine and Literary Miscellany* 11 (June–December 1822): 197.

On Visiting the Grave of Lieutenant Kirk, in Nepal

'Midst scenes as his own Grampians[1] wild,
    Here lies the Virtuous and the Brave—
On hills sublime his Cairn[2] is pil'd
    Where torrents dash—and pine-trees wave.

With Pilgrim-steps by sorrow led   5
    O'er Mountains wild, remote, and drear,
I come the bursting tear to shed,
    And kneel beside thy early bier.

I little thought of this thy doom,
    When in farewell I press'd thy hand,   10
Our trysting place thy mountain tomb!
    Amidst this far romantic land.

---

1. Grampians: the Grampian Mountains, in the Highlands of Scotland, one of the major mountain ranges in the country. Ben Nevis, the highest peak in the British Isles, is in this rugged range.
2. Cairn: in Scotland, a mound of stones marking a grave.

Where sweetly winds the past'ral Tay,[3]
    Thy native worth was early known,
Which still through Ind's subduing day,   15
    With undiminish'd lustre shone.

And now thy years of exile o'er,
    Thy breast beat high at Scotia's name:
Prepar'd to seek her happy shore,
    A Son she might be proud to claim.   20

But Heav'n which still directs the best,
    The long fond cherish'd wish denied—
Submissive to its high behest,
    Serene the Christian Soldier died.

On a Canary Bird

That died suddenly after nearly concluding the voyage to India.

Alas our little warbler's dead—
Its spark of Minstrel-fire is fled—
For ever hush'd the thrilling lay
That cheer'd us on our weary way!

Ah me, 'tis surely more than death   5
When dies the Minstrel's tuneful breath—
'Tis not these glazing eyes declare
That life no more shall brighten there:
But where's the power that bore along
So late the magic gift of song?   10
Can that high ton'd and heav'n-taught quaver
Be in a moment hush'd for ever?
In life—whence was its pealing tone,
In death—whence is its spirit gone!

How sweetly with the rising sun   15
    Thy matin[4] hymn'd the new born day:—

---

3. Tay: the longest river in Scotland, flowing from the Highlands to the Firth of Tay, where it empties into the North Sea.

4. Matin: a morning hymn or prayer service.

And must I ere the day be done
    Pour with my tears thy requiem lay!
O had I known thy last farewell
Was breath'd in that delighting swell,   20
Mine ear had drank with grief the strain
It never was to hear again.
And shall I not lament for thee
Companion o'er the dark blue sea—
Like us an Exile from green bowers   25
And sharer of our prison-hours—
For thee—with whom I claim a part
In Minstrelsy's extatic art—
For thee—with whom we've circled o'er
The wide, wide world—for thee no more.   30
O far from nature's living green
Thy song recall'd the rural scene—
Sweet as the Lark o'er Scotia's Lea[5]
Thy notes resounded o'er the Sea.

Haply thy now glad spirit roves   35
Delighted through thy native groves—
And from its cage and Ocean free
Wakes songs to woodland Liberty;
If so, I love such scenes too well
To wish thee back in prison-cell;   40
But we shall miss thy blithsome lay
On Ocean's long and dreary way—
And on sad India's blazing plains
Unblest by warbler's rural strains:
O till my native hills I see,   45
Sweet Minstrel, I shall mourn for Thee.

---

5. Lea: a pasture or meadow.

The Exile's Tribute

What Bard a votive lay may bring
    In honour of the Chief of Song?
    The loftiest lay would do him wrong,
Unless another Burns[6] should sing.

A pilgrim at our Minstrel's shrine,   5
    Where Nature wakes with morning's fire
    The echo of his thrilling lyre,
To stand in grateful tears be mine.

How oft when sad, and far away,
    The melting voice of Coila's Bard[7]   10
    In all the "joy of grief" was heard
To triumph o'er the exile-day.

Condemn'd 'neath tropic skies to roam
    Where scorching winds o'er deserts blew,
    The mountain daisy bathed in dew,   15
Restored the hills and streams of home.

There, where no bird's sweet warblings rise,
    To gladden India's dreary plain,
    I heard in Burns the laverock's[8] strain
Rejoicing in my native skies.   20

Wand'ring forsaken, and forlorn,
    The Bard of Love's entrancing power,
    Recalls the bliss of gloamin'-hour,
And vows beneath the trysting-thorn.

The friendships that beside the Tyne[9]   25
    Endears the scenes of joyous youth,
    Rush'd back thro' tears in all their truth
To live again in "Auld Land Syne."

---

6. Burns: Robert Burns, the national poet of Scotland, sometimes called simply "The Bard."

7. Coila: the poetic name for Kyle, a former district in Ayrshire. In his poem "The Vision," Burns declared Coila his muse.

8. Laverock: northern English dialect for lark.

9. Tyne: the River Tyne begins just east of Pencaitland, flows northeast, and empties into the North Sea three miles west of Dunbar, Scotland.

When far from my own village spire,
　　And idols claimed each horrid rite,　　　　　30
　　O, with what sacred, pure delight,
I worship'd at the Cottar's[10] fire!

And when to war the trumpet rung,
　　With what a high, exulting glow
　　The sons of Scotia met the foe　　　　　35
As men from Bruce and Wallace[11] sprung!

Where'er a home-sick exile mourns
　　The vanish'd joys of early years,
　　The anguish of impassion'd tears
Finds utt'rance in the song of Burns.　　　　　40

Kings may expire, and states decay,
　　But long as lovely Nature reigns,
　　Her laureate-bard's attending strains
Will hold their everlasting sway.

---

10. Cottar: poor tenant farmer, or cottager.

11. Bruce and Wallace: Robert the Bruce (1274–1329) and William Wallace (1272–1305) are two of Scotland's greatest heroes and are associated with Scottish independence and nationalism. During the Wars of Scottish Independence, Wallace was appointed commander of the Scottish Armies, and Bruce was crowned king of Scotland.

Horace Hayman Wilson

≈ ⌒

I N ADDITION to more than five hundred Sanskrit manuscripts, the Bodleian collection holds a fascinating notebook. An inch thick, bound in calf, it begins with ink drawings of English cottages and ends with portraits of Indian princes and caricatures of actors on the Calcutta stage. Interspersed are original, translated, and copied poems. Both the Sanskrit manuscripts and the commonplace book were assembled by a remarkable man: Horace Hayman Wilson (1786–1860), physician, amateur actor, employee of the East India Company, director of the Royal Asiatic Society, poet, and distinguished orientalist.

Wilson was born in London, the illegitimate son of George Paterson, deputy accountant general of the British East India Company, and Elizabeth Woolston (or Wilson). He attended Soho Academy, London, where he acquired a lasting love for the theater, and afterward he was trained at St. Thomas's Hospital, London. Admitted to the Royal College of Surgeons in 1805, he was appointed assistant surgeon to the East Indian Company three years later, no doubt thanks to his father's connections. Because of youthful holidays accompanying his uncle to work at the London mint, he was, on his arrival in Calcutta, recruited by the mint's assay master, fellow-surgeon and poet John Leyden. In addition to his medical duties, Wilson became Leyden's assistant. When Leyden departed for Java and subsequently died, Wilson succeeded him as assay master. In Wilson, the government found a man of talents similar to Leyden's—they shared a knowledge of chemistry, a strong interest in Asian languages, a love of letters, and prior medical training. Wilson seriously took up the study of Sanskrit and took an active role in the Chowringhee Theatre.

As was not uncommon for company officials in the late eighteenth and early nineteenth centuries, Wilson formed a liaison with an Indian woman, by whom he had a son in 1811. His biographer Penelope Devereux was unable to identify Wilson's partner, but she details his long-lasting love and support of this son. In an unpublished manuscript biography (British Library, Asia and Africa Collection, C 853), Devereux argues that one of the poems below, "The Brahman Maid," arose from Wilson's relationship with the mother of his first child. His later relationship, that with Elizabeth Kelly, was better documented; Devereux shows that Wilson met Elizabeth Kelly through the theatre, where she was an actor. Because Kelly was the wife of an enlisted soldier, Wilson's relationship proved a source of controversy some years later when he sought appointment to the new Boden professorship in Sanskrit at Oxford. With Kelly, Wilson had two sons whom he cared for, educated, and assisted in life. During the years of his relationship with Kelly, Wilson continued his studies and his scholarly activity as secretary to the Asiatic Society.

I deduce from Devereux's research that, as he sought the respectability necessary to return to England as Boden Professor, Wilson needed to overcome two obstacles—his less than respectable domestic situation and his lack of a university degree. According to Devereux, in 1828 Wilson dissolved his relationship with Elizabeth, settling upon her the very considerable sum of three hundred pounds a year and made further provisions for their sons' education. Shortly thereafter, he married Frances Sarah Parr Siddons, the daughter of an East India Company official and a fellow Anglo-Indian. In marrying Fanny, who was half his age, Wilson did not stray far from his beloved theatre, for his wife was the granddaughter of the famous actor Sarah Siddons. The elder Siddons had raised Fanny when she was sent home from India as a young girl. Like many Anglo-Indian children, Fanny had returned to Bengal in her teens, and there she soon met and married Wilson. Together they had seven daughters, six of whom survived to adulthood. After his marriage, Wilson was appointed to the Oxford professorship, and he moved his family to England, where he shortly took the B.A. from Exeter College.

During his time in India, Wilson showed himself to be a complex, perhaps even contradictory person. He intensely admired Sanskrit literature and much about Indian culture. He supported Indian education, which he believed should combine training in Indian languages and literatures with English and Western science. In the Orientalist/Anglicist controversy, he sided with those who wished the company to support learning in Indian classical languages. He also served on various local committees for the improvement of Indian education and supported the publication of schoolbooks in the vernacular languages. Though a great admirer of Indian learning, he was, as Paul Courtright has argued, nonetheless a firm believer in the superiority of Western civilization.

However contrary his views, Wilson believed strongly in the intellectual and literary abilities of Indian writers, as is clear in his relationships with H. L. V. Derozio and Kasiprasad Ghosh, both of whom dedicated poems to him. Though his Christian religious views were such that he was deemed qualified for the Boden professorship—which was designed with evangelical goals in mind—Wilson defended Derozio from the attacks of the Hindu College overseers who dismissed the young teacher on account of his freethinking religious views. Wilson was equally supportive of the young poet Ghosh, who might well have shared the conservative Hindu views of the overseers. In short, Wilson took the poems of Indian writers, living and dead, quite seriously and maintained an abiding enthusiasm, most especially for playwrights.

Wilson's major works included a translation of Kālidāsa's *Meghaduta* (*The Cloud Messenger*, 1st Calcutta edition, 1813), excerpted here, and *Select Specimens of the Theatre of the Hindus* (two volumes, 1826–27). He compiled a Sanskrit-English dictionary (1819; revised edition, 1831) and after returning to England translated the *Vishńu Puráńa: A System of Hindu Mythology and Tradition* (1840). His numerous general works were undertaken in part to support a growing family, and they included a continuation of James Mill's *History of British India*. Wilson's most important contributions to English language poetry in India were his translations, but included here also are two poems from his Calcutta notebook, probably revised fair copies of earlier drafts, that give the flavor of his early experience in India. The notebook contains other poems of historical significance as well, including a long meditation on the Taj Mahal and "Hymn of Hindu Women to Durga," which surely reflects his experiences of the Durga puja's prominence in Bengal.

Sources

Horace Hayman Wilson's commonplace book (c. 1828–1832), MS. Eng. misc. d. 1286, folios 83, 101–103, owned by the Bodleian Library, Oxford University, reproduced by their kind permission; Wilson, *The Mégha Dúta; or Cloud Messenger, A Poem in the Sanscrit Language by Cálidása* (London: Black, Parry and Co., 1814). See also Paul B. Courtright, "Wilson, Horace Hayman (1786–1860)," in *ODNB*.

The Brahman Maid

Along the West, above the Woods, the last bright streaks of day,
Their golden radiance scatter round, ere yet they fade away,
And by the holy wake I bend, with hopes like those rays bright,
As soon I fear to set them in sad and cheerless night.

Yet go my votive taper forth, within thy tiny boat,[1]   5
And flickering o'er the yellow stream in course prophetic float,
Whilst curiously I watch her with the sacred current glide.
And gather from thy voyage what may, my future fate betide.

For I have raised to stranger gaze, to foreign forms, mine eye
And with unholy love my breast has dared to breathe the sigh,   10

---

1. The traditional Hindu (in Bengal, both Hindu and Muslim) festival involved girls floating lamps on a stream, the fate of the tiny lamp foretelling the fate of their desires.

For one of other climes and speeds, and birth contemned to burn
And feel a flame that scarcely hopes and almost fears return.

For how could Brahma's sons endure a Daughter of their race
Should with an outcaste English Lord their heavenly tribe disgrace?
My parents—well—too well I know would sooner see me dead   15
Than to a partner so despised, so all detested, wed.

Such fatal union should it be, irrevocably must sever
The child that they have cherished—from their homes and hearts forever
Abandoned to the wide, wide world to sorrow, and to shame
The wretch who thus contaminates their still unsullied name.   20

And how could I consent to yield—the honor of my birth,
And hire a poor rejected worm—a scorn upon the earth
A Sudra[2]—worse—amid no caste however abject found
Doomed like a withered leaf to fall and rot upon the ground.

Yes, I would all the shame support—the sorrow and the sin,   25
And as more dreadful still, the stern abhorrence to my kin.
If, in that heart where mine has flown, I might but hope to prove
Some pity for my sacrifice—for all my suffering—love.

But no, the stranger rechs[3] not of the woes my hearth doth send
And could not for an Indian maid to pity condescend   30
Beyond the seas to brighter forms and fairer features shine,
And eyes where he would gladly read the thoughts he scorns from mine.

Though absence may awhile the blaze of those bright visions dim,
And meaner beauties for a time have even charms for him,
Yet should he, as he will, return to his paternal shore,   35
Their witchery would again enthrall as it enthralled before.

Then what of me, abandoned here, an outcaste and alone,
No home, no faith, no hand, no heart that I could call my own?
On to ungenial climes conveyed, the land of cloak and snow
And beson, that would be to me, more chill, more dark than those.   40

---

2. Sudra: a member of the fourth varna, or caste (the lowest). The trope of the sudra lover (or
the outcaste lover) is a common one in poetry of this period by Indian and British poets. The for-
eign lover is worse than the sudra because he is not Hindu and therefore is without caste. A more
common form of the trope occurs in many tales of Hindu/Muslim romances, which are equally
tragic. A woman who contracts an alliance with an outcaste becomes herself an outcaste.

3. Rechs: knows.

Ah me, whate'er I contemplate, where'er I turn mine eye,
I see one only solace left—one only hope—to die.
Tis so, for see the fated bark overwhelmed beneath the river
The light is quenched—and like the flame—my hopes are gone forever.

The Sudra Lover

Faint in the East, the first grey tints of morning gently spread,
And darkling yet I lonely stray, to sacred Ganges bed;
To mark the Brahmin's daughter, on the margins of the stream,
Salute with her pure orisons—the sun's returning gleam.

I know that it is madness all, such hopeless flame to nurse,   5
Debased the equal rights of man, by our primeval curse,
The law that all human good to Brahma's offspring gave,
And bade the hapless Sudra live the haughty Brahmin's slave.

Yet little should I heed the law, and should as little dread
To draw the wrath of men or gods unjust upon my head.   10
If I might hope from Malati one soft, one precious sigh,
Or win a kind returning glance from that soul searching eye.

But no, the teachers of her youth have other lessons taught,
And for a sudra she can own no fond, no tender thought;
Compassion for his abject state her gentle heart may move,   15
But horror in his homage lies—pollution in his love.

It hurts me not her steps to trace to every favourite spot,[4]
She passes with unheeding eye, as if she saw me not.
Or, if perchance a straggling glance upon my features light,
It quick recoils as startled, at some foul and hideous sight.   20

And, sooth to say, I cannot bear that look of chill disdain,
It sends a dart into my heart, a fire into my brain.
Remote I lurk, or in the gloom, or where may intervene
Some friendly bush or bank or tree whence I may gaze unseen.

---

4. This line may contain an error, as it would seem that it might in fact hurt the speaker to trace the beloved's steps.

What if I quit mine ancient faith and join the Moslem Lord   25
And underneath his banner dye with Brahmin's blood my sword?
Riches and rank around my brow shall with the turban twine
And with the iron grasp of power, shall Malati be mine.

Hence, horrid dream, could I consent from all she loves to tear,
The maid, and bid her bosom heave with anguish and despair,   30
To wreak on her revenge for wrongs, the work of man and fate,
And live to reap, and to deserve, her curses and her hate.

No. Let me unregarded still gaze from day to day,
And in my solitary love, thus look my life away
And haply heaven my present pangs may crown with future bliss,   35
And, in another life, reward my suffering in this.

Should then it be my lot to live great and renowned on earth,
And Malati should be condemned to some inferior birth
What rapture will it be to stoop low from my lofty sphere
And lift her up to happiness—to me—hark—she is here.   40

Song

Long years have passed, and now again
    My native home I see
The village green, the bowery land
    the stately old oak tree.
The church where oft in prayer I knelt,   5
    the school I truant fled,
The roof where once the parents dwelt,
    who now are with the dead.

And as I gaze on yonder stream
    the willow wanes above,   10
I dream as I was used to dream
    of Lucy and of love.
For there first my flame avowed,
    and heard her artless sigh.
I sought the world's unfeeling crowd   15
    and Lucy I left to die.

from *The Méga Dúta, or Cloud Messenger*

There in the fane a beauteous creature stands,
The first best work of the Creator's hands;[5]
Whose slender limbs inadequately bear
A full orbed bosom, and a weight of care;
Whose teeth like pearls, whose lips like *Bimbas* show,[6]   5
And fawn-like eyes still tremble as they glow.
Lone as the widowed *Chacraváci* mourns,[7]
Her faithful memory to her husband turns,
And sad, and silent, shalt thou find my wife,
Half of my soul, and partner of my life;[8]   10
Nipped by chill sorrow as the flowers enfold[9]
Their shrinking petals from the withering cold.

---

5. In *The Cloud Messenger*, Wilson translates a much-loved poem by Kālidāsa, acknowledged as one of the greatest Sanskrit lyric and dramatic poets. Here is excerpted the penultimate section of the poem. The poem is narrated by a yaksha, or nature spirit, who because he has offended the gods is sentenced to exile for the space of a year. He laments his separation from his faithful wife and commissions a cloud (associated with the monsoon) to visit her and tell her of his sorrow and continued love; this conceit provides the poet with an opportunity of describing the geography and natural beauties of northern India, which the cloud will pass over on its way to the lady. Wilson's poem is notable as the first English translation of Kālidāsa's masterpiece; his notes are longer than the text and conduct an implied argument defending the sensuality of Indian lyric poetry. In annotating this stanza, Wilson glosses "the first best work of the Creator's hands" thus:

Literally, the first creation of Brahmá: and *first* may refer to time, or to degree; it most probably here means best. So Milton, speaking of Eve,

"Oh fairest of creation, last and best
"Of all God's works."

(*Paradise Lost*, book ix, line 896)

We now enter upon perhaps the most pleasing part of this elegant little poem, the description of the Yacsha's wife. I may perhaps come under the denomination of those who, according to the illiberal and arrogant criticism of such a writer as a Mr. Pinkerton, prove, "that the climate of *India*," while it "inflames the imagination, impairs the judgment," when, standing in very little awe of such a poetical censor, I advance an opinion, that we have few specimens, either in classical or modern poetry, of more genuine tenderness or delicate feeling. [HHW]

6. The *Bimba (bryonia grandis)* bears a red fruit, to which the lip is very commonly compared. [HHW]

7. Wilson's lengthy note describes the *"Chacraváci* or the ruddy goose (*anas casarca*), more commonly known in *India* as the *Brahmany Duck."* He remarks, with numerous quotations, that these birds symbolize constancy in love and connubial affection.

8. Wilson quotes Milton, Horace, Propertius, Byron, and Mary Tighe in glossing this line, implying delicately that the original Sanskrit connotes both spiritual and physical union.

9. So in Lord Lyttleton's Monody:

A sudden blast from *Appenninus* blows,
Cold with perpetual snows;
The tender blighted plant shrinks up its leaves and dies. [HHW]

I view her now! long weeping swells her eyes,[10]
And those dear lips are dried by parching sighs;
Sad on her hand her pallid cheek declines,   15
And half unseen through veiling tresses shines;
As when a darkling night the moon enshrouds,
A few faint rays break straggling through the clouds.

Now at thy sight I mark fresh sorrows flow,
And sacred sacrifice augments her woe;[11]   20
I mark her now, with fancy's aid, retrace
This wasted figure and this haggard face;
Now from her favourite bird she seeks relief,
And tells the tuneful Sáricá[12] her grief,
Mourns o'er the feathered prisoner's kindred fate,   25
And fondly questions of its absent mate.

In vain the lute for harmony is strung,[13]
And round the robe-neglected shoulder slung;
And faltering accents strive to catch, in vain,
Our race's old commemorative strain: 30
The falling tear that from reflexion springs,
Corrodes incessantly the silvery strings;
Recurring woe still pressing on the heart,
The skilful hand forgets its grateful art,
And idly wandering strikes no measured tone,   35

---

10. In this she resembles the *Lesbia* of *Catullus*: "Her swollen eyes are red with weeping." [HHW]

11. Thus Laodameia to Protesilaus, in Ovid: "We offer incense up, and add our tears." The commentators, however, are not agreed how to interpret this passage in the original text. They seem, however, to conceive it means, that the approach of the Cloud reminding her of its being the period at which absent husbands usually return home; she recollects that the return of her own lord is proscribed, and therefore either falls in a swoon, or with excess of affliction. The sacrifice is to be performed to render the Gods propitious, or it is a sacrifice called *kákavali,* usually performed by women at the beginning of the rainy season. Some interpret *puré* "in the city," not "before, in front." [HHW]

12. The Sáricá (*gracula religiosa*) is a small bird, better known by the name of *Maina.* [HHW] Wilson goes on at some length describing the mina bird in Indian lore.

13. The lute is here put for the *Veena* or *Been,* a stringed instrument of sacred origin, and high celebrity amongst the *Hindus.* In *Bengal,* however, players on this instrument are very rarely met with, and amongst the natives of this province the *English* fiddle is its substitute. In the *Jatras,* or *Dramatic* performances, still current amongst them, I have seen the entrance of Na'reda, the traditionary inventor of the *Veena,* bearing in its stead a violin. The *Veena* is much the most harmonious and scientific of all the *Hindu* instruments of music; a description of it may be found in the first volume of the Asiatic Researches. [HHW]

Wilson provides further notes to this stanza, including references to European poetry.

But wakes a sad wild warbling of its own.
At times such solace animates her mind,
As widowed wives in cheerless absence find;
She counts the flowers now faded on the floor,
That graced with monthly piety the door,[14]   40
Thence reckons up the period since from home,
And far from her, was I compelled to roam;
And deeming fond my term of exile run,
Conceives my homeward journey is begun.

---

14. The *Hindus* pay a species of adoration to many inanimate objects: amongst others the door-way, or door-post, receives such homage as is rendered by hanging up a flower or a garland there once a month. [HHW]

John Lawson

JOHN LAWSON (1787–1825) followed three callings—printer, poet, and missionary. Something of a polymath, he was also a talented musician and a student of mineralogy and botany. Born in Trowbridge, Wiltshire, he early displayed a talent for carving. In 1803, he was apprenticed to a wood engraver in London, where, three years later, he joined the Baptist Church. Lawson began to think of a missionary career, which seemed to combine adventure with religious satisfaction and a rise in social status.

Upon offering his services to the Baptist Missionary Society, Lawson was approved for the Indian mission and set sail for India via the United States in 1810. He then settled for two years in Philadelphia. Either personal choice or transportation trouble caused by the Napoleonic Wars may have accounted for this delay. Whatever his motives, his choice of Philadelphia was scarcely coincidental, for the city was then the seat of much Baptist missionary activity. According to Henry Sweetser Burrage, who edited a collection of Baptist hymns, Lawson preached with great success in many American churches. Histories of American literature still name Lawson as an early American poet, on account of his volume *The Maniac, with Other Poems,* published by Hellings and Aitken in Philadelphia in 1811. Unsurprisingly, historians of American literature have discovered little about him, for by 1812 Lawson was in Calcutta.

In India, Lawson joined other Baptist missionaries at Serampore, a Danish settlement. The East India Company, at the time, did not permit missionary activity in territory it controlled. After 1815, however, when the renewal of the company's charter depended in part upon the company's acquiescence to the Evangelical party's desire to sponsor Indian missions, missions were accepted, and Lawson (among others) moved to Calcutta. In the early days of Lawson's residence, missionaries were eyed with considerable suspicion by the company, and according to one account, Lawson was imprisoned for refusing to leave Calcutta. As in the case of the famous Baptist missionary William Carey, the government had to concede the usefulness of Lawson's talents. In the print shop of the Baptist missionaries at Serampore, he had become an expert in the making of Chinese type. Lawson also taught Indian typographers how to produce both Bangla and other type fonts, for he was one of the few people in India experienced in punch cutting, that is, in making the molds for the pouring of foundry type.

After his ordination in 1816, Lawson became co-pastor of the Lall Bazar Chapel in Calcutta, an institution established in part by the contributions of such men as Francis Derozio, the father of the poet H. L. V. Derozio. In Calcutta, Lawson devoted his attention to education, pastoral duties, printing, and poetry. He set up a print shop in Calcutta and purchased a Bangla type font from Serampore to print tracts in Bangla prose and verse. He also made both Persian and devanagari fonts for printing tracts in Hindustani.

In Calcutta, Lawson also continued to publish poetry. His verse included subsequent editions of *The Maniac* (which was republished in London and Calcutta, with the Calcutta volume of 1825 listed as the third edition); *Woman: A Poem* (1820); *Orient Harping: A Desultory Poem in Two Parts* (1822); *An Elegy to the Memory of the Late Rev. Henry Martyn, with Smaller Pieces* (1823); and *The Lost Spirit: A Poem* (1825)—which was originally published in Calcutta along with a "tract in verse" which gave its title to the volume *Roland, A Tale*. After his death, friends published a pamphlet containing his hymns, *The Calcutta Melodies, Comprising Thirty-six Original Psalm and Hymn Tunes, by John Lawson, arranged by G. Mather* (1844).

Suffice it to say that William James would not have considered Lawson among the "healthy minded": from the Maniac to the freezing soldier in Napoleon's retreat from Moscow to the specter of Ugolino devouring his sons in the "tower of famine" to the delight in India's verdure coupled with despair for the damnation of her "heathen," Lawson seldom poetically indulged in a positive thought. Rather, the experience of severe depression characterizing the Maniac colored all his poetry. In his personal life, he seems to have managed, though, for pious memoirs of his death in 1825 record him as a loving father and husband.

Sources

John Lawson, *Orient Harping: A Desultory Poem in Two Parts* (Calcutta: Baptist Mission Press, 1822); Lawson, *The Lost Spirit: A Poem* (London: Francis Westley, 1825); and Lawson, *Woman in India* (London: printed for Samuel Lawson, sold by F. Westley, 1821). See also Lawson, *The Maniac, with Other Poems* (Philadelphia: Hellings and Aitkin, 1811); Lawson, *An Elegy to the Memory of the Late Rev. Henry Martyn, with Smaller Pieces* (London: Francis Westley, 1823); and Henry Sweetser Burrage, *Baptist Hymn Writers and Their Hymns* (Portland, ME: Brown, Thurston, 1888).

Hindoo's Complaint

Supposed to be spoken by one left to die on the banks of the River Ganges.

I.

DESPAIRING, I languish and die!
My heart heaves a sorrowful moan;
The soft flowing Ganges rolls by,
But hears not the long, the last groan.
Oh! where shall I seek for repose!   5
Where find the sweet haven of rest!
Eternity soon will disclose,
The misery begun in this breast.

II.

Bewildered and vain were my days,
On folly was founded my hope;   10
Now death the stern mandate obeys,
And strikes down the worm-eaten prop.
Ye hardened spectators of woe,
Who know not a sigh or a tear;
But a tear and a sigh you will know,   15
When lowly like me you lie here.

III.

Oh! listen—the tale is for you,
My orisons daily were paid,
While yet hung the bright drops of dew,
To the sun in his glory arrayed.   20
Then through the deep jungle I trod,
(There sleep the huge serpents by day)
There I culled from their darkest abode
The sweet-offering flowers of the spray.

IV.

With eager devotion, my hands   25
Consigned the weak babe[1] to the floods;
I burst through humanity's bands
To satisfy bloodthirsty gods.
My weakness did all things for them,
Whose power can do nothing for me;   30
Oh! who will the hurricane stem?
Oh! whither shall wretchedness flee?

V.

My father at work in the glade,
The trees of the Sunderbunds[2] felled;
There an infant I carelessly strayed,   35
And the parrot's gay plumage beheld.
I saw the wild tiger asleep,
In the shade where the rank hemlock grows;
Had he seen me, one swift glancing leap
Would have blasted the bud of my woes.   40

VI.

But I lived—to despair and to die;
I lived—but in madness to rave:
Oh! better a babe low to lie,
The grim tiger's bowels my grave.
Then my sorrows had surely been less;   45
But now (my heart aches at the thought)
I go to an unknown abyss!
I die—but my spirit will not!

---

1. Typical tropes of missionary writing included the notion that many Hindus practiced infanticide, immolated widows, and threw themselves under the wheels of the "car of Juggurnaut" (Jagganatha).

2. The area of jungle, swamp, and alluvial plain, forming the lower portion of the Ganges delta.

from *"Descent of Ganga"*

So seem'd the skies, yet not so lovely shone
Though radiant more, when Ganga fell from heaven.[3]
For gods came down to marvel at such show,
And with them all their grandeur. Elephants
Clad in caparison of richest gold   5
Stalk'd monstrous through th' ethereal plains, and all
The equipage of wondering deities;
Chariots, and horsemen, trod on silver clouds
And countless flaming cars roll'd rapidly;
Their drivers rob'd in spangled investments,   10
As if old Orion and Pleiades[4]
Had lent their jewels to bedeck the gods
On such august occasion. Thick and deep
They crowd, and upward lift their anxious eyes
To those blest realms where everlasting crags   15
And precipices rise interminable.
Down, thundering down, the holy prodigy
O'erleaping heavenly barriers, pours her floods,
A cataract madly roaring, foaming, swollen
With all the turbulent burden of vast oceans.   20
Then all that lives in waters headlong rush'd.
Leviathan plung'd his unwieldy course
Swift as the downward lightning, and with streak
Long stretch'd behind him, such as oft is seen
By mariners when the bloat animals   25
Cut their bright way amidst the storms of night.
The graceful dolphin swum of changeable hue,
But day shone not upon his glossy fins
To bring his golden beauties forth, for high
The column'd mists, and clouds of beauteous fowls,   30
Tower'd and obscur'd the sun. Unspeakable
Glory and grandeur mingled in confusion;
For marvellous sounds of rushing elements,
The torrent's voice, the roar magnificent
Of crazy billows, windy gusts, and surges   35
Foaming in wrathful wreaths, did howl and sing

---

3. Ganga: the Ganges River.
4. In Greek mythology, the constellation Orion is in eternal chase of the constellation Pleiades, the seven sisters.

The triumph of that day; and lambent fires
Deeply playing in seagreen depths, illum'd
The dwellers in dark floods of finny race
And shining vest, light tumbling in their courses,   40
Rejoic'd at holiday, and scene unusual.
The sky, the earth, the sea, teem'd with their objects
Diverse of form and being, divine and human.
Gods in dumb ecstasy throng'd the upper clouds,
Then with acclaiming voice, and plauding hands,   45
Mov'd in the heavens distinct at intervals,
Or seen in misty glances, as the show
Chang'd its disorder'd aspect. Alternate
Darkness and light, and twilight danc'd upon
Th' irregular assemblage. You might deem   50
That th' evanescent beauties of the day,
In storm and sunshine beaming—that the gloom
And garishness, and transient freaks nocturnal,
When galaxies, and dark bewildering tempests,
And northern lights, and shooting stars, together   55
Mix in their changeful sport—that the bright streaks
Of setting sun, cradled in radiance,
Suffusing with his firebeams endless fleeces
Climbing stupendous through the firmament,
Or rising moon of pensive countenance   60
Muffled in heavenly majesty—the forms
Fairest in earth and heaven, were here in one
Concentrated! What were the dribbling spout
Of western Niagara purling down
The gutter of her rocks? what were the streams   65
Of the fair Rhone sequester'd midst her hills
And placid plains? of the bold marching Rhine
Washing her blood-stained regions? the dark Po,
Slothful and solitary? the Wolga[5] drear,
Creeping in icy chains, and desolate?   70
What were their waves united, could they roll
From the hoar summit of th' amazing Alps,
Or heights (astounding mortal energies)
Of th' Appenines, compar'd with thy descent
Ganga, from heaven to earth? This rocking globe   75

---

5. Wolga: the Volga River.

Could scarce sustain the deluge! 'Twas nobly done,
O pious Bhagu-ratha,[6] thou prevail'dst!
The meed of praise be thine, blest of the gods!
O thou of potent merit! thou leddest the stream
Through the deep channels of the earth, to fill   80
The nether chambers where perpetual billows
Boom in perpetual darkness. 'Twas thy hand
Rein'd the proud floods, and showed the darkling rout,
Such as I erst have sung, to Patala[7]!

Then rose the sixty thousand sons, hailing   85
Th' immortal waters, emancipate by thee,
Daughter of heaven! and now thy votaries
Crowd to thy courses, and with blind belief,

---

6. Bhagu-ratha: see note below.

7. Lawson wrote an extensive note to the poem: "The tale of the descent of the Ganges is re-
lated to Rama by his conductor Vishwa-mitra. King Sagara had determined on offering the holiest
sacrifice, that is, the sacrifice of a horse. The warrior Ungshuman, grandson of Sagara, attended
the sacrifice. During the preparatory services, a serpent in [the] form of Ununta (a thousand-
headed dragon deity) arose from the earth, and seized the victim. The priests inform Sagara of the
event, who calls his sixty thousand sons together, and solemnly charges them to pursue the thief,
though he should have gone even to Patala, and destroy him, and bring back the horse. They, in
obedience to his command, depart, and with spades, clubs, crows [crowbars], &c. pierce the earth
to Patala, which disturbs the repose of certain deities, who apply to Bruhma [Brahma] to stop the
progress of these 'horse-seekers before they destroy all endued with life.' Bruhma foretells their
destruction. The sixty thousand sons, not finding the horse, return to their father, who commands
them to renew their digging; and after respectfully saluting their renowned elephants, they perceive
Kupila, (Vishnu,) and near him the horse feeding. Then follow the rencounter and its conse-
quences. Sagara sends Ungshuman to search out the fate of the sixty thousand sons. He travels the
road dug by his fathers—passes the elephants, 'eminent in eloquence,' who inform him that he shall
return with the horse. He travels till at length he beholds the remains of his fathers—a heap of
ashes. After bewailing their fate, he looks around for water, in order to perform the funeral obse-
quies, but looks in vain. The sovereign of birds, Soopurna, comforts him and tells him, it is not
proper to pour common water on the ashes, and that he must bring the Ganges from heaven for
this purpose; and that then the sixty thousand would arise to heaven. Upon this, Ungshuman takes
the horse, and returns to his father for the completion of the ceremony. Ungshuman himself is not
able to bring the Ganges from heaven, although he makes the attempt by retiring to the top of a
mountain to engage in sacred austerities. His son, Dwileepa, is equally anxious to effect this great
design, but is disappointed and dies. Bhugu-rutha the pious, the son of Dwileepa, is the highly
favoured one. He begins his course of severities, and his success is complete, as recorded in the
poem. This tale occupies the 32d, 33d, 34th, and 35th sections of the Ramayuna [Rāmāyaṇa]. A
brief outline of the descent of Ganga, or the tale of Sagara, may be found in the Rev. W. Ward's
View, &c. vol. ii. p. 207." Lawson refers to his fellow missionary William Ward, whose View of the
History, Literature and Mythology of the Hindus (Serampore, 1818) was a staple source of information on
forms of Hindu religion for missionaries as well as for other Europeans in the early nineteenth
century.

Since thy grand advent, wash themselves and live.
Thou art their only hope, their resurrection thou![8]   90

Thus have I told my tale. And now draw near
Ye blest enlighten'd men, ye gentle wights
Of weight, and worth, and vast rotundity,
Who fain would let the ignorant sleep on
And lose their souls, regardless of your own.   95
Investigate my long drawn story! Say,
Dare ye yourselves adventure on such faith?
If to applaud be just, to trust is safe;
If safe for heathens, why not safe for you?
Why praise in them what ye dare not believe?   100
If holy streams have power to save a soul,
Why hesitate to plunge? unless ye deem
Your nature more defiled than theirs can be,
More difficult to purge. And is it thus?
Then why that proud disdain, that mighty swell,   105
That strutting littleness of self-esteem,
When ye compare yourselves with them? Why boast
Of better blood and hue, of stronger mind,
Of higher intellect? O plunge, or cease
Th' ignoble strife. For once become consistent!   110
Give proof that ye believe in Hindoo gods,
That ye do love them, that ye dare commit
Into their hands your spirits, in weal or woe,
For life and death, and dread eternity;
Else, never more defend that vain belief   115

---

8. Lawson's note, with a lengthy quotation from Ward's *View*, reads, "All cast[e]s worship Gunga,
yet most of the ceremonies at the time of the daily ablutions, with the exception of some forms of
praise to this goddess, are in the name of Shivu [Shiva], and other gods. The Hindoos particularly
choose the banks of this river for their worship, as the merit of works performed here, according to
the promise of the Shasters, becomes exceedingly augmented, as the following extract from Gunga-
Vakya-Vulee will show. 'He who thinks upon Gunga, though he may be eight hundred miles distant
from the river at the time, is delivered from all! sin, and is entitled to heaven. At the hour of death
if a person think upon Gunga, he will obtain a place in the heaven of Shivu. If a person, according
to the regulation of the Sinister, be going to bathe in Gunga, and die on the road, he shall obtain
the same benefits as though he had actually bathed.—There are three million five hundred thou-
sand holy places belonging to Gunga; the person who looks at Gunga, or bathes in this river, will
obtain all the fruit which arises from visiting all these three million five hundred thousand holy
places. If a person who has been guilty of killing cows, Brahmuns, his gooroo, or of drinking spir-
its, &c touch the waters of Gunga, desiring in his mind the remission of these sins, they will be
forgiven. By bathing in Gunga, accompanied with prayer, a person will remove at once the sins of
thousands of births.'—See Rev. W. Ward's *View*, &c. vol. ii. p. 109."

Ye fear t' adopt yourselves! Idolaters!
Your bold defenders shrink, incompetent
To be upright. They libel their own faith,
And burlesque yours. The one, they cannot trust,
The other cannot brook. They lie in heart   120
When their smooth tongues would blab abroad your fame.
They love your faith, because they hate their own;
In this, they are but infidels, in that,
Accomplished hypocrites.—Leave we these lines
Of warm rebuke; leave we these curious modes   125
Of faith, and purity, and resurrection. My inkling Muse
Would whisper other secrets, and of thee
Whose deeds I did rehearse all sacredly
When in the realms below thou blow'st upon
Thy enemies, and slew them in thy wrath,   130
I sing; and all elate describe thy high abode.[9]

---

9. This line segues into another poem on heaven, in which Lawson appears to ridicule vegetarianism, among other things, though his irony is somewhat double-edged.

Thomas Medwin

⁓ ⁓

THOMAS MEDWIN (1788–1869) spent his childhood in Horsham, Surrey, where his father was a solicitor and steward to Charles Howard, Duke of Norfolk. Both in Surrey and at Syon House Academy, he was friend and companion to his younger second cousin, Percy Bysshe Shelley, whose family home was two miles from his own. Although his father intended Medwin to follow his path into the law, Medwin did not take to it. Nor did he have much sense of the value of money. His biographer Ernest Lovell conjectures that he had lived extravagantly in London and at Oxford, which he left without taking a degree.

No doubt despairing of his son's lack of direction, in 1812 Medwin's father bought him a cornetcy in the 24th Light Dragoons, then stationed in India; two years later, the elder Medwin purchased his son a lieutenancy at the cost of nearly one thousand pounds, exclusive of uniforms, passage to India, and other expenses. Medwin had additionally received the immense sum of three thousand pounds, with which he must have gratified his expensive tastes. Because he was the son of a tradesman and solicitor, Medwin expended much effort—including in his friendships with Lord Byron and Shelley—in living like a gentleman, a feature of his life that Lovell argues led on more than one occasion to financial ruin. For Medwin, as for many another young man of his generation, army and empire would have provided a solution to insolvency and disappointed parental expectations.

Medwin arrived in India in April 1813 and departed in October 1818, serving with his regiment primarily at Cawnpore (Kanpur, Uttar Pradesh). Although his promotion was not on merit but by purchase, he did see military action during the Maratha-Pindari war of 1817–18. For the young lieutenant, more disturbing than the light casualties of his regiment were the heavy losses from cholera suffered by much of Lord Hastings's army shortly after the capitulation of Sindia. Medwin recounted a night march in which more than eight hundred soldiers were left dying and dead along the way, a scene he touches on in his poem "The Pindarees." Though he was spared cholera, Medwin did not remain unscathed; he seems to have had a chronic liver complaint for the rest of his long life, probably a form of amoebic dysentery.

When his regiment was ordered home, Medwin received a leave of eighteen months to travel overland from northern India to Bombay, writing a travel diary along the way. The future biographer of Shelley and Byron, Medwin had an astonishing and unexpected moment shortly before his departure from India, when he found in a Bombay bookstall a copy of Shelley's *Revolt of Islam*. This discovery impelled him to renew his acquaintance with his cousin and childhood friend.

After his regiment was disbanded in 1819, Medwin went on half pay, and soon joined his friend and fellow officer from India, Edward E. Williams, and Williams's partner, Jane, in Geneva. Edward had served in a brother regiment in India, where he had met Jane Johnson, who left her abusive husband to live with Williams as his wife. The three old colleagues from India lived together for a year in Switzerland with great mutual affection. The Williamses named their son Medwin, and the poet dedicated his long poem *Oswald and Edwin* to Edward, who had provided the poet with additional anecdotes and details of Indian life. Edward Williams was shortly to become Shelley's most intimate friend, perishing with Shelley in the fatal boating accident on the Bay of Spezia in 1822.

After several months with the Williamses in Geneva, Medwin joined Shelley in Pisa in October 1820, and it was the circle of Medwin's friends—the Williamses and Edward John Trelawney, later a biographer of Shelley and Byron—whom we remember as intimate parts of the Shelley circle. Shelley recommended Medwin's poems, previously published as *Oswald and Edwin*, to Ollier in London, who in 1821 published a revised edition as *Sketches in Hindoostan*. Medwin went on to become a friend of Byron's as well, and after the poet's death at Missolonghi, Medwin published *Journal of the Conversations of Lord Byron*, followed some years later by "Memoir of Shelley," appearing serially in the *Athenaeum* (1832). Of the Byron volume, Medwin correctly predicted that he would be "assailed by a swarm of hornets" (Lovell, 161). Though Medwin would go on to publish fiction, as well as translations of Petrarch, Aeschylus, and the German poet Justinus Kerner, many of these later literary productions would be received with reference to the controversies and enmities occasioned by his account of Byron's intimate life and opinions.

Medwin's later life was checkered, to say the least, by disastrous speculations in art and in love. His marriage to a wealthy baroness was at first happy, but he ran through his wife's considerable fortune by buying worthless old paintings. He deserted her and their children and spent much of his old age in Germany. On the publication of his two-volume biography of Shelley, Mary Shelley perhaps unjustly accused Medwin of attempted blackmail—she wished him not to publish; he initially agreed but asked that she pay him 250 pounds for his expenses. Nonetheless, Medwin lived a long life and had considerable happiness in a long relation at the end with Caroline Champion de Crespigny. He is buried at Horsham, Sussex, where his tombstone commemorates him as "Friend and Companion of Byron, Shelley, and Trelawney" (Lovell, 331).

Though he was stationed in India for only six years and did not later return, Medwin's experiences there shaped his early poetry and also his later volume, *The Angler in Wales*. In *The Angler in Wales*, he fictionalized his own experiences. To lengthen the book to two volumes, Medwin recycled and revised earlier poems as well as selections from his Indian diaries. What appeared in *Oswald and Edwin* (1820) as a single poem about both a lion hunt and Oswald's tragic love for an Indian woman was revised into two poems—partly at Shelley's suggestion—in *Sketches in Hindoostan* (1821). Here the poem is subdivided into a narration of a lion hunt (and the tragic death of Edwin) and a separate poem, "The Pindarees," which narrates Oswald's love for a high-caste Indian woman whom he has rescued from bandits, or "Pindarees." In *The Angler in Wales,* this rescue is again revised, this time to suggest that Oswald rescued his love not from bandits but from a sati in which she was about to be burned on the pyre of her deceased husband.

In the first edition, Oswald appears as a vegetarian yogi who has gone native, who has eloped with an Indian woman, and who tracks the Pindaris through a network of spies. In the second edition, the spy network is omitted and Oswald appears heroic in his pursuit of the Pindaris. In the third version, the melodrama is increased and the poem substantially revised, at the level of individual phrases and rhymes.

The selection below is from *Sketches in Hindoostan,* reflecting Shelley's suggestions though not the poet's last (and not always best) thoughts. The passage excerpted here is the speech of Seta, Oswald's lover, who reflects on their love and her premonition that he will be injured or killed in fighting the Pindaris. In the remainder of the poem, Oswald successfully avenges the destruction of Seta's village and the death of her brother, but a rumor of his death causes her to die of grief. Oswald then becomes a yogi-like ascetic, grieving for his lost love. The poem closes at Oswald's tomb, and Medwin concludes in high romantic fashion. Although his other poems show Shelley's influence, here the Byronic is in the ascendant, modified by Anglo-Indian conventions and his reading of orientalist translations. "Music—the dance—the bowl, / Have their oblivious potions," the poet wrote, but a soul fed on love "spurns at all joys of grosser matter bred." Byron and Shelley combine in Medwin's poetic conceptions of his Indian subjects.

Shelley lamented that Oswald lived on in a morbid state but admitted, "[I]t is the spirit of the age & we are all infected with it" (*Letters,* 2:189). He found "The Pindarees" "fit for popularity," obviously alluding to the British craze for orientalist poems, but he regretted that Medwin included Indian words in the text, with their meanings relegated to the notes (*Letters,* 2:183–84). Despite Shelley's advice, Medwin retained footnotes and, in the company of the Williamses, was little troubled by what Shelley found to be an exotic vocabulary.

Sources

Thomas Medwin, *Sketches in Hindoostan, with Other Poems* (London: C. and J. Ollier, 1821). See also Medwin, *Oswald and Edwin, Sketches in Hindoostan, Ahasuerus,* ed. Donald H. Reiman (New York: Garland, 1978); Ernest J. Lovell Jr., *Captain Medwin, Friend of Byron and Shelley* (Austin: University of Texas Press, 1962); and Frederick L. Jones, ed., *The Letters of Percy Bysshe Shelley,* 2 vols. (Oxford: Clarendon Press, 1964).

from *"The Pindarees"*

"Speak not of parting, dearest! is it meet
This pulse should throb, when thine has ceased to beat?
When once a link of love like ours we sever,
The chain is snapped! unlinkable for ever!
 With none to solace—none to bless,   5
 Think'st thou that one of Seta's race,
 Would crawl self hated on the face
 Of earth's wide trackless wilderness,—
 Still linger here, condemned to cast
 A look despairing on the past,   10
 Exchanging for a heaven of light
 A universe of death and night?[1]
Where could the mourner turn, ah where,
That thought, corroding thought, would not be there?
For thee forsaking—nay forgetting all   15
Our creed enjoins, or mortals sacred call;
 Home—parents—caste—oh deem not I repine—
No Oswald, no! for ever blest the hour,
When rescued from the ruthless Zalim's power,[2]

---

1. Here Seta is worthy of her namesake, Sita, the heroine of the *Rāmāyaṇa* and a model of the
faithful wife. Abducted by the demon Rāvaṇa, Sita nonetheless remained chaste and, upon her
rescue by Rama, proved her virtue in a trial by fire. Seta asserts similar faithfulness to Oswald,
despite having left all that "mortals sacred call" through a liaison with a foreigner without caste. She
makes clear that this liaison has caused her to lose caste and to be rejected by her family, all for love
and the world well lost.

2. A "Pindaree" bandit chief. Reflecting nineteenth-century historical views, *Hobson-Jobson* may be
taken to provide a concise definition of "Pindaree" and summary of their conflict with the British:
the Pindaris "seem to have grown up in the wars of the late Mahommedan dynasties in the Deccan,
and in the latter part of the 17th century attached themselves to the Mahrattas in their revolt against
Aurangzib; the first mention which we have seen of the name occurs at this time. . . . During and
after the Mahratta wars of Lord Wellesley's time many of the Pindārī leaders obtained grants of land in
Central India from Sindia and Holkar, and in the chaos which reigned at that time outside the British
territory their raids in all directions, attended by the most savage atrocities, became more and more
intolerable; these outrages extended from Bundelkhand on the N.E., Kadapa on the S., and Orissa
on the S.E., to Guzerat [Gujerat] on the W., and at last repeatedly violated British territory. In a raid
made upon the coast extending from Masulipatam northward, the Pindāris in ten days plundered 339
villages, burning many, killing and wounding 682 persons, torturing 3600, and carrying off or
destroying property to the amount of £250,000. It was not, however, till 1817 that the Governor-
General, the Marquis of Hastings, found himself armed with permission from home, and in a posi-
tion to strike at them effectually, and with the most extensive strategic combinations ever brought into
action in India. The Pindāris were completely crushed, and those of the native princes who supported
them compelled to submit, whilst the British power for the first time was rendered truly paramount
throughout India." *Hobson-Jobson* and Medwin alike present this conflict as an effort to suppress ban-
ditry and chaos, though clearly the first edition of Medwin's poem also reflects the importance of the
conflict to the extension of British power in India (*Hobson-Jobson*).

Indissolubly sealed my fate with thine.   20
Oh no! I lived not, till I drew
That breath of thine,—those lips of dew!
    What did they not inspire!
The extasies my soul imbibed
Are in its essence still inscribed   25
    In characters of fire.
'Twas then you taught this heart of mine
To thrill in unison with thine.
To beat its mystic ebb and flow,
Self-conscious of thy joy or woe;   30
One tenement but holds our breath
In life—should be but one in death!
One urn should hold—enwrap one flame
The ashes of our mingled frame.
Is it for souls like ours to range?   35
Our natures thus we cannot change!
My Saumur—when she lost her mate,[3]
    (And shall a bird affections prove
    More tender than a woman's love?)
Remember how I wept her fate!   40
When anguish broke that heart in twain,
That may not reunite again:—
    Why is a paradise assigned
    To us, and not the feathered kind?
    Dear Oswald! sure that angel's veil   45
    I dreamt of (but your cheek is pale)
    That hid you from my arms this night
    Was but a visionary sprite
    Or, dearest, it were best to join
    My faith and creed at once to thine.   50
Yet in this amulet's a charm
To guard my frame from mortal harm;
Nay more—a stronger spell—'tis given
To pave the soul a way to heaven;
And claim for us those rights with man,   55
Untaught, unknown, in the koran;
What tho' our law forbids that one
Of woman kind presume to con
Verse that on meditation's wing

---

3. Saumur: a species of thrush. [TM]

Alone should seek the fountain spring 60
Of truth,[4] inspired in every line;
That stamps our Shaster[5] as divine—
Ah no! I cannot quit my shrine!
Tell me I need not kneel at thine!
For I was taught to love and spare 65
The habitants of earth and air;
To view beast, insect, bird, and tree,
As spirits in captivity;[6]
And thus a sisterhood I claim
With nature's universal frame; 70
Till all I hear or breathe or see
Image her deity to me.
Yon orbs on high—this little flower,
Are emblems of her love, or power;
This basil, that with mother's care[7] 75
I water—shield from sun, and air,
Is animate, and seems to know
From whom its life and fragrance flow;
This nightingale, whose notes dispense
Voluptuous pathos o'er the sense; 80
The fount that showers its chrystal light
On the dark tresses of the night;
The stream that ripples by unheard;
The breeze, amid the leaves unstirred,
That pants and trembles with delight 85
Of its own motion; and the air
With incense breathing every where
From flowers in slumber dreaming there;
All, all, is love: in such an hour
What wonder if the bird, the flower, 90
The fount, the stream, in such a calm,
Have each a soul to feel its balm,
A world of love and life to me,
A paradise while shared by thee:
Then by this cherished muntra[8] that I tear 95
Thus from my bosom—by this lock of hair

---

4. The excuse the Brachmans offer for not allowing the Vedas to be perused by the vulgar. [TM]
5. Shaster, shastra: a divine scripture or commentary, here referring to the Vedas.
6. This belief in Metempsychosis is universal. [TM]
7. The sweet basil, or toolsee [tulsi], is a sacred plant. [TM]
8. Muntra [mantra], a spell. [TM]

That ne'er has left till now, and must not part
With life's last throbbings from this widowed heart;
Oh by this mirror-ring[9] so often prest,
Thy image thus reflecting on my breast;
Or by that pledge of friendship that you wear,
A relic hallowed by affection's tear;
Oswald! by all by this more dear to you,
In pity, love, recall that word adieu."

100

9. The Hindu women wear a ring with a speculum. [TM]

Emma Roberts

EMMA ROBERTS (1791–1840) set out for India in 1828 with her sister Laura and her sister's husband, a captain in the British army. As was the custom for single British women, she initially lived with her sister's family at Agra, Cawnpore, and Etawah, where her brother-in-law was posted. After her sister's death in 1830, she moved to Calcutta and supported herself as a professional writer. Coming from a Welsh military family, Roberts learned early about financial independence. Her father died young, and she later assumed responsibility for her aging mother. After her mother's death, she traveled to India where she embarked fully on a literary career. She entered the Calcutta literary scene at a time when both Indian and British-born poets had created a lively, if small, literary culture.

Roberts made many friends, including the poet H. L. V. Derozio, who took charge of publishing her book of poems. She not only shared Derozio's enthusiasm for Byron, Landon, and the more radical British poets but also his ability to think beyond the usual moral and cultural assumptions of empire. As a professional writer, she saw the importance of marketing her work, and against the odds she managed to make poetry pay. Her only volume of verse, *Oriental Scenes, Dramatic Sketches and Tales* (1830), was sold in advance to more than 350 subscribers both in Calcutta and "up-country." Even in the twenty-first century, such a circulation would represent a respectable sale for a first volume of poetry. Roberts's list of subscribers constituted a virtual who's who of early-nineteenth-century literary culture in Bengal, and it included several book clubs sponsored by military regiments in the provinces.

Roberts published accounts of her travels in British and Indian periodicals and later collected many of these essays under the title *Scenes and Characteristics of Hindostan, with Sketches of Anglo-Indian Society* (1835). A second travel book, *The East India Voyager, or Ten Minutes Advice to the Outward Bound* (London, 1839), provided practical suggestions for prospective British travelers. A third, *Notes of an Overland Journey through France and Egypt to Bombay*, appeared posthumously in 1841.

Roberts told her readers how to pack a trunk, how to choose underwear for hot weather, and how many candles and how much wine to purchase for the sea voyage. A freethinking and independent woman, she did not shrink from providing ethical advice as well. She pointedly criticized British arrogance and racism, warning prospective military men in particular not to adopt the usual insular attitude of their peers. Many officers, she wrote in *The East India Voyager,* "remain for years in India without conquering a single prejudice or without seeing more than the mere external surface of a very small portion of the country" because the "native community" is beneath their notice. Her *East India Voyager* described the phrase "black fellow" as an "invidious epithet" and criticized the arrogance and even hatred with which many of her countrymen and women treated the Indian population. Unless Indians should "obtain the respect, consideration, and importance which seem so justly their due," she predicted, "it can scarcely be expected that they will continue to give their support to a government whose servants are resolutely opposed to their interests" (*East India Voyager,* 46, 105).

Roberts's prose writing on India influenced the poetry of her friend Letitia Landon, editor of the literary annual *Fisher's Drawing-Room Scrapbook.* The annuals, which were marketed as Christmas gift books in London and Calcutta, gained immense popularity with middle-class readers. Roberts's volumes of travel and poetry provided ideas for Landon's lucrative enterprise; the sketchbook of her friend Robert Elliott furnished illustrative materials. A few years after this collaboration, Roberts edited Landon's posthumous collection of verse and wrote a prefatory memoir of her friend, who had died shortly after accompanying her new husband to the Gold Coast of Africa. Roberts's poetry naturally reflects a much richer knowledge of India than Landon's, though clearly her approach to the topics of the day influenced her friend's work.

The longest and most effective poem in Roberts's *Oriental Scenes,* "The Rajah's Obsequies," engages reformist controversies in Calcutta, particularly arguments about women's rights that were central to Indian encounters with European culture in the wake of the French and American revolutions. Like her friend Derozio and many British and Indian writers of the time, Roberts takes sati (or suttee) as a locus for argument. Her militant heroine prophesies the doom of Hindu India in the wake of the Mughal conquest before she herself is reduced to a grisly "cloud of ashes on the gale." "The Rajah's Obsequies," like other poems in *Oriental Scenes,* relies upon the words of dramatized speakers. This device allowed Roberts to achieve a certain ironic distance from her position as an ambivalent representative of British imperialism. Roberts assumes directly or by dramatic triangulation a woman's voice, rather than—as was the custom of English poets—writing as a spectator or the omniscient narrator of ballads or epics. The trope of ruin in her poetry, while it reflects the imperialist historiography of the Muslim conquest, also evokes the inevitable demise of British imperialism.

Although Roberts's work generally resists the tropes of romantic longing and homesickness, her poem "Stanzas" exemplifies the typical stance of the male expatriate poet writing for the home market. Here, uncharacteristically, Roberts takes up the trope of exile and declares that she languishes for "a cottage home." Apart from this example, we find in Roberts a distance from the views of her fellow expatriates, which was certainly shaped by her unusual position as a single professional woman and was probably also formed by a Welsh skepticism about claims of English superiority. An eminently practical woman—author of a history, several travel guides, and a cookbook—Roberts generally preferred sympathetic descriptions of Indian scenery and the political controversies of the day to the exile's melancholy.

After four years in India, Roberts returned to London, but she did not remain there long. We can imagine that both financial necessity and her enthusiasm for Indian culture motivated her return, this time to Bombay (now Mumbai), where she became editor of a new newspaper, *The United Services Gazette*, in 1839. In the next year, she was taken ill while traveling and died at the home of a friend in Pune in 1840.

Sources

Emma Roberts, *Oriental Scenes, Sketches, and Tales* (London: Edward Bull, 1832). See also the first edition of Roberts's collection, titled *Oriental Scenes, Dramatic Sketches and Tales* (London: P. S. D'Rozario, 1830); Rosemary Raza, "Roberts, Emma (1791–1840)," in *ODNB*; Raza, *In Their Own Words: British Women Writers and India, 1740–1857* (New Delhi: Oxford University Press, 2006). For additional prose by Emma Roberts, see especially *Scenes and Characteristics of Hindostan, with Sketches of Anglo-Indian Society*, 3 vols. (London: W. H. Allen, 1835) and *The East India Voyager, or, Ten Minutes Advice to the Outward Bound* (London: J. Madden, 1839).

from *"The Rajah's Obsequies"*

The Younger Wife's Song

I love, I love my native vales![1]
The sighing of their perfumed gales
To me is sweet, and sweeter still
The music of the bubbling rill.

---

1. "The Rajah's Obsequies" is a long narrative poem, taking place in an undefined period before the Muslim conquest of northern India. Set in Benares (now Varanasi), it recounts the rajah's death, his funeral procession, and the sati (or suttee) of his two wives. Roberts enters the vigorous debate over the unusual but symbolically important practice, which encouraged wives, particularly Brahmins, to immolate themselves on the crematory pyres of their husbands. Excerpted here are the songs of the rajah's two wives followed by the poem's final stanzas.

Few are my years, but they have fled   5
In joy and sunshine o'er my head;
Happy my transient life has been,
And happier still life's closing scene.

Lord of my soul! I yield my breath
To snatch thee from the chains of death;   10
I claim the privilege divine,
Which makes thee more than ever mine!

Yes, to my thrice blessed hands 'tis given
To ope the saffron gates of heaven;
I bring, beloved, a boon to thee,   15
A pure and bright eternity.

Yon dazzling orb has golden courts,
And there the heaven-born lory[2] sports,
And thou with spirits blessed shalt dwell
Mid fragrant fields of aspohodel.   20

My soul shall pass to happy things,
With dainty plumes and glittering wings;
A Peri bird, I'll build my nest
On the *chumayla's* odorous breast.[3]

And that sweet state of being o'er,   25
Beside the Ganges' much loved shore
I'll spread my shining fins, and glide
A spark of silver on the tide.

The second transmigration past,
I'll reach my brightest, and my last—   30

2. Lory: a parrotlike bird of the family Loriinae, characterized by brilliant plumage. In *The Curse of Kehama*, Robert Southey alludes to the Indian "god of love" Camdeo "riding on his lory." See *The Curse of Kehama* (1810) in Southey, *Poetical Works, 1783–1810*, ed. Tim Fulford and Daniel Roberts (London: Pickering and Chatto, 2004), 5.

3. Roberts commented on this passage in a note: "The last words uttered by the Suttee are supposed to be oracular: they usually relate to the transmigrations which the parting spirit is destined to undergo." She then compared her work to H. L. V. Derozio's: "Mr. Derozio, in his very beautiful and truly Oriental Poem, 'The Fakeer of Jungheera,' has taken advantage of the license to depart from the beaten track, universally allowed, and has placed a highly poetical and spirited effusion, relating to things of far diviner nature than the transmigrations of the soul into the bodies of animals, on the lips of his heroine. I have followed his example by varying the parting address of Mitala from that of her sister victim, but can make no pretensions to the eloquence and harmony of Mr. Derozio's verse."

Shoot with my fire-fly lamp on high,
A star along the summer sky.

Then to the palace gleaming bright,
Turquoise, and pearl, and chrysolite,
My heavenly home, ascend and stray   35
For ever through the realms of day.

                *   *   *

The Elder Wife's Song

Think not, accursed priests, that I will lend[4]
        My sanction to these most unholy rites;
And though yon funeral pile I may ascend,
        It is not that your stern command affrights   40
My lofty soul—it is because these hands
Are all too weak to break my sex's bands.

I, from my earliest infancy, have bowed
        A helpless slave to lordly man's control,
No hope of liberty, no choice allowed,   45
        Unheeded all the struggles of my soul;
Compelled by brutal force to link my fate
With one who best deserved my scorn and hate.

Oh! better far it is to mount yon pile,
        And stretch my shuddering form beside the dead,   50
Than with a torturing effort strive to smile,
        And hide the bitter tears in silence shed—
That state of loathed existence now is o'er,
And I shall shrink from his embrace no more.

The tyrant sleeps death's last and endless sleep,   55
        Yet does his power beyond the grave extend,
And I this most unholy law must keep,
        And to the priest's unrighteous mandate bend,
Or live an outcast—reft of queenly state—
A beggar lost, despised, and desolate.   60

---

4. Here the younger bride concludes her song and the elder, Mitala, proudly flings aside her
gems and delivers these words "like an offended goddess."

Daughter and heiress of a princely line,
    From my proud birth-right I disdain to stoop;
Better it is to *die*, than inly pine,
    And feel the soul, the towering spirit, droop
Beneath the cruel toil, the years of pain,   65
The lost, degraded widow must sustain.

But could these weak arms wield a soldier's brand,
    Could these too fragile limbs sustain the fight,
Even to the death, Mitala would withstand
    This cruel custom, and uphold the right   70
Of woman to her share of gold and gems,
Sceptres and sway, and regal diadems.

Oh! is there none—not one amid the throng
    Pressing to view a deed by Heaven abhorred,
Whose brave heart, burning to avenge the wrong,   75
    Will at my adjuration draw the sword,
And god-like in an injured woman's cause
Crush at a blow foul superstition's laws?

Silent and moveless all!—Oh craven race
    Not long shall this fair land endure your sway;   80
Shame and defeat, and capture and disgrace
    Await the closing of a blood-stained day;
I see, I see the thickly gathering bands
Crowding in conquering ranks from distant lands!

The Persian Satrap, and the Tartar Khan   85
    The temples of your gods shall overthrow,[5]
And all the hundred thrones of Hindoostan
    Before the west's pale warriors shall bow,
Crouching where'er the banners of the brave,
The silver crescent, and the red cross, wave!   90

        *   *   *

Her song has ceased—but that bright eye.
    Still with prophetic frenzy glares,
And struggling with her agony
    Dries with its fires the springing tears.

---

5. This prediction relates to the outrages perpetrated by Aurengzebe. [ER]

She waves away the Brahmin band   95
    And mounts the funeral pile alone;
And the *Mussaul*'s enkindling brand
    Is on the heaped-up fagots thrown—
One long wild shriek, amid the crash
    Of gongs and drums and cymbals, drowned—   100
One burst of flame, a ruddy flash
    Gilding the green hill's distant mound—
One smoky column, whose dark veil
    Obscures the fast declining sun—
A cloud of ashes on the gale—   105
    And these unhallowed rites are done!

Stanzas

WRITTEN ON THE BANKS OF THE GANGES

Upon the Ganges' regal streams,[6]
    Through the wide landscape flow,
And gorgeously the noon-tide beams
    Upon its bosom glow;
But in a small sequestered nook,   5
    Beyond the western sea,
There rippling glides a narrow brook,
    That's dearer far to me.

The lory perches on my hand,
    Caressing to be fed,   10
And spreads its wings at my command,
    And bends its purple head;
But where the robin, humble guest,

---

6. Persons who have never quitted their native land, cannot imagine the passionate regrets experienced by the exile, who in the midst of the most gorgeous scenes pines after the humblest objects surrounding that home to which he dares not hope to return. The feeling may be perverse and wayward, but where all is strange, the very magnificence of the landscape is apt to revolt the mind, and many persons will, like the author, in a fit of despair, contrast the Ganges with some obscure rivulet, the magnolia with the daisy, to the disparagement of the mighty river and the monarch of flowers. To do justice to the sunny land of India, its visitors should have the power to leave it for Europe at pleasure; when the lot seems finally cast, the spirit becomes too much depressed to enjoy the dazzling novelties which give but too forcible an assurance that we are far from home. [ER]

Comes flying from the tree,
That bears its unpretending nest,   15
    Alas! I'd rather be.

The firefly flashes through the air,
    A meteor swift and bright,
And all the spangled atmosphere
    Gleams with its emerald light.   20
Though glory tracks that shooting star,
    With dazzling lustre blest,
The glow-worm's lamp is dearer far
    To my lamenting breast.

Flowers of rich and fadeless dies[7]   25
    The jungles overspread,
And with the breeze's faintest sighs
    Are sweetest perfumes shed.
The daisy, and the primrose pale,
    Though scentless they may be,   30
That gem a far, far distant vale,
    Are dearer still to me.

The lotus opes its chalices,
    Upon the tank's broad lake,
Where India's stately palaces   35
    Their ample mirrors make:
But reckless of each tower and dome,
    The splendid and the grand,
I languish for a cottage home
    Within my native land.   40

---

7. Lines 25–29 changed dramatically between the editions of 1830 and 1832. In the earlier publication, the language is completely different:

    Throughout the summer year the flowers
    In all the flush of bloom,
    Clust'ring around the forest bowers,
    Exhale their rich perfume;

Life's Changes

Mid gay and crowded festivals,[8]
In many a fair and glittering scene,
I tread those bright and gilded halls
Wherein thy feet so oft have been.
Familiar are the names to me   5
Which my new friends and flatterers bear,
Each sound comes linked with thoughts of thee;
But thou art—where?

The busy throng which thou hast known
In days gone by approach me now,   10
And every word and every tone
Reminds me of thy plighted vow.
They name thee not, but fancy brings
Thy voice upon the passing air,
Thy form is borne upon her wings;   15
But thou art—where?

The wreath which, when my humble song
Was breathed to careless ears in vain,
Thou fondly said'st should soon belong
To my unprized unvalued strain,   20
Is twined for me—upon my brow
In many a knot and cluster fair
Its blooming buds and blossoms glow;
And thou art—where?

Not thine the lips that whisper praise,   25
Not thine the bright and beaming eye
Turning on mine its ardent gaze,
Not thine the hope, not thine the sigh.
Another breathes a tender tale,
Another hovers round my chair,   30
Another trusts he may prevail,
For thou art—where?

---

8. This poem is excerpted from the 1830 edition of *Oriental Scenes;* Roberts did not include it in the second edition.

I know not if my once loved name
Now first before the world avowed,
As one who hopes her lay may claim   35
The homage of the busy crowd,
Though published wide, has reached thine ear,
Reviving thoughts which love will share—
I know not if it still be dear;
For thou art—where?   40

The North-Wester

Evening approaches, and the tropic sun
The western arch of ruddy heaven has won,
And, yielding to the balmy close of day,
Its scorching heat, its most oppressive ray,
Now 'mid ten thousand swiftly fading dyes   5
Looks smiling down from yonder roseate skies.
How beautiful, how placid, fair, and bright,
The gorgeous scene that greets its parting light!
The stately river's calm and waveless tide
In its deep slumber scarce is seen to glide;   10
So tranquil is the stream, the lotus crown
By some fond maid, or anxious lover thrown—
A bark of hope—unstirred upon its breast,
In lingering tenderness appears to rest.
The idle *goleeah*[9] from his flower-wreathed prow   15
With careless eye surveys the flood below;
And all the hundred oars that proudly sweep
The polished surface of the glassy deep,
Mocked by the lazy currents, vainly seek
To urge their shallops[10] round yon woody creek.   20
Its marble wings up springing from the shade
By the dark *peepul's*[11] glossy foliage made,
The waving *neem*,[12] the willow-like bamboo,

---

9. Gooleah: bowman, that is, the person at the front of a boat who oversees the rowers.
10. Shallop: a small pleasure boat with several rowers and an awning under which the passengers sit. On the Thames, the upper classes would often use shallops as leisure boats.
11. Peepul (pipal): the sacred fig, or bodhi tree.
12. Neem: a tall tree, with long narrow leaves.

And shrubs of fragrant scent and brilliant hue,
The Nazim's[13] regal palace proudly gleams   25
In pearl-like splendour in the evening beams;
While each surrounding crag and sun-kissed slope,
Crowned with the bright luxuriant mango tope—
Each vagrant creeper with its starry wreath,
Are softly mirrored in the stream beneath.   30

Where'er the wandering eyes delighted roam,
From groves embowering peeps the graceful dome
Of some small mosque, or holy Brahmin's cell,
Where the lamp glances, and the silvery bell
Makes gentle music in the balmy air;   35
No other sounds the listening echoes bear
On this calm eve, save snatches of sweet song
Which rise at intervals from yonder throng
Assembled on the terraced ghaut,[14] to fling
O'er Ganges' wave each flowery offering.   40
Sudden the fierce North-west breaks loose—and while
Half the bright landscape still is seen to smile,
The sultry air grows thick, the skies are dark,
The river swells, and now the struggling bark
Along the rushing wave is wildly driven,   45
And thunder bursts from every gate of heaven;
O'er tower and palace, hut, and holy fane,[15]
In frantic madness sweeps the hurricane;
And trees uprooted strew the earth; and air
Is filled with yells, and shrieks of wild despair.   50

The sun sinks down in splendour to the west,
The skies are in their richest colours drest;
And where a blackened wreck was seen to float,
A lamp within the palm nut's fragile boat
Glides tranquilly;—the stars shine forth—the vale   55

---

13. The brief but devastating storms, denominated in India North-Westers, are of frequent
occurrence during the rainy season. . . . The one described took place in the vicinity of Moorshed-
abad, the residence of the Nizam of Bengal, and it dispersed a splendid flotilla of boats belonging
to that prince. [ER] I have abridged Roberts's note.
  Moorshedabad (Murshidabad) was the capital of Bengal under the Mughals (located today in
the state of West Bengal), and Nizam was the title for the ruling prince of Bengal.
  14. Ghaut (ghat): a set of broad steps that lead down to a river.
  15. Fane: a church or temple.

Is vocal with the bulbul's[16] sweetest tale;
The air is gemmed with fire-flies; and the breeze
Is filled with perfume from the lemon trees:
The storm has passed—and now the sparkling river
Runs calm, and smooth, and beautiful as ever.   60

MOORSHEDABAD, AUG. 1828

---

16. Bulbul: a songbird from the family Pycnonotidae; the bulbul is often mentioned in Persian poetry, and the word is generally translated as "nightingale."

James Ross Hutchinson

JAMES ROSS HUTCHINSON (1796–1870), like many of the British-born poets in nineteenth-century India, hailed from Scotland and was by training a medical doctor. His best-known work, *The Sunyassee, an Eastern Tale, and Other Poems* (1838), was printed at the Baptist Mission Press in Calcutta. This long collection, more than two hundred pages in length, established Hutchinson as a significant poet among Anglo-Indians.

A patriotic Scot, Hutchinson dedicated the first edition of this volume of verse to "The People of Scotland: My Distant Friends!" and the next two editions to the president, vice president, and members of the Council of India. In his patriotic dedication to fellow Scots, he declared, "The following Poems were written, with the hopes of doing credit to myself, and consequently to you; to whom then could I dedicate them with so much propriety? Should these aspirations be, in any wise, realized, will you remember? And should they not, will you forget, that, I am, or was, YOUR COUNTRYMAN?"

Hutchinson collected his poems while on a medical leave in South Africa in 1837. During his stay there, he also purchased farms, for he intended to retire to the Cape. After twenty years of service as a surgeon on the Bengal Establishment, as secretary to the Medical Board of the Calcutta Presidency, and as the private secretary to the president of the Council of India, he did indeed retire to one of his farms, Belle Ombre, in Constantia, Cape Colony, where he died in 1870. He bequeathed his estates to his brothers on the condition that they reside there, but the estates were instead sold. Among his brothers was John Ross Hutchinson, a judge in Calcutta; another brother, Charles Hutchinson, had died in the Burmese campaign in 1825.

As a medical doctor, Hutchinson devoted considerable energy to the reform of Indian jails, for which he had medical responsibility. He inveighed especially against unsanitary practices giving rise to cholera and "hospital gangrene," or blood poisoning, often occasioned by the fetters prisoners were forced to wear. He published two editions of a detailed study and report: *Observations on the General and Medical Management of Indian Jails: And on the Treatment of Some of the Principal Diseases which Infest Them* (1845, second edition). This treatise drew on his previously published work on cholera, and it criticized Indian penal practices, suggesting that the British were far too inclined to imprison Indians, with pernicious effects for the

prisoners and their families. He argued, too, that prisoners should not be sub-
ject to immediate withdrawal of the opium to which many of them were addicted.
As a result of these observations, Hutchinson was, apparently, criticized in official
circles. He nonetheless retired with a high rank in the medical service.

The principal poem in Hutchinson's collection of verse, "The Sunyassee or
Pilgrim of India," does not lend itself to excerpts, but like his medical writings,
it betrays an independent spirit. Hutchinson has his hero compare the rise of
English power to "some vast Upas tree," a tree legendary for spreading poison;
the hero goes on to lament the English victory in the Maratha wars. Still, the poet
does end by wishing that his hero—who moves from fated love to war to banditry
to renunciation—could have known Christian consolation.

Hutchinson's lyric poems play on tropes common in the first half of the nine-
teenth century: star-crossed love, topographical appreciation of India's beauties,
translations from the Persian of Hāfiz, and—for Scots poets in India—a desire to
follow in the footsteps of Robert Burns. "Paraphrase," for example, takes as its
source the romantic trope of the harp hung upon the willow, which featured
largely in the bardic nationalism of Wales, Scotland, and Ireland and was taken
up most notably in India by H. L. V. Derozio. But Hutchinson also strikes an
original note. His elegy for his younger brother Charles betrays the horrors of
the Burmese campaigns, in which mortality from sickness far outpaced the casu-
alties of war.

Sources

The Literary Works of James Hutchinson, 3rd ed. (Cape Town, South Africa: Solomon, 1864). See
  also Hutchinson, The Sunyassee, an Eastern Tale, and Other Poems (Calcutta: Baptist Mission
  Press, 1838).

Elegiac Stanzas

And shall not I one feeble line essay,
To save thy name from dull oblivion's blight,
My more than brother;[1]—for affection's ray

---

1. These stanzas were written to the memory of my brother, Lieutenant Charles Hutchinson, of
the 42nd Regiment of the Bengal Native Infantry, who died in Arracan, on the 14th July, 1825, a
few days after the capture of that province. [JRH]

The first Anglo-Burmese war lasted from 1823 to 1826 and, despite tremendous mortality
from sickness among the troops, resulted in a British victory, with the Burmese renouncing their
claims upon Assam, Manipur, and other border areas.

On thee shone softer, with a purer light;
For that thou hadst our mother's eyes so bright   5
And wert the youngest, and her latest joy;
Hadst grown up 'mid our kindness;—our delight
Was centered in thee,—well the hero boy
Had those fond hopes fulfilled, our pride was to enjoy.

One year beheld him doff his school-boy garb,   10
And buckle on the panoply of war;
And graceful could he rein his prancing barb,
And ardent was his heart:—the only star
That shone for him was fame;—enough afar
In Arracan he sleeps,—his only grief,   15
To fall without one honourable scar:
But round his dying brow the victor's leaf
Was fresh—and 'twas his joy—his course, alas! too brief.

A column marks the spot where all remains
Of what was once so noble; and around,   20
On wooded eminence, and marshy plains,
The frequent, undistinguished, grassy mound,
(The cells of his companions) marks the ground
Where Pestilence gorged her thousands of the brave,
And all were sick—till there was heard no sound,   25
Nor prayer, nor volley o'er the soldier's grave,
To consecrate his bed—beyond the Maio's wave.[2]

Happy thy mother!—ere thy tale was known,
Her mind had been o'ershadowed, and the same
That fondly lighted up the youthful dawn   30
Of thine, was clouded, and the bright flame
Extinguished by disease—till she became
A sister's care, in this her helpless state;
And she will still repeat her Charles's name.
Peace be with her.—It was thy wish, and fate,   35
To sleep where thou hadst trod, with victory elate.

---

2. I was given to understand at the time, and I have since had no reason to doubt the accuracy
of the information, that the sickness and mortality among the troops in Arracan at the period in
question was so great, that it was deemed expedient to dispense with the customary military hon-
ours in burying the dead, with the view of obviating the disheartening and distressing effect which
their observance would naturally have produced on the sick. [JRH]
    Maio's wave: Mayo Bay on the coast of Burma.

Moonlight Scene

On Ganges' stream the moon shines bright,
And swift the skiff glides on its breast;
The waves are rippling in its light,
And all is fair and still, at rest.

The stately palm, its banks along,   5
High rears its head amid the trees;
There's scarce a breath to wake the song,
Its leaves sing, nightly, to the breeze.

A hundred barks at anchor ride,
The neighbouring city's walls below;   10
The lordly domes upon its side,
Far o'er the wave their shadows throw.

There is a stillness in the hour,
There is a magic in the scene,
That o'er the spirit hath a power,   15
To wake the thought of what hath been.

To Leilah

Oh! tell me, why thou art so dear?
What binds me in this spell to thee?
Thy voice is music to my ear,
Which hush'd—earth hath no charm for me;
Thou art the form my youthful fancy wrought;   5
Thou art the all this bosom ever sought.

Thy smile is dearer than the spoil
In glitt'ring heaps to miser's eyes;
The sigh is sweeter than thy smile,
That bids thy billowy bosom rise;   10
Though others fair as Parian marble glow,
As coldly burns the lamp of love below.

Thy large black eye, as saints' cast down,
Is like the lightning in its cloud;
Till eye meets eye, and wildly own 15
The love that flashes from its shroud;
That speaks at once the mind, uncurbed by art,
As sorrow melts—or passion fires the heart.

Thy breath is sweeter than the gale,
That's borne o'er Iran's garden queen;[3] 20
Thy voice is softer than the tale,
The Bulbul[4] sings to her at e'en;
Thy lip is redder than his blushing bride,[5]
To me more sweet than all the world beside.

What, though thy sun with deeper blush 25
That soft, soft cheek in envy drest?
In vain 'twould hide the tides that rush
And mantle o'er thy lovely breast:
Tho' fair the form that decks the northern dame,
How cold's her love to thy wild heart of flame. 30

Though I must teach me to forget
(O say not, to despair above,)
The all I ever loved, as yet;
Though ours, on earth, be hopeless love;
Yet shall my verse for evermore entwine 35
Thy cherished name inseparably with mine.

---

3. The rose is celebrated as the garden queen of Persia. [JRH]

4. The Bulbul, it is no doubt generally known, is the nightingale of the East. In India, the cages of these birds are generally covered over with calico, coloured or plain, but generally, I think, blue. Why they are kept in this darkened captivity I know not. Perhaps the subdued light thus occasioned is more congenial to them, and induces them more freely to pour forth their rich and mellow notes. [JRH]

5. The rose is fabled by the Persian poets as the bride of the Bulbul, or Nightingale. [JRH]

Song

What ails this heart o'mine?
What ails this watery e'e?[6]
What gars me aye turn cauld as death,
When I take leave o' thee?

What makes the hours o' day   5
Gae by sae light and free,
Till hours, like minutes, fast fell by,
Because they're spent wi' thee?

Why shuns sweet sleep these eyes?
The night seems long to me?   10
I see thee, hear thee, but by day;
At night I meet not thee.

Yet aft will sleepless fancy rife,
Like Seer's prophetic e'e,
With scenes which are, yet are not life,   15
In dreams return to thee.

Paraphrase

Far from our land
Driven by Jehovah's hand,
And exiles on a foreign strand,
We thought of Salem's sacred shrine,
And natal soil—the gift divine.[7]   5
    Our tears followed fast,

---

6. E'e: Eye.

7. Hutchinson paraphrases Psalm 137, in which the psalmist laments the Babylonian captivity, whereby Nebuchadnezzar II deported and exiled the Jews from the kingdom of Judah to Babylon. In the King James translation of the Bible, the psalm begins,

> By the rivers of Babylon, there we sat down, yea, we wept, when we
> remembered Zion.
> We hanged our harps upon the willows in the midst thereof.
> For there they that had carried us away captive required of us a song; and they
> that wasted us required of us mirth, saying, Sing us one of the songs of Zion.
> How shall we sing the Lord's song in a strange land?

Mingling with Babel's stream,
    That glided past,
  Like Joy's too fleeting dream;
O'er us poor captives and forlorn,   10
The willows seemed to droop and mourn,
Our harps upon their boughs we hung;
Neglected, tuneless, and unstrung.
    Regardless of our griefs and wrongs,
With taunting jeer our spoilers cried,   15
  "Come, sing us one of Sion's songs?"
"Never!" our bursting hearts replied.
How can our harps our cares employ,
Or captives strike the notes of joy?
Salem! should we forget thy land,   20
May cunning quit the faithless hand;
And speechless be the recreant tongue
Would wake for foes thy sacred song.
Remember, Lord, how Edom's race
Exulted in thy shrine's disgrace;[8]   25
Their cries of "Rase it," swelled the gale,
"Leave not a stone to tell its tale."
    And, Babylon, the time shall come,
When thy proud walls shall kiss the ground,
    And tenantless each hearth and home   30
Shall mingle with the dust around.
And happy he, who hath not felt
    The bliss in triumph to forbear,
Shall deal with thee as thou hast dealt,
    Unheeding of thy cries to spare.   35
Aye, blessed be the breast of steel,
    Unknowing for thy woes to feel,
Shall dash, despite their parents' groans,
    Thy children's heads against the stones.

---

8. Edom was contiguous to ancient Judea, in what is now the Negev Desert and adjacent Jordan. In the time of Nebuchadnezzar II, the Edomites helped plunder Jerusalem, an act that the psalmist excoriates in Psalm 137.

Henry Meredith Parker

≈⟩ ⟨⌢

L ITTLE IS known of Henry Meredith Parker's youth save that he perhaps
was a violinist at Covent Garden before going out to India as a clerk. He
was clearly a man of great wit and multiple talents. Once in India, he
managed to enter the Bengal Civil Service, where he rose through the ranks to
become a member of the Calcutta Board of Customs, Salt and Opium (later the
Board of Revenue). The British governor general William Bentinck declared
that Parker (1796–1868) combined the incompatible: "literary attainments and
excellence in dry official routine" (Laurie, 186).

Parker commenced by publishing verses under the pseudonym Bernard
Wycliffe and went on to publish both prose and verse in various Indian periodi-
cals from literary annuals to newspapers to sporting journals. His first volume of
poetry, *The Draught of Immortality* (1827), included Byronic echoes, a long transla-
tion from the *Mahābhārata* (the title poem), and a variety of ballads and songs.
Upon his retirement, Parker collected his miscellaneous writings in a volume he
titled *Bole Ponjis, Containing The Tale of the Buccanneer; A Bottle of Red Ink; The Decline and Fall
of Ghosts; and Other Ingredients.*

Parker's later publications included a collection of what he ironically called
"sermons" but which were actually essays: *The Empire of the Middle Classes.* These essays
were a reaction to the Indian rebellion of 1857 and, more proximately, to the
British government's abolition of the East India Company in 1858. Parker op-
posed this move—arguing that the English were as likely to fail in India as in
Ireland and that such a move was a mistaken continuation of evangelical folly.
Parker sarcastically dedicated his "sermons" to "that devout, earnest, and consci-
entious body of Englishmen, whose fervent zeal for Conversion has clearly
helped to create a fearful Mutiny, and will probably excite a National Rebellion
in India" (*Empire*, n.p.). Parker argued that, as Hindus had no wish to convert
Christians to their own religion, they could not but believe that evangelical fer-
vor proceeded from "advancement of our own worldly interests" (*Empire*, 17). A
similar inclination to skepticism and irony is evident in the lighter items in *Bole
Ponjis*, "the bowl of punch." The unease surrounding Parker's response to mid-
century Indian politics is prefigured in an earlier work, a futurist fiction titled
"The Meeting of the Oceans," published in 1835 in the *Bengal Annual.* In this story
of a twentieth-century deluge that followed the completion of a Panama Canal,
Parker betrayed a profound anxiety about cultural cataclysm.

Despite his imperial anxieties and later reactionary politics, Parker evidently was a man of many talents and was very popular in Calcutta literary circles. Both Kasiprasad Ghosh and H. L. V. Derozio dedicated verses to Parker, acknowledging his support of young Indian makers of verse.

Sources

Henry Meredith Parker, *The Draught of Immortality* (London: J. M. Richardson, 1827); *Bole Ponjis, Containing the Tale of the Buccanneer; A Bottle of Red Ink; The Decline and Fall of Ghosts; and Other Ingredients* (London and Calcutta: W. Thacker, 1851). See also Parker, *The Empire of the Middle Classes* (London: W. Thacker, 1858), and W. F. B. Laurie, *Sketches of Some Distinguished Anglo-Indians with an Account of Anglo-Indian Periodical Literature* (London: W. H. Allen, 1887).

from *"The Decline and Fall of Ghosts, with the History of Certain Apparitions which Afflicted the Author"*

I

Why should we sing of men and their misdeeds,
When mighty nature in her silent strength
Gives us more noble themes? First the heart bleeds
For human pain and misery: but at length
Grows callous as fresh woe to woe succeeds   5
I mean in our dark poems and romances,
(Heaven forbid 't should be so in real life,)
Where all the griefs the unhappy author fancies
Move one no more than parting with one's wife.

II

The time is past, too, when the mysteries   10
Of wild Udolpho made the cold flesh creep;[1]
Or sentimental bachelors, with knees
Of breeches half unbuttoned, lost their sleep

---

1. Udolpho: Ann Radcliffe's novel, *The Mysteries of Udolpho* (1794), a gothic tale of supernatural tension.

To snivel over Werter's[2] snivellings these
Were glorious days indeed; the author then,   15
Ambitious of lugubrious renown,
Had but in blood or tears to dip his pen
To terrify, to move, to win the town.

III

And are ye gone, for ever, blessed hours?
Alas for ever! is the sad reply,   20
Grub-street re-echoes it from all her bowers,
Romance-renowned Minerva[3] heaves a sigh,
(I mean the press, not goddess). Oh ye powers!
Who erst inspired sweet Matilda Dacres,[4]
And raised as many ghosts for Matthew Lewis[5]   25
As would have frightened forty undertakers,
And have ye gone from earth? Alas! how true is

IV

The observation of some learned Theban
That science is imagination's bane;
A truth which as true romance readers we ban,   30
But yet, ah us! the fact is very plain;
You might as well attempt to move Mount Leban
On as to persuade Sir Humphry Davy,
Or Mr. Brand, or Faraday, or Hatchet,[6]
That men e'er made the alkahest to save ye,   35
Or fix'd a shadow so that you might catch it.
* *

---

2. Werter: *The Sorrows of Young Werther* (1787), Johann Wolfgang von Goethe's novel, describes a tragic love affair.

3. Minerva Press was a publishing house known for publishing sentimental work.

4. Charlotte Dacre, who wrote under the pseudonym Rosa Matilda, wrote romance novels in the 1800s.

5. Matthew Lewis was a gothic novelist; his novel *The Monk* earned him the nickname Monk Lewis.

6. Davy, Brand, Faraday, and Hatchet: the British scientists Humphry Davy, William Thomas Brande, Michael Faraday, and Charles Hatchett.

XI

For who on earth, after a course of lectures
Attended at the Royal Institution,
Could tremble at a tale of moving pictures
Of goblins and of mysteries Rosicrucian;[7]   40
Why, miss of twelve years old would pass her strictures.
"Really, such trash is fit but for the nursery:"
In short we're spoilt for the mystic and the terrible.
Even our glorious Scott, the remark is cursory,
Could scarcely render his "White Lady" bearable.   45

XII

'Tis this alone has stopped what I intended,
The publication in nine volumes quarto,
Of a kind of "Vathek,"[8] rather more extended,
Filled with the eastern lore which I in part owe
To three weeks' residence at Budge, Budge, blended   50
With horror, witchcraft, mystery, love and murder;
And such descriptions! how on the bright river
Rich "bungalows" came sailing: who ere heard or
Told such things as I'd have told you—ever

XIII

Excepting Lady Morgan[9]—I'd prepared ye   55
An Orient tale with India for my stage;
Ghouls and Afreets had passed across and scared ye,
In any but this thrice incredulous age.
Mighty enchantments, too, I had not spared ye;
Peris had floated by on golden clouds,   60
Or glittered down to earth upon the ray
Of the red dog-star, robed in sparkling shrouds,
Woven from the moonlight dews of Himalay.
****

---

7. Rosicrucian: a secret society blending Christian ideas with Freemasonry and other orientalist-influenced notions.

8. Vathek: *Vathek, An Arabian Tale,* is a gothic novel written by William Thomas Beckford.

9. Lady Sydney Morgan's novel *The Missionary* was set in eighteenth-century India.

"But what's an eastern tale without a ghoul,
A little witchcraft, an afreet, and ghost: 65
A spirit in some cavern heard to growl,
A diamond palace, a magnetic coast?
All which would doubtless make the critics howl
In matter-of-fact and scientific days
Like these":—I thought, and in despair I threw   70
My beautiful MS. into the blaze,
So Science has to answer for that too.

Thus wrote I, my dear John Grant,[10] and thou didst usher my small lay into
the world in the spring-time of a friendship which will, I trust, flourish greenly
through all the seasons of life; defying the withering power of the tropical sun,
and if storms should arise, becoming like the Pine of Clan Alpine, rooted the
firmer, "the harder it blows."

As fellow-travellers in the realms of imagination, you and I may almost re-
gret that process which my rhymes attempted to describe. Yet even since the day
when those were conceived, our little domain of Faerie, surrounded on all
sides by the ocean of science, has become more and more circumscribed, till
like a tale written on the sands, each wave of the advancing tide threatens to
obliterate it for ever.

I know not whether we have reason to thank philosophy or not for the revo-
lution she has effected; of course there can exist but one opinion as to the in-
estimable benefit she has conferred on the human race, in rescuing mankind
from the cruelties of superstition; but could she not have been contented to
stop there? Alas! no; like an ambitious victor, she was satisfied with no con-
quest less than absolute; and having stormed the citadel, she now hurries to
plant her triumphant standard alike on the lonely moor, the blue misty moun-
tain, in the autumn grove, on the ruins of the old abbey, and by our winter
firesides. In short, philosophy makes endless war upon one of the most pre-
cious prerogatives of our imagination, because she sees in it a trace of that
power whose strength for evil she has broken: and without the slightest com-
passion for the innocent nature of our tacit resistance to her laws, she insists
that we shall relinquish this last remnant of the "wisdom of our ancestors," and
cease to believe in ghosts.

Truly it is hard to call upon us for the sacrifice of a sensation, when the en-
lightenment and politeness of the age have left us so few; and *that* the sensation
of ghostly apprehension, which has stood so deservedly high in the list of intel-

---

10. John Grant, a Scottish newspaper editor in Calcutta, was a patron of many aspiring writers.

lectual pleasing pains, as the assembly of ten thousand circles round the fires of
fifty years ago, while the winter storm raged without, for the mere purpose of
indulging in the dubious horrors of spectral narrations, sufficiently estab-
lished. Besides, to all persons of imagination, a belief in disembodied spirits
was an exquisite stimulus, stronger, cheaper, and more elegant than sal volatile
itself. Fancy the delight of your ruined Abbey, where you are forced, man and
horse, to take shelter from the tempest. Fancy your thunder-storm, the waving
boughs of the traditionary yew, the dull toll of a bell, so faint that the beating of
your own heart almost prevents it from being audible. Is it the distant village
clock sounding the hour of midnight through the storm? No! slow and solemn
it floats over the ancient graves like a warning of woe to come; it is the passing
knell borne by the rain-driving gusts up the long dark aisle of that solitary
ruin. At such moments what are the creature discomforts of the outward man?
The wet great coat; the nose so cold that your fingers are uncertain as to its
identity; the drenched hat, which performs the office of an aqueduct for the
conveyance of the chilly element down your shrinking back; nay, even the con-
trast between your actual state and that which you had proposed to yourself in
the snug, warm, and well-lighted parlour, with a brace of pheasants and a bottle
of old port before you—all, all are forgotten in the absorbing interest of your
situation. What deed of blood is to be disclosed? What injured nun, with one
finger on her pale lips and a lamp in her livid hand—but why should I pursue
so delightful a dream? Alas! if a man of *our* degenerate days were placed in the
awful situation I have endeavoured to conjure up to my mind's eye, his brutal
apprehensions would point to no other possibility than that of his getting a
cold and losing his supper; while he would infallibly attribute any visitations of
sight or sound, however unaccountable, either to the last cheerer he had taken
before starting, or to some derangements in the epigastric region. After all,
however, one could excuse men of science for their sins against the imagina-
tion; it is "their vocation, Hal": but we are reduced to despair when we see the
very high priests who minister at her altar, lift the veil which has so long con-
cealed the mysteries of her worship. We feel a mixture of grief and rage, such as
would indisputably fire the breasts of the rising generation, if the gentleman
who enacts Harlequin at Drury Lane were suddenly to step forward, and with a
low bow explain the process by which the dear children had been deluded into
an implicit belief that Mr. Grimaldi actually swallowed a hot poker forty feet
long, and subsequently created a vegetable man out of certain carrots, turnips,
and cabbages.

Sir Walter Scott,—that I should write it!—Sir Walter Scott hath done this
cruel deed. He hath lifted up the veil, he has exposed the pullies and the ropes;
and, in revenge I presume for the treatment which his White Lady received, has
waved his potent wand dispersing her and all her shadowy kindred "into thin
air" for ever.

The Indian Day

Dawn

Now come the delicate sighs of the soft gale,
First breath of dawn, the morn's sweet harbinger,
Which, as a herald, still precedes the pale,
Calm, silvery-mantled day-break.—There's a stir
Of life amongst the dewy opening flowers,   5
The hum of insects, and the ceaseless whirr
Of their light wings innumerous. Gem-like showers
Fall from the rustling leaves of waving trees,
While, in the west, the last star fades away,
Yet lingeringly, as lovers part at day   10
From 'neath their ladies' lattice. The cool breeze
Creeps on, as slumber steals o'er hearts at ease,
Fanning, with perfum'd wings and breathings light,
The sober footsteps of retiring night.

Sun Rise

Forth from the gorgeous east, as from an urn,   15
Spring mighty floods of rich and glorious light;
The heavens are bath'd in sun-shine, and are bright,
As if with smiles, and then all blushing burn
Like a bride's cheek, who hails her lord's return
From his first absence—who can marvel now   20
At that deep worship which the Ghebir[11] paid
To his resplendent god, from the hill-brow
Which new-born sun-beams clothed, whilst yet the shade
Of night lay pillow'd on the mists below?
Or who could view yon cloudy ocean, roll'd   25
In waves of ruby, amethyst, and gold,
Nor raise his heart to that First Cause, who bade
The fields of morning thus to be array'd.

---

11. Parker alludes to Walter Savage Landor's famous poem "Gebir," in which a prince of Spain
falls in love with his enemy the queen of Egypt.

Noon

Down from his blazing car the Lord of day
Hurls a fierce splendour through the sultry air,
Bright, fiery, piercing, as his arrows were
When, writhing at his feet, the Python lay.
The shadowless scene gleams dim through the white glare,
And the tam'd tiger gasps beneath the ray.
'Midst smoking marshes and hot reeds, the boar
Hides from the scorching blast, while the worn snake
Lies lank and torpid in the deepest brake.
The spirits of the southern whirlwind soar
Upon its burning breath, and hurry by
Each shatter'd cloud that o'er the dazzling sky
Casts a brief veil—so man, as frail, is driven
By passion's withering blast, from peace and heaven.

Evening

Thron'd amidst thunder-clouds, the dark toofaun[12]
Frowns grimly down upon the sinking sun,
With all his banners purple, black, and dun,
Unfurl'd for war.—The tribes of air have gone
Wheeling and screaming—flying from the gale
Like ocean mists;—A solitary sail
Shines through the gloom, and o'er the murky river,
Like hope's last light to hearts it leaves for ever.
Now bursts the storm in one terrific howl,
Wild as the din of hell. The lightnings pale
Glitter through rattling cataracts of hail.
The clouds rush down in floods, the heavens scowl,
Earth shakes, and all its groaning forests nod:
Kneel, man! and deprecate the wrath of God.

30
35
40
45
50
55

---

12. Typhoon. [HMP]

Night

The storm has past, and dewy silence rests
Upon the broad blue river, and the earth;
The scented air is cool, as tho' its birth
Had been 'midst Himalayah's frozen crests.   60
How calm, how silent—save where the plashing oar
Dips faint and far, rippling the lamp's pale beam
That shoots from mosque or temple on the shore,
Athwart the eddying Gunga's[13] holy stream.
And see! the rising moon: around her gleam,   65
The stars, bright satraps of her silver throne,
Lighting the hour when, sadly and alone
The exile muses.—What to him are these,
The East's resplendent skies and fragrant trees,
This clime of flowers and stars?—Alas! 'tis not his own.   70

---

13. The River Ganges. [HMP]

David Lester Richardson

DAVID LESTER RICHARDSON (1801–1865) was the single most influential teacher of British literature in nineteenth-century India. He was among the first to publish Indian poets writing in English, and his editorial activities did much to encourage literary English in Bengal. Born in London, Richardson appears not to have gone out to India until he was eighteen, and he returned to Britain on numerous occasions, eventually retiring to London, where he continued his Indian connections by editing the newspaper *Allen's Indian Mail*.

Like many other Anglo-Indians, Richardson experienced profound contradictions, even a disconnection, between his life and career in India and his role as a husband and father to a wife and children "at home" in Britain. On the one hand, he had an obvious enthusiasm for India, for educating Indian students, and for editing Indian belles lettres, yet on the other hand he possessed a highly conventional understanding of what an Anglo-Indian poet might write. The legacy of those contradictory inclinations is mixed; Richardson left us the fruits of his many significant publishing ventures, but he also left us many poems of futile longing for a rural England that perhaps never existed at all.

David Lester Richardson was born at the turn of the nineteenth century in London to Lieutenant Colonel David Thomas Richardson of the Bengal Army and Sara Lester Richardson. In 1819 he joined the family business, so to speak, enlisting as a cadet in the Bengal Native Infantry. The literary life, however, held more attraction for the young man than did the military, and only three years later he published his first volume of verse, *Miscellaneous Poems* (1822). While furloughed owing to illness in 1827–29, he returned to London and attempted to find a means of support outside of the military; against his father's advice that such ventures were likely to lose money, he founded and edited the *Weekly Review*. As his father predicted, Richardson was unable to make a living with this enterprise, and so he returned to military service in Bengal, where he became aide-de-camp to the governor-general, William Bentinck. In 1833, he retired as a major, having been invalided out. With his retirement nest egg and many connections in India, Richardson moved on to the next phase of his working life as an educator and editor.

From 1836 to 1843, Richardson served as a professor of English literature and later the principal of Hindu College. After quarrels over financial and governance matters with the Hindu College board, he served as the principal of Krishnagar College and of Hugli College near Calcutta, in all three of these institutions teaching young Bengali men. In his most important position, as the principal of the Hindu College, he exercised considerable influence on a generation of Bengali students, many of whom acknowledged his importance as a teacher of literature. Among others, Michael Madhusudan Dutt, who later became a leading Bangla poet, was strongly influenced by Richardson's teaching of Milton, Shakespeare, and the eighteenth-century British poets.

Richardson combined his career as an educator with much labor as an editor. As editor of the The Bengal Annual, The Orient Pearl, and the Calcutta Literary Gazette, he became the most important publisher of English belletristic writing in India. His anthology of English literature, first requested by Thomas Babington Macaulay for use in Indian English-medium schools, established a canon for northern India of English language verse written on the subcontinent. Unusually, Richardson included poems written by Indians and Anglo-Indians together in a section of Anglo-Indian verse. This collection of poetry in English, Selections from the British Poets, from Chaucer to the Poets of the Present Day (1840), became a standard text for schools and private reading, an important means for young Indian poets to learn about the British tradition. Of the periodicals he edited, the Literary Gazette established Richardson as an arbiter of literary taste. The Gazette was the most important northern Indian source for reviews of literature in English. Not surprisingly, a young poet such as Mary Carshore viewed Richardson as an authority worth both impressing and opposing when she argued that he and the Irish poet Tom Moore were mistaken in their romantic representations of young Indian women. Such women, she said, were unlikely to gad about at night in the way Moore described in his poem Lalla Rookh, and her cheeky dismissal of this and other evidence of ill-informed orientalism provoked Richardson's strictures in his review of her work. Carshore naturally took note of the opinions of the man whom they called "the Bulbul of India."

In addition to his editorial enterprises, Richardson published numerous volumes of poetry and criticism, including Sonnets and Miscellaneous Poems Written in India (1827), Literary Leaves (1836), Literary Chit-Chat, with Miscellaneous Poems (1848), and Literary Recreations (1852). An amateur botanist, he also brought out a delightful volume, Flowers and Flower Gardens (1855), which treated the techniques and tribulations of the Anglo-Indian garden.

Richardson's poetry had less impact than did his criticism or editorial work, but it incorporates many of the common tropes of expatriate verse in the period. In fact, his work could be viewed as a distillation of those tropes—which became the clichés—of expatriate writing. Seldom acknowledging the attractions of Indian scenes, friends, business, livelihood, or literature, these poems strike the same note again and again. They dismiss the complexities of expatriate life, as experienced by one who made his living from the imperial enterprise.

The poems included here owe much to Wordsworth, though they can in no way match Wordsworth's subtle use of the Italian sonnet form. Both "Sonnet—The Suttee" and "The Return from Exile" deploy tropes that by the time of their publication were highly conventionalized. The poet dismisses the sati as a "deluded victim"; equally conventionally, he imagines his own children shouting on the "sunny hills" in a bow to Wordsworth's "Intimations" ode. Nonetheless, Richardson's paternal longing gave rise to his most strongly felt and eloquently expressed sentiments. His children remained for him, in the phrase he borrowed from Milton, "phantoms of delight." One of his great sorrows was the death of one of his sons, who had come to India to enter military service. He laments in *Literary Recreations* the emotional toll on parents of separation from their children, declaring that "a state of exile is every way unnatural and breaks humanity's divinest links. The spirit of domestic happiness rarely wanders far from her native hearth." For Richardson, many years a resident in India, locating the domestic hearth was, in itself, a challenge. His poems reflect this divided and difficult effort.

Sources

David Lester Richardson, *Sonnets and Miscellaneous Poems Written in India* (London: Jones, 1827); Richardson, *Literary Leaves* (Calcutta: Samuel Smith, 1836; rev. ed. London, 1840); Richardson, *Literary Chit-Chat, with Miscellaneous Poems* (London: J. Madden, 1848); Richardson, *Literary Recreations; or, Essays, Criticisms and Poems: Chiefly Written in India* (London: W. Thacker, 1852).

Sonnet

On Hearing Captain James Glencairn Burns Sing (In India) His Father's Songs

How dream-like is the sound of native song
    Heard on a foreign shore! The wanderer's ear
    Drinks wild enchantment,—swiftly fade the drear
And cold realities that round him throng,
While in the sweet delirium, deep and strong,   5
    The past is present and the distant near!
    Such sound is sacred ever,—doubly dear
When heard by patriot exiles parted long
    From all that love hath hallowed. But a spell
Ev'n yet more holy breathes in every note   10
    Now trembling on my heart. *A proud Son sings*
    The lays of BURNS! Oh! what imaginings
Awake, as o'er a foreign region float
    These filial echoes of the father's shell!

           CALCUTTA, AUGUST 7, 1833

London, in the Morning

The morning wakes, and through the misty air[1]
In sickly radiance struggles—like the dream
Of sorrow-shrouded hope. O'er Thames' dull stream,
Whose sluggish waves a wealthy burden bear
From every port and clime, the pallid glare   5
Of early sunlight spreads. The long streets seem
Unpeopled now, but soon each path shall teem
With hurried feet and visages of care;
And eager throngs shall meet where dusky marts
Resound like ocean-caverns with the din   10
Of toil and strife and agony and sin.
Traders' busy Babel! Ah! how many hearts
By lust of gold to thy dim temples brought
In happier hours have scorned the prize they sought!

---

1. These sonnets descriptive of London and Calcutta are paired in Richardson's *Literary Leaves.*
The former rewrites William Wordsworth's "Composed upon Westminster Bridge."

View of Calcutta

Here Passion's restless eye and spirit rude
May get no kindred images of power
To fear or wonder ministrant.—No tower,
Time-struck and tenantless, here seems to brood,
In the dread majesty of solitude,   5
O'er human pride departed—no rocks lower
O'er ravenous billows—no vast hollow wood
Rings with the lion's thunder—no dark bower
The crouching tiger haunts—no gloomy cave
Glitters with savage eyes!—But all the scene   10
Is calm and cheerful. At the mild command
Of Britain's sons, the skilful and the brave,
Fair Palace-structures decorate the land
And proud ships float on Hooghly's breast serene![2]

Sonnet—The Suttee

Her last fond wishes breathed, a farewell smile
    Is lingering on the calm unclouded brow
    Of yon deluded victim. Firmly now
She mounts, with dauntless mien, the funeral pile
Where lies her earthly lord. The Brahmin's guile   5
    Hath wrought its will—fraternal hands bestow
    The quick death-flame—the crackling embers glow—
And flakes of hideous smoke the skies defile!
    The ruthless throng their ready aid supply,
And pour the kindling oil. The stunning sound   10
    Of dissonant drums—the priest's exulting cry—
The failing martyr's pleading voice have drowned;
While fiercely-burning rafters fall around,
    And shroud her frame from horror's straining eye!

2. The Hooghly provided access by boat to the interior of Bengal and in the nineteenth century
was still an active port. Here Richardson implicitly opposes a picture of imperial civilization to the
common image of India as home to natural and human savagery.

Consolations of Exile

Or an Exile's Address to His Distant Children

I.

O'er the vast realm of tempest-troubled Ocean—
    O'er the parched lands that vainly thirst for showers—
Through the long night—or when nor sound nor motion
    Stirs in the noon of day the sultry bowers—
Not all un'companied by pleasant dreams   5
    My weary spirit panteth on the way;
Still on mine inward sight the subtle gleams
    That mock the fleshly vision brightly play.
Oh! the heart's links nor time nor change may sever,
    Nor Fate's destructive hand, if life remain;   10
O'er hill, and vale, and plain, and sea, and river,
    The wanderer draws the inseparable chain![3]

II.

Fair children! still, like phantoms of delight,
    Ye haunt my soul on this strange distant shore,
As the same stars shine through the tropic night   15
    That charmed me at my own sweet cottage door.
Though I have left ye long, I love not less;
    Though ye are far away, I watch ye still;
Though I can ne'er embrace ye, I may bless,
    And e'en though absent, guard ye from each ill!   20
Still the full interchange of soul is ours,
    A silent converse o'er the waters wide,
And Fancy's spell can speed the lingering hours,
    And fill the space that yearning hearts divide.

---

3. And drags at each remove a lengthening chain—*Goldsmith.* [DLR]

III.

And not alone the written symbols show 25
    Your spirits' sacred stores of love and truth,
Art's glorious magic bids the canvas glow
    With all your grace and loveliness and youth;
The fairy forms that in my native land
    Oft filled my fond heart with a parent's pride, 30
Are gathered near me on this foreign strand,
    And smilingly, in these strange halls, reside!
And almost I forget an exile's doom,
    For while your filial eyes around me gleam,
Each scene and object breathes an air of home, 35
    And time and distance vanish like a dream!

IV.

Oh! when sweet Memory's radiant calm comes o'er
    The weary soul, as moonlight glimmerings fall
O'er the hushed ocean, forms beloved of yore
    And joys long fled, her whispers soft recall; 40
At such an hour I live and smile again,
    As light of heart as in that golden time
When, as a child, I trod the vernal plain,
    Nor knew the shadow of a care or crime.
Nor dream of death, nor weariness of life, 45
    Nor freezing apathy, nor fierce desire,
Then chilled a thought with unborn rapture rife,
    Or seared my breast with wild ambition's fire.

V.

From many a fruit and flower the hand of Time
    Hath brushed the bloom and beauty; yet mine eye, 50
Though Life's sweet summer waneth, and my prime
    Of health and hope is past, can oft espy
Amid the fading wilderness around
    Such lingering hues as Eden's holy bowers
In earth's first radiance wore, and only found 55
    Where not a cloud of sullen sadness lours.
Oh! how the pride and glory of this world
    May pass unmirrored o'er the darkened mind,
Like gilded banners o'er the grave unfurled,
    Or Beauty's witcheries flashed upon the blind. 60

VI.

Though this frail form hath felt the shafts of pain,
    Though my soul sickens for her native sky,
In visionary hours my thoughts regain
    Their early freshness, and soon check the sigh
That sometimes from mine inmost heart would swell   65
    And mar a happier mood. Oh! then how sweet,
Dear Boys! upon remembered bliss to dwell,
    And here your pictured lineaments to greet!
Till Fancy, bright Enchantress, shifts the scene
    To British ground, and musical as rills,   70
Ye laugh and loiter in the meadows green,
    Or climb with joyous shouts the sunny hills!
         CALCUTTA, SEPTEMBER 4, 1834

The Return from Exile

I.

As memory pictured happier hours, homesickness seized my heart,
I never thought of English land but burning tears would start;
The faces of familiar friends would haunt me in my sleep,
I clasped their thrilling hands in mine—then woke again to weep!

II.

At last my spirit's fevered dreams so wrought upon my frame,   5
That life itself uncertain seemed as some worn taper's flame,
'Till o'er the wide blue waters borne, from regions strange and far,
I saw dear Albion's bright cliffs gleam beneath the morning star!

III.

That radiant sight redeemed the past, and stirred with transport wild,
I paced the swift bark's bounding deck, light-hearted as a child;   10
And when among my native fields I wandered in the sun,
I felt as if my morn of life had only just begun.

IV.

The shining golden butter-cup—the daisy's silver crest—
The living gems of every hue on Nature's verdant breast—
The cheerful songs of British birds, that rose from British trees—   15
The fragrance from the blossomed hedge, that came on every breeze—[4]

V.

The white cot peeping from the grove, its blue smoke in the sky—
The rural group of ruddy boys, that gaily loitered nigh—
The silent sheep-besprinkled hill—the rivulet-watered vale—
The lonely lake, where brightly shone the fisher's sun-lit sail;—   20

VI.

Awhile these seemed illusions brief of beauty and delight,
A dear but transitory dream—a mockery of the night!
For often in my slumbering hours on India's sultry strand,
In visions, scarce less palpable, I hailed my native land.

VII.

But when upon my wildering doubts reflection flashed the truth,   25
Oh! Never in my childhood years, nor in my fervid youth,
So deep a rapture thrilled my breast as while I gazed around
And recognized the thousand charms that hallow English ground!

---

4. Richardson shifted this stanza from nostalgia for England to nostalgia for Britain; the last
two lines of the previous edition read, "Of English birds the cheerful songs that rose from English
trees— / From blossomed hedge, the fragrance fresh that came of every breeze—" [1840].

Honoria Marshall Lawrence

≈) ⌒

THE POEMS of Honoria Marshall Lawrence (1808–1854) provide an intimate look at the domestic life of an Anglo-Indian woman during the first half of the nineteenth century. Although she and her husband, Henry Montgomery Lawrence, published articles in the *Calcutta Review* and in Indian newspapers and jointly composed a novel with extensive verse epigraphs, Honoria devoted much of her literary labor to journals, letters, and privately circulated poetry.

Both Honoria Marshall and her husband came from Irish families, she being the twelfth of the fifteen children born to the Reverend George Marshall and his wife, Elizabeth. As a young woman, Honoria worked as a governess and gradually came to be a devout evangelical Anglican. She met her cousin and future husband while visiting relatives in London, where the two evidently spent a glorious and somewhat unconventional two weeks seeing the sights and talking incessantly. But Henry was to return to India shortly, and though he was already a commissioned officer, his income was not sufficient to support a wife and family in the way he wished. As Honoria Lawrence's journal makes clear, they corresponded from time to time over the next ten years until finally, after hearing—inaccurately—that Honoria had become engaged, Henry proposed first by proxy and then by letter.

With some trepidation (could love at first sight survive a ten-year separation?) Honoria embarked for Calcutta, trusting that her early first impression would be confirmed. Her experience was typical for women joining husbands or prospective husbands in India. On arriving in Calcutta, she found that Henry—who had been recently promoted to captain—had been delayed and was not on hand to meet her; when he appeared some days later, they were married with all possible speed, and he was immediately called back into service. Among the poems below is one reflecting their occupations in the first months of marriage, for Henry Lawrence had been seconded from the Army of Bengal to the revenue service as a surveyor. Honoria accompanied him, then, as throughout their marriage, acting as companion and coadjutor. He taught her to survey, and she conducted much of their varied correspondence. In his civil postings, Honoria assisted him in his work, always behind the scenes, and she took a significant role in their charitable endeavors, particularly in establishing the first Lawrence Military Asylum for children and orphans of British soldiers.

A glimpse of Honoria Lawrence's first years in India is provided by Henry Lawrence's assistant, Saunders Abbott, who met the newlyweds in the Himalayan foothills. In the dense jungle, Abbott recorded, "Tigers and wild elephants gave unmistakable signs of their presence. And, to my utter surprise, I found Mrs. Lawrence. . . . She was seated on the bank of a nullah, her feet overhanging the den of some wild animal, a portfolio on her lap, writing overland letters; her husband, at no great distance, laying his theodolite. In such roughings this admirable wife was delighted to share; and at other times she would lighten his labour by reading books he wished to consult, or making notes and extracts for his literary work. She was one in a thousand" (quoted in Raza, 126).

Honoria Lawrence soon found herself pregnant. In the sixteen years of her marriage, she had four children and survived one miscarriage. Her journal from the later years of her marriage records her trepidation at discovering she was pregnant in her mid-forties, for the doctors had warned her that it might prove dangerous, given her age and state of health; indeed, her death at age forty-six seems to have been from complications of pregnancy. Honoria and Henry Lawrence had two sons and two daughters. The poem below records their grief at the death in infancy of their first daughter. Lawrence's journals and her papers in the British Library record her constant concern for her sons, who were sent home to Britain for schooling, and for her brother, whose death is commemorated in the poem reproduced here.

After volunteering for duty in the first Anglo-Afghan War (where his combat duty was not in the end required), Henry Lawrence was appointed assistant to the governor general's agent for the Punjab and Northwest Frontier; he became the civil administrator of Ferozepore (now on the border with Pakistan), accompanied by his wife, and then served at Peshawar, afterward commanding Sikh forces in the Afghan campaign of 1842. In 1843, he was appointed British resident at the court of Nepal, and Honoria accompanied him there for nearly two years. She was one of the first European women ever to reside in Nepal, and she reported in her journals her happiness at being able to have a stable family life, her delight in Nepal, and her joint role in various literary activities undertaken with Henry.

Honoria returned to Britain in late 1845, while Henry served in the first Anglo-Sikh War, after which he was appointed resident at Lahore, with virtually unlimited authority over administration. Though he joined Honoria for some months on sick leave in Britain, Henry and Honoria soon returned to the Punjab, where during the last years of Honoria's life Henry found himself in bitter disagreement with his brother, John Lawrence (later viceroy of India), over the joint administration of the Punjab. After resigning in protest over the terms of land settlement in the Punjab, Henry took up an alternate post as the governor-general's agent in Rajputana. There Honoria died, at Mount Abu, in 1854. It was perhaps a blessing that she did not live to join her husband in his later posting in Oudh (Avadh); for, after months attempting to redress local grievances caused by the British annexation, Henry died in the siege of Lucknow during the uprising of 1857. Their elder son was afterward made a baronet, in recognition of his father's service. A biography and edited edition of Honoria Lawrence's journals (excluding her poetry) were published more than a century after her death.

Sources

Manuscript poems in the Lawrence collection, MS. Eur. F 85, Asian and African Studies Collection, British Library, printed by permission. "A Day in the District" appears in *Real Life in India* (London: Houlston and Stoneman, 1847). "The Soldier's Bride" appears in Herbert Benjamin Edwardes, *Life of Sir Henry Lawrence* (London: Smith, Elder, 1873). For Honoria Lawrence's letters and journals, see Maud Diver, *Honoria Lawrence: A Fragment of Indian History* (Boston: Houghton Mifflin, 1936); and John Lawrence and Audrey Woodiwiss, eds., *The Journals of Honoria Lawrence: India Observed, 1837–1854* (London: Hodder and Stoughton, 1980). See also Rosemary Raza, *In Their Own Words: British Women Writers and India, 1740–1857* (New Delhi: Oxford University Press, 2006).

August 21, 1841

KASAOLI

We gathered many a fragrant flower,[1]
To deck our pleasant bridal bower,
And life and joy their sunshine shed,
When first my love and I were wed.

Time passed—the bridal flowers might fade,   5
Sickness and care our brows might shade,
But then, the olive-branches sprung
To bid our hearts feel fresh and young,
And banish, with their joyous bloom,
Each passing breath of fear and gloom.   10

The thunderbolt of judgment flew—
And, where our tender nursling grew,
What rests to us, my husband, now?
—A narrow grave—a cypress bough!

---

1. Kasaoli (now Kasauli): a town in Himachal Pradesh, northern India.

Hush, hush, my heart, such deep complaint!   15
Forbid oh Lord! my soul to faint!
—Befits me more a thankful lay
To Him who gave and took away,
Withdrew our darling from our eye,
To shrine her with himself on high,   20
And gives us, while we watch her dust,
The humble faith, whose steadfast trust,
Can change the cypress bough of death
Into an amaranthine wreath![2]

And thou of one sweet bud bereft,   25
Yet ye, our first-born hope, is left;
And, had our sky been cloudless blue,
Could we have loved, as now we do?
The storms have made us cling for rest,
More closely to each other's breast.[3]   30

Jugduluk 8th January 1842

Where Kabul's hostile heights arise,[4]
And snow descends from Kabul's skies,
My brother's bloody bed was made,
My brother's tombless bones are laid.

---

2. Amaranthine wreath: a wreath made of fadeless flowers. Lawrence may allude here to Milton's "Lycidas" or Book II of *Paradise Lost* or, more probably, to John Keble's *Christian Year*, where, in poems for the feast of St. Michael and All Angels and the feast of St. Barnabas, the poet imagines saints and angels crowned with amaranth. Keble's poem for St. Barnabas's day aptly begins, "The world's a room of sickness where each heart / Knows its own anguish and unrest."

3. This poem appears on a recto page in one of Honoria Lawrence's manuscript notebooks (BL, MS. Eur. F 85, no. 88, 5) containing poems written between 1840 and 1843. On the verso page, Lawrence recorded the inscription on the tomb of her infant daughter, nicknamed "Mooniah": "Here rests the dust of Letitia Catherine / Daughter of / Henry Montgomery and Honoria Lawrence / She was born, the 10th of November, 1840 / And fell asleep, the 1st August 1841. / 'It is not the will of our Father in heaven, that one of these little ones should perish.'"

4. This poem commemorates the death of Lawrence's brother who was sent to India entrusted to her care shortly after she arrived. She and Henry finally procured for him a military place, but he was killed at the end of the first Afghan campaign (1839–1842), on the disastrous winter retreat from Kabul. The retreat commenced on January 8, 1842; those forces and camp followers who survived the slaughter reached the pass at Jugduluk on January 11, but only one British soldier made it finally to safety. The notebooks record two versions of this poem; the one given here is the second, and it appears to be a later revision.

Amid that whitening ghastly heap,   5
'Twere vain to seek thy place of sleep.
No—cold and heat their work have done
On thee—thou loved and slaughtered one.

Dark was the day—the day of death,
Where, before winter's icy breath,   10
Thy swarthy comrades sank around,
Blackening the snow-enveloped ground.

But thou was formed of nobler earth
The warrior's country gave thee birth;
And when the snow thy life blood drank   15
It was a British heart that sank.[5]

My Brother, could I there have stood,
Have striven to staunch thy gushing blood,
Been there to catch thy parting breath,
Then might I calmly tell thy death.   20

Could I within his ear have poured,
Conqueror of death! Thy living word,
Then might I dry my tears, and sing,
Where now, O Death, thy vanquished sting?[6]

Oh weak of faith—why thus afraid?   25
Needs the Most High thy puny aid?
Who made the spirit, cannot He
Speak to that spirit secretly?

Shewing the land where troubles cease,
Breathing around the breath of peace—   30
"Come home, my wandering, pardoned son,
Depart in peace, thou ransomed one."[7]

---

5. Lawrence made a major change in this stanza. An earlier version read, "It was an Irish heart that sank."

6. "O death, where is thy sting? O grave, where is thy victory?" I Corinthians 15:55.

7. "Lord, now lettest thou thy servant depart in peace, according to thy word." Luke 2:29. The last stanza alludes as well to the parable of the prodigal son.

The Soldier's Bride

Sutlej, November, 1842

"And wilt thou be a soldier's bride,
　　Girl of the sunny brow?
Then sit thee down and count thy cost,
　　Before thou take the vow!⁸

"Think—canst thou love with all thy soul,　　　　　5
　　Being thus loved again?
Enjoy no happiness apart?
　　Together smile at pain?

"Then, canst thou all this bliss forgo,
　　And bid thy heart not burst?　　　　　10
See all thy streams of pleasure dried
　　And bear the spirit's thirst?

"Wilt thou a lonely pillow press,
　　Wet with thy nightly tears?
Or start from dreams of agony　　　　　15
　　To sadder waking fears?

"And when thy child up towards thee lifts
　　His glad, unclouded brow,
Will not his question choke thy breath?
　　'Where is my Father now'?　　　　　20

"And thou, the weary day to watch
　　For tidings from afar;
While every breath of rumour breathes
　　Captivity and War!

"Daily to feel the sting of Death.　　　　　25
　　Canst thou thy heart inure?
And then—to be alone on earth—
　　Ah this canst thou endure?"

---

8. Sutlej: the easternmost branch of the Indus River. This ballad is dated from the poet's residence in the Punjab at Ferozepore.

Her lightsome eye was dimmed with tears,
 Her lip of roses quivered;   30
And oh her warm, elastic form
 With transient terror shivered.

'Twas but a moment—then her eye
 Shone with a luster pure.
"Yes—I *will* be a soldier's bride!—   35
 And in Love's strength endure.

"Distance divides not wedded hearts,
 Thought's pinion doth not tire,—
Nor can the waterflood of grief
 Quench Love's eternal fire!   40

"It is not for a sunny hour
 I plight my troth to his;
It is not on Earth's shifting sand
 We build our bower of bliss!

"We wed not, as prepared to find,   45
 The cloudless climes of fiction;
But look for storms and clouds to bring
 Our Father's benediction.

"I would not for all present joy
 My absent one resign—   50
No—rather let me wake and weep
 And feel that he is mine!

"The hour will come for us to meet,
 Souls in God's presence delighted,
On Earth—in Heaven—as He sees best,   55
 They shall be re-united.

"And seekst thou then by thoughts to cool,
 From hope like *this* to scare me?
No—gladly will I choose my path,
 And for the storm prepare me!"   60

God prosper thee, thou noble girl,
  And be thy guard and guide!
—But let no fainter heart resolve
To be a soldier's bride!

from "A Day in the District"

Part II. Day

Oh, pleasant, pleasant, are the hours[9]
We pass within these forest bowers!
And pleasant is the mango shade,
Wherein our bustling camp is laid,
And pleasant is it, as we sit,   5
T'indulge this idly rhyming fit,
And tell the dear ones far away,
How glides along the Indian day!

Come with me to our forest home!
  With many a charm 'tis gilt,   10
Nor change we howsoe'er we roam,
  The home within us built.
Are not all places where we rove
  Brightened alike by mutual love?
Is not maternal nature there,   15
Greeting us with her aspect fair?
In every spot, can we not lift
  The frank petitions, blending
With thanks for "every perfect gift"
  The Source of Good is lending.   20

---

9. Lawrence's notebook clearly indicates this poem to be a verse letter, describing for friends
and relatives in Britain her experiences in India. Immediately preceding this poem she wrote, "By
way of variety, you shall have a chapter of stanzas 'warranted genuine,' that is, the objects therein
described are those we really see." The poem has three parts; the first, omitted here, describes an
early morning march through the jungle by elephant and then on horseback. Part II was titled "A
Day in Camp" and the next section "Evening in the Village" when published in *Real Life in India*. The
published text has been corrected against the BL manuscript.

While yet the mid-day sun is high
Within the tent our tasks we ply,
The crowded table, thickly strewed
    With papers, maps and pens,
Bespeaks the Surveyor's abode,   25
    That busiest of men!
'Tis there the white-robed village chief
Obsequious comes, to tell his grief;
The Moslem Moonshee, seated low,
With busy look and gathered brow,   30
Full of th'important part he bears,
The Persian document prepares.
But, when the glowing noon is o'er,
    A pleasant seat is ours,
While near the mango-shaded door   35
    We pass the varied hours.
Sit by me here, look all around,
And say, if 'tis not fairy ground?
The vista's long and lofty shade
Opens upon the sunny glade,   40
Showing the fields of "living green,"
And shadowy thickets tangled screen.
In scarlet vest, the gay surcar[10]
Comes swiftly riding from afar,
And, as from a milk white stud he springs   45
With low salaam his message brings.
And look, where comes a loaded train
Of cattle bearing precious grain,
Sober their faces, their color dun,
They seem no children of the sun!   50
Not so their drivers, men who wear
The aspect of the mountaineer.
With jocund laugh and ready tongues,
The tasseled horn beside them slung,
Prepared alike for war or trade,   55
With matchlock, spear, and shield arrayed.
But hark! a song of rising cheer,
And bells, and drums, and horns I hear;
Yet, from amid this joyous shew,
There bursts a sound of female woe,   60

---

10. Sircar: head of affairs or accounts in government or in domestic households.

In palanquin of scarlet dye,
Close veiled from every curious eye,
The wailing bride they homeward bear—
And will she meet with comfort there?
Alas! not here does woman know   65
Domestic love's unclouded glow.
The husband is not here the friend,
Who loves, and loves her to the end,
And without this, life's fragrant lamp!
How dull were even the cheerful camp!   70

Part III. Evening

Quickly the evening sun descends,
And now a tempered radiance lends,
Forth let us hie, for evening's light
Unveils to us a glorious sight.
"The everlasting hills" are there,   75
The Himalaya's heights laid bare,
Creation's diadem! how bright
Their snowy crests and roseate light!
Like those fair hills the pilgrims viewed
        By Faith's far-piercing eye;   80
Serene in lofty solitude
        The untrodden summits lie.

Now sit we by the glassy tank
Upon its green and sloping bank,
And watch the herd of cattle grey   85
Sweep by us in their long array.
See India's dark, but graceful daughters
        With well-poised pitchers come,
Place on their heads the load of water,
        Then bear it lightly home.   90
Look at that lightning-stricken tree
        With branches white and bare,
The vulture's watch tower, there sits he
        And scents the jackal's lair.
Then, spreading wide his dusky wings,   95
From the sere bough he screaming springs.
        Now, as Night opes her starry eyes,
Come forth the thousands glittering flies,

Like floating stars around us play,
And sparkles o'er the bamboo's spray.   100
But, as our steps we homeward turn
We see the evening camp-fire burn,
And, from the lamp-illumined tent,
A long, low line of light is sent.
The red blaze shines on many a group   105
As round their fires they eager stoop;
On each bronzed form and glittering eye
The lights and shadows strongly lie,
Each party busy to prepare,
Day's labours o'er, their evening fare.   110
  And now the varied day is spent,
Return we to our cheerful tent;
There will we talk of bye-gone times,
Send back our thoughts to western climes
And dream that distant home is near,   115
And wish the absent loved ones here;
And then, in fond and thankful prayer
Commend them to our Father's care.[11]

---

11. To these lines Lawrence appended a note: "Take these lines as what they are, an attempt to describe what I have seen, and the overflowing of a happy heart."

Kasiprasad Ghosh

~⁀ ⁀

ORN IN Kidderpore, near Calcutta, Kasiprasad Ghosh (1809–1873) grew up in a high-caste Bengali family, members of which had for generations held government appointments, first under the Mughals and then under the British. He was a much-longed-for child. Following the death of their first son, his parents had undertaken a pilgrimage to Benares, seeking to ensure through religious rituals the birth of a son and heir. Some months later, Kasiprasad was born. As a sickly child and the eldest son, he was treated indulgently, but when he turned fourteen his father "reprimanded" him for being a poor scholar. As Kasiprasad admitted in an autobiographical essay written some years later, he "could scarcely read either English or Bengallee" (*Calcutta Literary Gazette*, November 1, 1834, 279). Though a bright boy, he had not profited from his father's instruction in English.

The young Kasiprasad's ignorance became a matter of general family consternation, and finally his grandfather intervened to suggest that the boy be sent to the Hindu College, which was then under the supervision of Horace Hayman Wilson (whose poems also appear in this volume). Either his ignorance was not so deep as his father feared, or he was a quick study. Admitted to the college in 1821, Kasiprasad soon rose to be head boy in the first class. With Wilson's encouragement, in 1827 Kasiprasad and the other students tried their hands at English poetry, and Kasiprasad clearly demonstrated poetic as well as intellectual talent. Although he later destroyed most of his juvenilia, he began very early to publish in the local newspapers, as was common at the time for British poets resident in India. At the age of twenty-one, he published a book of English language verse, *The Sháïr, and Other Poems*.

Kasiprasad's account of his life reveals a young man of considerable linguistic talents. Though a devout Hindu, he read and criticized the Bangla translation of the Gospel of Matthew then being published by missionaries at Serampore, and at their request he undertook to criticize and correct the translations of succeeding biblical texts. At the same time, he acquired what he called a "tolerable" knowledge of Persian, devanagari (written Hindi or Hindustani), and Sanskrit. The last accomplishment led, at least indirectly, to the texts anthologized here, which seek to create in English poetic forms a series of poems celebrating the major religious festivals of the Hindu year.

About his personal life, Kasiprasad commented in the same autobiographical reflection,

> I was first married at the age of seventeen, in 1825, and had a son in 1828. My
> wife dying in that year, I married again. . . . My father paid the debt of nature
> in 1831, and my second wife departed this life after she had been delivered of
> a girl, who died on the same day that she was born. . . . I have been again mar-
> ried, and God alone knows what length of life my third wife may enjoy. . . . On
> the death of my father, who left behind him six sons and four daughters, I was
> involved in a law-suit in the Supreme Court with my half brothers. . . . As . . .
> all my half brothers were then under age[,] I was . . . obliged to go to Court,
> where . . . we had to pay no less than 25,000 rupees as costs for this amicable
> settlement! (*Calcutta Literary Gazette,* 279)

This passage is, in many ways, an earnest of the man, for as an adult and head of
his family, Kasiprasad was at once a traditionalist, an admirer of English verse,
and a critic of the shortcomings—or worse—of the British administration.

Though he delighted in English language verse—and admitted that he pre-
ferred writing in English to writing Bangla verse—Kasiprasad was by no means
infatuated with things English. His first publicly presented essay critiqued the
first four chapters of James Mill's *History of British India.* Horace Hayman Wilson
found this essay particularly fine, and it was soon printed in the *Government Gazette*
and the *Asiatic Journal.* After leaving the Hindu College, Kasiprasad continued his
work as an essayist, historian, and journalist. He published essays on Bangla
literature and a history of the Marathas, and he went on to publish and edit a
weekly newspaper, the *Hindu Intelligencer,* fostering the careers of many aspiring
Bangla journalists. This effort he left off in 1857, following Lord Canning's
"gagging act," which severely restricted the native press.

One can glimpse Kasiprasad's mixture of broad-mindedness and conserva-
tism in his early volume, which is at once innovative—in adopting, adapting, and
mimicking English verse forms while treating Indian religious subjects—and
conservative. In later years, Kasiprasad became a supporter of the Dharma Sabha,
an organization devoted to promoting traditional Hindu values. He opposed fe-
male education and widow remarriage and objected to British and Bengali re-
formers' attempts to restrict child marriage and polygamy. At the same time, as
his remarks on "justice" indicate, he was willing to criticize what he saw as the
injustices of British rule.

Kasiprasad prefaced his only volume of English verse by claiming, accurately,
that he was the first "Hindu who has ventured a volume of English Poems." He
went on in his brief preface to explain that his motive for writing the "Hindu
Festivals" arose from a conversation with a friend in which his friend suggested
"the importance and utility of writing something by way of national poetry." The
poet argues that "having then no other Indian subject at hand which he could
make a choice of, but the Hindu Festivals; an account of which he had promised

to write for the *Calcutta Literary Gazette;* he versified them into small pieces of poetry, which were published in that journal." Though Kasiprasad sounds casual in his choice of subjects, clearly the Hindu festivals actually further his project of writing "something by way of national poetry." Here, as in many other nationalist and protonationalist instances, the nation is implicitly configured as Hindu; moreover, the poems in this sequence suggest a kind of cultural mimicry and—equally—a cultural reversal. It is not, for Kasiprasad, that Krishna is the Indian Jesus but rather that Jesus is the European Krishna. Moreover, Kasiprasad essayed a tour de force in English metrics, conquering various difficult forms, including the Spenserian stanza. This poetic sequence contained eleven sections, each celebrating a particular event in the religious calendar; three of these sections, each in a different verse form, are included here.

The nationalist, or protonationalist, implications of Kasiprasad's poetry went almost unremarked in his lifetime. Rather, as a young man he was taken up as an example of the Hindu poetic spirit. An engraving of his portrait was circulated through any number of British publications, from adult annuals to the *Juvenile Scrap-book,* and he was, at least in his twenties, viewed from Britain and in Anglo literary circles in India as a poetical figure.

Sources

Kasiprasad Ghosh, *The Shāïr, and Other Poems* (Calcutta: Scott, 1830). See also John Roselli, *Lord William Bentinck: Making of a Liberal Imperialist* (London: Chatto and Windus for Sussex University Press, 1974).

from "Hindu Festivals"

II. Rás Yátrá

Or a festival in commemoration of one of the many gambols of Krishna,
the Indian Apollo, with the milk-women.

I.

Young, beauteous maids are lightly dancing,
Their eyes like little carps are glancing,
Like puny lightnings those glances flash;
Like echoes through lone valleys ringing,
Of dulcet voices sweetly singing,   5
As onward they move their trinkets clash.

II.

Hark! they strike their music sweet,
Hark! they raise their voices meet,
Soft and mellow like the note
From the distant Koil's throat,[1]   10
When the morning's blooming ray
Is not lingering far away.

III.

They're crowned with fragrant wreaths of flowers,
Culled from the Jumna's greenest bowers,[2]
Where constant joy and rosy hours,   15
On pinions fleet fly smilingly;
And there the three bright nights beguiling
With fairy damsels sweetly smiling,
His time is youthful Krishna whiling,
In purple pleasure's ectasy.   20

---

1. Koil (also koël, kokilā, or koklā): an Indian bird of the cuckoo family, often poetically iden-
tified with the European nightingale.

2. The Jumna, or Yamuna, River is, like the Ganges, considered sacred. It flows through the
Mathura district of Uttar Pradesh, traditionally understood as the birthplace of Krishna and the
site of his gambols with the *gopīs*, or milkmaids.

IV.

Behold young Krishna's azure hue
Is like the spring-cloud's lovely blue,
With sparkling eyes like diamonds proud.
And there is Rádha by his side,
In budding youth and beauty's pride,   25
Like lightning clinging to a cloud.

V.

Like the bow that Káma[3] strings,
Are her lips of ruby light;
Whence the smiles that round she flings,
Like his darts of swiftest flight,   30
Pierce the youthful bosom deep,
Not, as feigned, with poison's pain,
But a softness, by which sleep
Griefs and cares—mischance's train.

VI.

The bright enchantress of the night   35
Is o'er them pouring fleecy light;
The stars but faintly burn above,
Like woman's languid eyes through love;
And the breeze that is breathing so gentle and gay,
Tells whence he has stolen the fragrance away.   40

DECEMBER 13, 1829

---

3. Káma: god of eros. Like Cupid, Káma is often depicted with a bow and arrow.

IV. Janmáshtami

Or Janma Yátrá, a festival in commemoration of the birth of Krishna.

I.

Lo! where the flaming east of brightening morn,
Proclaims the coming of the Lord of Day,
The various streaks that all the skies adorn.
Like angels shooting through the heavenly way,
To every clime the joyous news convey,   5
And nature fair who wept in dew-drops, wears,
Decked with a verdant smile, an aspect gay,
As beauty's visage being washed with tears,
More lovely, fair and beautifully bright appears.

II.

The woodland tribes salute the rising sun,   10
Or rove delightful or attune their song,
To fling his notes the Koil hath begun,
And others join him in the grove along
The sacred river, while the flowers among,
His lay so merrily bulbul sings,   15
As if the moments which to heaven belong,
Were given to him alone. The soft gale flings
The sighs of flowers and bears their odours on its wings.

III.

But hark! what noise invades the peaceful ear?
What shouts and joyful acclamations rise?   20
Why sounds of cymbals, drums, and pipes appear
As if to rend the vault of yonder skies?
Why should the people with astonished eyes
Crowd to the place where Nanda doth reside?[4]

---

4. Nanda: foster father of Krishna. Krishna was born to Devaki (the princess of Mathura) and
her husband, Vasudeva. Vasudeva feared Devaki's brother, the usurping king of Mathura, who had
threatened or killed all of his previous children. Vasudeva secretly took Krishna to Vrindavan to be
raised by the cowherd Nanda and his wife Yasoda. The poem commemorates this event, along with
Krishna's birth and his youthful dalliances with the *gopis*, or milkmaids.

Why many a learned, holy sage there hies
    Whose wealth is prayer and virtue is whose guide?
'Tis Krishna born to crush the demons and their pride.

IV.

Behold the power supreme revealed on earth,
    In mortal dress! His infant head is crowned
With beams of glory, and his promised birth   30
    With gladness fills the whole creation round.
The demons proud whose impious souls are bound,
    With ignorance's and delusion's chain,
Shrink at the holy conch-shell's herald sound,
    As if afflicted with a mortal pain,   35
And see with hopeless eyes their all endeavours vain.

V.

Look, look how beautiful! The new-born boy
    Reclines upon its mother's cautious arm,
Like young Hope resting in the breast of Joy,
    Around whom wantons every infant charm,   40
Which makes with future hope all bosoms warm
    Of thronging men and many a saintly sage,
Who gaze delighted on young Krishna's form,
    For now the long oppressive, baneful age
Will be no more ere long, and fiends will cease to rage.   45

VI.

Now soon the wicked king of demons foul,
    Will feel the dread result of all his hate;
And soon beneath the god's divine controul,
    Bow justly to his predetermined fate:
His power and impious glory, which so late   50
    Have spread sad terrors o'er the trembling land,
Even like a meteor from its blazing state,
    Will fall to nothing by th' almighty hand
Of Vishnu great and Bhagavati's high command.[5]
DECEMBER 19, 1829

---

5. Krishna is an avatar of Vishnu; the reference to Bhagavati here indicates Vishnu's consort
Lakshmi.

X. Káli Pujá

Or Syámá Pujá, a festival in honour of Káli or Syámá,
an emanation from the head of Durgá and the goddess of war.

I.

Most terrible Power![6] surrounding thee dance
    The direful disasters of war;
Like lightning terrific thy ominous glance
    Doth pierce through the heart from afar.

II.

Thy deeply black hue is like that of a cloud,   5
    Hanging dark in a sky overcast;
Thy breath is like that of the storm-god when proud,
    He rides on the hurricane-blast.

III.

Most terrible Power! like the bursting of thunder,
    Thy shoutings in battle are drear;   10
Which even the bravest of hearts ever sunder,
    With a blight of their hope and with fear.

IV.

A necklace of every great warrior's head
    By thee severed, thy person doth deck;
Which grinning with horrible life and with dread,   15
    And clashing, depends from thy neck.

V.

Dread honours on thee, awful goddess! await,
    While havoc, and slaughter, and fear,
In smiles that are ghastly—with pitiless fate,
    All wildly exult in thy rear.   20

---

6. The Kálī puja in Calcutta occurs nineteen days after the most important religious festival of
the year in Bengal, the Durga puja.

VI.

Most terrible Power! in the midst of thy brow,
    How blazingly burneth thine eye!
Like a red, fiery meteor, which direful doth glow
    At night in a cloud-darkened sky.

VII.

The flash of thy sword and the gleam of thy spear,   25
    When they sink in the enemy's heart,
Illumine the plain with a brilliancy drear,
    At which strength and all valour depart.

VIII.

With hideous attendants of many a form,
    When fiercely thou rushest to war;   30
Thou seem'st like a gloomy and fast-coming storm,
    Or the night in her dark-spreading car.

IX.

O! thou are all darkness, delusion and dread,
    Great Káli! most terrible Power!
Thou hast sprung from the beautiful Párvati's head[7]   35
    When wrath on her forehead did lower.

AUGUST 1, 1830

---

7. Kali is often identified, as she is here, as an emanation of Durga. Durga, in turn, is seen as a form of Párvatī.

The Vīnā

Or the Indian Lute

Lute of my country![8] why dost thou remain
Unstrung, neglected, desolate, and bound
With envious Time's and Ignorance's chain?
Ah lonely lute! who heareth now thy sound?
Which oft, as 'twere in gladness, did rebound   5
In courts, responsive to the tuneful band,
Who fired with various transports all around,
And whose unequalled spirit could command
Thy magic chords with love and rapture-kindling hand.

Though not a passer pays his tribute sigh,   10
Yet thus no more shalt thou unheeded be,
See Knowledge, heavenly maid, descending nigh,
Whose ever blessed vot'ries will string thee,
And give unto the world thy harmony:
When Time and Ignorance will try in vain   15
To hide thy sweet, triumphant minstrelsy;
But listening crowds shall press to hear thy strain,
And thou shalt be the pride—the joy of bards again.

Yet grant me, once beloved lute! to touch
Thy strings, where witching sweetness ever dwells,   20
My skill tho' scant, my feebleness tho' much,
Tho' spirits guard thee with their mighty spells.—
O! let me wake one note that sadness quells,
One heart-enchanting note, renowned of yore,
At whose despotic sway the heart but swells,   25
With all the ecstasy of fancy's lore,
When hope her many-coloured picture holds before.
FEBRUARY 1828

---

8. The Vīnā or Indian Lute is a fretted instrument of the guitar kind, usually having seven wires or strings and a large gourd at each end of the finger board; the extent of the instrument is two octaves; it is supposed to be the invention of Nareda (the greatest of celestial saints and the son of Brahma) and has many varieties, enumerated according to the number of strings, &c. *Am. Co.*—Mr. Wilson's *Sanscrit Dictionary.* Page 841. For a more particular account of this instrument, see *Asiatic Researches* Vol. I. Page 295. [KG]

Kasiprasad's poem owes much to British romantic notions of the bard and to H. L. V. Derozio's poems, especially "The Harp of India."

Henry Louis Vivian Derozio

ENRY Louis Vivian Derozio (1809–1831) was one of those rare poets who at an early age achieved both passionate engagement with and skeptical detachment from his circumstances. In Derozio's case, the circumstances were complex. Although his mother, Sophia Johnson, was born in England and his father came from Portuguese and Indian ancestors, Derozio is claimed as the first Indian poet writing in English. Many of his poems and much of his journalistic writing addressed issues of Indian identity and India's future. Rather than defining India through appeals to ethnicity, religion, or nature, Derozio explored these issues in a global philosophical and literary context. His own hybrid identity and philosophical training enabled him, even during his short life, to write poems that have had a lasting impact on Indian writing in English.

Derozio's religious upbringing and his political background were as multifarious as his ancestry. His paternal grandfather, initially a Catholic, joined the Baptist Church as an adult, and thus Derozio's father, Francis, grew up in an atmosphere of evangelical piety. The Baptist Church in Calcutta shared a common mission with Catholic and Anglican congregations but was distinguished from them by its British working-class affiliations. Baptists in Bengal supported Indian education for all classes and sponsored the largest independent publishing enterprise on the subcontinent. The poet's father was raised in this milieu, and his mother also appears to have been a Baptist. Francis and Sophia had five children (three boys and two girls); Henry was the middle son. His father, an accountant for the British firm James Scott and Co., was ambitious for the children. He sent his youngest to Scotland to study and sent Henry not to a religious academy but to one of the best schools in Calcutta: Dhurmatola Academy. There the poet studied with the Scottish schoolmaster David Drummond and was imbued with the philosophy of the eighteenth-century Scottish Enlightenment (Locke, Hume, Reid, and Dugald Stewart). Derozio's poetry gives evidence that he was widely read in the European classics and contemporary literatures as well. Derozio's early years thus were a mix of influences—intellectual, linguistic, religious, and political. His identity was multiple, his ambitions literary.

After leaving school, Derozio entered his father's business for several months and then assisted his uncle on his indigo plantation, but neither occupation was congenial. He began publishing verse under the pseudonym "Juvenis" in Calcutta periodicals, and he began writing prose as well. His writings, his intellectual precocity, and his reputation as an excellent student among the Scots schoolmasters of Calcutta landed Derozio his next and most exciting employment. At the tender age of seventeen, he was appointed teacher of history and philosophy at the Hindu College. A preparatory and postsecondary school, the Hindu College was then under the supervision of its famous principal, the Scotsman and former watchmaker David Hare. Hare was a freethinker in matters of religion and politics alike, and he found in the young Derozio a promising teacher.

Derozio proved a charismatic instructor for boys scarcely younger than himself. He and many of his students were caught up in discussions of philosophical, religious, and political questions. They began the Hindu College Academic Association, a lively extracurricular debating society, and because of their challenge to all sorts of orthodoxies, they came to be known collectively as "Young Bengal." To his eventual discomfort, Derozio's Hindu students declared their religious skepticism; some of his teenaged charges went so far as to eat beef and drink beer in imitation of the British and in defiance of their parents' religious custom. In 1831, outraged parents demanded Derozio's resignation. Though he honestly argued that he never preached atheism but only taught his students to debate philosophical and religious questions, Derozio was forced to resign.

For the remaining months of his life, Derozio drew on his experience as a journalist and editor to launch a newspaper, the *East Indian*. This publication evinced his strong support of the "East Indian" cause, which advocated for the rights of persons of mixed European and Indian descent. Despite his relative youth, he was a leader in the public agitation for the rights of East Indians, who sought justice under British law and equal employment opportunities, both of which the East India Company denied them. Indeed, in 1822, the Supreme Court in Calcutta declared that most East Indians could not be considered British subjects. Derozio played a significant role in the ensuing public petitions to the British parliament.

The clarity of his thinking about the relationship of East Indians to Hindus and Muslims and to British power is evident in Derozio's prose. In 1829, for example, he published a short reflection—really a manifesto—"On the Colonization of India by Europeans." Here he argued against the proposal that Europeans be allowed to buy land and thus to colonize India. He argued "that colonization would not be beneficial" unless the British government intervened to admit "natives and Indo-Britons to a participation of privileges on a similar footing, as far as practical and expedient, with the Europeans." "It is only by such a measure that discontent can be prevented from brooding into rebellion," Derozio warned, "and the arts and sciences, when established, can produce benefits both to the governors and governed, to Britain, and to this . . . our oppressed and neglected native country." Derozio concluded by quoting the English utilitarian philosopher Jeremy Bentham to argue that Britain should ensure that India be governed in accordance with the principle of "the greatest good of the greatest number" (Mukhopadhyay, 317–19).

Derozio's fame rests not on his controversial prose but on the way in which issues of identity and political equality inform his poetry. His sonnets "The Harp of India" and "To India—My Native Land" have remained important for generations as simultaneously representing the stimulus of English language poetry and the first poetic expression in English of an emergent Indian nationalism.

The poet was celebrated in his time for two volumes of verse: *Poems* (1827), finished when he was only eighteen, and *The Fakeer of Jungheera, a Metrical Tale, and Other Poems* (1828). Given the influence of his Scottish mentors Drummond and Hare and the support of the Scotsman John Grant, then editor of the *India Gazette*, it is not surprising that Derozio was influenced by the Scottish poet Thomas Campbell and by Thomas Moore's *Irish Melodies*. The trope of the harp hung upon the willow is integral to Moore's work and shapes Derozio's poems "The Harp of India," "Tasso," and "To India." The silent harp, which is based on the persecution of Welsh bards at the time of the English conquest of Wales, appears repeatedly in Scottish and Irish poetry of the period as a trope for cultural nationalism; it was adopted by English poets as a form of nostalgia for a preindustrial age. For Derozio, in contrast, the untuned harp represented the cultural power of an imaginary India, evoked from a mythic past as an aid to visualizing a quite different future.

Letitia Landon (L.E.L.) and George Gordon, Lord Byron, also had their impact on the young poet. That Derozio read their work shortly after its London publication testifies to the creation by 1820 of a common literary culture among Calcutta, London, Edinburgh, and Dublin. The poet and journalist Emma Roberts, a friend of Derozio's, would have provided a direct link to L.E.L. From both L.E.L. and Byron, Derozio derived romantic attitudes of self-dramatization, particularly those of the spurned lover and the melancholy poet. He also tried his hand at Byron's cultural satire in his very youthful "Don Juanics." Byron's radical politics, and to a lesser extent Shelley's, were crucial influences as well. No doubt Byron's death at Missolonghi, where he was supporting the Greek nationalist cause, and Byron's critique of what he saw as a hypocritical and oligarchic British society in the final cantos of *Don Juan* had their effect on the young poet in India, as they did on young poets in Britain.

With a poetic maturity surprising for his age, Derozio attempted to bring these European influences to bear on a nationalist or protonationalist politics by engaging the legends and stories of India. Here, like many British poets including Byron and Moore and like many contemporary English language poets in India, he wove such stories into "Oriental" tales—melodramatic stories of valor, star-crossed lovers, rescues, and fatal conflicts between conflicting loyalties. Like his contemporaries, Derozio implicitly furthered a historical model that read the Muslim conquest of India against a mythic golden age of Hindu culture, though he avoided both the negative image of Islam and the suggestion that British rule was, at some point, destined to restore the glories of India.

Derozio's long poem *The Fakeer of Jungheera* partakes of this historiography at the same time that it takes a position on sati, or the ritual burning of Hindu widows. The poet is clearly critical of the practice. His lengthy footnotes constitute an essay endorsing the British utilitarian critique of sati. Derozio's heroine, Nuleeni, the daughter of a Muslim ruler, is captured and married off to a Hindu whom she does not love, but she remains secretly in love with a robber bridegroom, who disguises himself as a fakir, or religious hermit. After her husband's death, her lover rescues her from the flames at the moment when she is to be consumed as a sati, but coincidentally he is soon killed by Nuleeni's father in a battle. At this point, Nuleeni herself dies clasping her lover's corpse in a curious approximation of the death she had earlier avoided. Although this poem, Derozio's longest, is not his most powerful, it is the most representative of his time.

Before he could publish a third volume of verse or make the *East Indian* fully into the newspaper he had envisioned, Derozio was taken ill at the age of twenty-two. He died of cholera and was buried on December 26, 1831. After his untimely death, Derozio was celebrated both for his accomplishments and for his unrealized potential. In later years, he was often memorialized as the "Indian Keats." Numerous poets wrote verses to his memory, and to this day he is commemorated in an annual ceremony and wreath-laying at his grave in Park Street Cemetery, Kolkata.

Sources

H. L. V. Derozio, *Poems* (Calcutta: Baptist Mission Press, 1827); Derozio, *The Fakeer of Jungheera, a Metrical Tale, and Other Poems* (Calcutta: Samuel Smith, 1828). See also Rosinka Chaudhuri, ed., *Derozio, Poet of India: The Definitive Edition* (New Delhi: Oxford University Press, 2008); Chaudhuri, "An Ideology of Indianness: The Construction of Colonial/Communal Stereotypes in the Poems of Henry Derozio," *Studies in History*, n.s. 20, no. 2 (2004): 167–87; and Abirlal Mukhopadhyay, with Derozio Commemoration Committee, eds., *Song of the Stormy Petrel: Complete Works of Henry Louis Vivian Derozio* (Calcutta: Progressive Publishers, 2001).

To the Pupils of the Hindu College

Expanding like the petals of young flowers
I watch the gentle opening of your minds,
And the sweet loosening of the spell that binds
Your intellectual energies and powers
That stretch (like young birds in soft summer hours)   5
Their wings to try their strength. Oh how the winds
Of circumstance and freshening April showers
Of early knowledge and unnumbered kinds
Of new perceptions shed their influence,
And how you worship truth's omnipotence!   10
What joyance rains upon me when I see
Fame in the mirror of futurity,
Weaving the chaplets you have yet to gain,
Ah then I feel I have not lived in vain.

Freedom to the Slave

> And as the slave departs, the man returns.
> *Campbell*

How felt he when he first was told
    A slave he ceased to be;
How proudly beat his heart, when first
    He knew that he was free!—
The noblest feelings of the soul   5
    To glow at once began;
He knelt no more; his thoughts were raised;
    He felt himself a man.
He looked above—the breath of Heaven
    Around him freshly blew;   10
He smiled exultingly to see
    The wild birds as they flew,
He looked upon the running stream
    That 'neath him rolled away;
Then though on winds, and birds, and floods,   15
    And cried, "I'm free as they!"

Oh Freedom! there is something dear
    E'en in the very name,
That lights the altar of the soul
    With everlasting flame.   20
Success attend the patriot sword,
    That is unsheathed for thee!
And glory to the breast that bleeds,
    Bleeds nobly to be free!
Blest be the generous hand that breaks   25
    The chain a tyrant gave,
And, feeling for degraded man,
    Gives freedom to the slave.
                FEBRUARY, 1827

The Harp of India

Why hang'st thou lonely on yon withered bough?
    Unstrung, for ever, must thou there remain;
Thy music once was sweet—who hears it now?
    Why doth the breeze sigh over thee in vain?—
    Silence hath bound thee with her fatal chain;   5
Neglected, mute, and desolate art thou,
    Like ruined monument on desert plain:
O! many a hand more worthy far than mine
    Once thy harmonious chords to sweetness gave,
And many a wreath for them did Fame entwine   10
    Of flowers still blooming on the minstrel's grave:
Those hands are cold—but if thy notes divine
    May be by mortal wakened once again,
    Harp of my country, let me strike the strain!

To India—My Native Land

My country! in thy day of glory past
A beauteous halo circled round thy brow,
And worshipped as a deity thou wast—
Where is that glory, where that reverence now?
Thy eagle pinion is chained down at last,   5
And groveling in the lowly dust art thou:
Thy minstrel hath no wreath to weave for thee
Save the sad story of thy misery!—
Well—let me dive into the depths of time,
And bring from out the ages that have rolled   10
A few small fragments of those wrecks sublime,
Which human eye may never more behold;
And let the guerdon of my labour be
My fallen country! one kind wish from thee!¹

from *The Fakeer of Jungheera*

O! this is but the world's unfeeling way
To goad the victim that it soon will slay,²
And like a demon 'tis its custom still
To laugh at sorrow, and then coldly kill.
Yet dreaming sophists in this world there be   5
Who tell us man for man has sympathy,
Who say that tears arising out of pain
Soon see themselves reflected;—but 'tis vain—
Sure social love dwells not beneath the skies,
Or it is like the bird of paradise,   10
Which lights we know not where, and never can
Be found alive among the haunts of man.

---

1. The poem, with no title, appears as the introduction to Derozio's volume *The Fakeer of Jungheera*. The title is conventionally given in the numerous reprints of the poem.

2. Derozio's long narrative poem is written mainly in octosyllabic couplets. At this point in the narrative, the heroine, who has been married against her will, is about to immolate herself upon the pyre of her deceased husband and the priests have sung their ritual praise of her wifely devotion. Preceding the widow's narration, the poet comments on the practice of sati as the music rises, a music he describes as mocking "the solemn scene / And her who shall be something that had been."

Ye who in fancy's vision view the fires
Where the calm widow gloriously expires,[3]
And charmed, behold her ere she mounts the pile;   15
Her lip illumined by a radiant smile,
Her tearless eye disowning fear's controul
Lit to reveal the heavenward soaring soul;
In hope exulting till life's hour be past,
With ardent faith, devoted to the last;   20
Fresh in the spotless loveliness of youth,
And all the native purity of truth:—
Ye who are lost in fancy's wondrous maze
At love you see not—O! could once you gaze
On those whom martyrs now you fondly deem—   25
'Twould break the magic of your golden dream!
To see the beauteous but the purchased flower,
The toy that pleases but a passing hour,
The suffering victim to the altar driven,
And bid to hope for happiness in heaven—   30
A heaven beyond the limits of her thought,
A bliss her spirit never yet had sought—
Ah! haply then might pity mourn above
Degraded nature, not exalted love!

---

3. Derozio appends a note here, which is essentially the beginning of an extended essay (continued in an additional note as well) arguing against the common treatment of widows in India. His note reads, in part, "The whole of this passage has reference to a mistaken opinion, somewhat general in Europe, namely, that the Hindu Widow's burning herself with the corpse of her husband, is an act of unparalleled magnanimity and devotion. To break those illusions which are pleasing to the mind, seems to be a task which no one is thanked for performing; nevertheless, he who does so, serves the cause of Truth. The fact is, that so far from any display of enthusiastic affection, a Suttee [sati] is a spectacle of misery, exciting in the spectator a melancholy reflection upon the tyranny of superstition and priest-craft. The poor creatures who suffer from this inhuman rite, have but little notion of the heaven and the mission years of uninterrupted happiness to which their spiritual guides tell them to look forward. The choice of immediate death, or a protracted existence, where to be only must content their desire, is all that is offered to them; and who under such circumstances would hesitate about the preference? the most degrading and humiliating household offices must be performed by a Hindu Widow; she is not allowed more food than will suffice to keep her alive; she must sleep upon the bare earth, and suffer indignities from the youngest members of her family; these are only a few of her sufferings. The philanthropic views of some individuals are directed to the abolition of widow-burning; but they should first ensure the comfort of these unhappy women in their widowhood,—otherwise, instead of conferring a boon upon them, existence will be to many a drudge, and a load." Derozio's poem was published in 1828; William Bentinck, the governor-general of Bengal, outlawed sati in British India in 1829.

Tasso

While Tasso continued in this melancholy
situation, he is said to have written the fol-
lowing elegantly simple and affecting lines.

Tu che na vai in Pindo
Ivi pende mia cetra ad uncipresso,
Salutala in mio nome, e dille poi
Ch'io son dagl' anni e da fortuna oppresso.

Life of Tasso

In *such* a cage, sweet bird, wast thou confined?[4]
    Alas! their iron hearts no feeling knew;
Yet, while thy spirit in a prison pined,
    And while thy grief almost to madness grew,
Thy minstrelsy was wafted on each wind,   5
    On every breeze thy fame triumphant flew,
And spake, through every land, of thy immortal mind.
Upon a cypress bough thy harp was hung,
Silent, neglected, mournful, and unstrung;
Such fate befitted not a harp of thine;   10
    Yet, while th' oppressor breathed, such was its doom;
But now by bards who worship at thy shrine
    'Tis crowned with flowers of everlasting bloom.

---

4. Tasso: Torquato Tasso (1544–94), an Italian poet best known for *Jerusalem Delivered*. He was
confined for seven years in a madhouse by the duke of Ferrara. Over the years, many legends
swirled around this action, cited here by Derozio as an ultimate injustice. Derozio quotes for his
epigraph the preface to John Hoole, ed. and trans., *Jerusalem Delivered* (Exeter: Edward Little, 1810),
I:xxxvii.

Sappho

> And love too much, and yet cannot love less.
>
> *Don Juan, Canto 4.*

Her love was like the raging of a storm,
    Sweeping all things before it; and her song
Was like her soul of passion, wild and warm;
    She could not brook a slight, or suffer wrong;
And when her heart the treacherous wound received   5
    From him who should have sheltered her from harm,
And soothed her every sorrow when she grieved,
    O! how the gushing blood did inly flow!
    O! how she wept his falsehood, and her woe!
Hers was melodious mourning; like the dew   10
    Her bright tears fell, for madness made her weep;
Too soon her gold-winged pleasures flew,
    Too soon she sank into a slumber deep—
Lo! high Leucadia now can tell where she doth sleep.[5]

MAY, 1827

---

5. Derozio celebrates the Greek poet Sappho (c. 610–570 B.C.E.), very likely attracted by the stories of her exile from her home in Mytilene on the island of Lesbos, her love for the girls in her household, and the legend that because of unrequited love she threw herself into the sea from the heights of the Leucadian rock. Derozio's view of Sappho may have been influenced by Letitia Landon, whose poetry he admired.

Henry Page

HENRY PAGE (c. 1814–1846) was reared in an evangelical Baptist family in what is now Bihar. His father, Captain Henry Edwin Page, was the fort adjutant at Monghyr. Thanks to his father's piety, we know something about the poet's background. Born in the west of England, Henry Page's father came from a family of some twenty children. As a young man, he joined the Indian Army, and after leading what his biographer describes as a dissipated life, in 1812 he married Jane Morgan in Calcutta. The couple had five children. Some years later, Henry Edwin Page persuaded his wife, along with their children, to be baptized in the Baptist Church. Jane Morgan's own origins are a mystery. She may have had both Indian and British ancestry, for her children were clearly brought up speaking Hindustani or perhaps Bangla, as well as English, and her son Henry identified strongly in his poetry as Indian rather than British.

Some ten years after the father's death in 1829, his son Henry and his daughter Charlotte contributed elegiac poems to a spiritual biography of their father. Written by Andrew Leslie (the father of the poet Mary Leslie, whose work appears in this volume), the biography details Henry Edwin Page's contributions to the church and his care for both his children and his much younger brother. That both Henry Page and his sister Charlotte D'Oyly contributed poetry to Henry Edwin's memorial volume allows us to conjecture something of the poet's milieu. Like Mary Leslie in the next generation and like Henry Louis Vivian Derozio, who would have been his contemporary, Henry Page seems to have found many of his metaphors and concerns rooted in his religious upbringing. In contrast to Mary Leslie, who was politicized toward a conflicted British patriotism by the uprising of 1857, both H. L. V. Derozio and Henry Page were influenced by the radical critique of the British establishment, which is characteristic of the early Baptists in Bengal. Upon leaving the church in his teens, Derozio embraced an Enlightenment skepticism in religious matters, while Henry Page appears to have remained a Christian. His poetry suggests, however, a strong identification with Derozio on personal and patriotic grounds. Though Page was probably a bit younger than Derozio, his poetry indicates that he and Derozio may have been friends or acquaintances. Certainly Page viewed Derozio as a model for poetry and as a champion of India; Page is likely to have identified with his famous contemporary on ethnic as well as intellectual grounds. He applauded in verse Derozio's "patriot heart" and wished that Derozio might return to waken India's slumbering spirit.

In "The Land of Poesy" (1842), a long poem in three books, Page laments that India had been laid "grov'ling low / Upon a field of endless woe" by British conquest, and at the end of Book III, he evokes Derozio by name, lamenting Derozio's untimely death and wishing for his return in spirit. In "The Land of Poesy," Page clearly hopes to position himself as Derozio's successor, and that desire is equally evident in Page's elegy for Derozio, written ten years after the elder poet's death. Henry Page identified himself as Indian and even imagined poetry creating the social and political awakening that would make such an identification a matter of great pride.

Sources

Henry Page, *The Land of Poesy* (Calcutta: Baptist Mission Press, 1842). See also A[ndrew]. Leslie, *Memoirs and Remains of the Late Captain H. E. Page of the Service of the Hon. East Indian Company; and Fort-Adjutant at Monghyr,* 2nd ed. (Calcutta: Baptist Mission Press, 1840).

from *"The Land of Poesy"*

And even now methinks I tread
    That far sequester'd spot,
By some celestial angel led,
Or spirit from the sacred dead,
    In deep and hallow'd thought—   5
No stranger step may wander there,
    Nor voice, to muse unknown,
Be heard—yet Poesy, in pray'r
May I approach thy temple, where
    The laden altars groan   10
'Neath costly gifts, from every land,
Presented by some suppliant hand?

Gems from the fertile earth, and flow'rs
    Of richest, deepest dye
From heav'n's unseen, transcendent bow'rs;—   15
Yet mine shall be the tear that pours
    From mortal's sorrowing eye—

Accept it then—'tis for the land
    With grief I call mine own;
For Slavery with a ruthless hand
E'en there, alas! hath fix'd his brand
    Of deathless shame alone—
Would that my soul could but forget
This source of madd'ning, dark regret!—

India, my country! once how bright,
    How spotless was thy fame!—
Not brighter heav'n's ethereal light!—
And oh! how matchless was thy might!
    Ere yet thy victors came,
From Albion, o'er the tossing wave,
    In England's pow'r array'd,
And to the summer breezes gave
Their banners, while each warrior brave
    Drew forth his battle-blade,
And, hapless, laid thee grov'ling low
Upon a field of endless woe.

Oh! I would drop a burning tear
    Upon thy listless breast
To rouse the pride that slumbers there,
And passions wake which should not share
    So long inglorious rest;—
I'd tell thee what thou once hadst been—
    A nation great and free!—
On earth, like some far-famed queen,
Amidst her loyal subjects seen
    In new-born majesty!
Receiving all the homage due
From hearts to every virtue true;

I'd speak of all that once was dear
    To thee, in happier hour,
And all thou didst but late revere—
Glory's enchanting, bright career,
    And honor, virtue, power!—
But oh! how lifeless, dead art thou
    To every noble thought,
Which like a diadem, ere now

20

25

30

35

40

45

50

55

So proudly sat upon thy brow,
    And shone, as if that naught
But death—more welcome than despair—
Were doom'd to quench its luster fair.   60

Yet India, while I humbly tread
    The long-untrodden way,
Which to immortal fame has led
Thy poets, and around thee shed
    Unrivall'd glory's ray,   65
Should I, perchance, be haply taught
    The silent harp to wake,
When'er to thee I turn a thought,
By oft remembrance sadly brought,
    E'en for my country's sake   70
With gentler hand I'll touch each string,
With kinder, deeper feeling sing.—

This is Poeta's land—Behold!
    The mighty Tiber here
Still flows along her banks of gold   75
In crystal stream, as sung of old,
    And Rome, proud empire, there,
Yet unsubdued, now lifts her head
    With dazzling honors crown'd;
There too Olympus, mountain dread,   80
And Tempe's sweet and flow'ry mead[1]
    Are blossoming around—
The calm retreat where gods had stray'd
To drink the breath of cooling shade,

More precious to the lip of care   85
    Than nectar's sparkling bowl—
I love to breathe this hallow'd air—
It brings me back to things that were,—
    To feelings of the soul,
And dreams of bliss in childhood's scene,   90
    Alas! untimely cast,
With every hope that once had been,
Beyond the gulf which rolls between

---

   1. Tempe: vale near Mount Olympus in Thessaly, Greece, a favorite haunt of Apollo and the Muses.

The present and the past;
And, like a faded fantasy,   95
Is only seen by memory!—

            .   .   .   .   .

All, all is hush'd in fearful calm—
    I cannot linger here,
And yet, amid this strange alarm,
There is one other youthful form,   100
    Which I, advancing, near,—
One other marble monument,
    On which my thoughts would rest,
One other—he whose knee is bent
In supplication eloquent,   105
    Whose hands upon his breast
Clasped, bespeak some fond desire
Lurks hidden in that soul of fire.

'Tis he—Derozio, bent in pray'r
    That India's harp too long   110
Has silent hung—Oh! could we bare
That heart, and only witness there
    Emotions which no tongue,
Nor mortal language, can reveal,—
    Reviv'd, full well I know,   115
All India would awaking feel
A pride it could not then conceal,
    All India's bosom glow
With fire to strike the harp again
He oft had woke to happy strain.   120

And may this be?—perhaps not so,
    And yet methinks there are
Some few who *feel*—else why this slow
Returning hope comes even now
    To cheer me from afar?—   125
I may no longer muse—'Tis past
    The magic twilight hour,
And night her shadowy veil hath cast
O'er every object—while the last,
    Faint echo from yon tow'r   130
Is hush'd, as if to hear me tell
Thee, sweet Poeta, fare thee well.

Stanzas to the Memory of Henry Louis Vivian Derozio

Pride of the East! thy memory
    Comes like a magic spell
Upon the soul of poesy,
    Or like the holy swell
Of music from that happy land   5
    Where fairy muses string
Their harps with well-attuning hand,
    And all in concert sing.

Pride of the East! perchance again
    The harp that silent long   10
May yet on India's sunny plain
    Awake another song,
But oh! the hand which most it lov'd,
    Which best attuned its strings,
Is cold in death—the heart unmov'd—   15
    The soul hath spread its wings,

And India's pride fled far away!—
    He sung—a nation's voice
Welcom'd the high aspiring lay,
    And India did rejoice,   20
That still amid the general wreck
    Of her proud eastern fame,
One spark of bright poetic fire
    Had kindled into flame;

One gifted mind, unfetter'd, rang'd   25
    Beyond oblivion's grasp;
And Pride, that long had been estrang'd,
    With one convulsive gasp,
Rose from the gloomy depths of time,
    And breath'd another soul,   30
With thoughts that in a patriot's heart
    Would brook no stern control!

He sung—'twas in life's early day—
    Oh! had he longer sung,
The sun which in such bright array   35

From th' east exulting sprung,
How in its proud meridian height,
    And ere it gain'd the west,
Would it have burn'd with crimson light,
    And blaz'd with gilded crest!   40

But no, 'twas else—a vengeful cloud,
    Gorg'd with red lightning's fire,
And breathing thunder's summons loud,
    Arose in blackness dire;
A cloud by Death there hurried forth   45
    To meet that blazing sun,
And quench the light which shone on earth
    Ere yet its course was run.

And thus, O Minstrel of the East!
    Thy sun was clouded o'er;   50
But tho' thy strain hath hapless ceas'd
    And thou art now no more,
An echo still in every heart
    Shall breathe sweet melody,
And many a tear unbidden start   55
    To thy sad memory!

AUGUST 2, 1841

Sir John William Kaye

≈ ⌒

S IR JOHN WILLIAM KAYE (1814–1876) began his writing career later in
life. As a privileged young man, he was able to complete his schooling at
Eton College and the Royal Military College, Addiscombe, the latter of
which he referred to as "a great nursery of Indian Captains" (Kaye, *History*, 1:147).
In 1832, Kaye was commissioned in the Bengal Artillery as a cadet. He soon was
promoted, but plagued with poor health he retired from the army in 1841 at age
twenty-seven. Kaye stayed on in India, beginning his writing career at the *Bengal
Hurkaru*, Calcutta's first daily newspaper. In 1844, Kaye left the *Hurkaru* to start his
own publication, the *Calcutta Review*, writing over fifty articles for the journal and
acting as editor. During these years he also wrote a novel, *Long Engagements: A Tale of
the Affghan Rebellion.*

Kaye returned to England and began publishing prolifically. He joined the
home civil service of the East India Company, and in 1858 when the government
of India was transferred directly to the Crown, he succeeded John Stuart Mill as
the secretary of the Foreign Department of the India Office. During this time,
he produced his major historical work, *A History of the Sepoy War in India, 1857–58.*
Christopher Herbert has argued that Kaye's history, his most notable work, was
composed "under the sign of very extreme ambivalence" (196). As Herbert puts
it, Kaye attempts to see British conduct during the Mutiny as honorable, yet over
hundreds of pages he describes both British conduct during the Mutiny and the
behavior leading up to it as fatally wrong and morally bankrupt. Kaye, Herbert
says succinctly, "rehearses a great litany of British folly, rapacity, and injustice,
the causes to which he attributes Indian rebelliousness. Arrogance, besetting
national vanity, and other debilitating flaws of character cause British govern-
ment in India to be productive, despite all good intentions, of widespread injus-
tice and maladministration" (195). For Kaye, as for many another poet whose
work appears in this collection, triumphalist imperialism was never truly a ten-
able option.

Recognized by the government for his service, Kaye was made Knight Com-
mander of the Order of the Star of India, He retired in 1874 to a country resi-
dence in Carmarthenshire, Wales. His last book, *Essays of an Optimist*, published in
1870, collected many of the occasional pieces he had written for *Cornhill Magazine.*

Sources

John William Kaye, *Poems and Fragments* (Jersey: privately printed, 1835). See also John William Kaye, *A History of the Sepoy War in India, 1857–58.* 3 vols. (London: Allen, 1877 [1864–1876]); Christopher Herbert, *War of No Pity: The Indian Mutiny and Victorian Trauma* (Princeton, NJ: Princeton University Press, 2008); and E. J. Rapson, "Kaye, Sir John William (1814–1876)," *ODNB*.

Composed at Sea, by Moonlight

Sept. 1833

The moon hath clomb the top-most Heaven
　　And looks down on the wave,
Like the eye of hope which gleams upon
　　The darkness of the grave.

I am sitting now beside the helm　　　　　　　5
　　Watching the waters black
Close with a low and sullen roar
　　Behind our vessels track.

On, on, she goes like a pawing steed
　　As though she felt delight　　　　　　　10
In the freshness of the evening breeze
　　And the beauty of the night.

She almost seems like us to know
　　That her course is well nigh run,
And is giving a bounding spring at the last　　15
　　That the goal may be bravely won.

How beautifully white she gleams
　　In all her proud array,
You can see the shadow of each rope
　　As clearly as by day;　　　　　　　20

And as you look on her many sails
    From the helm unto the prow
It were not difficult to think
    As I am thinking now,

That the spreading canvas over-head   25
    The mariners asleep,
And the huge pointed guns were like
    A camp upon the deep;

Whilst the helms-man's eye on the compass-light
    Is fixed as on a spell;   30
And he stands scarce moving by the wheel
    Mute as a sentinel.

I fain would have no thought of home
    But that they will intrude,
And rise in sunny voice up,   35
    To mock my solitude.

I would not think of that which is
    To me a thing denied;
It is enough that I am here
    What boots then aught beside?   40

The future is before me now,
    Why think I of the past,
I have been happy, may be still;
    My sun is not o'er-cast.

But there is one to whom my thoughts   45
    In spite of all will stray,
And why should they be checked for none
    More hallowed are than they.

My mother—my dear mother—why
    Should I check one thought of thee?   50
For if it makes me sad at times
    I love not gaiety.

And more than all, on such a night
    So calm—so pure above;
For what can be more calm and pure   55
    Than is a mother's love?—

'Tis said that unto sever'd hearts
    Some solace it doth lend
To think the orb that smiles on you
    Is smiling on your friend.   60

But Heaven 'mongst other blessed things
    Has me denied this one,
For the sun now shines on thee,
    The moon upon thy son.

Written on Recovering from Sickness

Sept. 1834

I

I stood upon the shores of Hindustan
A solitary man;
And a voice came pealing across the sea
Unheard by all but me;
And the voice said "Up; and begone my son,   5
This land is not for thee."

II

"Why hast thou left thine own sweet country's bowers,
And all its world of flowers?
Why hast thou left a home of quiet bliss
For such a clime as this?   10
Up; and begone, my son, and quit this land;
Thou know'st not what it is."

III

"Why should'st thou leave a shore, where all is green,
Fresh, lovely, and serene;
To seek a country far across the sea   15
Where winds blow parchingly.
And grim disease comes stalking o'er the plain
Ready to light on thee."

IV

"Dost thou seek glory?—Why abroad then roam?
Have we not that at home?   20
Dost thou seek riches?—Oh! believe me, Son,
That such a goal when won
Will not repay thee for the weary race
Thou, seeking it, hast run."

V

But stubbornness was in my heart; and I   25
        Turn'd away silently:
Yet still I could but hear the warning voice—
        "Methinks, thou dost rejoice
In this thy exile"—then I answer made
"Alas! 'twas not my choice."   30

VI

Much did I marvel what the voice could be
        That spoke so kind to me;
And I cried out—"Those tones, oh! whose are they
        That now I hear—oh! say:
Me-thought at first it was my mother's voice   35
That thought has died away;"

VII

"And now I know not"—Then the voice replied
        "I am thy Friend—thy guide
Thou has none such throughout this teeming earth;

E'en from thy very birth,
I have watched o'er thee; and I charge thee now
Reseek thy father's hearth."—

VIII

Then sickness came upon me; and I lay
    For many a weary day,
Cursing the hour when first I saw the light:
    At morn I pray'd for night,
And when night came I long'd for day to burst
Upon my straining sight.

IX

Then I had visions, though I never slept
    But aye my senses kept—
Wild, troubled visions which I could not quell
    Although I knew right well,
That my distempered brain saw many things
Which were invisible.

X

And as I lay upon the bed of pain,
    I heard the voice again;
"My son, dost thou believe me?"—and I cried
    "Oh! my best friend—my guide—
Whatever thou mayest be, relieve me, and
Thou shalt be deified."

XI

Then the voice said—"Thou needst not repine,
    The hand, which smote, is mine;
And I smite whom I love.—Yet I will save
    Thy body from the grave;
And when thou standest up, thou wilt regard
The counsel which I gave."

XII

And out I spake—"Whatever thou may'st be
    Who thus dost counsel me—
Thou unembodied, formless eloquence
    Whence comest thou—oh! whence?—   70
And the voice answered in the gentlest tones"My name is Providence."

Sonnet

Burial at Sea

Oh! 'tis a fearful thing to stand beside
    A dead man's coffin on a foreign sea,
    And think in dreariest solitude that he
Afar from his own father-land had died,
    Without one friend to smooth his dying pillow,   5
Without one loving eye to shed a tear,
    When his soul fled, they gave him to the billow,
Unwept, unhonoured—In the waters drear,
I heard a plunge, and saw the white foam rise,
    Then looked around me; but in no man's eyes   10
    Could I see aught unwonted; soon we parted,
    One here, one there; but all most joyous-hearted,
    A cloud on no one's brow: and can it be,
That scenes like these, weak man, stir up no thought in thee.

E.L.

I N 1846, a most interesting volume of verse was privately printed at the Baptist Mission Press in Calcutta. It was signed "E.L.," and its dedication indicated that the author was an American woman. The author prefaced her volume thus: "To America, this Volume is Affectionately and Dutifully Inscribed by One of her Absent Daughters Calcutta April 14th, 1846." The poet seems to have envisioned her readers as forming a circle of friends, near and far, for the volume includes many poems dedicated to her sister, named here "Francesca Carolina," and numerous other poems addressed to particular friends in the crises of their lives. Following her inscription to America, the poet provided a brief poem by way of a preface, conceiving her poems and their readers in terms of social exchange:

> Dear Reader:—
> 'Tis Friendship's wish to gratify
> That now this volume meets thine eye;
> Its faults are great, its merits less,
> Nor can it boast attractive dress:
> Yet O, receive my humble muse,
> And let your kindness be like dews
> From heaven that nurse the lonely flower,
> Which else would die before its hour.
> To thee, to her dear native land,
> She looks from India's burning strand,
> And thinks of blessings home doth bring,
> While here she sits with folded wing:
> If she a "Leisure Hour" beguile,
> Then deign to cheer her with thy smile.

E.L. folded her wings in Calcutta, but it is impossible to say whether she afterward flew home to America. She appears, despite her homeward thoughts, to have loved India, its delights marred only by the vicissitudes of infant mortality and separation from family.

What we can say with reasonable certainty about E.L. does not go far enough, as yet at least, to provide a positive identification. Her poetry invites a biographical reading, and insofar as internal evidence can be trusted, she was presumably born in the United States and embarked for India as an adult. She seems to have traveled between Boston and Calcutta and to have anticipated meeting her husband in Calcutta. Her poetry gives evidence that she was a devout Christian, yet she seems to have been reasonably open-minded for her time, writing in "Some Things that I Love" that her "orient friends" were more Christian than those who called themselves Christian. Though she wished her Indian friends to have contrite hearts, she seems to have been content with their virtues and their friendship. Clearly, E.L. had at least one child, for she speaks from experience in a poem intended to comfort a friend. And she clearly had significant learning. Her poems include learned footnotes in the orientalist manner (particularly with respect to botany), and they contain words in Bangla and Hindi (or Hindustani), Greek, and French. E.L. also recorded that she studied en route to India, completing exercises in Hindustani, Arabic, and French. E.L. either became a teacher in India or was intimate with women who were teachers, and her study seems to have been aimed partly toward this profession. The poem "Kádambiní" is unique among those in this volume in representing the multilingual context of Indian speech and writing. The poet provides footnotes in Indian script and, unusually for the 1840s, uses diacritical markings in her transliterations. Most interesting of all is her effort to represent vernacular code switching, as the poem re-creates an adult language learner's conversation with a child. Each has set out to learn the other's language, but neither can yet speak it. And so the poem is conducted in that mix of language held in common by beginning language learners.

The Christian subtext of E.L.'s volume may be what has led to its misattribution. For more than a hundred years, E.L. was misidentified as Lydia Lillybridge Simons, an American woman who traveled to Burma with the famous missionary Adoniram Judson and his third wife, Emily Chubbuck Judson. Lydia Lillybridge is identified in several sources as the author of *Leisure Hours,* but internal evidence shows that she could not have written these poems. Multiple sources record that Lillybridge departed Boston with the Judsons in July 1846; *Leisure Hours,* however, is datelined Calcutta, April 14, 1846. E.L.'s poems were almost certainly in circulation in Calcutta before Lillybridge arrived in South Asia. The poems of the volume, moreover, bespeak a much longer acquaintance with India than Lillybridge could possibly have had by 1846. E.L.'s knowledge of local botany and her bow to the poems of Kasiprasad Ghosh, whose volume *The Shāïr and Other Poems* had been published in 1830, imply that she arrived in India some years before 1846.

E.L.'s references to Kasiprasad's poetry are especially interesting, because tributes between poets in this period tended to run in the other direction, with Indian poets dedicating their work to British-born poets rather than vice versa. Another notable exception to this rule is another female poet, Emma Roberts, who a decade earlier dedicated her work to her friend H. L. V. Derozio. E.L. is not as accomplished a poet as Roberts, Derozio, or Kasiprasad, but her work provides an insight into how an American woman viewed the landscape and society in which she found herself.

Perhaps most affecting—and unusual—is E.L.'s strong personal attachment to Indian friends and places, reflected clearly in her poem and prose on Vrindavan (which she calls Gupta-Brindiabon). E.L. seems to have loved India, even while missing her American friends and family. Before a projected departure to America, she lamented more than she rejoiced. "India's a hallowed spot to me," she wrote. India, E.L. said, was her "adopted soil!"

Source

E.L., *Leisure Hours; or, Desultory Pieces in Prose and Verse by E.L.* A Private Edition (Calcutta: Baptist Mission Press, 1846).

Lines

On reading the "Sháïr and Other Poems by Kásiprasád Ghosh."

> List! List! what mournful sigh is that that
>   sweeps
> Along the gale, and falls upon the ear!—
> It is the broken-hearted "Shair" who weeps
> The love of his beloved "Armita" dear.

Bright emanation from th'empyreal skies!
    Genius and Poesie's favorite son thou art;
Thy lyre,—Oh! how tenderly it breathes!
    Entrancing with a spell the raptured heart.

The feelings of a tender, noble soul   5
    When crushed by stern adversity 'tis laid,
Thy ready pen, e'er dipp'd in living truth,
    Hath faithfully and fully here portrayed.

Thy strains so sweet, so pure, so seraph-like,
    Flow gently from the living Fount within;   10
That fount of quenchless, wild, poetic fire,
    Which, burning on, a deathless fame shall win.

The magic of thy harp has thrilled my soul,
　　Thy pages e'er a healing balm convey,—
Those lines of living truth I oft con o'er　　　　　　　　　　15
　　With joy and comfort in the darksome day.

More worthy hands than mine will twine the wreath
　　Of laurel round thy high, majestic brow;
And to thy lofty, noble—heaven-born mind
　　Their spirits with humility will bow.　　　　　　　　　　20

Oh may thy crown, preserved by heaven's own dews,
　　Be one *indeed immortal,* that shall bring
Thee greenest bays, unmingled with the rue,
　　Whose native soil drinks of the "Living-Spring."

To thee I bring this humble votive lay,　　　　　　　　　25
　　Accept the offered tribute, and may Fame
Extending far and wide, my friend esteemed,
　　"Each passing year add honors to thy name."

A Fragment

On Board the Norfolk at Sea, Bound to Calcutta

From Tithonas' couch ere Aurora arose,[1]
The cerulean gates of the sky to unclose,
My matins were chanted, my lessons prepar'd,
And I to my little *escritoire* repair'd.
Here with French, Hindost'hani, Arabic display'd,　　　　5
With a pen from the quill of an Albatross made,
I translated three pages, then thought of three friends,
Two[2] at home, *one*[3] I hope where the graceful palm bends.
Reclining absorb'd in profound reverie,
My fancy-led mind rose unfetter'd and free,　　　　　　10
Though sober-hued *pensées* would now and then fling
Their saddening shades o'er my fluttering wing.

---

1. Tithonas, hopelessly in love with the goddess, was given immortality but not eternal youth by
Aurora, goddess of the dawn.
　2. My dear sisters whom I left in America. [EL]
　3. My beloved husband in Calcutta. [EL]

To the Koil

Sweet Koil! on my "Champá" tree,[4]
Oh sing thy loveliest notes to me;
See! here I sit all isolate,
And for thy welcome song I wait.

Monotonous then sing away,   5
Just on the threshold of sweet May;
Suspend not thou thy gentle note,
That was on April's breeze[5] afloat.

In this hot, and burning sphere,
Thou sooner visitest the year   10
Than where dull Caurus, whistling past,
Unites with Borelean blast.—[6]

Where powder'd snow is borne along
On pinions—dancing to the song
Of hoary, blust'ring Winter, drest   15
In surplice white, and icy vest.

Where the merry sleigh-bells jingle,
And the ears with cold do tingle,—
Where icicles bedeck each branch,
And snow in sudden avalanche   20

Descends from all the laden eaves;
While frigid arms, with diamond leaves,
Are sparkling 'neath the half warm gaze
Of Sol, who 'round coquettish plays.

Bright bird! thou tell'st of all that's sweet,   25
Benignant nature at our feet—

---

4. Koil: cuckoo. [EL]
    This note was attached to the poem's title in E.L.'s published volume. The champá is a highly ornamental and sacred tree (*Micheliachampaca* sp., L., also *M. rheedii*), a kind of magnolia, "whose odorous yellow blossoms are much prized by Hindus, offered at shrines, and rubbed on the body at marriages," according to *Hobson-Jobson*.
    5. Vide Babu Kasiprasad Ghose's [Ghosh's] Poems, "on the vernal air's afloat." [EL]
    6. Caurus, Borelean blast: Caurus, the personification of the northwest wind (storm wind); Borelean blast, that is, Borean, relating to the north wind.

From her full lap in generous show'rs
Fair Flora's treasures rich she pours.

Pomona, too, with open hand,
Her gifts doth lavish o'er the land;   30
Of verdure bright that crown'st the spring,
Continue, Koil, e'er to sing.

Thy notes, though mournful to my ear,
I cannot bid thee disappear;—
Mournful,—and oh, what they impart,   35
So like the music of —— heart:—[7]

That patient heart, through a long day
Of sorrow, 'neath affliction's sway,
Bends meek—submissive—still bears on,
Though left, like me, almost alone.   40

Then sit, dear bird! and sing to me,
All lonely in my "Champá" tree;—
Through those sweet, mournful notes of thine,
A voice I hear all but divine.

Kádambiní

A Fragment

To India's clime a lady came—[8]
But not to acquire wealth or fame;
Benevolence inspired her heart,
And made it joy from friends to part,—
From heart-dear friends in Christian lands,   5
That she might help unloose the bands
Of superstition, which do bind
In captive chains the untaught mind.

---

7. An assemblage of clouds. [EL]
   This note was attached to the poem's title in E.L.'s published volume. E.L. also gives the deva-
nagiri script here and in the notes reproduced below—as indicted here by dashes.
   8. In this poem, E.L. may be describing work that brought her to India, but there is no cer-
tainty of this.

Across the broad Atlantic wave,
Whose billows roll o'er many a grave,   10
A worshipper of Jagannáth,[9]
Despatched to her an urgent note:—
"Oh! come to us, I pray you would,
To India come, and do us good;
I have a little daughter dear,   15
'The god' has given me this year;
I wish indeed that Mistress L.
Would give advice, and kindly tell
Me how I am to educate
My daughter, ere it be too late."   20
God gave the Hindu this desire,
Imbued his friend with holy fire;
She read the lines that he had traced,
His wish before her Maker placed,
And prayed the Lord his will to shew,   25
And help her his blest will to do.

On Gangá's shore now see her stand,
A female, lone, in distant land;
Yet knowing that the Lord designs
Enlightenment for Hindu minds,—   30
And hope that from the heaven-taught tongue,
That she shall hear the joyful song
Of glory to the Christian's God,
And Jesus for his cleansing blood,
Supports her weak and sinking heart,   35
And bids all doubts and fears depart.

Having arrived at the far-famed
"City of Palaces," so named;[10]
Her work commenced, the Lord doth bless,
And strengthen her with promised grace.   40
The Rájá brings to her his child,
A lovely one, with face as mild
As Chandra, whom some castes address,
In Purnimá[11] the hand they kiss.

The lady spake:—the child came near,   45
"Here is an English Pustak, dear,[12]
With pretty stories, pictures too,
Brought from America, for you."
"Bahut khush, do ham ko," lisped the child,[13]
And giving it, the lady smiled;   50
Then Kádambiní, laughing, took,
And ran and hid the little book.
Then peeping from behind the door,
Said, "Bibi, * * * * *"[14]
"Bahut achchhá, dear, very well,   55
Han, bánán kara, you shall spell."[15]
The father decks, in orient style,
A school-room for his darling child;
Where zephyrs through the palm trees play,
And flowers exert a pleasing sway;   60
With roses blushing, sweet to see,
Is my own Padma Karabí![16]
On branches of the Dálim-phul,[17]
Rest the sweet Koil and Bulbul;[18]
The sacred "Bata-gách" is there,[19]   65
With incense filled of Hindu prayer;
The rites performed with Gangáá-jal,[20]
By Bráhman priest, at Sandhyá-kál;[21]
Its purifying influence,
Some say, absolves from all offence.   70

Biní begins to read and chat,
Her bangled feet crossed on the mat:
O'er shadowed by her raven hair,
Her dark eyes beam with luster rare,

---

12. Pustak: book.
13. Bahut khush, do ham ko (Hindi): very happy, give me.
14. Bibi: in this context, the term means "lady." The asterisks are E.L.'s, probably indicating a rush of the child's speech that the American woman cannot yet understand.
15. Bahut achchhá (Hindi): very good, very well; bánán kara (Bangla): you spell.
16. Padma Karabí: red-blossomed flower.
17. Pomegranate. [EL]
18. Bulbul: Indian "nightingale."
19. Bata-gách: banyan tree.
20. Water of the Ganges. [EL]
21. Sunset. [EL]

Like brilliant diamonds in the dark,   75
Lit up with the immortal spark.
The lady loves her pupil-child,
And gazes on those orbs so mild,
Which an undying mind reveal,
Bearing the stamp of Heaven's own seal.   80

Michael Madhusudan Dutt

≈⟩ ⟨≈

MICHAEL MADHUSUDAN DUTT [Datta] (1824–1873) had a voracious intellect and equal ambition. Growing up in Calcutta in the middle of the nineteenth century, he absorbed the multiple and hybrid influences of a newly global literary culture. Michael Madhusudan was conversant in many languages—Persian, English, Bangla, Sanskrit, French, Tamil, Telugu, Hebrew, Greek, and Latin. In drawing together these multifarious influences, he made himself into the first modern Bangla poet. Along with his contemporary, the novelist Bankimchandra Chattopadhyay, he shaped a wholly new approach to the written tradition of Bangla literature. His new style yoked the tropes, forms, and themes he found in European, Indian, and Persian literatures.

The young Madhusudan began writing, not in Bangla, the language of the village where he was born, but in English. As a middle-class boy who had to make his way in the world, he was expected to be multilingual. When he was still a child, his father moved the family from their home village, which is now in Bangladesh, to Kidderpore, then on the outskirts of Calcutta. Consequently, as Clinton Seely speculates in his introduction to Michael's epic, while Bangla remained the language that Madhusudan spoke at home, English became his "first language, if not chronologically, at least with respect to his command of it" (13). His father, Raj Narain Dutt, was a pleader in the Sudder Diwani Adalat Calcutta (that is, the chief civil court) and thus was educated in Persian, the legal language at the time. Madhusudan apparently learned Persian as well as English and other European languages, for he entertained his friends with recitations from the Persian poet Hāfiz.

At thirteen, Madhusudan was enrolled in the Hindu College, where he remained for five years. The legacy of Henry Derozio, the charismatic young teacher and poet, was still strong. Derozian admiration for things European and Derozian skepticism mingled in the heady intellectual air of Calcutta with the critique of Hinduism that was being forwarded in very different ways by the Brahmo Samaj (a religious movement aimed at purifying Hinduism along the lines of a relatively abstract and monotheistic theology) and by Christian missionaries. Young literati still conceived passionate admiration for Byron, Shelley, and Landon, enticed nearly as much by the poets' politics as by their poetry. At the same time, David Lester Richardson, the chief lecturer in English literature and sometime principal of the Hindu College, imbued his students with an enthusiasm for

Shakespeare and Milton. The young Madhusudan took in all these influences and determined to become a great poet and to travel to England. In an early poem, sounding much like his teacher D. L. Richardson, he wrote,

> I sigh for Albion's distant shore
> Its valleys green, its mountains high;
> Tho' friends, relations, I have none
> In that far clime, yet, oh! I sigh
> To cross the vast Atlantic wave
> For glory, or a nameless grave!

But his early ambitions were to be postponed, for his father determined, as any good Indian father might with a son turning eighteen and dangerously interested in things foreign, that it was time for Madhusudan to be married.

Accordingly, in 1842 Raj Narain arranged a marriage for his son and informed Madhusudan that he was to wed in three months' time. The form of Madhusudan's resistance was to convert forthwith to Christianity. While it is clear from his letters and verse that Madhusudan was a convinced Christian, it is equally evident that one motivation for his precipitous conversion was to make it impossible for a Hindu family to allow their daughter to marry him. The marriage, not surprisingly, never occurred; equally predictably, a rift developed between father and son.

Moreover, at this time no Christians were allowed in the Hindu College, so Madhusudan had to leave school before completing his course of study in the upper, or postsecondary, division. After a lapse of some months, about which we know little, he enrolled in Bishop's College, as the sole Indian student. At that time, Bishop's College served British students and those of mixed European and Indian parentage, most of whom were studying for the Anglican priesthood. Despite his relative isolation, Madhusudan made friends, pursued his studies avidly, and even considered becoming a missionary, though perhaps more as a means of support than out of a confirmed vocation. At college or afterward, he studied Hebrew, English, Greek, and Latin as well as Sanskrit, Tamil, and Telugu.

For reasons that are not entirely clear, but perhaps owing to his father taking a second and then a third wife, Madhusudan determined to move to Madras (now Chennai). There he became employed as a teacher in the Madras Male Orphan Asylum. A few months later, the twenty-four-year-old married Rebecca Thompson, then seventeen and a student in the sister school. According to Clinton Seely's and Ghulam Murshid's researches, Rebecca was the daughter of a British father and an "Indo-Briton" mother.

Along with learning new Indian languages, teaching for the first time, and courting his bride, Madhusudan completed his first volume of verse, *The Captive Ladie,* in 1849. Here for the first time we find him adopting on the title page the name Michael Madhusudan. His name, his poems, and his wife all reflected his fascination with things English. It is even possible, given his estrangement from his father, that he chose the name Michael as much for its Miltonic and Wordsworthian as for its Christian archangelic resonances. In Wordsworth's pastoral poem, "Michael," an old shepherd recounts how his son of that name left for the city to make his living and was never heard from again. Issues of filial duty inform not only Michael's adopted name but also his later epic. But still more to Madhusudan's liking may have been the fact that Milton's Michael, the prince of archangels, provides Adam with a view of the future of the world and all its glories before escorting the fallen pair into their long exile from Paradise.

Eager for the response to his first volume, Michael Madhusudan was perhaps chagrined by its mixed reception among the literary tastemakers in Calcutta. He was reportedly chastened by the advice given to him by John Drinkwater Bethune, a famous educationist at the time, that he should stick to Bangla. "We do not want another Byron or another Shelley in English," Bethune wrote in a curiously double-edged formulation; "what we lack is a Byron or a Shelley in Bengali literature" (Seely, introduction, *The Slaying of Meghanada*, 26–27).

In Madras, Michael worked as a journalist, published an additional volume of English verse titled *Visions of the Past*, and managed to support a growing family. Michael and Rebecca had four children, but when he returned to Calcutta some years after his marriage, his family did not accompany him. In Madras he had entered a relationship with Henrietta Sophia White, who moved with him first to Calcutta and then to London when he finally realized his ambition of traveling to England. In London he studied law, and he and Sophia moved on to Paris and then to the more affordable Versailles while he waited to be called to the bar. After this brief residence in France, he practiced law, without notable success, in Calcutta, possibly because of his alcoholism. He died in considerable poverty at age forty-nine.

Despite financial difficulties, in the last twenty years of his life Michael Madhusudan created a body of work that has had a lasting impact on Bangla literature. He became the first poet to write sonnets in an Indian language. Between 1858 and 1862, he published five plays, three narrative poems, and a volume of lyrics in Bangla, in addition to translations. He created the greatest Bangla literary epic, the *Meghanadavadha kavya* (*The Slaying of Meghanada*), which, in all its Miltonic difficulty, has had a lasting impact on Bengali literary culture. A recent translation by Seely of *The Slaying of Meghanada* has made Michael's magnum opus available to English speakers for the first time. To follow up the poem's influence within India, however, I include a brief section of translation by Roby Datta. Even this brief sample in translation shows how Michael Madhusudan's apprenticeship in English language poetry culminated in a new idiom, combining both classical Indian and European traditions of epic.

Michael Madhusudan's English language volumes, *The Captive Ladie* and *Visions of the Past*, from which the other selections are taken, allow us to see the beginnings of a talent that expressed itself more fully and forcefully in Bangla writing. To generations of Bengali readers, Michael Madhusudan's work has been a touchstone and a challenge, bringing together European and Indian traditions to form a new, if highly elaborate, vernacular verse.

Sources

Michael Madhusudan Dutt, *The Captive Ladie (An Indian Tale) in Two Cantos* (Madras: Advertiser Press, 1849); *Michael madhusūdana racanāvalī,* ed. Kṣetra Gupta (Kalikātā [Calcutta]: Sāhitya Samsada, 1965); Dutt, *The Slaughter of Meghanad,* trans. Roby Datta, in *Poems, Pictures and Songs* (Calcutta: Das Gupta, 1915). See also Michael Madhusudan Dutt, *The Slaying of Meghanada: A Ramayana from Colonial Bengal,* trans. Clinton B. Seely (New York: Oxford University Press, 2004); Ghulam Murshid, *Lured by Hope: A Biography of Michael Madhusudan Dutt* (New Delhi: Oxford University Press, 2003).

Sonnet

Oh! how my heart exulteth while I see
These future flow'rs, to deck my country's brow,
Thus kindly nurtured in this nursery!—
Perchance, unmark'd some there are budding now,
Whose temples shall with laureate-wreaths be crown'd   5
Twined by the Sisters Nine; whose angel-tongues
Shall charm the world with their enchanting songs.
And time shall waft the echo of each sound
To distant ages:—some, perchance, here are,
Who, with a Newton's glance, shall nobly trace   10
The course mysterious of each wandering star;
And, like a God, unveil the hidden face
Of many a planet to man's wondering eyes,
And give their names to immortality.

Sonnet

Oft like a sad imprisoned bird I sigh
To leave this land; though mine own land it be;
Its green robed meads,—gay flowers and cloudless sky
Though passing fair, have but few charms for me.
For I have dreamed of climes more bright and free   5
Where virtue dwells and heaven-born liberty
Makes even the lowest happy;—where the eye
Doth sicken not to see man bend the knee
To sordid interest;—climes where science thrives
And genius does receive her guerdon meet;   10
Where man in all his truest glory lives,
And Nature's face is exquisitely sweet;
For those fair climes I heave the impatient sigh,
There let me live and there let me die.

Hymn

Long sunk in Superstition's night,
By sin and Satan driven,—
I saw not,—cared not for the light
That leads the blind to Heaven.

I sat in darkness,—Reason's eye   5
Was shut,—was closed in me;—
I hasten'd to Eternity
O'er Error's dreadful sea!

But now, at length thy grace, O Lord!
Bids all around me shine: 10
I drink thy sweet,—thy precious word,—
I kneel before thy shrine!—

I've broken Affection's tenderest ties
For my blest Savior's sake;—
All, all I love beneath the skies,   15
Lord, I for Thee forsake!

King Porus—A Legend of Old

'We never shall look upon his like again!'
—Shakespeare[1]

'When shall such a hero live again?'
—Byron[2]

I

Loudly the midnight tempest sang,[3]
Ah! it was thy dirge, fair Liberty!
And clouds in thundering accents roar'd
Unheeded warning from on high;
The rain in darksome torrent fell,   5
Hydaspes' waves did onward sweep,
Like fiery Passion's headlong flow,
To meet th'awaken'd calling deep;
The lightning flashed bright—dazzling, like
Fair woman's glance from 'neath her veil;   10
And on the heaving, troubled air,
There was a moaning sound of wail!
But, Ind! thy unsuspecting sons
Did heedless slumber,—while the foe
Came in stealthy step of death,—   15
Came as the tiger, noiseless, slow,
To close at once its victim's breath!
Alas! they knew not 'midst this gloom,
This war of elements, was nurst,—
Like to an earthquake in the womb   20
Of a volcano,—deep and low—
A deadlier storm—on them to burst!

---

1. Shakespeare, *Hamlet*, act 1, scene 2, lines 393–94. Hamlet says of his father, "He was a man, take him for all in all. / I shall not look upon his like again."
2. George Gordon, Lord Byron, "The Giaour," line 6.
3. Porus, whose kingdom was located in what is now the Punjab, fought the battle of the Hydaspes (Jhelum) river against Alexander the Great in 326 B.C.E. After Porus's defeat legend has it that Alexander was so impressed with the king's nobility that he returned the kingdom to Porus. Porus is believed by historians to have held the position of a Macedonian subordinate ruler, not so much a king as a vassal until he was assassinated sometime between 321 and 315 B.C.E. after the death of Alexander. In any case, owing to heavy casualties, the battle of the Hydaspes had the effect of halting Alexander's further progress, and hence it paved the way for the rise of the Mauryan kingdom. In retelling this story, Datta draws on the genre of the Oriental tale, at once using the king's heroism as a source of national pride and implying, as Western writers of such tales often did, that India had lost much of her past glory.

II

'Twas morn; the Lord of Day
From gold Sumero's palace bright,[4]
Look'd on his own sweet clime,   25
But, lo! the glorious flag,
To which the world in awe once bow'd,
There in defiance waved
On India's gales—triumphant—proud!—
Then rose the dreadful yell,—   30
Then lion-like, each warrior brave
Rushed on the coming foe,
To strike for freedom—or the grave!
Oh Death! upon thy gory altar
What blood-libations freely flow'd!   35
Oh Earth! on that bright morn, what thousands
Rendered to thee the dust they ow'd!
But 'fore the Macedonians driven,
Fell India's hardy sons,—
Proud mountain oaks by thunders riven—,   40
That for their country's freedom bled—
And made on gore their glorious bed!

III

But dauntlessly there stood
King Porus, towering 'midst the foe,
Like a Himala-peak   45
With its eternal crown of snow:
And on his brow did shine
The jewell'd regal diadem.
His milk-white elephant
Was deck'd with many a brilliant gem.   50
He reck'd not of the phalanx
That 'round him closed—but nobly fought,
And like the angry winds that blow
And lofty mountain pines lay low,
Amidst them dreadful havoc wrought,   55
And thinn'd his crown's and country's foe!
The hardiest warriors, at his deeds,

---

4. Sumero [Sumeru]: the world mountain, sometimes called Mount Meru, around which the
sun and moon were said to circle.

Awe-struck quail'd like wind-shaken reeds:
They dared not look upon his face.
They shrank before his burning gaze,   60
For in his eye the hero shone
That feared not death:—but high—alone—
A being as if of lightning made,
That scorch'd all that is gazed upon—
Trampling the living with the dead.   65

IV

Th' immortal Thund'rer's son,
Astonish'd eyed the heroic king;
He saw him bravely charge
Like his dread father,—fulmining:—
Tho' thousands 'round him clos'd,   70
He stood—as stands the ocean rock
Amidst the lashing billows,
Unmoved at their fierce thundering shock
But when th'Emathian conqueror
Saw that with gaping wounds he bled,   75
'Desist—desist!'—he cried—
'Such noble blood should not be shed!'
Then a herald was sent
Where bleeding and faint,
Stood, 'midst the dying and the dead,   80
King Porus,—boldly, undismayed:
'Hail, brave and warlike prince!
Thy gen'rous rival bids thee cease—
Behold! there flies the flag,
That lulls dread war, and wakens peace!'   85

V

Like to a lion chain'd
That tho' faint—bleeding—stands in pride—
With eyes, where unsubdued
Yet flash'd the fire—looks that defied;
King Porus boldly went   90
Where 'midst the gay and glittering crowd
Sat god-like Alexander;
While 'round Earth's mightiest monarchs bow'd.

King Porus was no slave;
He stooped not—bent not there his knee,—   95
But stood, as stands an oak,
In Himalayan majesty.
'How should I treat thee?' ask'd
The mighty king of Macedon.
'Ev'n as a King,' replied   100
In royal pride, Ind's haughty son.
The conq'ror pleas'd,
Him forth releas'd:
Thus India's crown was lost and won.

VI

But where, oh! where is Porus now?   105
And where the noble hearts that bled
For freedom—with the heroic glow
In patriot bosoms nourished—
—Hearts, eagle-like that recked not death,
But shrank before foul Thraldom's breath?   110
And where art thou—Fair Freedom!—thou
Once goddess of Ind's sunny clime!
When glory's halo round her brow
Shone radiant, and she rose sublime,
Like her own towering Himalye   115
To kiss the blue clouds thron'd on high!
Clime of the sun!—how like a dream—
How like the bright sun-beams on a stream
That melt beneath gray twilight's eye—
That glory hath now flitted by!   120
The crown that once did deck thy brow
It's trampled down—and thou sunk low;
Thy pearl, thy diamond and thy mine
Of glistening gold no more is thine.
Alas!—each conquering tyrant's lust   125
Has robb'd thee of thy very dust!
Thou standest like a lofty tree
Shorn of fruits—blossoms—leaves and all—
Of every gale the sport to be,
Despised and scorned e'en in thy fall!   130

The Slaughter of Meghanad

Translated by Roby Datta from the Meghanadavadha kavya, Book I

When, fallen in front of fray, the chief of heroes high[5]
Heroic-arm'd, did go adown until the town of Death
Right early,—say, O Goddess fair with nectar-flowing speech,
What hero great was chosen out unto the captain's post,
And sent again to battle by the Lord of Demonkind,   5
And foe of Raghav;[6] by what scheme the source of Demon's hope,
Great Indra's Victor, Meghanad, invincible on earth,
The Lord of Urmila destroy'd, and drove out Indra's dread.
I bow unto thy lotus-feet, all dull of intellect
I am, I call yet once again on thee, O white of hand,   10
Speech-Goddess! Just as, mother mine, thou didst alight and sit
Upon Valmiki's[7] tasteful tongue, as on a lotus-throne,
What time with sharply-shotten shaft, all in a wood profound,
The crane together with his bride the fowler pierced full deep,
So to thy bounden thrall do come, and be thou kind, O good!   15
Who knows thy majesty divine throughout this world all around?
The man who was the worst of men among all human kind,
On theft intent, the same became, thro' favour of thy gift,
Immortal, as immortal is the Lord of Uma fair!
O thou boon-giver, by thy boon the robber Ratnakar   20
Was Ratnakar of poesy! 'Tis at thy touch divine

---

5. The fourteen-syllabled blank verse used here has a pause usually at the eighth syllable and occasionally at the seventh. The original metre is entirely syllabic and has natural accents as in French. Michael Dutt's model in this legendary epic was Homer. He did not live to finish his projected national epic called "The Conquest of Ceylon," which was to imitate Vergil and to vie with the projected "Arturiad" of Milton. His favourite European authors were Homer, Vergil, Ovid, Dante, Petrarch, Tasso, Milton, and Camoens; and to some extent Shakespeare. He gave Bengal the blank verse, the Italian sonnet, the *vers libres*, and several choice lyrical metres, as well as the literary drama. [RD]

6. The poet asks the goddess of poetry to allow him to sing and celebrate the death of Meghanada, the son of the demon king of Lanka, Rāvaṇa. Michael's epic recounts the story of the *Rāmāyaṇa* but from a different perspective. The poem does not focus primarily on the sufferings and accomplishments of Rama, the warrior prince—the brother of Lakshman and husband of Sita, who vanquished Rāvaṇa, the ruler of Lanka and lord of the Rākṣasas or demons; rather, it focuses on Rāvaṇa's famous son, Meghanada, and his heroic death in combat with Rama.

7. Ratnakar the robber became Vālmīki the bard; so runs the Indian tradition. He is called the Homer of India, and is known all over the country through Krittibas, Tulsidas, and other Mediaeval writers. [RD]

Michael says that Vālmīki, divinely inspired by the goddess of music and poetry, Sarasvatī, has become as immortal as the "Lord or Uma," that is, as immortal as Shiva himself.

The beauty of a sandal-tree the poison-tree doth bear!
Ah, mother! such a virtue great may there be in thy thrall?
But then, the one that worthless is among her progeny,
Dull-brained, the parent's tenderness is shown forth unto him   25
The most of all. So thou uprise, uprise, O kindly One,
All world's beloved! I'll, mother, sing, with high thoughts flowing o'er,
A mighty song; uprise, and shield thy thrall with shadowing feet.
And thou, too, gentle Goddess, come, thou honey-making bee,
O Fancy! from the poet's mind, as from a flower-fraught wood,   30
Take mead, and build a honeycomb, from whence all Gouda's folk,[8]
Contented, shall imbibe their fill of nectar evermore.

JUNE, 1908.

---

8. Gouda: ancient name for Bengal.

Shoshee Chunder Dutt

I N A fictionalized autobiography published in his *Bengaliana*, Shoshee Chunder Dutt recalled his youth. While still fresh from school, the young poet fantasized his future, his brain "stocked with quotations from Shakespeare, Milton, and Bacon." "The melodious warblings" of David Lester Richardson were still "rumbling in his head." Fired by the famous headmaster of the Hindu College, the youth was eager to "start a newspaper or a magazine; nothing, in his estimation, was easier: or, better still, he could write books for the edification of mankind in general, and the Hindu race in particular; or he might become a pedagogue, and for the benefit of others unload his brain of the perilous stuff that was playing the deuce with it." All of this seemed easy, Shoshee wrote, but his "papa shook his head." The youth forthwith joined the "respectable firm of Smasher, Mutton, and Co."

Shoshee Chunder Dutt (1825–1886) did not, like his alter ego, work for Smasher, Mutton, and Co. though he too was obedient to "papa." Rather than joining a trading firm, he went to work for the government treasury and eventually rose to the very responsible position of registrar in the Bengal Secretariat. At his retirement after thirty-four years of service, he was named Rai Bahadur, a high order of merit bestowed by the government on distinguished civil officers.

The cousin of Govin Chunder, Hur (Hari) Chunder, and Greece (Girish) Chunder Dutt, Shoshee (Sasi) shared the family passion for literature, a passion he passed on to his nephew Romesh, whose guardian he became. The family's literary tastes and accomplishments were such that Shoshee's teacher Richardson called them the "Rambagan nest of singing birds" (Das, 16). Even during his employment as a civil servant, Shoshee wrote incessantly. In 1884, he brought out his collected English works in ten volumes. These included a volume of verse, a three-volume novel, ethnographic studies, journalism, a history of Bengal, and various humorous pieces. His collection of essays, *Bengaliana,* is notable for its indirect criticism of British arrogance and ineptitude, often presented through dialogues between the author's autobiographical surrogate and various of his British colleagues and superiors. These exchanges touch on British racism, unequal pay for equal work, and even the causes of dissatisfaction that led to the rebellion of 1857 and to the development of nationalism. As Alex Tickell has argued, Shoshee's work exhibits a gradual identification with British interests;

yet the multiple voices in Bengaliana suggest that such identification was as conflicted as it was genuine.

Shoshee's volume of verse, *A Vision of Sumeru, and Other Poems,* is equally conflicted. The volume is divided into four major sections: the long title poem, a section titled "Indian Ballads," a collection called "Lays of Ancient Greece" (frankly imitative of Thomas Babington Macaulay's famous *Lays of Ancient Rome*), and a section of miscellaneous poems. "A Vision of Sumeru," often imitative of Milton, is caught between the claims of Christian dogmatism and Hindu protonationalism. It draws on traditions of orientalist poetry and translation, on traditional descriptions of Hindu deities, and on the dominant tropes of Christian evangelical literature.

Though Christianity triumphs in the title poem of Shoshee's *Vision of Sumeru,* his prose creates a more complex social reality than his poetry, for its idiomatic rendering of Indian English and its oblique treatment of political and social inequalities establish a wide range of reference. Shoshee's story "The Republic of Orissá; A Page from the Annals of the Twentieth Century" is both striking and somewhat unusual; written in 1845, it imagines a successful twentieth-century rebellion against the British, a war of independence prompted by the British introduction of slavery to India. More typical are Shoshee's later prose works, which—no doubt partly in response to greater censorship by the British government—take a more satiric and less direct approach. Even the subtitle of *Bengaliana—A Dish of Rice and Curry, and Other Indigestible Ingredients*—implies that India exceeds comfortable digestion by the British stomach. Shoshee Chunder Dutt's poetry is more serious in tone than the prose, more apologetic in the religious sense of that term, and thus more deeply conflicted in its implied politics. In the tones of a much belated romanticism, the poet can only lament his widowed country's former glory.

Sources

Shoshee Chunder Dutt, *A Vision of Sumeru, and Other Poems* (Calcutta and London: Thacker, Spink and Co., 1878); Dutt, *Bengaliana: A Dish of Rice and Curry, and Other Indigestible Ingredients* (Calcutta: Thacker, Spink, 1879). See also Dutt, *Selections from "Bengaliana,"* ed. Alex Tickell (Nottingham: Trent Editions, 2005); and Harihar Das, *Life and Letters of Toru Dutt* (London: Oxford University Press, 1921).

from "A Vision of Sumeru, Canto Third"

XXXII

My dream is o'er; Sumeru's gods—
Sumeru's self hath passed away,[1]
By lightning blasted and by thunder scath'd.
Within the deep Tartarean dell,[2]
Perchance yet tortured, unforgiven,   5
Unpitied, unreprieved, they rave and roar;
But in high heaven their ancient sway
    They hold no more:
On bleak Vycant no archéd bower
A shed to Vishnu now affords,   10
    Umbrageous and obscure;
Nor Lakshmi loiters there her prime;
    In breathing[3] beauty bathed:
Kailása grey, by thunder riven,
Brightens no more 'neath Umá's spell,   15
    Its happy fields grown wild;
Nor Siva comes to reassert
His iron rule thereon again:
Indra, with his *Cinnaras* mild,[4]
And *Apsarás* born of the main,   20
Hath *Swarga* gay renounced and left,
His halls all echoless and cold—
    Inglorious in repose;
And never more may ye behold
    The gods and sprites so deft   25
Wanton upon the craggy mound,

---

1. Sumeru: sacred mountain at the center of Hindu and Buddhist cosmologies, the abode of Brahma and other gods. Later in the stanza, the poet refers also to Vycant (Vaikuntha) and to Kailasa (Kailash), the sacred mountain abodes respectively of Vishnu and his consort Lakshmi and of Shiva and his consort Pārvatī (Uma). These sections are the two penultimate sections of Shoshee's long poem, which has to this point recounted a contest between Jesus and the Hindu pantheon, in which Christianity triumphs but only after many pages of verse recounting the beauties and powers of the Hindu gods in Miltonic terms.

2. Tartarean dell: hell, a realm even below Hades.

3. The body of Lakshmi, according to the *Puráns*, breathes of the lotus, the fragrance being perceptible from a great distance. [SCH]

4. Indra: the lord of heaven. He is also referred to here by his epithet "Swarga," or Svargaloka; he is accompanied by "Cinnaras" and "Apsarás," that is, beautiful female spirits associated with him and often with Mount Kailash.

Or in the woody glades,
Or happy walks, and sylvan shades,
 Move loftily and slow;
Or where resistless torrents sweep,   30
Or milder streamlets gently flow,
Or where the ocean surges bound,
 Fit haunts for such as they!
 Sing songs, or play, or sleep,
In morning hour, or at bright noon,   35
Or when the mists of evening close,
 Or 'neath the autumn moon.
That day, when Bruhmá was uncrown'd,[5]
With him to hell they did depart,
By fiery tempest whirl'd away;   40
Eternal justice doom'd them all
Who had their lot together wound,
And none may them again recall
To envied bliss, and boundless power,
 And dignity sublime.   45

XXXIII

My dream is o'er, and past their reign
From dark Himávan's shaggy brow;[6]
And every art of man once more
Their ancient service to restore
Is fruitless now and vain.   50
Glory on earth! Jehovah's sway
Alone endureth now!
Alone it passeth not away.

---

5. Bruhmá: Brahma.
6. Himávan's shaggy brow: Himavat, god of snow, or here the personification of the Himalayan peaks previously described.

My Native Land

I

My native land, I love thee still!
There's beauty yet upon thy lonely shore;
    And not a tree, and not a rill,
    But can my soul with rapture thrill,
        Though glory dwells no more.   5

II

My fallen country! on thy brow
The ruthless tyrants have engraved thy shame,
    And laid thy haughty grandeur low;
    Yet even thus, and even so,
        I love to lisp thy name.   10

III

What though those temples now are lone
Where guardian angels long did dwell;
    What though from brooks that sadly run,
    The naiads are for ever gone—
        Gone with their sounding shell!   15

IV

And haunted shades and laurel bowers
Resound not now the minstrel's fiery lay,
    And, e'en though deck'd with orient flowers,
    They ne'er recall those witching hours,
        For ever passed away: 20

V

My heart yet may not cease to burn
For thy sweet woodlands, and thy sunny shore;
    Though oft unconscious it will turn,
    Unconscious sigh, unconscious yearn
        For glorious days of yore!   25

VI

Those days of mythic tale and song,
When dusky warriors, in their martial pride,
Strode thy sea-beat shores along
While with their fame the valleys run,
And turn'd the foe aside.   30

VII

Then sparkled woman's brilliant eye,
And heaved her heart, and panted to enslave;
And beauteous veils and flow'rets shy,
In vain to hide those charms did try
That flash'd to woo the brave.   35

VIII

My fallen country! where abide
Thy envied splendour, and thy glory now?
The Páthán's and the Mogul's pride,
Spread desolation far and wide,
And stain'd thy sinless brow.   40

IX

In freedom's shrine, the slave alone
Now dwells—a lasting monument of thy shame!
The mighty and the brave are gone;
Thy hallow'd triumphs overthrown—
The trophies of their fame!   45

X

But still the sun his noon-tide ray
Darts proudly on thy mountains towering round;
And heedless winds with streamlets play,
As slow they murmur on their way,
Through th' lovely, classic ground.   50

XI

And human naiads love to roam
Where reckless sweep thy regal rivers bold;
    By temple, and by shatter'd dome,
    Of gods the consecrated home,
        The hallow'd shrines of old!   55

XII

And beauty's eye retains its fire,
What though its lightnings flash not for the brave;
    And beauteous bosoms yet aspire,
    With passion strong and warm desire,
        To wake the crouching slave.   60

XIII

My country! fallen as thou art,
My soul can never cease to heave for thee:
    I feel the dagger's edge, the dart
    That rankles in thy widow'd heart,
        Thy woeful destiny!   65

XIV

I cannot choose but love thee yet;
And, while I rove thy fragrant meads along,
    I only wish I could forget
    That thy sun hath for ever set,
        Sweet land of love and song![7]   70

---

7. The following beautiful stanza was added to a presentation copy of the poem by the late Rev.
J. H. Parker:—

    Nay, not *for ever* set thy sun;
Truth's brighter, holier sun shall rise to shine:—
    See, even now, the dawn begun,
    A glorious course thou yet may'st run,
    Beneath the beamings of that 'Sun
        Of Righteousness' Divine. [SCH]

Govin Chunder Dutt and
The Dutt Family Album

G OVIN CHUNDER DUTT (1828–84) is often remembered as the father
of the poet Toru Dutt, but his own poetry and the poems of his remark-
able extended family reveal the impact of English language literary edu-
cation in colonial India. Govin's grandfather, Nilmoni Dutt, was a wealthy
resident of Rambagan, Calcutta, who was known equally for his hospitality, his
considerable library in several languages, his liberal opinions, and his piety.
This last attribute led him to spend more than was perhaps wise on various
Hindu pujas and charities, and it was left to his son Rasamoy Dutt to rebuild the
family fortune. This Rasamoy did, becoming at the same time known for his civic
virtue and his learning. Appointed judge of the Court of Requests in Calcutta,
he also served on the managing committees of both the Hindu College and the
Sanskrit College.

Rasamoy provided an English-medium education for his sons at the Hindu
College, where Govin studied under the tutelage of David Lester Richardson
(whose poems appear in this volume). There Govin and his brothers, cousins,
and nephews came under the spell of English poetry. Individually and collec-
tively, they composed numerous volumes of English language verse along with
novels and histories. Their joint literary enterprise is best symbolized by the
cover of *The Dutt Family Album,* published in London in 1870. The green cover with
gilt embossing depicts a cluster of three birds on branches intertwined with the
title design; a fourth bird perches just above them. Symbolically, the three
brothers—Govin, Hur, and Greece (their Anglicized names)—shared the anony-
mous authorship of the volume and are joined by their nephew Omesh. Of the
four authors, Omesh and Govin produced the lion's share of the contents. Ac-
cording to Romesh Chunder Dutt (another nephew, who wrote many volumes of
prose and verse), Govin wrote 66 of the 197 poems and Omesh produced 73.
There is, to my knowledge, no complete account of the authorship of each poem,
although the British Library does hold a copy whose contents has been anno-
tated, and Theodore Dunn in *The Bengali Book of English Verse* (1918) makes many
reliable attributions. Here I reproduce poems from the volume, noting, where
sources are reliable, the authorship of each.

The Dutt Family Album is prefaced by an anonymous statement in which the writer (I suspect Govin) declares that the authors are "foreigners, natives of India, of different ages, and in different walks of life, yet of one family, in whom the ties of blood relationship have been drawn closer by the holy bond of Christian brotherhood. As foreigners educated out of England, they solicit the indulgence of British critics to poems which on these grounds alone may, it is hoped, have some title to their attention." Here, the writer of the preface points to the peculiar position of his family, for the conversion of most of the extended family had been a matter of some note in Calcutta. It resulted in relative social isolation, particularly for the women of the family, some of whom (such as Govin's wife, Kshetramoni Mitter Dutt) became devout Christians.

Govin's conversion, his admiration of European poetry, his frustration at being passed over for advancement in his government post, and the early death of his only son prompted him to take his wife and daughters to Europe for an extended period, first to France and then to England. *The Dutt Family Album* was assembled during this period, and the poems it contains reflect the complex circumstances of the extended family. The family had perhaps intended to remain longer in Europe, but the illness of their elder daughter, Aru, precipitated a return to Bengal, where Aru and her sister, both of whom shared the family delight in poetry, died very young of tuberculosis. Both before and after her death, Govin saw to it that Toru's poetry was published in India and in Paris and London. In his later life, Govin served as honorary magistrate and a justice of the peace in Calcutta, and he and Kshetramoni engaged in various charitable works.

Sources

Poems are from *The Dutt Family Album* (London: Longmans, Green, 1870); attributions are the editor's, relying primarily on Harihar Das, *Life and Letters of Toru Dutt* (London: Humphrey Milford, Oxford University Press, 1921) and Theodore Douglas Dunn, *The Bengali Book of English Verse* (Bombay: Longmans, Green, 1918).

from *The Dutt Family Album*

Home

No picture from the master hand
    Of Gainsborough or Cuyp may vie
With that which at my soul's command
    Appears before mine inward eye
In foreign climes when doomed to roam—   5
Its scene my own dear native home.

What though no cloud—like hills uprear
    Their serried heights sublime afar!
What though the ocean be not near,
    With wave and wind in constant war!   10
Nor rock nor sea could add a grace,
So perfect seems the hallowed place.

Casuarinas[1] in solemn range
    At distance look like verdant hills,
And winds draw from them music strange,   15
    Such as the tide makes when it fills
Some shingle-strown and land-girt bay
From men and cities far away.

And round, as far as eye can reach
    What vivid piles of foliage green!   20
Mango and shaddock, plum and peach,
    And palms like pillars tall between:
An emerald sea surrounds the nest,
A sea for ever charmed in rest.

What roses blossom on the lawn!   25
    What warblers on the bamboo boughs,
Lithe and elastic, swing at dawn,
    And pour their orisons and vows!

---

1. Casuarina: evergreen tree native to Australasia, Southeast Asia, and the western Pacific, imported to Bengal in the nineteenth century. An evergreen, it is known for its feathery foliage and for the sound it makes in the wind, as it often thrives near the ocean. Toru Dutt's poem "Our Casuarina" is among her best known work.

What dew upon the greensward lies!
How lovingly look down the skies! 30

And at high noon when every tree
  Stands brooding on its round of shade,
And cattle to the shelter flee
  And there, in groups recumbent laid,
Gaze ruminant—what deep repose 35
Lies on the landscape as it glows!

But most at evening's gentle hour
  The reign of Peace is clearly read,—
In the blue mists which hail her power,
  Pavilions rich and banners spread,— 40
While 'mid the hush is heard the tone
Of night's sweet minstrel—hers alone.

As star by star leaps out above,
  As twilight deepens into night,
As round me cluster those I love, 45
  And eye meets eye in glances bright,
I feel that earth itself may be
Lit up with heaven's own radiancy.

[GOVIN CHUNDER DUTT]

Lines Written Some Time After

The glory of the scene hath fled,
  The light no more invests the place,
Wherefore appears thus nature dead?
  And whence the darkness on her face?
Where are the rainbow colours fair, 5
And the bright throne of Peace—oh, where?

Well said the poet when he sung
  'A kingdom is to me my mind,'[2]

---

2. "My mind to me a kingdom is" begins one of the most famous of Elizabethan lyrics, often attributed to Edward Dyer. It has been in print continuously since the late sixteenth century, when it appeared in William Byrd's *Psalmes, Sonets, and Songs*.

The shadow of one sorrow flung
    Athwart it, makes this change unkind.   10
Gone are those love-reflecting eyes
That made the scene a paradise.

Well, be it so. We have on earth
    No city for continuous stay;
As children of the second birth   15
    We seek another far away;
Nor, with our hands upon the plough,
Dare we look back and break our vow.

And is it sin to contemplate
    That when the final goal we gain   20
Some visions of this earthly state
    May full maturity attain,
The links now broken then be bound,
The pearls here scattered there be found?

        [GOVIN CHUNDER DUTT]

Wordsworth's Poems

(See Preface to The Excursion)

This volume is a Gothic church—no less,
    And every separate poem but a part
    Of a great edifice, built with rarest art,[3]
A cell, or oratory, or carved recess,
Or but a simple leaf—wreath winding round   5
    A marble pillar, in the sombre light,

---

3. Govin quotes the 1814 preface to Wordsworth's poem *The Excursion*, in which Wordsworth describes his previous and as yet unpublished poem, *The Prelude*, as an antechapel to the Gothic church that is *The Excursion*: "[T]he two Works have the same kind of relation to each other, if he may so express himself, as the ante-chapel has to the body of a Gothic church. Continuing this allusion, he may be permitted to add, that his minor Pieces, which have been long before the Public, when they shall be properly arranged, will be found by the attentive Reader to have such connection with the main Work as may give them claim to be likened to the little cells, oratories, and sepulchral recesses, ordinarily included in those edifices" (http://www.bartleby.com/145/ww397.html). By implication, the short poems of The Dutt Family Album are "little cells, oratories, and sepulchral recesses." Govin travels in his mind's eye to Wordsworth's Lake District, where he imagines its dominant peak, Helvellyn. There is no evidence that Govin ever actually managed to travel to Wordsworth country.

Or an emblazoned window flashing bright,
Fair in itself, but fairest where 'tis found;
Each delicately symmetrical—but the whole
Ravishing with loveliness the 'prisoned' soul.   10

The labour of a lifetime, and the work
    Of one inspired, the prophet of his age.
    What deep philosophy and experience sage
And tender sympathies here retired lurk
In simplest verses. Oh, beloved book!   15
    With thee and but one other, which to name
    Even with thee would matter be for blame,[4]
Contented could I glide o'er life's calm brook
Until it mingle with the mighty sea,
And time be swallowed in eternity.   20

Nor deem this praise extravagant or strange,
    For without travel here I have its joys,
    And sitting by my hearth where naught annoys,
O'er hills and oceans by these spells I range.
Is it not grand to see Helvellyn rear   25
    Its lofty summit to the azure sky,
    Or mark the lake below faint-gleaming lie,
A mirror for all objects far and near,
Bare rocks, and woods arrayed in vivid green,
And cheerful homesteads through the foliage seen?   30

And should an English landscape ever pall,
    With all its wide diversity of hills
    And trees and waters, lo! the fresh breeze fills
Our swelling canvas at the Poet's call!
Where shall we wander? In the fields of France?   35
    Or classic Italy's wave-saluted shores?
    Or dearer Scotland's barren heaths and moor
Or Staffa's natural temple,[5] where in trance
One shadowy beings may behold? Command,—
All wait the movement of the enchanter's wand.   40

---

4. Probably the Bible.
  5. Fingal's cave on the uninhabited island of Staffa in the Scottish Inner Hebrides was made famous by James McPherson in his pseudo-medieval Ossian poems, in which the eponymous Fingal is made a hero. The cave was visited by poets from Wordsworth onward and celebrated by the composer Felix Mendelssohn in his Hebridean Overture in 1829.

Hail, ye Rydalian laurels that have grown
    Untended by the Poet's calm abode,
    And in the footpaths that he often trod
Wrapt in deep thought, at evening time, alone.
No Delphic wreath he wanted, when he found   45
    Nature unveiled in all her loveliness;
    But these wild leaves and wilder flowers that bless
Our 'common earth' he prayed for, and she bound
His brows therewith; and see, they never fade,
A crown of amaranth by her own hands made.   50

        [GOVIN CHUNDER DUTT]

Lines (Written While on a Visit to Kalighat)

    They know full well that God hath said
        Thou shalt not bend in fear
    To stock, nor stone, nor carved thing,
    Nor ever to their altars bring
        The first fruits of the year.   5

    Still grim Idolatry with pomp,
        O'er India's realm doth reign;
    For still its fell and baneful power
    Is owned in palace, hut, and bower,
        In city, town, and plain.   10

    Where'er we turn we see them rise,
        Those temples huge and grand,
    To hideous idols consecrate:
    Alas for man's degraded state!
        Oh, woe to this fair land!   15

    But most they fear that goddess dread,
        Reeking with blood and wine,
    And prince and peasant trembling bring
    Their rich or humble offering
        To her ensanguined shrine.[6]   20

---

6. Kalighat: the most important temple in Calcutta, dedicated to the goddess Kali.

The farmer, ere he sallies forth
   To reap his waving field,
The diver, ere he goes to brave
The dangers of the treacherous wave,
   To her their homage yield.   25

The traveller, by his guide despoiled,
   Belated and betrayed,
As night with darkness brings despair
And unknown sounds are in the air,
   In awe invokes her aid.   30

Her dreaded name is shouted high
   Where deepens most the fray,
It nerves the warrior's wearied hand
To wield anew the flashing brand,
   And join the wild mêlée.   35

Great God, tho' *all* may not have heard,
   Still *many* know Thy name,
And tho' Thy bounties they receive,
Yet recklessly Thy path they leave,
   And glory in their shame.   40

Woe, woe to this devoted land,
   Woe to this erring race,
That thus the evil way they choose,
And with hard wilful hearts refuse
   Thy proffered Love and Grace.   45

But Thou art merciful, O Lord,
   And Thou alone canst save:
Oh, let the day-spring clear arise,
Oh, open Thou their blinded eyes,
   Send freedom to the slave.   50

[UNATTRIBUTED]

The Hindu Convert to His Wife

Nay, part not so—one moment stay,
    Repel me not with scorn.
Like others, wilt thou turn away,
    And leave me quite forlorn?
Wilt thou too join the scoffing crowd,   5
The cold, the heartless, and the proud,
    Who curse the hallowed morn,
When, daring idols to disown,
I knelt before the Saviour's throne?

It was not thus, in former hours,   10
    We parted or we met;
It was not thus, when Love's young flowers
    With hope and joy were wet.
That kindling cheek, averted eye,
That heaving breast and stifled sigh,   15
    Attest thy feelings yet.
It was not thus, reserved and cold,
Like strangers, that we met of old.

Remember, love, thy sacred vow,
    Ah, once so dear to thee!   20
Then part, as thou wert parting now:
    Then—then abandon me.
Remember how we often strayed,
Cheek touching cheek, where none surveyed
    Beneath the banyan tree;   25
And swore (Love witnessed us) to bide,
In life or death, still side by side.

Canst thou forget the grief and joy,
    In fond affection shared,
The day that beamed upon our boy,   30
    The brief months he was spared
To bless us with his cheering light:
The sullen, rayless, stormy night,
    When Death his weapon bared,
And laid beneath his savage blow   35
Our fondest hopes and wishes low?

Canst thou forget how, sick and sad,
  We sauntered by the stream,
Which o'er its pebbles murmured glad
  Beneath the lunar beam? 40
Canst thou forget how, all apart,
We heard each other's beating heart,
  And summoned many a dream,
Too bright, too beautiful to last,
Back from the dim and shrouded past? 45

O ever-drooping eyes, whose glance
  May lions wild subdue!
O star-crowned forehead's meek expanse!
  O lips of coral hue!
O sable locks, that shade and deck 50
The marble of the swan-like neck,
  Can ye continue true
While feelings change, and, tempest-tost,
Love strives awhile, and then is lost?

When others blamed, I was not grieved; 55
  At others' scoff or jeer
My passive bosom never heaved,
  Nor shed mine eyes a tear.
But thou, so trusted, cherished, proved,
So loving, and so dearly loved; 60
  Thou, too, alas! to veer.
This scarce my swelling heart can bear,
This—this must drive me to despair!

Yet better thus;—the sinner's tear
  Will reach the Holy throne, 65
Though he may meet no kindness here,
  And weep—apart—alone.
When e'en a sparrow cannot fall
Unmarked by Him that cares for all,
  Will He not guard His own? 70
Friends may desert and foes oppress,
But He assuredly will bless.

At morn or eve whene'er I bend
  In grateful love the knee,

The words with swiftest wings ascend   75
    That form my prayer for thee.
May He whose accents raised the dead,
Who shone in darkness, and it fled,
    Thy Guide and Guardian be,
And kindling in thy breast the flame.   80
Constrain thee, love, to bless His Name.

[GOVIN CHUNDER DUTT]

The Hindu Wife to Her Husband

An English lady, visiting an odalisque, in-
quired what pleasure her profusion of rich
ornaments could afford, as no person ex-
cept her husband was ever to behold them.
'And for whom,' replied the fair barbarian,
'do you adorn yourself?—is it for other
men?'—The Crescent and the Cross.

I

Oh, not for strangers do I wear
The jewels in my flowing hair,
Nor yet for others' eyes array
My limbs in vestments rich and gay:
Nor wish that even friends should see,   5
The smile that's only meant for thee.

From pleasures of this life debarred,
They tell me that my lot is hard,
That, forc'd like prison'd bird to pine,
Such joys as theirs can ne'er be mine;   10
That beauty, wit, and gems are vain
If hidden they must thus remain.

They tell me that in festal hall,
To be admired and prais'd by all,
To feel one's self—O triumph high!—   15
The cynosure of every eye,
The fairest of the fair to be:
This, this is life,—bright, glad, and free.

From such advice I turn away,
It only serves to lead astray: 20
The dance, the crowd, are not for me,
I envy not their liberty:—
Happy as queen upon her throne,
I love to dwell among mine own.

Is there no peace for them at home,   25
That restless here and there they roam?
And are they of their lords so tired,
That they should seek to be admired
By friends and strangers? Thus can they
Mid dance, and song, and jest, be gay?   30

For thee alone, my love, I wear
The jewels in my flowing hair,
For thee the glance, for thee the smile,
For thee this heart which knows no guile:—
And blest, supremely blest I'll be   35
With one kind word and look from thee.

[OMESH CHUNDER DUTT]

The Caves of Elephanta

Across the harbour we gaily sped,
    The white waves laughing round our prow,
Serenest skies hung overhead,
    And joy sat throned on every brow.

Hills after hills on all sides rose,   5
    A dreary mountain scenery;
No trees but stunted shrubs disclose
    The region's stern sterility.

Sometimes a lonely mosque we past,
    At distance white as ocean-foam;   10
And once a pile of buildings vast,
    With an immense far-gleaming dome.

Till having reached the loneliest spot,
  We leapt upon the yellow sand,
And wandered up—the Caves we sought,   15
  The wonder of this wondrous land.[7]

A sudden turn displayed to sight
  A lofty staircase made of stone,
Part basking in meridian light,
  And part in sombre shadow thrown.   20

High up it went—and higher still,
  Receding far and farther yet:
Are fairies dwellers on this hill?
  A sight of fairies shall we get?

In sooth, no wonder had it been   25
  To see one stand on every stair,
And on the top a fairy queen
  With diamonds in her floating hair.

Up, up we went till tired—at last
  A terrace through the brambles gleams,   30
And then in all their grandeur vast
  The caves—surpassing all our dreams.

O lofty pillars from the rock,
  The solid rock cut out, that bear
The ponderous roof, and mind no shock   35
  Of elements, but their fury dare!

O lions guarding inner shrines
  For ages with a gaze sublime!
O walls where sunlight never shines
  That mock the ruthless hand of time!   40

O cistern that hast ever owned
  The purest waters maids may draw!

---

7. The Caves of Elephanta: located on an island in Bombay harbor, the caves are beautiful rock-cut temples (dating from the fifth to eighth centuries) dedicated to Shiva. Elephanta is now a UNESCO world heritage site. Govin might have visited the caves when he moved his family south shortly after their conversion to Christianity, but I have found no certain attribution of the poem.

O images of gods dethroned
    That chill the gazer's heart with awe!

Speak, for ye can, who reared these halls,   45
    What strange mutations they have seen,
Reveal a mystery that appals,
    And tell us all that here hath been.

Speak, for ye can, with what a pomp
    The rites inaugural were held,   50
With sound of fife and drum and tromp
    And incantations darkly spelled.

Speak, for ye can, what thousands came
    In worship here to bow the knee,
While altars blazed with bickering flame   55
    And blood of victims bubbled free.

Speak, for ye can, what priests in bands,
    What statesmen with their thoughtful brows,
What travellers from distant lands,
    And maids with gifts, here paid their vows.   60

Speak, for ye can, at dead of night
    What prayers and hymns rose hence to powers
That quench the spirit's conscience light,
    The noblest of our earthly dowers.

Speak, for ye can—all silent still!   65
    The past remains a mystery,
And shall remain, for 'tis His will:
    What He conceals no man may see.

Only this much may fancy guess—
    Perchance the king whose mandate made   70
The wonder in the wilderness,
    When it was finished, proudly said:

'Is not this Babylon the great
    That I have reared in strength of power
To show my majesty and state?'   75
    The doom went forth that very hour.

And now the remnants—Pride—behold!
    A lonely wilderness again.
Where are the gems and cloth of gold?
    Where is the king and all his train?   80

The guns of Portugal have done
    Their shattering work amid these gods;[8]
The banyan lo! a niche hath won,
    And to the south wind's whisper nods;

The snails on Brahma's forehead crawl,   85
    The blind-worms dwell in Siva's eye,
On Durga's cheek the raindrops fall,—
    Or are they tears for days gone by?

On breasts no Bramin's hand might soil
    Each upstart stranger writes his name: 90
Such the result of earthly toil,
    And such the end of human fame.

[UNATTRIBUTED]

---

8. Bombay was in the hands of the Portuguese for some years beginning in 1534; it was leased to the British East India Company in 1668.

To Lord Canning

Though a thousand pens condemned thee, mine still should write thy praise;
Though a thousand tongues reviled thee, mine still should paeans raise;
For factious clamours heeding not, that only call for blood,
True to thy duty and thy race, Lord Canning, thou hast stood.[9]

What is the meed of thy deserts? Let history blush to tell!   5
A foul memorial of recall sent o'er the ocean's swell;
And from the press—a press, alas! long held in honour too—
The daily sneer for justice done, as God hath taught to do!

Is this the meed of thy deserts? No, no, it cannot be,
All England's best and noblest are heart and soul with thee!   10
And India's swarthy children, from hill and field and town,
Lift up the voice with one acclaim, and blessings summon down.

And the next age—shall it not hear, with wonder and with awe,
How amidst rancour, hate, and strife, thou sternly gavest the law?
'He governed all alike'—'twill say—'all races and all creeds,   15
He judged not men by skin or faith, he judged them by their deeds.'

And the next life? Is there not one when God shall judge us all,
The peasant from his cottage and the ruler from his hall?
Then who shall justified appear, and who shall win the crown?
The man that strove for duty, or the man that sought renown?   20

All that a bold wise heart can do—all that a righteous may,
Was done the bursting storm to quell in India's evil day!
But a heavy task is still on hand, for an omniscient God
Hath women's blood and children's seen run reeking on the sod.

Yes, a heavy task remains behind—a 'burden's laid on thee,'   25
Thou hast been chosen Minister—such is thy destiny;

---

9. Charles John Canning (1812–1862), Viscount Canning, was the governor-general and then viceroy of India. Although his policies in Oudh (Avadh) helped precipitate the rebellion of 1857, he refused to countenance summary execution and other indignities perpetrated against the native inhabitants during and after the uprising. Although he saw to it that the rebellion was put down, his resistance to British jingoism and hunger for revenge earned him the contemptuous nickname "Clemency Canning." Canning's sense of justice is celebrated here.

Oh, pray—for highest counsel pray!—of such shalt thou have need,
For 'vengeance is a fearful thing'—and vengeance is decreed.

Strike thou and home, but not in wrath—fulfil a high command;
Avenging angels weep to smite a sin-o'erburdened land: 30
Strike, mourning, at the word of God, and hold at His behest
These words in water are not writ—'The merciful are blest.'[10]

It is not for her trampled flag that England bares her sword;
It is not for a just revenge upon a murderous horde;
It is to prove to blood-stained men, self-blinded of their sight,   35
That evil hath no chance with good or darkness with the light.

But guiltless blood, where'er it flows, in black or white men's veins,
Is precious in the sight of Him who trieth heart and reigns;
Oh, watch it be not shed in vain!—Oh, act as heretofore!
And let a wreath-encircled name one priceless wreath have more.   40

[GOVIN CHUNDER DUTT]

---

10. Govin quotes the Beatitudes: "Blessed are the merciful, for they shall obtain mercy"
(Matthew 5:7).

Mary Seyers Carshore

ORN IN Calcutta to Irish Catholic parents, Mary Seyers (1829–1857)
lived all her life in Bengal and the North West Provinces (now Uttar
Pradesh) and was educated mostly at home. She published only one vol-
ume of verse in her lifetime. Such biographical information as we have comes
from the preface to the second edition of the volume, *Songs of the East*, which was
written by her still-grieving sister more than ten years after Mary Carshore's
death at Jhansi in the uprising of 1857. Carshore's poetry was informed by—and
responded critically to—the dominant trends of late romanticism and the tropes
of an Anglo-Indian poetry of exile.

Mary Seyers's father was an official in the East India Company's opium ser-
vice; he was posted from Calcutta to the vicinity of Fatehpur Sikri (near Agra)
while she was still a child. At this point, Fatehpur would have felt rather remote
from the centers of British culture in India, and Mary's sister makes clear that
the girls were educated at home in a traditionally genteel way. Their access to
books came largely by mail from Calcutta, but evidently their mother managed to
share a strong love of poetry with her children. Like most Anglo-Indian women
of her time, Mary had no formal training in Indian vernaculars or Indian or
European classical languages; nonetheless, her poems reveal avid attention to
the latest poems from London and a delight in Indian vernacular songs. Brought
up to middle-class accomplishments, Mary seems even from childhood to have
played the guitar and to have composed her own songs.

In her teens, Mary spent one year at the newly founded school for girls run by
the nuns of Loretto Convent in Calcutta. After some months, her sister reports,
she fell ill and was taken home by her mother. Subsequently, the girls' mother
returned to Calcutta with her daughters, perhaps to separate Mary from an un-
suitable attachment or to provide eligible suitors for her daughters, or both. At
any rate, in her sister's words, Mary, though having many admirers, could not
"easily forget the name of one, whom obedience to a father's stern decree alone
had caused her to give up" ("Memoir," v). Mary evidently did not find a suitable
partner in Calcutta, and to make matters worse, on their return to Fatehpur the
family found that their house had burned. The Hindoo College at Benares, hear-
ing of their loss, commissioned several portraits from her father, and in subse-
quent months Mary assisted him with these paintings.

On April 8, 1850, at the age of twenty-one, Mary Seyers married William Samuel Carshore. She probably wed despite her family's objections, for Mary's sister observes that events proved that their father had been wise to oppose the match. At the time of their marriage, William Carshore was a collector of customs in salt and was known for his extravagant living. In the memoir, we are told that through clever management Mary managed to pay off her husband's debts in two years. She and William had several children, including an eldest son, Clarence, who was born while his father was on trial for an unspecified crime, of which he was, in the end, acquitted. Clarence's death in infancy and the subsequent move to Jhansi are recorded in Mary's elegiac poem, "To Clarence in His Grave."

In the years immediately after her marriage, Carshore prepared her first volume of poems for the press; the volume was printed under the name Mrs. W. S. Carshore in 1855. In prefacing the volume, she at once protested her diffidence and expressed her confidence in her work. Referring to herself, as was customary, in the third person, she wrote, "Born and reared on Indian soil, she cannot boast an extensive or intimate acquaintance with the literature of the West, and her only object in publishing the following tales and songs has been, to give a more correct idea of native customs and manners, than she has yet observed Europeans to possess, seconded of course by that instinctive thirst for fame implanted in the human breast. This acknowledgement she trusts will disarm the severity of those who might otherwise be disposed to be too critical."

In fact, the volume was reviewed positively in Calcutta, with the exception of a critical review by David Lester Richardson, who seems to have taken offense that Carshore dared to criticize Tom Moore, the Irish poet, correcting his idea of "native customs and manners." Though the volume of poems takes on traditional orientalist tropes and the Anglo-Indian trope of exile, the poems cannot be easily assimilated to either, for Carshore claims local knowledge, a knowledge that is implicitly gendered and experiential. The poet, for example, refuses an identification with Ireland for herself, though she acknowledges the importance of rural Ireland for her father's imagination; similarly, rather than speaking of herself as an exile, she makes common cause with Letitia Landon, mourning Landon's trampled grave in western Africa and implying that both she and Landon are neglected poets of empire.

Carshore's sister makes clear that Mary was preparing additional poems for the press at the time of her death. As fears mounted during the early days of the Indian uprising of 1857, Carshore wrote to a friend saying that she had buried her volume, her "undying child," in her garden. The poet's foresight, or foreboding, was fulfilled when a few weeks later she was among the Europeans assembled in the fort at Jhansi. Here, in one of the most famous or infamous moments of the rebellion, the Europeans who had negotiated a safe passage from the besieged fort to the river were all massacred en route. Mary's sister prefaced the second edition of Carshore's poems with an anguished account of her death. Like the other European women at Jhansi, Mary witnessed the murder of her husband and then her children before she was killed. Her sister writes, "How she stood and uttered no cry, and sought no means of escape, unless she was bound, is to me a mystery, knowing her energetic, impulsive character, and her deep, tender, yearning love for her darlings. But suffice it to say they were all murdered and then thrown into a well" (xvi).

In concluding her memoir, Carshore's sister quoted the judgment of a mutual friend: "Those who criticize her books should rather dwell on what such a talented woman might have become, with opportunities and education, than on what she was" (xviii). Despite her limited opportunities for study and travel and despite her early death, Mary Seyers Carshore managed to create a poetry unique in its attempt to depict the domestic life, the actual "customs and manners," of provincial Anglo-India.

Sources

Mary Carshore [Mrs. W. S. Carshore], *Songs of the East* (Calcutta: D'Rozario, 1855), 2nd ed. (Calcutta: Englishman Press, 1871). 1871 edition contains her sister's memoir of Mary Carshore's life.

Parrot of the Far Land

Hindoostanee Song, Translated to the Original Air

From crystal founts I'll give thee drink,
    Where many a rosy garland
Hangs o'er the green and grassy brink,
    O Parrot of the far land!
O Parrot of the far land!   5

I'll give thee food and liberty
    To soar in yon blue-star land,
O Parrot of the far land!

If thou tell me where he strays,
    And why his footsteps wander,   10
Whose weary ways and sad delays
    Have made this heart grow fonder.
O Parrot of the far land!

Bridal Song

The sounds of the tasa[1] are telling
    The hour of the bridal is come;
The notes of the marfa[2] are swelling
    To welcome the bride to her home.

The "nowbut"[3] is now celebrating   5
    The names of the new-wedded pair;
The silver mohaffas[4] are waiting,
    The day is propitious and fair.

The mehndee[5] is fresh in its blossom,
    The roses are sweet for thy bosom;   10
Then cull them while bright, and prepare thee tonight,
    And steep thy white robes in the cussoom.[6]

Thou askest the stars what they fate thee,
    I ask them thy features, my bride!
Perhaps I may see thee, to hate thee,[7]   15
The moment we meet shall decide.

What is it to love and adore?
    I never loved woman before;
O! thine be the duty, with goodness and beauty,
    To teach me that holiest lore.   20

---

1. "Tasa" is a musical instrument formed of an earthen vessel with goat or other skin drawn over the face of it, to answer the purpose of a drum. [MSC]

2. "Marfa." A similar instrument of a large kind. [MSC]

3. "Nowbut." A complete band. [MSC]

4. "Mohaffa." A species of litter for carrying a bride. [MSC]

5. "Mehndee." Henna or Indian myrtle. [MSC]

6. "Cussoom." Safflower. [MSC]

7. It so often happens that the bridegroom having fondly pictured to himself a lovely being whom he is about to behold his own, is presented with an ugly or deformed woman, older than himself. This is not unfrequently the case when bribery has been resorted [to,] to induce the matchmakers to give a favorable misrepresentation of a long unmarried daughter. Such a disappointment must naturally lead to unhappiness and dislike. When the pair however are betrothed in childhood, while the girl is not yet subjected to rigid confinement, the boy has a chance of forming a correct judgement of the kind of wife he has to expect. These marriages are generally more fortunate. [MSC]

Here Carshore takes a very different tack from the usual missionary objection to child marriage.

But away with doubt, sorrow, and care,
  Good omens the Brahmins declare:
The Fates have relented—the stars have consented;
  The day is propitious and fair.

Bridal Song

Translated to the Original Air

May the hour of marriage be happy and blest,
Blessed and happy, and happy and blest;
May the hour of marriage be happy and blest;
May its brightness be seen like the east in the west.
  May the hour of marriage, &c.   5

Long may thy smile, fairest bride! beam with gladness,
Long be all joy near thee, far from thee sadness,
Be thou happy and blest.
  May the hour of marriage, &c.

Song

Translation

At first how fondly didst thou love me, dearest!
  At first how fondly, dearest, didst thou love!
The stars bear witness far above thee, dearest!
  The stars bear witness, dearest, far above!

But, when this captive heart was fettered to thee,   5
  Thy love how quickly didst thou disavow!
And now, alas! it is my lot to woo thee,
  And it is thine, love! to disdain me now.
At first how fondly didst thou, &c.

The Ivied Harp

The cord that rung sweetly, has ceased to ring,
The cold blast of sorrows has severed the string;
The harp that sung softly hangs mute by the deep:
The stern voice of anguish has hushed it to sleep.
Around and around it the ivy has clung,   5
Yet silent it hangs there, untuned and unstrung;
O! where is the minstrel who tuned it before
To magical numbers?—speak Africa's shore,
For there unremembered the Poet is laid:[8]
No marble to cover, no willow to shade,   10
Untombed and exposed to fierce Africa's ray,
Is the spot where reposes her hallowed clay.
She sleeps there, afar from the land of her birth,
In a grave scarce distinguished from the commonest earth;
Scarce marked, save alone by a rude level plot,   15
Laid with coarse earthen tiles to discover the spot;
Intersecting the beaten and narrow bye-way,
Where feet undiverted tread o'er it each day;
Round the name of the minstrel while laurel leaves wave,
Rude strangers profanely are trampling her grave.   20
Long years have rolled o'er her, with sunshine and rain,
But the voices of spring cannot wake her again;
It is well, for again could the minstrel awake
To behold the unkindness her heartstrings would break.
But the spirit is departed of heavenly flame,   25
Whose halo illumined the temple of fame,
To regions from whence it can never return,
Neglect as ye will the cold dust of the urn.
Then rest secure, England! thy accuser is far,
Even her ashes repose 'neath a strange foreign star,   30
Then rest thee unquestioned, there's none to upbraid thee,
Since they dare not to tell thee the things that degrade thee,
The living thou feedest with vain empty breath,
And 'tis thus thou rewardest thy children in death.

---

8. This alludes to the grave of L.E.L. [Letitia Elizabeth Landon] which lies sadly neglected, and
I have not a whit exaggerated a description I read of it lately given by a visitor at the Cape. [MSC]
Letitia Landon (L.E.L., 1802–38) was a famous and highly successful English poet, reviewer, and
editor of annuals. She died in mysterious circumstances of an overdose of prussic acid at Cape
Coast Castle, West Africa, a few months after her marriage to George Maclean, who was then gov-
ernor of the outpost. The inquest was hurried, according to press reports, and Landon was buried
under the pavers in the courtyard of the fortress.

To Clarence in His Grave

Ah! did I ever dream,
    While thou wert with me shedding light and bliss
In every tender gleam,
    Of thy dear eyes, in every infant kiss.

Did I then dream that we   5
    Should quit that home thou mad'st bright, to find
Another far from thee
    More blest, and that thou should'st be left behind,

Be left behind alone
    To slumber on that solitary plain,   10
With but a sculptured stone
    Upon thy breast to tell where thou art lain.

O Hermit, sleeping there
    Beneath the solid house that stands above,
Whose dwelling none may share,   15
    Except the ghost of fond maternal love.

What tho' removed so far,
    My spirit haunts that sacred spot,
There memory's treasures are
    Too dearly valued to be e'er forgot.   20

And tho' I may not steep
    Thy urn with tears of grief o'er past delight,
Around it still I creep
    In dreams and waking fancies of the night.

I see the slender grass   25
    Around thy sepulchre still sigh and wave,
More blest than I, alas!
    To sigh beside thy solitary grave.

I see across the sky
    The bending trees their branches o'er thee stoop,   30
More privileged than I,
    Above thy silent tomb they still can droop.

I see the earth where lie
　　Thy precious relics in their sacred rest,
Ah! happier far than I,   35
　　It still can hold thee on its parent breast.

Poetical Letter to Mrs. V...

I greet you, lady. I received
Your missive, which hath much relieved
My mind of doubts, that you were nought
But some fair myth by fancy wrought.
Is it true then, and can it be,   5
That earth contains a soul like thee?
Alas! so very like a dream
Thy coming and departure seem.
I almost fear that some rude hand
Will wake me from a happy sleep,   10
And truth, at reason's stern command,
Dispel the visions I would keep.
But then I cast my eyes around,
And there, upon the abandoned ground,
Are traces of the vanished tent   15
Whereon my thoughtful gaze is bent.
And, searching inward, there I find
Some jewels thou hast left behind,
High thoughts and holy words that dwell
Within my bosom cherished well.   20
That more than outward marks to me
Attest the fond reality,
Thou art no fancied shape of dreams
To vanish with the morning gleams;
No bright, illusive beau ideal,   25
But loving, true, unchanged and real;
And I shall see thee yet again
To know and love thee better then;
O my dear Lady,—writing dear,
My heart cries dearest low and clear,   30
But then 'tis always best to show
Less than is felt,—than once to know,

You feel not half of what you say,
O my dear Lady, therefore, pray,
Think of me sometimes as you may,   35
And when your nightly prayer is given,
Repeat my lowly name to heaven,
Thus wilt thou, when at closing day
Thy better thoughts resume their sway,
Think of me, tho' I merit not   40
From thee—from any one—a thought,
For I with traits of good and ill,
And all my faults, I love thee still;
And will, tho' fate and distance sever,
Affectionately yours, be ever   45
       Mary Carshore.

Song

Translation

Go where the streamlet is gracefully wending,
Go where the waters are breaking and blending;
     Thy home is afar, girl!
      Away from the river,
      And yonder's a star girl!   5
      Beginning to quiver;
Then hasten away, girl, away from the river!
Haste from the streamlet that's gracefully wending,
Haste from the waters dividing and blending;
     Thy vases of water   10
      Are over full, maiden
     Thy slender waist, daughter,
      Bends thrice over-laden;
Then haste from the river away, gentle maiden.

To Annie

I met thee in the festive hall,
The lamps were bright upon the wall;
But O! the light of beauty's glance,
That flashed at moments thro' the dance,
    Outshone them all, outshone them all.   5

And yet amidst a scene so fair,
Where love met beauty everywhere,
Why didst thou then appear to me,
With thy mild placid brow to be
    The brightest there, the brightest there?   10

I met thee in each humbler call
Of life, and then, methought, the ball
Flung not around thee charms so sweet,
As thus amidst the good to meet
    Thee best of all, thee best of all.   15

It was not beauty's short control,
It was the sweetness of thy soul
Which shed a more enduring grace;
Not o'er thy eyes, not o'er thy face,
    But round the whole, but round the whole.   20

Lines to a Withered Shamrock

"O say, thou withered leaf and sear,
    "Where sprang thy parent stem?
"On what sweet shore did'st thou appear
    A green and living gem?

"What field or hedge did'st thou adorn,   5
    "O poet's hallowed leaf?
"In what wild meadow wast thou born,
    "Or proud domain of chief?"

"Upon a Western Island fair,
    "Old ocean's brightest gem,   10

"I sprang to breathe the forest air
    "Upon my parent stem."

"How cam'st thou hither, withered leaf,
    "Across the rolling sea?
"A messenger of joy or grief   15
    "Hast thou been sent to be?

"Frail traveler of the watery waste,
    "With spells of memory fraught,
"O'er deserts wild, o'er oceans traced,
    "What errand hast thou brought?"   20

"A sister culled me for her prize
    "On Erin's sainted shore;
"The tears that filled her deep blue eyes
    "Were almost rolling o'er.

"She sent me to beguile and cheer   25
    "An exile's pilgrimage;
"And like a seal affixed me here
    "Upon her written page.

"I've told the exile's heart a tale
    "Of childhood's fields and flowers;   30
"I've told him of his native vale,
    "And of his boyhood's hours.

"The music of the lark and thrush,
    "His own loved Island tongue,
"Have in one wild melodious gush   35
    "Fond memory's echoes rung.

"The violet's scented breath I bade
    "To sweep across his soul;
"The voices of his home I made
    "Around his heart to roll.   40

"I've told him that unchanged and true
    "Are those he left behind;
"His native breeze around him blew
    "And bore him there in mind.

"I've shown him where his childhood played,   45
          "Each field and glen and hill;
"The dim and fragrant hawthorn shade,
          "The lane unaltered still.

"I've brought unto his face a smile,
          "And gladness to his heart;   50
"And taught him to forget the while
          "An exile's weary part."

"O blessed art thou, thou withered leaf.
          "Thy mission pure and high;
"And tho' thy verdant bloom were brief,   55
          "Thou'lt live when others die."

Sir Edwin Arnold

⁀

E DWIN ARNOLD (1832–1904), an indefatigable writer and editor, was best
known for his poetic re-creation of the life of the Buddha, *The Light of Asia*,
and for his enterprise as a newspaper editor who sponsored reporting
expeditions around the globe. During the period of his greatest productivity as a
poet, Arnold wrote more than six thousand leading articles for the *Daily Telegraph*.
As chief editor of that paper from 1873, he dispatched reporters on numerous
expeditions, including most famously the joint effort with the *New York Herald* that
sent Henry Morton Stanley to Africa.

Unlike many poets we might properly think of as Anglo-Indian in the Victo-
rian sense—poets who were born in or spent the majority of their lives in India—
Arnold lived only briefly on the subcontinent. He spent five years in India
(1857–61) as principal of the Deccan Sanskrit College in Pune. There he studied
Indian languages, including Sanskrit and Persian, though he never claimed for
himself a mastery of the languages that his biographers have since claimed for
him. Undoubtedly Indian culture had a profound influence on Arnold, and it
was by allying that influence with an earlier interest in poetry that he produced
his most famous work.

Arnold's accomplishments as a poet began while he was still a young student.
He earned a scholarship to University College, Oxford, where he graduated B.A.
in 1854 and M.A. in 1856. At the beginning of his university career he won the
Newdigate prize for his poem "The Feast of Belshazzar." His *Poems Narrative and
Lyrical* was published in Oxford in 1853.

Years later, Arnold achieved his greatest success with *The Light of Asia* (1879)
which went into many editions in Britain and America and was translated into
numerous languages. This work, with its implicit endorsement of Buddhist
views, aroused great enthusiasm and provoked great hostility. One critic called
Arnold a "poetizer and paganizer." To quell such criticism, the poet endeavored
a parallel volume on the life of Jesus, which he called *The Light of the World* (1891).
It was on all accounts a failure, and perhaps for that reason Arnold returned to
translation. Arnold's versified life of the Buddha had been preceded by a volume
of Sanskrit translations, *The Indian Song of Songs: From the Sanskrit of the Gîta Govinda of
Jayadeva* (1875). *The Light of Asia* was followed by an additional volume of transla-
tions or transcreations, *Indian Idylls, from the Sanskrit* (1883).

The *Indian Song of Songs* and *The Light of Asia* were intended by their author as part of a trilogy—expounding the beauties of Hinduism, Buddhism, and Islam. The third volume in this endeavor appeared in 1883 as *Pearls of the Faith; or, Islam's Rosary, Being the Ninety-Nine Beautiful Names of Allah (Asmâ-el-husnâ) with Comments in Verse from Various Oriental Sources (As Made by an Indian Mussulman)*. Arnold's long title reveals much about his "poetizing" and "paganizing" strategies, for he often takes on an "Oriental" persona, surrounding translated passages with poetry supposed to be by a practitioner of the religion in question. He sums up his approach in the preface to *Pearls of the Faith*: "I have thus at length finished the Oriental Trilogy which I designed. In my 'Indian Song of Songs' I sought to transfer to English poetry a subtle and lovely Sanskrit idyll of the Hindoo theology. In my 'Light of Asia' I related the story and displayed the gentle and far-reaching doctrines of that great Hindoo prince who founded Buddhism. I have tried to present here, in the simple, familiar, and credulous, but earnest spirit and manner of Islam— and from its own points of view—some of the thoughts and beliefs of the followers of the noble Prophet of Arabia."

Arnold's global—if imperialist—sensibility is indicated in his personal life. He was twice widowed and three times married—to a British woman, to an American woman, and to a Japanese woman. His later efforts include a prose work, *East and West* (1891), presenting a positive view of Japan. He was made companion in the Order of the Star of India upon Victoria's being proclaimed empress of India, and the king of Siam awarded him the order of the White Elephant to honor his contributions to the appreciation of Buddhism.

Sources

Edwin Arnold, *The Light of Asia; or, The Great Renunciation (Mahâbinishkramana)* (London: Longmans, Green, 1891). See also Arnold, *Pearls of the Faith* (London: Trübner, 1883); and J. P. Phelan, "Arnold, Sir Edwin (1832–1904)," in *ODNB*.

from *The Light of Asia, Book the Sixth*

But Buddh heeded not,[1]
Sitting serene, with perfect virtue walled
As is a stronghold by its gates and ramps;
Also the Sacred Tree—the Bôdhi-tree—

---

1. This passage records the Buddha's enlightenment. It follows a lengthy account of the Buddha's meditation under the bodhi tree, during which he defeats Mara, the lord of the world. In defeating Mara, the Buddha has defeated death.

Amid that tumult stirred not, but each leaf   5
Glistened as still as when on moonlit eves
No zephyr spills the glittering gems of dew;
For all this clamour raged outside the shade
Spread by those cloistered stems:
                    In the third watch,—   10
The earth being still, the hellish legions fled,
A soft air breathing from the sinking moon—
Our Lord attained *Sammâ-sambuddh;*[2] he saw,
By light which shines beyond our mortal ken,
The line of all his lives in all the worlds,   15
Far back, and farther back, and farthest yet,
Five hundred lives and fifty. Even as one,
At rest upon a mountain-summit, marks
His path wind up by precipice and crag,
Past thick-set woods shrunk to a patch; through bogs   20
Glittering false-green; down hollows where he toiled
Breathless; on dizzy ridges where his feet
Had well-nigh slipped; beyond the sunny lawns,
The cataract, and the cavern, and the pool,
Backward to those dim flats wherefrom he sprang   25
To reach the blue; thus Buddha did behold
Life's upward steps long-linked, from levels low
Where breath is base, to higher slopes and higher
Whereon the ten great Virtues[3] wait to lead
The climber skyward. Also, Buddha saw   30
How new life reaps what the old life did sow;
How where its march breaks off its march begins;
Holding the gain and answering for the loss;
And how in each life good begets more good,
Evil fresh evil; Death but casting up   35
Debit or credit, whereupon th' account
In merits or demerits stamps itself
By sure arithmic—where no tittle drops—
Certain and just, on some new-springing life;
Wherein are packed and scored past thoughts and deeds,   40
Strivings and triumphs, memories and marks
Of lives foregone:
            And in the middle watch

---

2. Sammâ-sambuddh: *samma-sambodhi* (the Pali term) is the full or perfect enlightenment at-
tained by the Buddha.

3. Ten great Virtues: the Pāramitās or Pāramīs, also known as the ten perfections. These are the
ten virtuous qualities that are said to lead to Buddhahood.

Our Lord attained *Abhidjna*[4]—insight vast
Hanging beyond this sphere to spheres unnamed,   45
System on system, countless worlds and suns
Moving in splendid measures, band by band
Linked in division, one, yet separate,
The silver islands of a sapphire sea
Shoreless, unfathomed, undiminished, stirred   50
With waves which roll in restless tides of change.
He saw those Lords of Light who hold their worlds
By bonds invisible, how they themselves
Circle obedient round mightier orbs
Which serve profounder splendours, star to star   55
Flashing the ceaseless radiance of life
From centres ever shifting unto cirques
Knowing no uttermost. These he beheld
With unsealed vision, and of all those worlds,
Cycle on epicycle, all their tale   60
Of Kalpas, Mahakalpas—terms of time
Which no man grasps, yea, though he knew to count
The drops in Gunga from her springs to the sea,
Measureless unto speech—whereby these wax
And wane; whereby each of this heavenly host   65
Fulfils its shining life and darkling dies.
Sakwal by Sakwal,[5] depths and heights he passed
Transported through the blue infinitudes,
Marking—behind all modes, above all spheres,
Beyond the burning impulse of each orb—   70
That fixed decree at silent work which wills
Evolve the dark to light, the dead to life,
To fulness void, to form the yet unformed,
Good unto better, better unto best,
By wordless edict; having none to bid,   75
None to forbid; for this is past all gods,
Immutable, unspeakable, supreme;
A Power which builds, unbuilds, and builds again,
Ruling all things accordant to the rule
Of virtue, which is beauty, truth, and use: 80
So that all things do well which serve the Power,
And ill which hinder; nay, the worm does well

---

4. Abhidjna (abhijñā): extraordinary knowledge or insight.

5. Sakwals (cakkavāḷaṃ): world systems, vast circular planes covered with water in the center of which stands Mount Meru. Each system has its own sun and moon. They exist in infinite numbers.

Obedient to its kind; the hawk does well
Which carries bleeding quarries to its young;
The dewdrop and the star shine sisterly   85
Globing together in the common work;
And man who lives to die, dies to live well
So if he guide his ways by blamelessness
And earnest will to hinder not but help
All things both great and small which suffer life.   90
These did our Lord see in the middle watch.

    But when the fourth watch came, the secret came
Of Sorrow, which with evil mars the law,
As damp and dross hold back the goldsmith's fire.
Then was the Dukha-Satya[6] opened him   95
First of the "Noble Truths"; how Sorrow is
Shadow to life, moving where life doth move;
Not to be laid aside until one lays
Living aside, with all its changing states,
Birth, growth, decay, love, hatred, pleasure, pain,   100
Being and doing. How that none strips off
These sad delights and pleasant griefs who lacks
Knowledge to know them snares; but he who knows
Avidya—Delusion—sets those snares,
Loves life no longer but ensues escape.   105
The eyes of such a one are wide, he sees
Delusion breeds Sankhâra,[7] Tendency
Perverse; Tendency Energy—Vidnnân—
Whereby comes Namarûpa, local Form
And Name and Bodiment, bringing the man   110
With senses naked to the sensible,
A helpless mirror of all shows which pass
Across his heart; and so Vedanâ grows—

---

6. Dukha-Satya: the truth of suffering, the first of the Four Noble Truths in Buddhism.

7. Here Arnold recapitulates and simplifies the twelvefold chain of codependent origination of Buddhist doctrine. I gloss his text, using for simplicity's sake Arnold's version of Pali diacritical markings. In Buddhist cosmology, the twelvefold chain begins with ignorance, Avidya, that is, ignorance of the Four Noble Truths, the truths of suffering and impermanence; ignorance leads to Sankhâra, mental constructs or formations; Sankhâra (or Saṃskāra) leads to Vidnnân (Vijñāna), or dualistic consciousness, which in turn leads to Namarûpa, or categories (name and form, the psychological and physical constituents that make up a human being); this in turn links to the six senses; as a result of the senses, feeling, or Vedanâ, grows, which in turn gives rise to desires—to Trishna, craving or thirst, and to the Upâdânas, or attachments. These desires produce action—and action is/produces karma—which in turn leads to rebirth.

'Sense-life'—false in its gladness, fell in sadness,
But sad or glad, the Mother of Desire,   115
Trishna, that thirst which makes the living drink
Deeper and deeper of the false salt waves
Whereon they float, pleasures, ambitions, wealth,
Praise, fame, or domination, conquest, love;
Rich meats and robes, and fair abodes and pride   120
Of ancient lines, and lust of days, and strife
To live, and sins that flow from strife, some sweet,
Some bitter. Thus Life's thirst quenches itself
With draughts which double thirst, but who is wise
Tears from his soul this Trishna,[8] feeds his sense   125
No longer on false shows, files his firm mind
To seek not, strive not, wrong not; bearing meek
All ills which flow from foregone wrongfulness,
And so constraining passions that they die
Famished; till all the sum of ended life—   130
The *Karma*—all that total of a soul
Which is the things it did, the thoughts it had,
The 'Self' it wove—with woof of viewless time,
Crossed on the warp invisible of acts—
The outcome of him on the Universe,   135
Grows pure and sinless; either never more
Needing to find a body and a place,
Or so informing what fresh frame it takes
In new existence that the new toils prove
Lighter and lighter not to be at all,   140
Thus "finishing the Path"; free from Earth's cheats;
Released from all the Skandhas[9] of the flesh;
Broken from ties—from Upâdânas—saved
From whirling on the Wheel;[10] aroused and sane
As is a man wakened from hateful dreams.   145
Until—greater than Kings, than Gods more glad!—
The aching craze to live ends, and life glides—
Lifeless—to nameless quiet, nameless joy,
Blessed NIRVANA—sinless, stirless rest—
That change which never changes!   150

---

8. Trishna: craving, desire, thirst.
9. Skandhas: The five skandhas refer to five aggregates of existence: form, sensation, perception, mental formations, and consciousness.
10. The Wheel: samsara, the wheel of life, death, and rebirth.

Greece Chunder Dutt

GREECE (GIRISH) CHUNDER DUTT was the youngest son of Rasamoy Dutt of Calcutta, and thus brother to Govin and uncle to Aru and Toru Dutt, whose poetry also appears in this volume. Like his brothers, Greece (1833–1892) was given an English language education, and with them and his nephew Omesh, he contributed to *The Dutt Family Album* (1870). He reprinted several of his *Album* poems in later collections: *Cherry Stones* and *Cherry Blossoms. Cherry Blossoms* reprints poems, sometimes for the third time, though with few changes.

The poems reproduced here indicate Greece's Christian piety, his identification with British poetic traditions, and the poet's complex and contradictory fascination for Hindu sacred spaces. Epigraphs and poetic forms in Greece's two volumes are often borrowed from Tennyson and from Walter Scott. Like others in his family, Greece took up Christian subjects and also versified traditional Indian stories.

Sources

Greece Chunder Dutt, *Cherry Stones* (Calcutta: P. S. D'Rozario, 1879), and *Cherry Blossoms* (London: T. Fisher Unwin; Calcutta: Thacker, Spink, 1887).

Sonnet

A Persian's mansion, near the Vacool trees,[1]
    That bound the College green, with its array
    Of Ethiop porters, oft in boyhood's day,
When Fancy wove the subtlest webs with ease,
Recalled the age when Sinbad ploughed the seas,   5
    With bales of spicery from far Cathay.
    It was a stately pile of granite grey,
With carved pilasters, and quaint balconies.
Exotic plants with gaudy blossoms starred
    Its terraces; a marble dolphin flung,   10
    In the wide court, a limpid column high;
The windows of the upper rooms were barred,
    But through the lattice-work, with creepers hung,
    Glanced now and then an arm, or lustrous eye.

Samarsi

Samarsi the bold is the pride of his clan,
But he owns not an acre in broad Rajasthan;[2]
Samarsi the bold is the hope of the true,
But his sporran is empty, his henchmen are few,
For the Moors o'er the Jumna in triumph have come,   5
And Samarsi the bold is an exile from home.

Though the Moslem now feasts in his hall and his bower,
And the crescent flag flutters from temple and tower,
Though the chase and the forest, the pass and the height,
Are watched by the soldiers by day and by night,   10

---

1. The Vacool is the Mimusops Elegengi, a large timber tree remarkable for the delightful fragrance of its flowers. There are splendid specimens of this tree in the [Hindu] College green, Potuldanga, and in the gardens of the Raj at Agra, as also in the enclosed gardens of the palace at Deeg [in Rajasthan]. [GCD]

2. "Samarsi" is a metrical imitation of Byron's "Destruction of Sennacherib," and it is heavily influenced both by Walter Scott's narrative poetry and by the orientalist fascination for James Tod's *Annals and Antiquities of Rajasthan, or the Central and Western Rajput States of India*. For details of the story that Greece has versified here, see Tod, *Annals,* chapter 5, "Annals of Mewar," which describes the exploits of Samarsi.

Samarsi the bold is as merry as when
His will was the law in his loved native glen.

For the roebuck still bounds by the dark haunted lake,
And the partridge still springs from the deep tangled brake,
And the perch and the salmon in silv'ry shoals gleam,   15
At morning and noontide in pool and in stream,
And spite of their warders on hill and on plain
Samarsi can harry his father's domain.

Though an outlaw decreed by the chiefs of the foe,
Samarsi has homage from high and from low,   20
For the copsewood is heavy by Saloombra park,
And the vale of Banmora at noonday is dark,
And he's ready, aye ready, right firmly to stand
By the wood or the pass with his sword in his hand.

In the cave of Pokurna, beneath the green hill,   25
Where the throstle keeps time to the soft-crooning rill,
Samarsi at nightfall, unknown to the Moor,
Lights his watch-fire in peace, when his labours are o'er,
And revels in freedom till morning again
Gives the signal to mount and ride down to the plain.   30

On an Old Romaunt

When the night is dark and dreary, and the north wind whistles shrill,
And the snow storm drives in fury down the gorges of the hill,
Like the necromancer's mirror, when his magic perfumes burn,
Mocking Time, these curious volumes make the glorious Past return.

Fast as ripples on the river, or cloud-shadows on the grass,   5
As I read their quaint old pages, down my curtained chamber pass
Mitred priest, and hospitaller, armed and mounted for the fray,
Bands of bronzed condottieri, maidens fair as laughing May.

All that fancy loves to cherish, of the grand old feudal times,
Palmer guides, and weary pilgrims, wending home from distant climes,   10
Trembling Jews with jewel caskets, border chiefs who own no law,
Quivered bands of merry archers, mustered on the 'greene shaw.'

Norman holds, embattled belfrys, gyves, and chains, and dungeons dim,
Winding stairs, and blazing beacons, ancient arms grotesque and grim,
Pensive nuns, in quest of simples, in the lonely midnight hour,   15
Adepts o'er alembics chanting uncouth rhymes of mystic power.

Foreign marts, Venetian Doges, bales of precious merchandise,
Stately streets in Flemish cities, burgher crowds in peaceful guise,
Mighty dukes by guards attended, foresters in kirtles green,
Silver fonts and flaring tapers, ladies sheathed in jewels' sheen.   20

Moorish forts in far Grenada, portals barred and turbans blue,
Gardens green as blissful Eden, crystal fountains fair to view,
Divans in the proud Alhambra, fairy mosques of Parian stone,
Groups of Moors and whiskered Spaniards tilting round the Soldan's throne.

And enrapt I gaze in silence, like a child before a show,   25
Heedless in my joy and wonder, how the golden moments flow,
Till the cock's shrill ringing clarion breaks the spell and clears the air,
And I find me silent seated in my old accustomed chair.

The Taj Mahal

1.

Tax not the prince with pride,
    Or foolish greed of Praise
That with the mushroom's growth
    Developes and decays,
Who built by Duty urged,   5
    With taste and pious care,
Above his buried Love,
    This cenotaph so fair;—

2.

This triumph grand of Art,
    This dream in marble pure,   10
That shall unharmed by Time,
    For ages yet endure,

And witness give to all,
　　How well she played her part,
As consort and as friend　　　　　　　　　　15
　　To him who owned her heart,

3.

How constant was her soul,
　　That feared no adverse shock,
But seemed a structure firm,
　　Let deeply in the rock,　　　　　　　　　20
How noble were her aims,
　　How holy and how high,
Like minarets sublime,
　　That strive to pierce the sky;

4.

'Tis known a mighty queen,　　　　　　　　25
　　Blest servant of the cross,
Felt humbled and subdued
　　When (mindful of her loss,
And of his tender love,
　　With whom her youth was spent)　　　30
At Frogmore she upreared,
　　A stately monument.

Sonnet

Like a great temple built to Nature's God,
　　Kanchun uprears his stately form in air;[3]
　　A crown of stainless snow his turrets wear,
And virgin forests o'er the basement nod.
No tourist seeks him, but the fissures broad　　　5
　　That trench his ample side, the glaciers bright
　　On his wide slopes, are sacred to my sight;
The ground on which he stands is sainted sod.

---

3. Kanchun: Kangchenjunga, third highest mountain in the world (after Everest and K2) in Nepal on the border with Sikkim. Its name literally means "The Five Treasures of Snows." The people of Sikkim consider its summit sacred.

When life hangs heavy, and sharp cares and woes
    Vex the smooth current of my tranquil mind,   10
While sunset bathes his loftiest cone in light,
How often peaceful thoughts and calm delight,
    And soothing hopes, and sadness mild I find,
In his rich colours and his still repose!

Sonnet

Benares

Broad stairs that lead down to the water's side,
    Huge images of stone, and temples wrought
    By Zeal directed by artistic thought,
The swart ascetic full of wrathful pride,
And bands of bathers near the sacred tide,   5
    By restless conscience from each province brought,
    Were all that first the startled vision caught,
As from the ghaut[4] our barge commenced to glide:
The scene was such as once Persepolis
    Or mighty Babylon to prophets gave;   10
A lurid grandeur that spake not of bliss,
    Clothed every object and rehearsed this stave,
Avert thine eyes, although it seems to fair,
The town is cursed, Jehovah's wrath is there.

---

4. Ghaut: ghat, or landing place. In Benares (now Varanasi), the ghats allow bathers to descend stairs into the river to bathe in the holy waters. The poem takes an uncompromisingly negative view of the holiest Hindu pilgrimage site in India, its most ancient continuously inhabited city.

Mary Eliza Leslie

AT THE TIME of the Sepoy Rebellion, the most widespread and violent of many Indian uprisings against British authority, Mary Leslie was twenty-three years old, already an experienced poet with one book to her credit (*Ina and Other Poems*, 1856). As the bloody events of 1857 unfolded, Leslie (1834–?) wrote a long sonnet sequence, which became at once a diary of the rebellion and an expression of her moral and personal dilemma. Leslie's poems grew from her ambiguous place as a woman who was identified with British India but was marginal to its structures of power.

The daughter and granddaughter of Baptist missionaries, Mary Leslie wrote at a time when Protestant Christianity in India was increasingly identified with British nationalism. Leslie's sonnet sequence, published in 1858, furthers many tropes that became standard mutiny lore in the years that followed. Leslie found herself, somewhat to her own surprise, praying for divine vengeance on the rebels. She presented British women and children as heroines and martyrs and praised British heroes, especially Sir Henry Lawrence and Henry Havelock. Yet Leslie concluded that the rebellion marked a sorrowful centenary of empire, ending in "deep griefs, and wailings, and low sighs."

Unlike many of her Anglo-Indian peers, Leslie was born in India and anticipated living her whole life there. India was, in that sense, her only country—she had spent but a few childhood months in Britain, and she was no doubt more at ease in Bengal than London. Leslie's father, Andrew, was a Scotsman who came to India in 1824. A printer, who like many of his trade began his adult life a self-educated man, Andrew had been steeped in the Scottish Enlightenment. On professing a missionary vocation, however, he was sent by the Baptists to study in Bristol and was ordained before his departure for the subcontinent. He was soon posted to Monghyr in Bihar, where his first wife—also a missionary—shortly died; afterward, he married the daughter of his predecessor, the missionary John Chamberlain. With her, he had a son and, in 1834, a daughter, Mary. In 1842, Leslie was called to the Lower Circular Road Baptist Church in Calcutta, where he remained until his death in 1870, gradually involving his daughter in his educational and missionary efforts. His biographers characterize Leslie as a man of elegant scholarship; whether through his tuition or with the help of other teachers, Mary acquired a knowledge of languages, including Greek, Italian, and German. She probably also spoke and wrote Bangla and Urdu.

Mary Leslie spent many years working in education, particularly the education of Indian women. She is characterized in the preface to her book *Eastern Blossoms: Sketches of Native Christian Life in India* as a zenana visitor (that is, an educational missionary to upper-caste women living in seclusion). Edward Storrow in his introduction to *Eastern Blossoms* refers to her "long residence in Calcutta, and noble efforts in behalf of native female education," which "in addition to unusual personal culture" enabled her to write about Indian women. Leslie wrote three volumes best characterized as missionary literature: *Eastern Blossoms* (1875), The *Dawn of Light: A Story of the Zenana Mission* (London, 1868), and *A Child of the Day: A Brief Memorial of Mrs. H. C. Mukerji* (Calcutta, 1882). Each embodies evangelical narrative conventions, focusing on personal stories of conversion, and evinces a relatively strong empathy with the Indian women who are its subjects.

Although Leslie's prose provides a typical picture of female missionary life in nineteenth-century India, her poetry is of more historical and aesthetic interest. The poems of *Sorrows, Aspirations, and Legends from India* have a vivid immediacy, for all their bloody-minded and nationalist sentiments. In contrast, the poems of Leslie's last volume of lyrics, *Heart Echoes from the East; or, Sacred Lyrics and Sonnets*, represent the best Christian devotional poetry written in English in nineteenth-century India. Though reviews were scant—and those mixed—and though the verse is marred by the occasional solecism that might have benefited from an editor, *Heart Echoes* is remarkable for its metrical experimentation and its devotional fervor. Leslie is clearly aware of and allies her verse with English devotional practice from Henry Vaughan to Reginald Heber and John Keble, whose *Christian Year* she acknowledges frequently in her epigraphs.

Given the political trauma of the Mutiny and the increasing dogmatism of evangelical Christianity in India, it is not surprising that Leslie's last volume of verse is intensely personal, the poems focused entirely on individual spiritual struggle. Contemporary accounts make clear that Leslie moved from the Calvinism of her Baptist upbringing to a more forgiving Arminianism among the Calcutta Methodists. Her verse owes its antecedents to George Herbert, as well as to Keble and to biblical prose and poetry—in both the King James version and in Luther's German.

Sources

Mary Eliza Leslie, *Sorrows, Aspirations, and Legends from India* (London: John Snow, 1858); Leslie, *Heart Echoes from the East; or, Sacred Lyrics and Sonnets* (London: James Nisbet, 1861). See also Leslie, *Eastern Blossoms: Sketches of Native Christian Life in India* (London: John Snow, 1875) with an introduction by Edward Storrow; Henry Sweetser Burrage, *Baptist Hymn Writers and Their Hymns* (Portland, ME: Brown, Thurston, 1888); and Thomas Evans and David Hooper, *A Welshman in India: A Record of the Life of Thomas Evans, Missionary* (London: Clarke, 1908).

from *Sorrows, Aspirations, and Legends*

XII

Death of Sir H. M. Lawrence

Our best! our bravest![1] Has Death's darksome cloud
Drifted above thee too? We lift our eyes,
And missing thy clear light within our skies
Fall back to solemn moaning long and loud;
And thoughts of sorrow press and throng and crowd   5
Upon the heart crushed with its sad surprise,
And yearning as if from a dream to rise,
Which pictures thee wrapt in a bloody shroud.
Yet strive we our deep agony to quell,
Pressing it down with stifled sob and start,   10
And saying softly, "It is well, O well
For him from this blood-crimsoned land to part,
Leaving the foe-encircled citadel
For the calm rest and bliss near God's own heart!"

XIV

"How long, O Lord?"

A voice came stealing down yon azure steep:—
"How long, O Lord, holy and just and true?
Our blood yet reddens with its crimson hue
The ground wherein our martyred bodies sleep,
And fearlessly our cruel murderers keep   5
High revel, and their wonted sports pursue,
While gorgeous trains of pomp and retinue

---

1. Sir Henry Montgomery Lawrence was a British soldier and administrator, killed in the 1857 rebellion at the siege of Lucknow. See the introduction to the poems of his wife, Honoria Marshall Lawrence, in this volume.

Through the wide city's squares and purlieus sweep."
And we, who little thought such cry would spring
From our hearts even in their wildest hours,   10
Catch up the burning spirit, uttering
Its echo in the midst of tearful showers:—
"How long, Lord God most mighty? Quickly bring
Thine arm down clothed with all its venging powers!"

XXXV

1857 continued

We lift our voices, praying:—Let the gone
Be gone, O God. O fling Thou down and break
Our cup of sorrow, so that none may take
Hereafter ought like it to look upon,
And, tasting, drink with deep and bitter moan.   5
Pity us, O our God. These moments rake
The smouldering embers up, and darkly make
Past agonies remembered one by one
Too vividly for utterance, and hot tears
Come rushing into lately dried-up eyes,   10
To think of our first glorious Hundred Years
Of rule, aye widening under Eastern skies,
Not ending with loud, jubilant heart-cheers,
But with deep griefs, and wailings, and low sighs.

from *Heart Echoes*

VI

"Then came Jesus, the doors being shut."
John 20:26

I am alone, O Saviour; all my doors—
    My heart's doors—are close barred at this still time.
Now let Thy feet be heard along the floors,
    The while Thy priestly garments softly chime.

O come and shew to me Thy wounded side,　　　　　　　　5
　　Thy hands yet red with blood—Thy very own!—[2]
Thy pierced feet,—O, Though Great Crucified,
　　The ruddy memories of Thy thorny crown!

I would behold them all; for faith is weak,
　　And hope is dim, and love has grown a-cold;—　　10
O come!—earth's spell shall at Thy presence break,
　　Time and eternity their depths unfold:

And I shall fall down at Thy feet and say,
　　"My Lord! my God!" and then my eyes will dim
With tears of gladsome love, and all my way　　　　15
　　Henceforward will be as the way of him

Who, after his dark dreary unbelief,
　　Lived calmly on a life of holy faith,
Preaching his Master's word in joy and grief,
　　Dying, 'neath tropic suns, a martyr's death.　　20

VII

> "Lord, I believe; help Thou my unbelief."
>
> *Mark 9:24*

"Lord, I believe; help Thou my unbelief."
　　So spake the father through his blinding tears,
　　And instantly the load of many years
Was lifted, and the worn lad found relief.

Lord, I believe; but with a faith so weak　　　　　　5
　　I cannot even name it hope or trust:
　　My soul lies low and moaning in the dust,
I tremble, daring scarce to rise and speak,

---

2. The poet compares herself to Jesus' disciple Thomas, sometimes called Doubting Thomas, who declared that he could not believe in the resurrected Jesus unless he could touch Jesus's wounded hands and side; when Jesus appears to the disciples (in the chapter of John that Mary Leslie quotes here), he beckons Thomas to touch him, and Thomas responds with a declaration of belief. Thomas in his after years is said to have embarked on a mission to the Parthians, traveling into northern India and thence sailing south to the Malabar coast. He is believed to have died in India and to have been buried in the town of Mylapore, though there is no reliable historical evidence to confirm his place of burial.

Knowing not what to say. O Thou whose ear
    Caught the full meaning of those broken tones,   10
    Severed the faith from earth's low fearing moans,
Be near me, too, my whispering faith to hear!

Turn not my prayer away, O Crucified!
    Hush Thou the unbelief which rises high,
    Threatening to drown faith's feeble infant cry—   15
Strengthen the faith so frail, so weak, so tried.

"Lord, I believe; help Thou my unbelief!"
    With faltering tones I say this faltering prayer;—
    Let all I bring to Thee Thy mercy share,
Bind Thou my loved in Thy salvation's sheaf!   20

XXIII

> "Jesus. . . . having loved His own who were
> in the world, He loved them to the end."
> *John 13:1*

Love me too till the end, my God, my Saviour,
    Though my behaviour
Be very wilful, and ofttimes unheeding
    I hear Thy pleading,
Like to a child whose moods are ever changing   5
From joy to sorrow, love to coldness, ranging.

My God! my Saviour! Thou who changest never,
    Yet still for ever
Continuest the same, bear with my weakness,
    While I in meekness   10
Kneel down before Thee, O Thou ever loving,
To seek from Thee Thy favour never moving.

I know that life without Thee would be dreary;
    Its labour weary;
Its sweetness comes from Thy exceeding favour;   15
    Thy love gives savour
To that which else, though ringed with joy and brightness,
Would still be nought but one unbroken whiteness.

Yet still to syren voices oft I listen,
    My eyes oft glisten 20
With joy at visions of earth's fading beauty,
    And thought of duty
Passes away, and I turn madly chasing
The fleeting sounds, the momentary blazing.

Lord! my Redeemer! even though I wander, 25
    And trifles ponder,
Cease not to love me; let Thy arm uphold me,
    And close enfold me
Unto Thy breast, whereon I ever leaning
May look up to Thy face of love-full meaning, 30

Until the end, when with Thee in Thy glory,
    My life-time's story
May come before me, all my joy increasing,
    So that unceasing
I may with seraphs join Thy praises singing, 35
Low at Thy feet my blood-bought amaranth flinging.

XVII

The Gathering Home

They are gathering homeward from every land
    One by one,
As their weary feet touch the shining strand
    One by one,
Their brows are enclosed in a golden crown, 5
Their travel-stained garments are all laid down,
And clothed in white raiment they rest on the mead,
Where the Lamb loveth His chosen to lead,
    One by one.

Before they rest they pass through the strife 10
    One by one,
Through the waters of death they enter life
    One by one
To some are the floods of the river still
As they ford on their way to the heav'nly hill, 15

To others the waves run fiercely and wild,
Yet all reach the home of the Undefiled
     One by one.

We too shall come to that river side
     One by one,   20
We are nearer its waters each eventide
     One by one,
We can hear the noise and dash of the stream
Now and again through our life's deep dream,
Sometimes the floods all the banks o'erflow,   25
Sometimes in ripples the small waves go
     One by one.

Jesus! Redeemer! we look to Thee
     One by one,
We lift up our voices tremblingly   30
     One by one,
The waves of the river are dark and cold,
We know not the spots where our feet may hold;
Thou who didst pass through in deep midnight,
Strengthen us, send us the staff and the light,   35
     One by one.

Plant Thou Thy feet beside as we tread
     One by one,
On Thee let us lean each drooping head
     One by one,   40
Let but Thy strong arm around us be twined,
We shall cast all our fears and cares to the wind,
Saviour! Redeemer! with Thee full in view,
Smilingly, gladsomely, shall we pass through,
     One by one.   45

Sir Alfred Comyn Lyall

≈⁀

S IR ALFRED COMYN LYALL (1835–1911) was born into a distinguished family with Scottish roots. His father was a philosopher and rector of Harbledown, Kent; his uncle, the chairman of the East India Company and an MP for London; and another uncle, dean of Canterbury Cathedral. Lyall and his younger brother were taken, so to speak, into the India branch of the family "business," his younger brother after becoming governor of the Punjab.

After studying at Eton College as a foundation scholar, Lyall joined the last class of young men appointed through patronage to the Indian Civil Service. In preparation for Indian service, he was sent to Haileybury College, and three years later, in 1856, he arrived in Calcutta. He was appointed assistant magistrate in the Bulandshahar district, but the rebellion of 1857 began soon after. Lyall saw service as an occasional cavalryman (on one occasion, his horse was shot out from under him). The fighting took him across northern India and won him a medal, but he had mixed feelings about enforcing the prosecution of the mutineers when at the conclusion of the conflict he was appointed to restore civil order in his old district of Bulandshahar. The war and his early service in India caused Lyall to lose his religious faith and perhaps some of his faith in human nature. He is described by Eric Stokes as a "liberal authoritarian." His work as an Indian administrator, while able, was in some measure compromised both by his sense of irony and by his suspicion of British contempt for Indians and British faith in liberal reforms.

In the course of his career in India, Lyall held numerous responsible appointments, ranging from commissioner of West Berar to home secretary in Calcutta and (after a stint in Rajasthan) foreign secretary to the government in Calcutta. In this last position, Lyall found himself unable or unwilling to oppose Lord Lytton's forward policy in Afghanistan, which led to the Second Anglo-Afghan War. Upon Lytton's replacement, however, Lyall persuaded the new viceroy, Lord Ripon, to retreat from Afghanistan; reach an accord with the current strongman, Abdur Rahman (a former ally of Russia); and retain only border positions. As Lyall's biographer Katherine Prior puts it, Lyall was "twice decorated for pursuing contradictory policies." In the remainder of his time in India, Lyall was promoted to a position as lieutenant governor of the North West Provinces, yet in this highly desirable position, he found himself resisting Lord Ripon's reform measures. Lyall's liberalism was tempered almost entirely by his belief that should their traditional institutions be too quickly changed Indians would rise up against the British and by his belief that social stability required the conciliation of large landholders.

Lyall retired to England in 1887 at age fifty-two, hoping for a subsequent appointment as viceroy of India. He served for fifteen years on the Council of India, and he wrote numerous essays for the *Edinburgh Review, The Cambridge Modern History*, and *Encyclopedia Britannica*. His essays were collected in two volumes, and he wrote biographies of Alfred Tennyson and Warren Hastings. His book of poems, *Verses Written in India*, appeared in 1889, followed in 1891 by his most famous work, a history titled *The Rise and Expansion of the British Dominion in India*. Lyall's verses evidence the sources of his ambivalence about British policies, British reformism, and the moral and historical claims of the empire—in these poems his early experiences in the rebellion of 1857 clearly shape both his cultural attitudes and the irony and skepticism that marked both his literary endeavors and his political attitudes.

Sources

Alfred Comyn Lyall, *Verses Written in India*, 3rd ed. (London: Kegan Paul, Trench, Trübner, 1903). *Verses* went through six "editions" (more properly, six printings) between 1889 and 1903, all of them substantially identical. See also Katherine Prior, "Lyall, Sir Alfred Comyn (1835–1911)," in *ODNB*.

Retrospection

1857–1882.

Well; I've walked the jail, and the Courts I've seen,
The school is in order, the streets are clean,
  And the roads are swept and mended;
The treasury's right, you've got the keys?
So now, at the spring of the evening breeze,   5
Just leave me to linger among those trees,
  I'll come when the twilight's ended.

Yes, the garden now looks spruce and trim,
Yet the old trees still, though decayed and grim,
  Stand waving as if they knew me;   10

All else is changed since I saw the ground,
(How the roses bloom on that sloping mound!)
And the long lean branches swaying around
  With their shadowy arms pursue me.

As I cross the flower-bed, laid with taste   15
Where the old grove sheltered a sandy waste,
  How soft the geraniums gleam in
The light of a dusty crimson sky!
Yes, only the trees remember, and I,
Things once spoken, and done, hard by   20
  The spot where we now stand dreaming.

That year when the tempest of mutiny broke,
And the empire swayed like a storm-bent oak,
  When the sepoys gave no quarter;
When Islam had risen and Delhi fell,   25
And this plain was a furnace hot as hell;
We were camped, three English, beside that well:
  We had nothing but shade and water.

Hour after hour, till the day was spent,
We had watched our restless regiment,   30
  And the soldiers whispering round us
In the glaring noon-tide heat; and yet
Our hearts sank low when the red orb set,
And the soft dark night like a falling net
  In its unseen meshes bound us.   35

He was my Colonel and she was his wife;
We had little comfort or hope in life;
  And he said "Is it worth complaining,
As you look at the sullen sepoys' line,
That they bide but the hour and await the sign   40
That shall end our cares in the fierce sunshine
  And the ills of a rough campaigning?

"It shall never be heard in the English host
That I lost my colours and left my post
  From a treacherous band to hide me;   45
We are trapped and hemmed in this cursed wood,
Yet stand I ready" ('twas there he stood)

"To die as a Christian soldier should,
　　With my wife and my friend beside me."

Then he clasped her close in a warm embrace,　　　　50
And he took my hand; but I marked her face
　　And the flashing glance she gave me:
For the mutinous eyes said, "Life is sweet
　　While nerves have courage and hearts can beat;
Will you crouch like a hare at the hunter's feet,　　55
　　Will you die like a fool, or save me?"

So I saddled in silence our horses three,
And I brought them there, to that tamarind tree,
　　And the night, as now, was falling,
And the air was heavy, as now, with scent,　　　　60
And just outside at the sepoy tent
The armed sentry came and went,
　　We could hear his comrades calling;

And I whispered "Up; 'twill be lighter soon,
See the faint foreglow of the rising moon,　　　　65
　　Let your wife mount quick—God speed her,
Her Arab can gallop, he needs no lash,
We can break their line with a sudden dash;
But a man may fall when the volleys flash,
　　So will you ride last, or lead her?"　　　　70

Lightly the lady to saddle sprung;
But the other's hand to the bridle clung,
　　And he said "Do ye all betray me?
I serve the Queen, and I trust the Lord;
Shall I stain mine honour and break my word?　　75
I move not hence while I wear this sword,
　　And I charge you both, obey me."

Then none for a moment spoke or moved;
One look she gave me, the woman I loved,
　　And said but one word, "Listen";　　　　80
As there came one tap of the sepoy's drum,
And the light air shook with the tramp and the hum
Of a moving crowd, and I said "They come,
　　I can see their bayonets glisten;

"They come; You boast of a soldier's faith,   85
Will it screen your wife from a cruel death?
     Remember the troth you plighted,
And your home in the far-off summer days,
And a young life lost for an empty phrase";
But he said "Wherever I stay, she stays: 90
     We shall meet our end united."

Then I cried, "'Tis the craze of a fevered brain,
Will you take your hand from her bridle rein,
     Will you mount and ride?" "No, never,"
He said. And she bent from her saddle low,   95
And she touched my cheek and whispered "Go,"
With her eyes all full of despair and woe;
     "Good-bye sweetheart, for ever!"

And then? One shot, and her rein was free,
And fast and furious I and she   100
     Out of the grove were flying;
The white smoke rose, and the leaves were stirred,
But only the solemn branches heard
Or sound or motion, of sign or word,
     As he lay beneath them dying.   105

A shout, a volley, a rushing ride:
The low moon led us, and side by side
     We followed from dark to dawning
Over the streams and the silent plain;
All sights and shadows and sounds again   110
And figures are flitting across my brain;
     And the meeting of eyes at morning.

Yes; this was the hour, and that was the spot,
And the mute trees know who fired that shot,
     But the secret well they're keeping;   115
How they beckon and bend in the gathering gloom
O'er the sloping mound where the roses bloom!
Can that be an old forgotten tomb,
     Is it there that the Colonel's sleeping?

The Amir's Soliloquy

1881.

"Latest news from Afghanistan promises ill
for future tranquility. The Amir has failed
in conciliating the Duranis, there is jeal-
ousy at Herat. . . . the Kohistanis are dis-
contented. . . . the Ghilzais are restless,
Lughman tribes are showing uneasiness. . . .
No doubt the situation is far from reassur-
ing, and calls for great tact and administra-
tive ability on the Amir's part."
—Times telegram, 15th December, 1881.

Scene.—The Bála Hissar at Kábul. The Amir soliloquises:

Thus is my banishment ended; it's twelve long years, well nigh,[1]
Since I fought the last of my lost fights, and saw my best men die;
They hunted me over the passes, and up to the Oxus stream,[2]
We had just touched land on the far side as we saw their spearheads gleam.

Then came the dolorous exile, the life in a conquered land   5
Where the Frank had trodden on Islam; the alms at a stranger's hand;
While here in the fort of my fathers my bitterest foe held sway;
He was ten years building his kingdom, it all fell down in a day.

May he rest, the Amir Sher Ali,[3] in his tomb by the holy shrine;
The virtues of God are pardon and pity, they never were mine;   10
They have never been ours, in a kingdom all stained with the blood of our kin,
Where the brothers embrace in the war-field, and the reddest sword must win.

---

1. Here Lyall recapitulates the complex military and diplomatic history of Afghanistan in the period preceding and including the Second Anglo-Afghan War (1878–1880). The speaker of the poem is Abdur Rahman Khan (1840–1901), who was emir of Afghanistan from 1880 to 1901. Abdur Rahman was the grandson of Dost Mohammed Khan, who had established the Barakzai dynasty in Afghanistan.

2. Oxus: Oxus river, which Abdur Rahman crossed, fleeing his uncle who suspected him of rebellion.

3. Dost Mohammed had nominated his third son, Sher Ali, as his successor—passing over Abdur Rahman's father. Though Abdur Rahman's father came to terms with Sher Ali, Abdur Rahman was suspected by Sher Ali of raising resistance in the north.

And yet when I think of Sher Ali, as he lies in his sepulchre low,
How he died betrayed, heartbroken, 'twixt infidel friend and foe,
Driven from his throne by the English, and scorned by the Russian, his guest,   15
I am well content with the vengeance, and I see God works for the best.[4]

But all His ways are warnings; and I, God's slave, must heed
How I bargain for help with the Káfir, or lean on a venomous reed;
For never did chief more sorely need Heaven for his aid and stay
Than the man who would reign in this country, and tame Afgháns for a day.   20

I look from a fort half-ruined on Kábul spreading below,
On the near hills crowned with cannon, and the far hills piled with snow;
Fair are the vales well watered, and the vines on the upland swell,
You might think you were reigning in Heaven—I know I am ruling Hell.

For there's hardly a room in my palace but a kinsman there was killed,   25
And never a street in the city but with false fierce curs is filled;
With a mob of priests, and fanatics, and all my mutinous host;
They follow my steps, as the wolves do, for a prince who slips is lost.

And they eye me askance, the Mollahs, the bigots who preach and pray,
Who followed my march with curses till I scattered Ayúb[5] that day;   30
They trusted in texts and forgot that the chooser of kings is a sword;
There are twenty now silent and stark, for I showed them the ways of the Lord.

And far from the Suleiman heights come the sounds of the stirring of tribes,
Afreedi, Hazára, and Ghilzi, they clamour for plunder or bribes;
And Herát is but held by a thread; and the Usbeg has raised Badukshán;   35
And the chief may sleep sound, in his grave, who would rule the unruly Afghán.

Shall I stretch my right hand to the Indus, that England may fill it with gold?
Shall my left beckon aid from the Oxus? the Russian blows hot and blows cold;

---

4. Abdur Rahman raised a successful rebellion against Sher Ali and saw to it that his father was
put into power, but after some months in power, following his father's death, Abdur Rahman and
his uncle were defeated by a returning Sher Ali and were forced to flee into Persia, where Abdur
Rahman put himself under the protection of the Russians. On Sher Ali's death in 1879, Abdur
Rahman again entered Afghanistan, eventually negotiating with the British for their withdrawal
subsequent to the Second Afghan War. Kandahar, however, remained under dispute.
   5. Sher Ali's son Ayub Khan marched on that city from Herat and was finally defeated by Abdur
Rahman, who thus began to consolidate his rule in Afghanistan, a process that took years and in-
volved punitive actions against many tribal groups who opposed him. *Mollah* is now commonly
spelled *mullah.*

The Afghán is but grist in their mill, and the waters are moving it fast,
Let the stone be the upper or nether, it grinds him to powder at last.[6]   40

And the lord of the English writes, "Order, and justice, and govern with laws,"
And the Russian he sneers and says, "Patience, and velvet to cover your claws;"
But the kingdoms of Islam are crumbling—and round me a voice ever rings
Of death and the doom of my country—shall I be the last of its kings.

---

6. Lyall alludes to Luke 20:18, "Whosoever shall fall upon that stone shall be broken; but on whomsoever it shall fall, it will grind him to powder."

Aru Dutt

～ ⌒

WHEN SHE died at age twenty of tuberculosis, Aru Dutt (1854–1874) left behind a series of translations from the French. Two years later, her sister, Toru, published these along with many more of her own translations in a volume Toru called *A Sheaf Gleaned in French Fields.*

The elder daughter of Govin Chunder and Kshetramoni Mitter Dutt, Aru shared with her sister a degree of education most unusual for women of their time and place. Although very few women in Bengal were literate, both their mother and all of the children—Toru, Aru, and Abju, their brother—were educated in English and, to some extent, in Bangla. The Dutt family, since the days of Toru's great-grandfather Nilmoni Dutt, had a particular interest in reform and education, including the education of women. Aru's grandfather Rasamoy Dutt was a sympathizer with the work of Rammohan Roy (who had been a friend of Nilmoni's), the founder of what became the Brahmo Samaj, an influential movement for social reform in Hinduism. These reformist attitudes, coupled with an unusual degree of what we might call ecumenical thinking stemming from Rasamoy's interest in comparative religions, eventually led to the conversion to Christianity of a considerable portion of the Dutt family.

Aru's uncle Kissen was baptized on his deathbed by his brother Girish (Greece Chunder Dutt), who was not yet a Christian; Kissen's dying request was for his brothers' conversion. After Kissen's death, Aru's uncles Greece and Hur Chunder and her father Govin Chunder Dutt, along with their families, were baptized; thus, the Dutt brothers set their families apart from friends and relatives and created a tight-knit community whose intellectual life revolved around Christian piety and English poetry.

The other important event of Aru's childhood was the death of her brother, Abju. Partly in response to this death and partly to provide a change of scenery and a much-longed-for trip to Europe, some months after Abju's death the family embarked for France, where Toru and Aru were enrolled in a small *pensionnat.* In 1871, the family moved to England, where they settled for nearly two years in Cambridge. There Toru and Aru attended the higher lectures for women at Cambridge, and they met, among others, Anne Clough, who had just become head of the newly founded Newnham College, the first women's college at the university. The sisters studied French as well as other subjects, and they had, in addition, private tuition in piano and voice. Clearly, Govin recognized the extraordinary talents of his daughters and devoted much love, energy, and money to their education, permitting them a degree of freedom not always accorded their British or Bengali counterparts. Eventually, however, Aru showed clear symptoms of the tuberculosis that was to kill her and her sister, and the family chose to return to Bengal, where she died a few months later.

After Aru's death, Govin played an important role in publishing *A Sheaf*, arranging for printing, contributing poems himself, and assisting with proofreading; work on this volume was clearly a labor of love for Toru and Govin as they attempted to cope with their loss. Though Aru is now primarily known for her close relationship to and collaboration with her sister, her translations, few though they be, have intrinsic charm as well as novelty. In addition to the translations reproduced here, *A Sheaf* contains one poem that I believe to be original with Aru: "The Mother's Birthday" is attributed to an "anonymous" poet and followed by Aru's initial. To my mind, "The Mother's Birthday" bears the marks of the sort of juvenilia that would have been much appreciated in the Dutt family circle. Aru—or "anonymous"—invokes a beloved mother thus:

> Thou so good, O! thou so perfect,
> > Who lovest us with so much love,
> Mamma with joy we hail thy birthday,
> > Day all other days above.
> In exchange of all our presents,
> > Of our songs composed for thee,
> Of our field-flowers and our roses,
> > Give us kisses tenderly.

Such a poem, whether an original composition or not, surely marks the familial devotion characteristic of Aru Dutt's childhood.

Aru Dutt's translations are taken from the first edition of *A Sheaf Gleaned in French Fields*. Toru's final note to the volume speaks of Aru's verse in the third person: "The pieces signed A. are by her dear and only sister Aru, who fell asleep in Jesus, on the 23rd July, 1874, at the early age of twenty years."

Source

Toru Dutt, *A Sheaf Gleaned in French Fields* (Bhowanipore, Bengal: Saptahik Sambad Press, 1876).

The Young Captive

André Chénier

The budding shoot ripens unharmed by the scythe,[1]
Without fear of the press, on vine-branches lithe,
    Through spring-tide the green clusters bloom.
Is't strange, then, that I in my life's morning hour,
Though troubles like clouds on the dark present lower,   5
    Half-frighted shrink back from my doom?

Let the stern-hearted stoic run boldly on death!
I—I weep and I hope; to the north wind's chill breath
    I bend,—then erect is my form!
If days there are bitter, there are days also sweet,   10
Enjoyment unmixed where on earth may we meet?
    What ocean has never a storm?

Illusions the fairest assuage half my pain,
The walls of a prison enclose me in vain,
    The strong wings of hope bear me far;   15
So escapes from the net of the fowler the bird,
So darts he through ether, while his music is heard
    Like showers of sweet sound from a star.

Comes Death unto me? I sleep tranquil and calm,
And Peace when I wake stands by with her balm,   20
    Remorse is the offspring of crimes;
My welcome each morning smiles forth in all eyes,
My presence is here to sad brows, a surprise
    Which kindles to pleasure at times.

The end of my journey seemed so far to my view;   25
Of the elm-trees which border the long avenue,
    The nearest are only passed by;

---

1. "La jeune captive" was composed by André Chénier (1762–1794) while he was imprisoned during the French Revolution. A constitutional monarchist, Chénier began his brief career writing neoclassical poems. "La jeune captive," published posthumously, was one of his most popular poems and was dedicated to Mademoiselle de Coigny, imprisoned with him at Saint-Lazare; Charlotte Bronte has her character Caroline Helstone recites this poem in her novel *Shirley.* Chénier's work also influenced Alexander Pushkin and Victor Hugo. The reference to Pales in line 40, indicating the classical goddess of sheepfolds, is part of Chénier's mythological machinery.

At the banquet of life I have barely sat down,
My lips have but pressed the bright foaming crown
    Of the wine in my cup bubbling high.   30

I am only in spring,—the harvest I'd see,
From season to season like the sun I would be
    Intent on completing my round;
Shining bright in the garden,—its honor and queen;
As yet but the beams of the morning I've seen,   35
    I wait for eve's stillness profound.

Oh Death, thou canst wait; leave, leave me to dream,
And strike at the hearts where Despair is supreme,
    And Shame hails thy dart as a boon!
For me, Pales has arbours unknown to the throngs,   40
The world has delights, the Muses have songs,
    I wish not to perish too soon.

A prisoner myself broken-hearted and crushed,
From my heart to my lips all my sympathies rushed,
    And my lyre from its slumbers awoke;   45
At these sorrows, these wishes, of a captive, I heard,
And to rhyme and to measure I married each word
    As softly and simply she spoke.

Should this song of my prison hereafter inspire
Some student with leisure her name to enquire,   50
    This answer at least may be given,—
That grace marked her figure, her action, her speech,
And such as lived near her, blameless might teach
    That life is the best gift of heaven.

The Emigration of Pleasure

Madame Viot

Affrighted by the ills that war[2]
    Had drawn upon unhappy France,
Pleasure sought in regions far,
    Encouragement and countenance.
Through Germany and Spain to pass   5
    Was weary work for miles and miles,
The Spaniard never jokes, alas!
    And the German never smiles.

To Russia next. His hopes are vain,
    The killing climate in a week,   10
Benumbed and sickened all his train,
    And robbed the colours from his cheek.
By Catherine[3] he was begged to take
    The halls of snow that flashed like gold,
But could he, even for her sake,   15
    Expose his life to death by cold?

To England now. He wandered wild,—
    And on the same fool's-errand bent;
The Lord Mayor, fat, grey and mild,
    Conducted him to Parliament.   20
Pleasure is courteous,—full of grace,
    But from the truth he never shrinks,
'I cannot stay i' this horrid place,
    Where everybody yawns and nobody thinks.'

Once more adrift,—on, on to Rome   25
    Where burned the Muse's altar-fires!
Ah me! it was only the home
    Of a sick old man and some friars.
When he asked for Horace's verse,

---

2. Madame Viot (Marie-Anne Henriette Payan de l'Estang) was born in Dresden in 1746 and studied languages, including German, Latin, Italian, and English. She wrote poems, opera, letters, and the famous *Éloge de Montaigne*, a discourse on Montaigne's philosophy and his virtues. She died in Bagnols, France, in 1802.

3. Catherine II, empress of Russia (Catherine the Great).

Doggrel hymns were sung through the nose,　　　　　30
　　He felt he'd fallen from bad to worse,
　　And tears in his eyes unbidden rose.

Poor Pleasure! How get back to France?
　　That was the question for him now,
Without papers or money, small his chance!　　　　35
　　A loan,—but who would a loan allow?
Heaven-helpt, he reached the country dear,
　　And there at last saw Liberty;
What has a pet spoilt-child to fear
　　Who falls with tears at his mother's knee?　　　　40

Morning Serenade

Victor Hugo

Still barred thy doors!—The far east glows,[4]
　　The morning wind blows fresh and free,
Should not the hour that wakes the rose
　　Awaken also thee
　　　No longer sleep,　　　　　　　　　5
　　　Oh, listen now!
　　　I wait and weep,
　　But where art thou?

---

4. Victor Hugo (1802–1885), the French poet, playwright, novelist, and statesman, was a hero
to both Toru and Aru Dutt. Toru translated his work extensively, and she comments in her printed
annotation of Aru's poem, "It would be absurd to make any comment on Victor Hugo in a short
note at the end of a book. His name is among the great ones of the earth. With Shakespeare, Mil-
ton, Byron, Goethe, Schiller, and the rest, his place has long been marked in the Valhalla of the
poets. Sings England's latest poet,—a poet indeed, in spite of his many serious aberrations.
　　　"Thou art chief of us, and lord;
　　　Thy song is as a sword
　　　Keen-edged and scented in the blade from flowers;
　　　Thou art lord and king; but we
　　　Lift younger eyes and see
　　　Less of high hope, less light on wandering hours;
　　　Hours that have borne men down so long,
　　　Seen the right fail, and watched uplift the wrong."
　　Here Toru Dutt quotes Algernon Charles Swinburne, "To Victor Hugo in Exile," which she
may have known either as reprinted by Edmund Gosse in *English Odes* (1890) or from Swinburne's
Poems and Ballads (1866).

All look for thee, Love, Light, and Song;
    Light, in the sky deep red above,   10
Song, in the lark of pinion strong,
    And in my heart, true Love.
      No longer sleep,
        Oh, listen now!
          I wait and weep,   15
          But where art thou?

Apart we miss our nature's goal,
    Why strive to cheat our destinies?
Was not my love made for thy soul?
    Thy beauty for mine eyes?   20
      No longer sleep,
        Oh, listen now!
          I wait and weep,
          But where art thou?

Toru Dutt

TORU DUTT (1856–1877), like her predecessor H. L. V. Derozio, became a remarkably accomplished poet in a remarkably short time. Derozio is frequently called the "Indian Keats." In a similar fashion, Toru Dutt has often been compared to the Brontës. Like Emily Brontë, Toru was precocious and intellectually a free spirit. Like Charlotte, she survived her siblings only to die young herself. Although she was barely twenty-one at the time of her death, Toru Dutt was the first Indian woman to write poetry in English—and it was extraordinary poetry.

Writing in English, or writing at all, was an unusual accomplishment, for very few Indian women in the nineteenth century learned English or other European languages. Not many were literate in any Indian language. Dutt's poetry, however, was much more than a "first" for Indian women; it created a new idiom in Indian English verse.

Like Michael Madhusudan Dutt's, Toru Dutt's poems arose from a multilingual and cosmopolitan sensibility. Both poets brought together blended materials from the traditional tales and poetry of India with formal qualities from British and European poetic traditions. But in contrast to Michael's ornate style and his turn to Bangla verse, Toru chose to write all the verse she had time to create in English. She possessed a strong lyric sensibility, as well as a technical facility for meter and lineation, and she brought to formal English verse a powerful idiomatic diction.

This sensibility owed much to Toru Dutt's family background as well as to her education. She was born into a distinguished, if unusual, Bengali family, the youngest of three children. Two major events shaped her childhood: when she was six years old, her family converted to Christianity; and when she was eleven, the only son in the family, her fourteen-year-old brother, Abju, died.

Even before their religious conversion, the Dutts had been a westernized and very literary family. Toru's father, Govin Chunder, her uncles Greece (Girish) Chunder and Hur Chunder, and her cousin Omesh collectively authored a volume, *The Dutt Family Album,* in 1870. Although this collection was not particularly well received, probably because the tide was already turning toward explicit nationalism, it indicates the Dutt family's wide reading in European literatures. Toru and her siblings shared this literary culture. In her letters to her English friend Mary Martin, Toru recounted reading *Paradise Lost* so often that she and her brother and sister learned the first book of Milton's epic by heart.

Toru's precocity and her extraordinary memory led her to serious study of languages. She was accomplished in French, the language of her one completed novel and the source language for many of her verse translations. She was fluent in English. She of course spoke Bangla and wrote it as well, and she was learning Sanskrit at the time of her death. That her father enabled both his daughters and his son to study intensively was in itself highly unusual. During their residence in England, Govin encouraged his daughters to attend the lectures for women at Cambridge University, something many a father—British or Indian—might have forbidden.

While one might educate one's daughters and remain within the pale of Hindu society, conversion to Christianity was a different matter altogether. Conversion marked a drastic change for Govin's extended family, most of whom, except his mother, were baptized with him. This step essentially made the Dutt family outcaste. They became socially unacceptable, no longer invited to dinner parties and other social events among their Hindu acquaintances. It is not surprising that shortly after their conversion Govin took his family to Bombay (now Mumbai) for a year. Not long after their return to Calcutta in 1864, Toru's brother died, making more painful an already difficult situation.

In 1869, when Toru was thirteen, the Dutts traveled to France. Toru, Aru, and their mother were among the first Bengali upper-class women to travel abroad. After some months at school in a *pensionnat* in Nice, the girls moved with their parents to Cambridge, England, where the sisters continued their studies. Probably about this time, Toru and Aru began to think of themselves as writers, with Toru taking the lead in translating French romantic poetry. It is probable also that Aru contracted tuberculosis while at Cambridge, for the family removed to the British coast and some months later returned to Bengal, where the twenty-year-old Aru died in 1874.

After her brother's and sister's deaths, Toru became particularly close to her father. Clearly the two provided emotional and intellectual companionship for each other. Beginning in 1874, Toru published regularly in the *Bengal Magazine* and the *Calcutta Review*, including essays on Derozio and on Leconte de Lisle, the French Creole poet from Mauritius. The recent editor of her work, Chandani Lokugé, argues that both these essays reflect Toru's interest in mediating between cultures, perhaps fueled by her sense of her own place as culturally double. Lokugé describes the poet as an exile in her own city. In fact, the Dutts spent much time at their country residence, Baugmauree, which formed Toru's appreciation for nature and gave rise to some of her best-known poems.

In the three short years between her sister's death and her own, Toru was often ill, reporting to a friend in 1877 that she had suffered with an unremitting cough for months. Yet in this period she published a volume of translations, *A Sheaf Gleaned in French Fields,* and completed enough original poetry for a second volume, published posthumously as *Ancient Ballads and Legends of Hindustan*. She also wrote two novels—one in French, *Le journal de Mademoiselle d'Arvers*, and one incomplete novel in English, *Bianca*—though she may have drafted these prose works during her years in Europe.

A Sheaf Gleaned in French Fields was published first in Calcutta and then reprinted by Edmund Gosse in London. Gosse, who had a hand in publishing several Indian writers of English language poetry, first "discovered" Toru Dutt when he pulled her "thin and sallow packet with a wonderful Indian postmark" from the slush pile at the newspaper where he regularly reviewed books. This most "unattractive orange pamphlet" of verse, as Gosse called it, gave him a shock, "surprise and almost rapture" at the quality of the poetry. Gosse subsequently published a review of the volume and instigated the London publication of *Ancient Ballads and Legends* by Kegan Paul. To this volume, he attached a memoir of the poet. Gosse's response to Toru Dutt was not unlike that of John Drinkwater Bethune to Michael Dutt, for he approved Toru's "turning to the legends of her own race and country for inspiration." In her poems on stories taken from the *Ramayana*, Gosse said, Toru Dutt seemed "to be chanting to herself those songs of her mother's race to which she always turned with tears of pleasure."

But of course, from Toru Dutt's perspective, both her Anglicized father and her less Anglicized mother were of the same "race" as she, and her genius was to combine sources of inspiration. In this she resembled both Michael Dutt and Derozio and also her favorite English poet, Elizabeth Barrett Browning. Indeed, the political engagement with European continental politics in a poem such as "France, 1870" strongly resembles Barrett Browning's similar engagement with the Italian Risorgimento and with French politics. At the same time, it draws on a Calcutta tradition—the radical enthusiasm of men such as David Hare and Derozio for the project of the French Revolution.

Toru's poems celebrating the natural world, including "The Lotus" and "Our Casuarina Tree," are equally cosmopolitan, rewriting European precedents in a fully realized local context. The latter poem begins with a line that, as Lokugé shows, borrows from Milton's description of Satan in *Paradise Lost;* it is equally inspired by Wordsworth's poem "Yew Trees." Similarly, in "The Lotus," Lokugé identifies precedents in William Cowper's poem "The Lily and the Rose" as well as "The Indian Passion Flower" from *The Dutt Family Album*. Among the ballads and legends, the most intimate poem, "Sîta," borrows from Pope's "Windsor Forest" for its allusion to the peacock "whirring from the brake." In each of these instances, Toru Dutt melds traditions, using her broad reading to increase the range of comparison and at the same time integrating allusions in a lyrical voice all her own.

One of Toru Dutt's last poems perhaps best captures the complexity of her lyric voice. In "The Tree of Life," she has a vision of an angel who relieves her pain and fever and binds her brows with sprays of silver and gold. At once a premonition of death and a vision of the poet crowned with laurel, and hence immortalized, "The Tree of Life" creates a delicate emotional balance. It vindicates the young poet's vocation and at the same time suggests the emotional debt to her father and caretaker; her father, himself a poet, is refused the crown, though whether this is because he will outlive his child or because his talents lie in family life rather than in art is left unclear. The straightforward diction and the careful pentameter of "The Tree of Life" create a poem of understated power.

Not long after completing this poem, on August 30, 1877, Toru Dutt died of tuberculosis. She is buried in the Church Missionary Society Cemetery in Calcutta.

Sources

Toru Dutt, *A Sheaf Gleaned in French Fields* (Bhowanipore: Saptahik Sambad Press, 1876); Dutt, *Ancient Ballads and Legends of Hindustan* (London: Kegan Paul, Trench and Co., 1882). See also Edmund Gosse, preface to Dutt, *Ancient Ballads and Legends of Hindustan;* Harihar Das and H. A. L. Fisher, *Life and Letters of Toru Dutt* (Oxford: Oxford University Press, 1921); and Chandani Lokugé, ed., *Toru Dutt: Collected Prose and Poetry* (New Delhi: Oxford University Press, 2006).

À mon Père

The flowers look loveliest in their native soil
Amid their kindred branches; plucked, they fade,
And lose the colours Nature on them laid,
Though bound in garlands with assiduous toil.
Pleasant it was, afar from all turmoil,   5
To wander through the valley, now in shade
And now in sunshine, where these blossoms made
A Paradise, and gather in my spoil.
But better than myself no man can know
How tarnished have become their tender hues   10
E'en in the gathering, and how dimmed their glow!
Wouldst thou again new life in them infuse,
Thou who hast seen them where they brightly blow?
Ask Memory. She shall help my stammering Muse.[1]

---

1. In this elegant postscript and dedication to *A Sheaf Gleaned in French Fields,* Dutt modestly calls upon her father to supplement with memory the vividness of the poems in their original language. At the same time, she implicitly invokes the memory of her sister, with whom she learned French.

Sîta

Three happy children in a darkened room!
What do they gaze on with wide-open eyes?
A dense, dense forest, where no sunbeam pries,
And in its centre a cleared spot.—There bloom
Gigantic flowers on creepers that embrace   5
Tall trees; there, in a quiet lucid lake
The white swans glide; there, "whirring from the brake,"
The peacock springs; there, herds of wild deer race;
There, patches gleam with yellow waving grain;
There, blue smoke from strange altars rises light,   10
There, dwells in peace, the poet-anchorite.
But who is this fair lady? Not in vain
She weeps,—for lo! at every tear she sheds
Tears from three pairs of young eyes fall amain,
And bowed in sorrow are the three young heads.   15
It is an old, old story, and the lay
Which has evoked sad Sîta[2] from the past
Is by a mother sung. . . . 'Tis hushed at last
And melts the picture from their sight away,
Yet shall they dream of it until the day!   20
When shall those children by their mother's side
Gather, ah me! as erst at eventide?

Near Hastings

Near Hastings, on the shingle-beach,[3]
      We loitered at the time
When ripens on the wall the peach,
      The autumn's lovely prime.
Far off,—the sea and sky seemed blent,   5
      The day was wholly done,
The distant town its murmurs sent,
      Strangers,—we were alone.

---

2. The poet chooses to recall her mother's recitation of the Bangla verse tale of Rama and Sita, appropriately so, as Sita is understood to be the very type and epitome of the faithful wife.
    3. Shingle-beach: beach of pebbles and stones.

We wandered slow; sick, weary, faint,
  Then one of us sat down,   10
No nature hers, to make complaint;—
  The shadows deepened brown.
A lady passed,—she was not young,
  But oh! her gentle face
No painter-poet ever sung,   15
  Or saw such saintlike grace.

She past us,—then she came again,
  Observing at a glance
That we were strangers; one, in pain,—
  Then asked,—Were we from France? 20
We talked awhile,—some roses red
  That seemed as wet with tears,
She gave my sister, and she said,
  "God bless you both, my dears!"

Sweet were the roses,—sweet and full, 25
  And large as lotus flowers
That in our own wide tanks we cull
  To deck our Indian bowers.
But sweeter was the love that gave
  Those flowers to one unknown,   30
I think that He who came to save
  The gift a debt will own.

The lady's name I do not know,
  Her face no more may see,
But yet, oh yet I love her so!   35
  Blest, happy, may she be!
Her memory will not depart,
  Though grief my years should shade,
Still bloom her roses in my heart!
  And they shall never fade!   40

France, 1870

Not dead,—oh no,—she cannot die!⁴
    Only a swoon, from loss of blood!
Levite England passes her by,
Help, Samaritan! None is nigh;
    Who shall stanch me this sanguine flood?   5

Range the brown hair, it blinds her eyne,
    Dash cold water over her face!
Drowned in her blood, she makes no sign,
Give her a draught of generous wine.
    None heed, none hear, to do this grace.   10

Head of the human column, thus
    Ever in swoon wilt thou remain?
Thought, Freedom, Truth, quenched ominous,
Whence then shall Hope arise for us,
    Plunged in the darkness all again!   15

No, she stirs!—There's a fire in her glance,
    Ware, oh ware of that broken sword!
What, dare ye for an hour's mischance,
Gather around her, jeering France,
    Attila's own exultant horde?   20

Lo, she stands up,—stands up e'en now,
    Strong once more for the battle-fray,
Gleams bright the star, that from her brow
Lightens the world. Bow, nations, bow,
    Let her again lead on the way!   25

---

4. In "France, 1870," the poet alludes to the defeats in the Franco-Prussian war; France is
fallen, but "Levite England passes her by." In a reversal of Jesus's parable of the good Samaritan, no
one reaches across ethnic or nationalist lines to succor the struggling nation. Despite the lip service
paid to freedom in Britain, no good British Samaritan comes to the aid of France.

The Tree of Life

Broad daylight, with a sense of weariness!
Mine eyes were closed, but I was not asleep,
My hand was in my father's, and I felt
His presence near me. Thus we often passed
In silence, hour by hour. What was the need   5
Of interchanging words when every thought
That in our hearts arose, was known to each,
And every pulse kept time? Suddenly there shone
A strange light, and the scene as sudden changed.
I was awake:—It was an open plain   10
Illimitable,—stretching, stretching—oh, so far!
And o'er it that strange light,—a glorious light
Like that the stars shed over fields of snow
In a clear, cloudless, frosty winter night,
Only intenser in its brilliance calm.   15
And in the midst of that vast plain, I saw,
For I was wide awake,—it was no dream,
A tree with spreading branches and with leaves
Of divers kinds,—dead silver and live gold,
Shimmering in radiance that no words may tell!   20
Beside the tree an Angel stood; he plucked
A few small sprays, and bound them round my head.
Oh, the delicious touch of those strange leaves!
No longer throbbed my brows, no more I felt
The fever in my limbs—"And oh," I cried,   25
"Bind too my father's forehead with these leaves."
One leaf the Angel took and therewith touched
His forehead, and then gently whispered "Nay!"
Never, oh never had I seen a face
More beautiful than that Angel's, or more full   30
Of holy pity and of love divine.
Wondering I looked awhile,—then, all at once
Opened my tear-dimmed eyes—When lo! the light
Was gone—the light as of the stars when snow
Lies deep upon the ground. No more, no more,   35
Was seen the Angel's face. I only found
My father watching patient by my bed,
And holding in his own, close-prest, my hand.

Sonnet—The Lotus

Love came to Flora asking for a flower[5]
    That would of flowers be undisputed queen,
    The lily and the rose, long, long had been
Rivals for that high honour. Bards of power
Had sung their claims. "The rose can never tower   5
    Like the pale lily with her Juno mien"—
    "But is the lily lovelier?" Thus between
Flower-factions rang the strife in Psyche's bower.
"Give me a flower delicious as the rose
    And stately as the lily in her pride"—   10
"But of what colour?"—"Rose-red," Love first chose,
    Then prayed,—"No, lily-white,—or, both provide";
    And Flora gave the lotus, "rose-red" dyed,
And "lily-white,"—the queenliest flower that blows.

Our Casuarina Tree

Like a huge Python, winding round and round
    The rugged trunk, indented deep with scars
    Up to its very summit near the stars,
A creeper climbs, in whose embraces bound
    No other tree could live.[6] But gallantly   5
The giant wears the scarf, and flowers are hung
In crimson clusters all the boughs among,
    Whereon all day are gathered bird and bee;
And oft at nights the garden overflows
With one sweet song that seems to have no close,   10
Sung darkling from our tree, while men repose.

5. The two most important literary antecedents of this text are William Cowper, "The Lily and the Rose" and Alfred Tennyson, *Maud,* particularly the latter's famous lyric "Come into the Garden, Maud." In Hindu and Buddhist iconography, the lotus connotes purity and spiritual realization arising from the muck of creation. The goddess Lakshmi (associated with wealth, beauty, and wisdom) is often depicted on a full-blown lotus. Thus Toru substitutes her own version of beauty, inspiration, and poetic power for conventional European ones—the lotus, combining the red and the white, exceeds even Juno's beauty.

6. The casuarina, an evergreen, is native to Southeast Asia and Australasia, and its Bangla name, *belati jhāu,* literally means "foreign tamarisk." It is famous for the sound it makes in the wind. Both Govin Chunder Dutt (Toru's father) and David Lester Richardson wrote poems on the casuarina. The most important literary allusions here are to Milton's garden of Eden (the python echoing Satan); to Keats, "Ode to a Nightingale"; and most explicitly to Wordsworth, "Yew Trees."

When first my casement is wide open thrown
　　At dawn, my eyes delighted on it rest;
　　Sometimes, and most in winter,—on its crest
A grey baboon sits statue-like alone　　　　　　　　15
　　Watching the sunrise; while on lower boughs
His puny offspring leap about and play;
And far and near kokilas hail the day;[7]
　　And to their pastures wend our sleepy cows;
And in the shadow, on the broad tank cast　　　　20
By that hoar tree, so beautiful and vast,
The water-lilies spring, like snow enmassed.

But not because of its magnificence
　　Dear is the Casuarina to my soul:
　　Beneath it we have played; though years may roll,　　25
O sweet companions, loved with love intense,
　　For your sakes, shall the tree be ever dear!
Blent with your images, it shall arise
In memory, till the hot tears blind mine eyes!
　　What is that dirge-like murmur that I hear　　　　30
Like the sea breaking on a shingle-beach?
It is the tree's lament, an eerie speech,
That haply to the unknown land may reach.

Unknown, yet well-known to the eye of faith!
　　Ah, I have heard that wail far, far away　　　　35
　　In distant lands, by many a sheltered bay,
When slumbered in his cave the water-wraith[8]
　　And the waves gently kissed the classic shore
Of France or Italy, beneath the moon,
When earth lay trancèd in a dreamless swoon:　　　40
　　And every time the music rose,—before
Mine inner vision rose a form sublime,
Thy form, O Tree, as in my happy prime
I saw thee, in my own loved native clime.

Therefore I fain would consecrate a lay　　　　　　45
　　Unto thy honour, Tree, beloved of those
　　Who now in blessed sleep, for aye, repose,

7. Kokilas: cuckoos.
8. Water-wraith: alluding to John Logan's poem "The Braes of Yarrow" and Wordworth's "Yarrow Visited September 1814."

Dearer than life to me, alas! were they!
   Mayst thou be numbered when my days are done
With deathless trees—like those in Borrowdale,   50
Under whose awful branches lingered pale
   "Fear, trembling Hope, and Death, the skeleton,
And Time the shadow";[9] and though weak the verse
That would thy beauty fain, oh fain rehearse,
May Love defend thee from Oblivion's curse.   55

---

9. See Wordsworth, "Yew Trees," in which he writes that beneath the shade of the ancient yew, spirits may appear even at midday:

                       ghostly Shapes
May meet at noontide; Fear and trembling Hope,
Silence and Foresight; Death the Skeleton
And Time the Shadow;—there to celebrate,
As in a natural temple scattered o'er
With altars undisturbed of mossy stone,
United worship.

John Renton Denning

≈ ∽

IN HIS less than flattering review of John Renton Denning's *Poems and Songs* (1888), Oscar Wilde opined that Denning's poetry shows "an ardent love of Keats and a profligate luxuriance of adjectives." Ever the lover of art, Wilde credited some of Denning's serious poetry with "wonderful grace and charm" but complained that the "get-up of his volume, to use the slang phrase of our young poets, is very bad indeed, and reflects no credit on the press of the Education Society of Bombay." A few years later, the *Calcutta Review* was perhaps more unkind than Wilde. Ignoring the fact that many of Denning's satiric poems were published before Rudyard Kipling's fame, the Calcutta reviewer dismissed the poet by suggesting that his book should be called "Kipling Echoes." Nonetheless, the reviewer conceded, "Mr. Denning has quite obviously a muse of his own and she deserves to be allowed to speak in her own natural style" (*Calcutta Review*, 123 [1906]: 334]).

The Kipling/Denning contest was earlier decided in a different way. W. E. Stanley, in editing *Patriotic Song: A Book of English Verse*, choose in 1903 to include three of Denning's poems and only one of Kipling's. In fact, Denning and Kipling inhabited similar territory in that both extended a much older tradition of satirizing British India and all its denizens. By the time of Denning's birth in 1858, this tradition was three generations old, having commenced with the publication of the anonymous Quiz's *Qui Hi* (an excerpt appears in this volume).

Along with John Horsford, John Renton Denning is one of only two common soldiers who appear in this volume. The dedication of his first volume, *Poems and Songs,* is addressed to the Duke of Connaught, who was then commander in chief of the Bombay Army. Denning confesses that poetic ambition came to him years earlier when he served "as a private soldier in the 1st Battalion Rifle Brigade" under Connaught's command. He goes on, as authors of such prefaces frequently do, to describe his path toward poetry and his diffidence toward his audience: "Fortune, I confess, made me a soldier; although Nature, under whose influence I came first, made me in some sort a stringer together of rhymes. . . . I have now been a soldier nearly ten years; and although those ten years cannot quite be looked upon as belonging to the 'piping time of peace;' yet, so far as I myself am concerned, I seem to have used the pen, as indeed is the actual case, with more freedom than I have used the sword." His brigade, the poet said, had "brought forth few poets; perhaps for the reason that Mars would be a rough foster-mother at best."

Though his foster-mother was Mars and his literary mother perhaps the poetic muse, we know little of John Renton Denning's actual mother (and father) save that he was born at Lambeth in June 1858. By 1888, he was in Poona (now Pune) and stayed with the army for at least ten years. His poetry gives evidence of some training in grammar, probably Latin, and his pseudonym (J.A.N.) indicates that he probably also wrote for newspapers, given the then common practice of signing journalistic contributions with initials. He is listed on the title page of *Indian Echoes* as author of "Chelsea Jeanie" and "In a Dák Bungalow" and the two volumes of poetry, *Poems and Songs* and *Soldierin'*. In 1911, Denning published in Bombay a short travel book, *Delhi: The Imperial City*. He also published a more practical book, *Shorthand in Three Lessons*. Given that he was fifty-eight at the time, this publishing history suggests he retired in India.

One doubts that, like John Horsford, Denning resigned a university fellowship to flee England under an assumed name. Yet despite a reasonably strong education, he was precluded from becoming a commissioned officer owing to his class, economic situation, or perhaps personal misadventures. The poem included here is typical of the military ballads in *Soldierin'* with their emphasis on common soldiers, their trials and difficulties. As Denning says in the prefatory note to *Indian Echoes*, many of his poems appeared in such Indian newspapers as the *Pioneer*, the *Madras Mail*, the *Civil and Military Gazette*, and the *Times of India*. John Renton Denning's poetry exhibits all the ambivalence of the situation—commiseration with the common British soldier and the Indian farmer, disdain for those who pursue the profits of empire without counting the costs, and disgust at empire as a land grab. At the same time, he expressed patriotism in such conventional terms that the same imperial land grab appeared ameliorative of India's condition.

Sources

John Renton Denning, *Soldierin': A Few Military Ballads* (Bombay: Indian Textile Journal Co., 1899). See also Denning, *Poem and Songs* (Bombay: Education Society's Press, 1888); and Oscar Wilde, *Reviews by Oscar Wilde* (London: Methuen, 1908).

Enteric

Jones of 'C,' pegged out las' night, they've carried 'im inter the stiffun's ward;
What did'e die of ?—Padri sez: 'All men die by the will o' the Lord.'
Will o' the Lord, and Gawd ha' mercy, Gawd ha mercy upon 'is soul!
The soul that we'll parade for,—arms reversed—this afternoon,
An' the clay we'll slowly foller through the slush o' the monsoon,   5
  Wi' the muffled cymbals meetin',
  An' the muffled drums a-beatin,
In a strangled smothered rumble of a route march roll!
  Thump 'n roll 'n roll 'n thump,
  Till yer thouat gits in a lump,   10
While the men wot's left in barracks 'ears the music on the wind
  An' gits the 'ump
  Wailin' music on the wind
   So Gawd Rest you, Jones of 'C';
  Solemn music on the wind   15
  Ter the grave's eternitee!
With a pioneer-made coffin from the workshops—issued free!

  Oh 'ere it is enteric, boys, an' there it is enteric, boys,
  In all the big cantonments, boys, from Quetta to Lahore.
   From Poona to Cawnpore   20
   An' another bloomin' score,
  It's enteric—'teric—'teric—everlastin'—evermore—
   Wot shrivels up an' flummixes the soldier!

Enteric's wors'n the C. D. plague—an' all the hell o' the Lal Bazar,[1]
Enteric's wors'n the men we fight from the Irriwaddy to Kandahar!   25
Sooner I'd face a Burmese gingall,[2] chancin' the rip o' the nails an' wire.
  Or a spell o' chol'ra dodgin'—or storm a stiff stockade,
  Or starve upon the frontier when the 'dibs' is bein' made.
  Than ter find the doctor writin'
  That *my* bit o' service fightin'   30
Is ter skirmish through a battle wi' the fever fire!
  Fire wot comes ter burn an' slay
  When it dries yer up like 'ay,
While yer sorter go on dreamin' lazy-like as though yer dead

---

1. Venereal disease.
2. Gingall: a long tapering gun, borne by two men and fired by a third (*Hobson-Jobson*).

Night 'n day!   35
Mos' the same as if yer dead
    An' yer feel so blasted weak
When they raises of yer 'ed,
    That you'd like ter swear or shriek;
But yer tongue's a bit o' leather shriveled dry agin yer cheek!   40

    Oh 'ere it is enteric, boys, an' there it is enteric, boys,
    In all the big cantonments, boys, from Nagar to the Doon,
    From Sibi to Rangoon,
        Carn't yer stop it, stop it soon?
    For enteric—'teric—'teric, mornin'—midday—arternoon,   45
        Is a puttin' outer mess the British soldier!

Our barrick walls is white 'n 'igh, an' *pucka*[3] built by the Public Works,
But under the flags 'n roun' the lines[4] is where the dratted enteric lurks,
'Teric lurks fer the young recruity, 'cruity, 'cruity an' orficer too,
Wot comes ter guard an empire full o' gritty, blindin' plains,   50
Where creation fairly shrivels 'fore the busting o' the rains!
    Where the *mussick* is forgotten,
    Don't it pend, an' ain't it rotten—
While the *pani*[5] is a-squoojin' an' a-drippin', droppin' through!
    From the inside, green an' rank   55
    As a famine stricken tank;[6]
Not fit fer pup not pyah—black or white, or man or beast,
    But ain't it drank?
    Fightin' man or dyin' beast,
        Though it's charcoal—gravel—sand,   60
    An' it's filtered an' it's chattied[7]
    In the barracks on a stand,
Still the bhisti-bag's enteric poisons Atkins in the land![8]

    Oh, 'ere it is enteric, boys, an' there it is enteric, boys,
    In all the big cantonments, boys, from Pindi to Bombay,   65
    From Mhow to Mandalay

---

    3. Pucka: a well-built structure, usually of masonry.

    4. Under the flags 'n roun' the lines: under flagstone pavers and in the ditches where soil, feces, and so forth leach into the water and cause disease, especially during the monsoon.

    5. Pani: water.

    6. Tank: reservoir open to the air and used often for bathing and for drinking water.

    7. Chattied: placed in water pots designated for drinking; the filtering is obviously ineffective.

    8. Bhisti-bag: water bag; Atkins: nickname for the common British soldier.

Whirraru! an' 'ip 'ooray!
It's enteric—'teric—'teric ev'ry blasted, blazin' day
Wot fills chock-full the graveyard wi' the soldier!

Jones of 'C' is inter the pit! one more volley—the third 'n last; 70
If *that* could roll right over the sea, wouldn't the tears be fallin' fast!
Fallin' fast for the young recruity, 'cruity, 'cruity o' twenty years,
Wot guards six foot of Empire underneath that Empire's sod
That 'olds so much of England!—death o' man an' will o' God!
Men who've 'elped it on by sleepin', 75
Clean away from wimmen's weepin',
An' the useless, silly sobbin' o' the salt, home tears!
Back ter barracks—back ter camp
With a swingin', ringin' tramp,
An' the band wi' suthin' lively fer ter set our 'earts at rest 80
Through the damp!
'Earts at rest—the dead is dead,
We're alive an' pretty fit;
'Nother tuppence in the bank,
Ain't it better ter forgit 85
The chum wot's 'time-expired' everlastin' in the pit?

Oh, 'ere it is enteric, boys, an' there it is enteric, boys,
In all the big cantonments, boys, from Lucknow to Dagshai,
From Bhuj to Loralai,
Ain't the doctors fit ter cry, 90
'Cos enteric—'teric—'teric euchres[9] all their reason why
An' everlastin' swallers up the soldier!

---

9. Euchres: derived from the card game of that name, the slang usage implies that the doctors
have failed to make their trumps and have been defeated.

Rabindranath Tagore

W HEN HE arrived in London in June 1912, Rabindranath Tagore (1861–1941) brought with him a slim manuscript notebook. On board the ship from India, he had finished translating a series of his Bangla poems into English. Then, in a confusion of underground trains and transfers, the manuscript disappeared.

Fortunately, his son retrieved the notebook from among the umbrellas, caps, and hats in the Underground's lost property office. This notebook soon became Tagore's first English book, *Gitanjali*. It was largely on the basis of this collection that a few months later the Nobel committee awarded its prize in literature.

That a slim book by a poet already famous in Bengal but little known outside India would catapult its writer to international fame was wholly unexpected. In 1912, readers of English could have—and in some measure still have—only a refracted understanding of Tagore's significant achievements, but *Gitanjali* found popularity because it spoke to its literary and historical moment. It allowed anti-imperialists to celebrate a poet who could serve as the antithesis of Rudyard Kipling, who had been awarded the Nobel some five years earlier. Kipling's poetry, fairly or not, had come to stand for a resolutely British imperialist point of view, while Tagore could be identified with a broader understanding of the moment of nationalist struggle.

Tagore arrived in London at a particularly fraught moment in British imperial politics, for the British government had just rescinded the partition of Bengal after months of protest and had declared an intention to move the capital of British India from Calcutta to Delhi. Meanwhile, the Irish Parliamentary Party held the balance of power in the House of Commons, and strikes, lockouts, and petitions in Ireland were the daily news. The latest version of an Irish Home Rule bill was debated over many months in 1912 and 1913.

Politics was not the only arena undergoing considerable ferment—poetry and religion were experiencing their own upheavals. In 1912, Ezra Pound, Hilda Doolittle, and Richard Aldington invented imagism; Harriet Monroe founded *Poetry* magazine with Pound as her "foreign correspondent"; and Kipling published his *Collected Verse*. The climate was right for a new voice in poetry and for a new emphasis on East-West religious exchange. *Gitanjali* capped more than two decades of growing European fascination with Indian religions, dating at least from the 1893 Parliament of World Religions held in Chicago. It spoke to the multiple political needs and cultural understandings of its British and American audiences.

In this moment of political, cultural, and poetic activity, *Gitanjali* and Rabindranath Tagore made a significant impact. Although *Gitanjali* in no way fully captured the poet's work, through its lens the world came to see Tagore. Published first in a limited edition in London and then in more popular editions attracting broader audiences in Britain and America, the volume could not wholly capture a man of notable complexity—a poet, writer of drama and fiction, essayist, political and humanitarian being, educationist, musician, and painter.

Of course, before his London literary debut, Rabindranath Tagore was already a distinguished writer. Born in 1861 to one of the most prominent families in Bengal, he was the youngest son in a family of fourteen children. His grandfather Dwarkanath built a fortune (and also mortgaged a considerable part of it). His father, Debendranath, both frugal and pious, consolidated the family's fortunes and continued the family's deepening support of Brahmo Sabha, later called the Brahmo Samaj. This Hindu reform movement combined rationalist and Christian Protestant ideas with Hindu ideas and practices; members of the Brahmo Samaj advocated for social as well as religious reforms, valuing education and opposing many social inequalities stemming from caste and gender. Rabindranath's religious views and poetic practice owed much to Brahmo ideals as well as to Bengali Vaishnava devotional poetry.

Tagore owed much, as well, to highly talented older brothers, for he was remarkably resistant to formal schooling. Many years later in his autobiography, he recounted the tortures of school and of rote learning of all kinds. With particular verve, he described the pains of learning English, its impenetrability, and the soporific effect of the books, the tutor, and the dim lamp that cast its pale glow over these evening sessions. In the midst of his account, the poet recalled—or imagined?—that his tutor took the boys to the operating amphitheater of the medical college, where they were terrified at the sight of an amputated leg. English lessons held similar terrors, for the language came already dissected: "[A]t the gateway of every reading lesson stood sentinel an array of words, with separated syllables, and forbidding accent marks like fixed bayonets, barring the way to the infant mind" (*My Reminiscences*, 43). Despite the boredom of English lessons, the young man read widely via loaned books from his elder brothers. He read everything he could in Bangla, studied Sanskrit with more passion for the poetry than the grammar, and progressed in English verse as well. In his teens, he translated *Macbeth* into Bangla verse. He recalled that in his youth, "our literary gods . . . were Shakespeare, Milton and Byron," though he faulted English poets for putting personal passion above all else and thus reducing the whole human experience to one of its elements (*My Reminiscences*, 180). His resistance to traditional schooling aside, Tagore received a thorough education thanks to his elder brothers and to the atmosphere of literary and cultural excitement that pervaded the household. The lessons in Sanskrit, in sciences, in Bangla (at school and at home), and in English were rescued from dullness by the intellectual ferment centered in the Tagore joint family mansion. His elder brothers and his sister-in-law Kadambari Devi encouraged his youthful literary endeavors.

Tagore's personal suffering from traditional schooling eventually found its way into a passion for education, and he devoted much of his life and energy to the school he founded at Santiniketan in 1901. This school, along with the university eventually founded there and its sister institution, Viswa Bharati in Calcutta, required both administrative oversight and endless fund-raising. Legend has it that the poet exclaimed upon the Nobel announcement that he could, at last, fix the school's drains. The many foreign tours Tagore undertook after 1913—to the United States, Europe, China, Japan, Russia, and Great Britain—allowed him to meet other writers, to foster international understanding, to escape his sadness at the early deaths of three of his children and his wife, and, not least, to raise money for his educational experiments. Santiniketan was designed to foster the whole child and the child's love of learning. Unlike his English tutor, who literally unwrapped a package containing human lungs to explain the marvels of human speech, Tagore wrote that he "always thought the whole man spoke" (*My Reminiscences*, 42). In poetry and fiction and in education alike, Rabindranath sought to cultivate the whole person.

This effort entailed work in many genres and gave rise to essays on political, social, aesthetic, and religious topics. Tagore was a fervent supporter of Indian independence and an equally fervent believer in avoiding war and cultivating international harmony; his literary writings were attuned to the needs of women, though he arranged marriages for his female children; he protested the partition of Bengal, leading an important march through Calcutta, yet strongly disapproved of the potential for Hindu-Muslim conflict in the development of Indian nationalism; he admired but disagreed with Gandhi over such issues as birth control and the cult of the spinning wheel. Throughout his life, Tagore returned to the themes of nonviolence, communal harmony, and sympathy with the poor, even though the practical application of these priorities often led to controversy and criticism when they caused him, at various times, to distance himself from political activism. In 1915, at the height of his post-Nobel fame, Tagore accepted a knighthood from the British—not a move designed to endear him to radical nationalists. But he won sympathy in his public renunciation of the honor in 1919, following the Amritsar massacre (in which British troops fired on a crowd who were protesting the repressive policies of internment without trial).

Tagore's literary oeuvre was no less complex than his political views. English speakers, even now, can have only a partial understanding of the variety and accomplishments of his work. Rabindranath could be said truly to have made modern Bangla what it is. In Bengal to this day, Rabindranath need not be referred to by name—to invoke "our poet" suffices. Working in multiple genres, he built upon the innovations in literary Bangla of writers such as Ishvarchandra Vidyasagar (essayist, reformer, and educationist); Bankimchandra Chattopadhyay, who essentially invented the Bengali novel; and the poets Michael Madhusudan Dutt and Biharilal Chakravarti. He also wrote dramas, short stories, novels, narrative poems, satiric poems, essays, and autobiography. William Radice calls him a "perpetual innovator" in the arts, including music and painting. His many hundreds of songs profoundly shaped Bengali vocal music.

In *Gitanjali*, Tagore selected 103 poems from ten collections of his Bangla verse, primarily from *Naivedya* (1901), *Kheyā* (1906), *Gītāñjali* (1910), and *Gītamāla* (1914). *Gitanjali*, though it drew on several of his published collections of lyrics, was not, in the strictest sense, quite a translation at all: in some cases, he combined poems, and he turned his complex metered and rhymed verse into English prose poetry. As Sisir Kumar Das makes clear in his authoritative edition of Tagore's English writings, the poet was contemplating self-translation from about 1901 onward, and his resolution to translate his own work into English prose (or prose poetry) took shape after about 1905. In part, Tagore wished to replace what he viewed as unsatisfactory translations by others, objecting to their transformations of his work into English meter.

Though the larger English-speaking public would not come to know him until the publication of *Gitanjali*, there were some in the London literary scene who had heard of Tagore and were familiar with some of the earlier translations of his work. And so upon arriving, manuscript in hand, he received a formal welcome, thanks largely to the attentions of William Butler Yeats, Ezra Pound, and the painter William Rothenstein. Rothenstein arranged for one of Tagore's poems, translated by Ajit Chakravarti, to appear in *The Nation* on the day preceding his arrival. Shortly thereafter, a dinner in the poet's honor drew more than seventy of the city's most prominent cultural figures, featuring a toast by Yeats and testimonials by numerous other guests. Rothenstein was enthusiastic about Tagore's manuscript, and he and his friends arranged that the first printing would be by the India Society's press, to be released as a limited edition in November 1912. Macmillan brought out editions in Britain and the United States shortly thereafter, and Yeats famously provided a preface.

In Yeats's preface, we can see clearly the contours of Tagore's British and American reception. In it, Yeats compared Tagore anachronistically but, characteristically for Yeats, to a troubadour and a medieval saint. Thus Tagore, who though a traditionalist in his way was also a modernist, came to be understood, in Europe and America at least, partially through orientalist tropes. Tagore appeared to many admirers as a guru and a bard—not as a reformer, satirist, educationist, or experimental poet. His modified traditional dress (appearing as a guru's robes to his audiences) and his lectures on religious topics in America only increased this impression. As Mary Lago observed in *Imperfect Encounter*,

Tagore's advent in London might be taken as an example of how *not* to present an Indian poet to a Western audience. For, especially after the Nobel Prize, an inevitable backlash occurred. Ezra Pound, for one, saw the "Tagore" phenomenon as the sensation of the year but soon experienced ennui at Tagore's success. As Das puts it, Tagore almost simultaneously found an impact as a poet and as a "preacher or prophet" (*English Writing*, 18), a role that cast him as the successor to Swami Vivekananda in America. In a backwards manner, this image projected onto him by others would shape the volumes that appeared quickly after the success of *Gitanjali*. There was a sense in which his later writing reduced Tagore to a one-dimensional role as "mystic." The poet reflected in later years that in his translations he did himself a "great injustice" (Das, *English Writing*, 22).

Tagore was a poet, not a saint; he was consciously experimenting with poetics and remaking the literature of both Bengal and Britain. Although numerous critics have drawn comparisons between Tagore's English prose poems and the verse of the Christian Bible, this analogy, to my mind, derives in part from the poems' reception as a kind of mystical literature in the West. For though his English diction seems to echo biblical verse, Tagore was acutely aware of contemporary European poetics and was also in effect participating in the creation of the modernist prose poem. Tagore's English prose poems can be understood as a deliberate intervention in the British poetic scene, and these in turn, led to his further experiments in Bangla.

Shortly after publishing his volumes of English self-translations (the prose poems of *Gitanjali, The Gardener, The Crescent Moon, Fruit Gathering, Lover's Gift*, and *Crossing*, all published between 1912 and 1918), Rabindranath began to experiment with prose poetry in Bangla. These experiments he collected in *Lipikā* in 1919. Though these poems went largely unremarked, ten years later, in the thick of the controversy over modernist Bengali poetics, Tagore began once more to write in this form, publishing a poetry "distinctly different from his earlier writings," as Das puts it (*History*, 2:214–16).

Until recently, Tagore's multiple self-reinventions as a poet and his experiments with poetic language were almost inaccessible to English readers. English translations have only begun to do justice to his complex and extended literary career. Tagore's self-translations, in *Gitanjali* and especially in the series of volumes that followed it over the next decade, arguably do an injustice to the Bangla originals. The 150th anniversary of the poet's birth in 2011 promises to bring a further series of translations and reprinted volumes in conjunction with critical assessment by bilingual scholars that may lead to a fuller understanding of his work in Britain and America.

Sources

Rabindranath Tagore, *Gitanjali* (London: Macmillan, 1913); Tagore, *The Gardener* (New York: Macmillan, 1913). See also Sukanta Chaudhuri, ed., *Rabindranath Tagore: Selected*

Poems, Oxford Tagore Translations (New Delhi: Oxford University Press, 2004); Sisir Kumar Das, ed., *The English Writing of Rabindranath Tagore*, vol. 1, *Poems* (New Delhi: Sahitya Akademi, 1994); Das, *A History of Indian Literature, 1800–1910*, vol. 2, *Western Impact: Indian Response* (New Delhi: Sahitya Akademi, 1991); Mary Lago, ed., *Imperfect Encounter: Letters of William Rothenstein and Rabindranath Tagore, 1911–1941* (Cambridge, MA: Harvard University Press, 1972); Lago, *India's Prisoner: A Biography of Edward John Thompson, 1886–1946* (Columbia: University of Missouri Press, 2001); William Radice, trans. and ed., *Rabindranath Tagore: Selected Poems* (London: Penguin Books, 2005); and Tagore, *My Reminiscences* (New York: Macmillan, 1917).

from *Gitanjali*

5

I ask for a moment's indulgence to sit by thy side. The works that I have in hand I will finish afterwards,

Away from the sight of thy face my heart knows no rest nor respite, and my work becomes an endless toil in a shoreless sea of toil.

To-day the summer has come at my window with its sighs and murmurs; and the bees are plying their minstrelsy at the court of the flowering grove,

Now it is time to sit quiet, face to face with thee, and to sing dedication of life in this silent and overflowing leisure.[1]

11

Leave this chanting and singing and telling of beads! Whom dost thou worship in this lonely dark corner of a temple with doors all shut? Open thine eyes and see thy God is not before thee!

He is there where the tiller is tilling the hard ground and where the path-maker is breaking stones. He is with them in sun and in shower, and his garment is covered with dust. Put off thy holy mantle and even like him come down on the dusty soil!

---

1. Sisir Das argues in his notes to *The English Writing* that "[t]he *Gitanjali* poems indeed have deep links with the Upanishadic conception of Godhead, as has often been claimed by Indian critics, but they have neither the authoritarian voice of the Upanishadic seers nor their apocalyptic vision. They are more indebted so far as verbal texture is concerned, to the Bhakti poems of medieval India in general and the love-symbolism of Bengali Vaishnava poets in particular. . . . The original poems are marked by simplicity of diction, structural compactness and effortless rhyming and cadence. . . . The translations, though in prose, retain the haunting quality of the original to a great extent" (1:601–2).

Deliverance? Where is this deliverance to be found? Our master himself has joyfully taken upon him the bonds of creation; he is bound with us all for ever.

Come out of thy meditations and leave aside thy flowers and incense! What harm is there if thy clothes become tattered and stained? Meet him and stand by him in toil and in sweat of thy brow.

35

Where the mind is without fear and the head is held high;

Where knowledge is free;

Where the world has not been broken up into fragments by narrow domestic walls;

Where words come out from the depth of truth;

Where tireless striving stretches its arms towards perfection;

Where the clear stream of reason has not lost its way into the dreary desert sand of dead habit;

Where the mind is led forward by thee into ever-widening thought and action—

Into that heaven of freedom, my Father, let my country awake.

64

On the slope of the desolate river among tall grasses I asked her, "Maiden, where do you go shading your lamp with your mantle? My house is all dark and lonesome—lend me your light!" She raised her dark eyes for a moment and looked at my face through the dusk. "I have come to the river," she said, "to float my lamp on the stream when the daylight wanes in the west." I stood alone among tall grasses and watched the timid flame of her lamp uselessly drifting in the tide.

In the silence of gathering night I asked her, "Maiden, your lights are all lit—then where do you go with your lamp? My house is all dark and lonesome,—lend me your light." She raised her dark eyes on my face and stood for a moment doubtful. "I have come," she said at last, "to dedicate my lamp to the sky." I stood and watched her light uselessly burning in the void.

In the moonless gloom of midnight I asked her, "Maiden, what is your quest holding the lamp near your heart? My house is all dark and lonesome,—lend me your light." She stopped for a minute and thought and gazed at my face in the dark. "I have brought my light," she said, "to join the carnival of lamps." I stood and watched her little lamp uselessly lost among lights.

81

On many an idle day have I grieved over lost time. But it is never lost, my lord. Thou hast taken every moment of my life in thine own hands.

Hidden in the heart of things thou art nourishing seeds into sprouts, buds into blossoms, and ripening flowers into fruitfulness.

I was tired and sleeping on my idle bed and imagined all work had ceased. In the morning I woke up and found my garden full with wonders of flowers.

82

Time is endless in thy hands, my lord. There is none to count thy minutes.

Days and nights pass and ages bloom and fade like flowers. Thou knowest how to wait.

Thy centuries follow each other perfecting a small wild flower.

We have no time to lose, and having no time we must scramble for our chances. We are too poor to be late.

And thus it is that time goes by while I give it to every querulous man who claims it, and thine altar is empty of all offerings to the last.

At the end of the day I hasten in fear lest thy gate be shut; but I find that yet there is time.

When my play was with thee I never questioned who thou wert. I knew nor shyness nor fear, my life was boisterous.

In the early morning thou wouldst call me from my sleep like my own comrade and lead me running from glade to glade.

On those days I never cared to know the meaning of songs thou sangest to me. Only my voice took up the tunes, and my heart danced in their cadence.

Now, when the playtime is over, what is this sudden sight that is come upon me? The world with eyes bent upon thy feet stands in awe with all its silent stars.

I dive down into the depth of the ocean of forms, hoping to gain the perfect pearl of the formless.

No more sailing from harbour to harbour with this my weather-beaten boat. The days are long passed when my sport was to be tossed on waves.

And now I am eager to die into the deathless.

Into the audience hall by the fathomless abyss where swells up the music of toneless strings I shall take this harp of my life.

I shall tune it to the notes of for ever, and, when it has sobbed out its last utterance, lay down my silent harp at the feet of the silent.

In one salutation to thee, my God, let all my senses spread out and touch this world at thy feet.

Like a rain-cloud of July hung low with its burden of unshed showers let all my mind bend down at thy door in one salutation to thee.

Let all my songs gather together their diverse strains into a single current and flow to a sea of silence in one salutation to thee.

Like a flock of homesick cranes flying night and day back to their mountain nests let all my life take its voyage to its eternal home in one salutation to thee.

from *The Gardener*

64

I spent my day on the scorching hot dust of the road.

Now, in the cool of the evening, I knock at the door of the inn. It is deserted and in ruins.

A grim *ashath*[2] tree spreads its hungry clutching roots through the gaping fissures of the walls.

Days have been when wayfarers came here to wash their weary feet.

They spread their mats in the courtyard in the dim light of the early moon, and sat and talked of strange lands.

They woke refreshed in the morning when birds made them glad, and friendly flowers nodded their heads at them from the wayside.

·But no lighted lamp awaited me when I came here.

The black smudges of smoke left by many a forgotten evening lamp stare, like blind eyes, from the wall.

Fireflies flit in the bush near the dried-up pond, and bamboo branches fling their shadows on the grassgrown path.

I am the guest of no one at the end of my day.

The long night is before me, and I am tired.[3]

---

2. Ashath: ficus or banyan tree.

3. *The Gardener,* unlike *Gitanjali,* contains a more or less random selection of poems spanning the first thirty years of Tagore's career; unlike the earlier volume, this one was not designed with a single thematic arc.

65

Is that your call again?

The evening has come. Weariness clings round me like the arms of entreating love.

Do you call me?

I had given all my day to you, cruel mistress, must you also rob me of my night?

Somewhere there is an end to everything, and the loneness of the dark is one's own.

Must your voice cut through it and smite me?

Has the evening no music of sleep at your gate?

Do the silent-winged stars never climb the sky above your pitiless tower?

Do the flowers never drop on the dust in soft death in your garden?

Must you call me, you unquiet one?

Then let the sad eyes of love vainly watch and weep.

Let the lamp burn in the lonely house.

Let the ferry-boat take the weary labourers to their home.

I leave behind my dreams and I hasten to your call.

67

Though the evening comes with slow steps and has signalled for all songs to cease;

Though your companions have gone to their rest and you are tired;

Though fear broods in the dark and the face of the sky is veiled;

Yet, bird, O my bird, listen to me, do not close your wings.

That is not the gloom of the leaves of the forest, that is the sea swelling like a dark black snake.

That is not the dance of the flowering jasmine, that is flashing foam.

Ah, where is the sunny green shore, where is your nest?

Bird, O my bird, listen to me, do not close your wings.

The lone night lies along your path, the dawn sleeps behind the shadowy hills.

The stars hold their breath counting the hours, the feeble moon swims the deep night.

Bird, O my bird, listen to me, do not close your wings.

There is no hope, no fear for you.
There is no word, no whisper, no cry.
There is no home, no bed of rest.
There is only your own pair of wings and the pathless sky.
Bird, O my bird, listen to me, do not close your wings.

82

We are to play the game of death to-night, my bride and I.

The night is black, the clouds in the sky are capricious, and the waves are raving at sea.

We have left our bed of dreams, flung open the door and come out, my bride and I.

We sit upon a swing, and the storm winds give us a wild push from behind.

My bride starts up with fear and delight, she trembles and clings to my breast.

Long have I served her tenderly.

I made for her a bed of flowers and I closed the doors to shut out the rude light from her eyes.

I kissed her gently on her lips and whispered softly in her ears till she half swooned in languor.

She was lost in the endless mist of vague sweetness.

She answered not to my touch, my songs failed to arouse her.

To-night has come to us the call of the storm from the wild.

My bride has shivered and stood up, she has clasped my hand and come out.

Her hair is flying in the wind, her veil is fluttering, her garland rustles over her breast.

The push of death has swung her into life.

We are face to face and heart to heart, my bride and I.

Laurence Hope
[Adela Cory Nicolson]

～⌇ ⌇～

ADELA CORY NICOLSON (1865–1904) was born in Gloucestershire, England, to parents who had spent their adult lives in India. Her father, Arthur Cory, a colonel in the Indian army, was then on home leave. After her parents' return to India, Adela was cared for by relatives and was educated in England and for a short time in Italy. She joined her parents in Lahore at the age of sixteen. There her father, who had retired, edited the *Civil and Military Gazette,* and his daughters for some years assisted him in his work. This same Lahore newspaper employed the young Rudyard Kipling a few years later. Both Adela and her sister Annie Sophie went on to write poetry and fiction, her sister becoming famous for sensational novels she signed with the name "Victoria Cross."

In 1889, Adela Cory married Malcolm Nicolson, some twenty-three years her senior. He was then a colonel in the Indian army and an expert linguist, having passed interpreter's examinations in Baluchi, Brahmi, Persian, and Pushto. Shortly after their marriage, he saw service in the punitive expedition against the Pathans in the Zhob Valley (the route from the British Northwest Frontier to what is now Quetta, Pakistan). Colonel Nicolson was rapidly promoted in the first years of their marriage, becoming lieutenant general by 1899. He saw service in North Africa and took Adela with him, inspiring her volume *Stars of the Desert* (1903). The couple returned to India shortly after Nicolson received his pension in 1893. He died in Madras in 1904. It seems evident, so far as can be judged from the implicit autobiographical elements of her verse, that Adela Nicolson was obsessed with death, though little else can be said with certainty. Only a few weeks after her husband's death, she took her own life. Her collected poems were edited by her son Malcolm Joceline Nicolson.

Adela Nicolson went by two alternative names—she was called Violet by her husband and friends, and she published under the pseudonym Laurence Hope. Her first volume of verse was published in 1902 under the oddly elliptical title *The Garden of Kama and Other Love Lyrics from India, Arranged in Verse by Laurence Hope* (London: Heinemann). It was compared, both positively and negatively, to the poems of Swinburne, to Fitzgerald's *Rubáiyát of Omar Khayyám,* and—perhaps most aptly—to the poems of the Decadents. Thomas Hardy's response to this and the volumes published in the next two years best sums up the positive reactions to Laurence Hope. In a heavily edited obituary, Hardy claimed, "The author was still in the early noon of her life, vigour, and beauty, and the tragic circumstances of her death seem but the impassioned closing notes of her impassioned effusions" (Millgate, 213). Hardy went so far as to compare Nicolson's two volumes, *The Garden of Kama* and *Stars of the Desert*, to Elizabeth Barrett Browning's *Sonnets from the Portuguese*, which likewise made some tangential claim to be translations or imitations—but with no obvious resemblance to any originals. Nicolson's poems, though far more limited in range than Hardy suggested, were wildly popular in their time and are still in print.

In his obituary notice, moreover, Hardy hinted at another dimension of Laurence Hope's verse. He praised her "Sapphic fervour," a phrase which, according to Michael Millgate, he added on his fourth revision to the obituary. Nicolson's choice of a masculine pseudonym combined with an intensely personal, if not morbid, sensibility, and the impression of sexual ambiguity or, rather, of indeterminancy, was further reinforced by the tremendous popularity attained by the four poems set to music in 1902 by Nicolson's friend Amy Woodeforde-Finden. Woodeforde-Finden's "Four Indian Love Lyrics," as Edward Marx makes clear, remained popular for fifteen or more years. "Pale Hands I Loved Beside the Shalimar" became one of the most popular Edwardian parlor songs, and it took on a further orientalist tinge in a recording by Rudolph Valentino, who was soon to figure as the romantic eastern hero of the silent film *The Sheik*.

Reviews of Laurence Hope are themselves an education in decadence and an indication of the emergence of the New Woman, of British and American willingness to project an unfettered eroticism on India, and of the divided minds of readers. For reviewers at once delighted in the poet's erotic or romantic intensity and, on occasion, deplored her amateur diction and technical skills.

Sources

Laurence Hope, *India's Love Lyrics Including the Garden of Kama, Collected and Arranged in Verse* (London: William Heinemann; New York: John Lane, 1912). The publishing history for Nicolson is complex, as Heinemann and Lane published in London and New York under separate imprints, while Lane copyrighted the 1902 edition of *The Garden of Kama*. See also F. L. Bickley, "Nicolson, Adela Florence (1865–1904)," rev. Sayoni Basu, *ODNB*. Edward Marx, *The Idea of a Colony: Cross-Culturalism in Modern Poetry* (Toronto: University of Toronto Press, 2004); and Michael Millgate, ed., *Thomas Hardy's Public Voice* (Oxford: Oxford University Press, 2001).

Till I Wake

When I am dying, lean over me tenderly, softly,
Stoop, as the yellow roses droop in the wind from the South.
So I may, when I wake, if there be an Awakening,
Keep, what lulled me to sleep, the touch of your lips on my mouth.[1]

Kashmiri Song

Pale hands I loved beside the Shalimar,[2]
Where are you now? Who lies beneath your spell?
Whom do you lead on Rapture's roadway, far,
Before you agonise them in farewell?

Oh, pale dispensers of my Joys and Pains,   5
Holding the doors of Heaven and of Hell,
How the hot blood rushed wildly through the veins
Beneath your touch, until you waved farewell.

Pale hands, pink tipped, like Lotus buds that float
On those cool waters where we used to dwell,   10
I would have rather felt you round my throat,
Crushing out life, than waving me farewell!

---

1. "Till I Wake," "Kashmiri Song," and "Valgovind's Song in the Spring" were included in the cycle set to music by Woodeforde-Finden. There were numerous editions of Woodeforde-Finden's musical settings, the first published in 1902.

2. The Shalimar (or Shalamar) Gardens in Lahore were already world-famous in Nicolson's time and are now a UNESCO world heritage site. Built by the Mughal emperor Shāh Jāhan, beginning in 1641, the gardens contain more than four hundred fountains fed by an elaborate irrigation system.

Valgovind's Song in the Spring

The Temple bells are ringing,
The young green corn is springing,
    And the marriage month is drawing very near.
I lie hidden in the grass,
And I count the moments pass,   5
    For the month of marriages is drawing near.

Soon, ah, soon, the women spread
The appointed bridal bed
    With hibiscus buds and crimson marriage flowers,
Where, when all the songs are done,   10
And the dear dark night begun,
    I shall hold her in my happy arms for hours.

She is young and very sweet,
From the silver on her feet
    To the silver and the flowers in her hair,   15
And her beauty makes me swoon,
As the Moghra[3] trees at noon
    Intoxicate the hot and quivering air.

Ah, I would the hours were fleet
As her silver circled feet,   20
    I am weary of the daytime and the night;
I am weary unto death,
Oh my rose with jasmine breath,
    With this longing for your beauty and your light.

---

3. Moghra (mogra): a tall growing shrub of the jasmine family, with fragrant flowers.

Atavism

Deep in the jungle vast and dim,
That knew not a white man's feet,
I smelt the odour of sun-warmed fur,
Musky, savage, and sweet.

Far it was from the huts of men   5
And the grass where Sambur[4] feed;
I threw a stone at a Kadapu[5] tree
That bled as a man might bleed.
Scent of fur and colour of blood:—
And the long dead instincts rose,   10
I followed the lure of my season's mate,
And flew, bare-fanged, at my foes.

     *   *   *

Pale days: and a league of laws[6]
Made by the whims of men.
Would I were back with my furry cubs   15
In the dusk of a jungle den.

---

4. Sambur: a deer.
5. Kadapu: a South Asian tree, *Mitragyna parvifolia*, known in the lumber trade as *kaim*.
6. Asterisks are the poet's.

Rudyard Kipling

~⌒) ⌒

RUDYARD KIPLING, born in Bombay, spent his youth in India and in England. Though often identified simply as a British imperialist, Kipling (1865–1936) viewed himself as straddling two cultures, a feeling complicated by the sense of desolation and abandonment he felt in England as a child. His best-known works reflect the kinship and fascination he felt for India: *The Jungle Books, Just So Stories,* and the novel *Kim.* Kipling also wrote a series of fine short stories and many early poems based on his understanding of ordinary British life in India.

Despite living most of his life outside of India, the depth of Kipling's feeling for his birth-country is apparent in his prefatory tribute to Bombay in *The Seven Seas:* he called himself the son of Bombay. Because he no longer lived in India, he said, he existed "under an alien sky," yet clung to Bombay's hem as "a child to the mother's gown." Thus, ironically, the poet most often identified with British imperialism employed a metaphor that transformed Bombay into his mother, nurturer, and protector.

Kipling's early experience in India was profoundly shaped not only by place but also by his family. He came from an artistic and unusual household. His mother, Alice Macdonald, was the eldest of an intelligent and witty group of sisters, each of whom achieved distinction in her own life or through her children. Alice's sister Georgiana married the painter Edward Burne-Jones; another married the highly successful painter Edward Poynter; and a third married an industrialist turned politician and reared an only child, Stanley Baldwin, who became prime minister of Britain. Kipling's father, like his mother, was the child of a Methodist minister. Rather than follow the family profession, John Lockwood Kipling abjured all formal religious ties in favor of a career in art. Immediately following his marriage to Alice Macdonald, John Lockwood Kipling took up a post teaching art in India.

Rudyard seems to have enjoyed an idyllic babyhood, in and out of his father's studio and the temples, markets, and bazaars of Bombay. But following upper-class Anglo-Indian custom, Rudyard and his sister were sent to England. Kipling was five years old. Oddly, the children were not sent to live with members of Alice's lively extended family. Thomas Pinney argues that perhaps Alice felt estranged from her sisters or imagined that they would not welcome her children.

By all accounts, the young Rudyard was a tempestuous handful, having been spoiled by his Indian ayahs and indulgent parents, though this fact alone cannot adequately explain the parents' decision abruptly to leave their very young children with total strangers. Rudyard and his three-year-old sister, Alice, or "Trix," were deposited with the Holloway family in Southsea (now Portsmouth) without forewarning or explanation. Kipling did not see his parents again for five years.

In his autobiography, Kipling called the domicile in Southsea the "house of Desolation." How badly Rudyard and Alice were treated is difficult to know, but certainly Mrs. Holloway's fire-and-brimstone religion, her evangelical emphasis on Bible reading, and the experience of abandonment were to have lasting effects on Kipling the writer. The miserable years at Southsea were brightened by vacations with the Burne-Joneses and visits with cousins in the artistic milieu of the extended Pre-Raphaelite circle.

Finally relieved of Southsea, Kipling was sent in 1878 to the United Services College, a new school for sons of the less well-off among British Army officers. Most of the pupils at the college were destined for the army, and the imaginative and myopic Rudyard seemed at first ill-suited to school life. Gradually he made friends, and the principal, a family friend, proved a congenial spirit, giving the boy the run of his library and reviving the school paper as a vehicle for Kipling's talents. On leaving the college, Kipling was neither enough of a scholar nor rich enough to think of university, but his mother used her considerable connections to secure a position for him as a cub reporter on the *Civil and Military Gazette* (Lahore).

And so at sixteen Kipling was reunited with his family—to all appearances quite happily—in their home in Lahore (now Pakistan), where his father been appointed head of the new Mayo School of Art and of the Lahore Museum. The family shared literary endeavors, writing poems, satiric pieces, short prose pieces, and stories. The tradition of the Christmas annual (favored by D. L. Richardson in Calcutta fifty years earlier) lived on, and the Kiplings jointly produced the Christmas supplement to the *Gazette*, publishing *Quartette* in 1885. Exhibiting great energy and talent as a journalist, Kipling was soon given many opportunities to write feature stories, fiction, and poetry, in addition to editing news and taking on the many mundane tasks assigned to reporters on small papers. At the end of his time in India, he was transferred to the *Pioneer* (Allahabad). His work allowed him the opportunity to travel a good deal in northern India and to mingle in all kinds of society. It also sharpened his already considerable observational skills and taught him to write quickly and under a deadline. Though underage, Kipling became a Freemason and found in the Lodge one of the few social institutions in India comprising both Indians and Europeans from very different religious and social backgrounds. Like his later hero Kim, Kipling moved in and out of varying social milieus, a flexibility that allowed him to bring finely tuned observations of speech and habits to his writing. While there is no doubt that these observations veer into classist, racist, and misogynist stereotypes, they also provide the very texture that is responsible for his work's success.

Seldom has a writer been as prolific as Kipling, or so early famous. *Departmental Ditties*, first published in an official-looking wrapper tied up with red tape, were an instant hit, the first edition selling out immediately. From that moment on, Kipling's prose and verse were immensely popular, to the point that his critical reputation was at times jeopardized by his popularity. In 1907, he became the first English writer to win the Nobel Prize in Literature (and one of the youngest writers ever so recognized). Because he steadfastly refused honors from the British government, he was never officially put forward as a candidate for poet laureate. He also turned down an offer of knighthood and ignored pressure to stand for Parliament, despite his often public engagement in political controversy. At his death in 1936, when of course he could no longer decline official honors, his ashes were buried in Westminster Abbey.

Although much of Kipling's long and prolific career lies beyond the scope of this anthology, even his early poems on Indian subjects evince the vigor of language and narrative, the reporter's eye for vivid detail, and the contradictory elements that would shape his later work. Not all critics see Kipling's work as embodying contradictory elements; some instead view him as entirely univocal, an unequivocal champion of empire. Kipling's credentials as an imperialist are not in doubt—he was a friend and admirer of Cecil Rhodes, a defender of the British hegemony in and after the Anglo-Boer War, a fierce opponent of Irish home rule and independence, and a fierce opponent of female suffrage. General readers and critics since his time have engaged in a lively debate, pitting a jingoist, masculinist, and racist Kipling on one side against a heroic chronicler of empire on the other.

In recent years, a more nuanced take on Kipling has emerged from these controversies. Edward Said's foreword to Kipling's *Kim* might stand as one example. Though he argues that Kipling was, for historical reasons, oblivious to the contradictions of empire, Said points out that Kipling represented an India that "he obviously loved but could never properly have" (46). In a similar vein, Maria Cuoto speaks of Kipling as "not quite pukka enough to belong to the sahib caste" (73). Calling attention to Kipling's marginal position as a journalist rather than an Indian civil servant and his class position as neither university man nor officer, Cuoto argues that this position gave rise to his "characteristic contradictions" (80).

The literary critic Daniel Karlin, refusing to mitigate the abhorrent aspects of Kipling's politics through an appeal to history, introduces the Oxford edition of Kipling's work by arguing eloquently that we must know Kipling the way we know a city—we may dislike many of its inhabitants, but it is a major part of the country. In Karlin's view, as in Cuoto's, Kipling always knew himself to be an "outsider." For an artist, this position was both a blessing and a curse. Karlin puts it bluntly: "England was not, and never became, Kipling's native land" (xxv). Rather, Karlin argues, citing the mutual admiration of Kipling and Henry James (another outsider, for that matter), that if anything, storytelling—the craft of fiction—was Kipling's home, a place where all the vernaculars he observed or made his own might find form and meaning.

Kipling's poems in this selection are chosen from the early years of his career; they do not represent the darkening of his vision during and after the First World War, nor do they illustrate the range of his later verse. Rather, *Departmental Ditties, Barrack-Room Ballads and Other Verse,* from which these selections are principally taken, reveal both Kipling's originality and his debts to the conventions of English language poetry in nineteenth-century India. As the title suggests, the volume of poetry is divided into three sections, and in each are poems that owe their ancestry to particular traditions. First, the satiric sketches of Anglo-India in *Departmental Ditties* are close cousins to *Lays of Ind* (1873) by Aliph Cheem (Arthur Yeldham), which had gone through many editions by the time of Kipling's first newspaper verse in Lahore. Behind both Kipling and Yeldham are other anonymous satirists, who from the beginnings of Anglo-India were willing to pillory the pretensions and worse failings of their society. From Quiz's *Qui Hi,* published in 1816, to Yeldham's *Lays,* British India, particularly, had been ripe for satire. But Kipling was writing within other conventions as well. One of the most important sources for the *Barrack-Room Ballads* was less literary than popular—they took important inspiration from the late-Victorian music hall. Published in the final section among the "other verses," moreover, are narrative poems such as "The Last Suttee," which finds its source in orientalist romance, and "Lament of the Border Cattle Thief," which, like many Indian English poems that preceded it, owes something to the border ballads of Scotland as well as to the politics of the Afghan border. Then there are the language and tropes of the Christian Bible that permeate all of Kipling's early verse, despite his agnosticism. His early days in Southsea, where Bible reading was meted out as punishment, left an indelible mark on Kipling's language and style.

Sources

Rudyard Kipling, *Departmental Ditties, Barrack-Room Ballads and Other Verses* (New York: United States Book Co., 1890); rev. ed. (Garden City, NY: Doubleday, Page, 1926). See also Maria Cuoto, "Rudyard Kipling," in *An Illustrated History of Indian Literature in English,* ed. Arvind Krishna Mehrotra (Delhi: Permanent Black, 2003); Daniel Karlin, ed., *Rudyard Kipling: A Critical Edition of the Major Works,* Oxford Authors (Oxford: Oxford University Press, 1999); Kipling, *Something of Myself* (London: Macmillan, 1937); Edward Said, foreword to Rudyard Kipling, *Kim* (London: Penguin Books, 1987).

prefatory poem to *Departmental Ditties*

I have eaten your bread and salt,
    I have drunk your water and wine,
The deaths ye died I have watched beside,
    And the lives that ye led were mine.

Was there aught that I did not share   5
    In vigil or toil or ease,—
One joy or woe that I did not know,
    Dear hearts across the seas?

I have written the tale of our life
    For a sheltered people's mirth,   10
In jesting guise—but ye are wise,
    And ye know what the jest is worth.

The Story of Uriah

> "Now there were two men in one city; the
> one rich and the other poor."

Jack Barrett went to Quetta[1]
    Because they told him to.
He left his wife at Simla[2]
    On three-fourths his monthly screw:
Jack Barrett died at Quetta   5
    Ere the next month's pay he drew.

Jack Barrett went to Quetta.
    He didn't understand
The reason of his transfer
    From the pleasant mountain-land: 10
The season was September,
    And it killed him out of hand.

---

1. The poem's title references the biblical story of David and Bathsheba, in which David sleeps with Bathsheba and then sends her husband, Uriah the Hittite, to die in battle. The story is found in 2 Samuel 11. Quetta was an important British military station, first occupied in 1876. It is located in present-day Pakistan.

2. Simla: a town at the base of the Himalayas, and the summer capital of British India.

Jack Barrett went to Quetta,
    And there gave up the ghost,
Attempting two men's duty   15
    In that very healthy post;
And Mrs. Barrett mourned for him
    Five lively months at most.

Jack Barrett's bones at Quetta
    Enjoy profound repose;   20
But I shouldn't be astonished
    If *now* his spirit knows
The reason of his transfer
    From the Himalayan snows.

And, when the Last Great Bugle Call   25
    Adown the Hurnai[3] throbs,
When the last grim joke is entered
    In the big black Book of Jobs,
And Quetta graveyards give again
    Their victims to the air,   30
I shouldn't like to be the man
    Who sent Jack Barrett there.

Gunga Din

*The bhisti, or water-carrier, attached to regiments in India, is often one of the most
devoted of the Queen's servants. He is also appreciated by the men.*

[THIS BALLAD IS EXTENSIVELY PLAGIARIZED]

You may talk o' gin an' beer
When you're quartered safe out 'ere,
An' you're sent to penny-fights an' Aldershot it;[4]
But if it comes to slaughter
You will do your work on water,   5

---

3. To travel from Simla to Quetta, one would enter the mountains by way of the Hurnai (also
Harnai) Pass. The pass was an important point of defense because it was a possible route of inva-
sion from the northwest.

4. Karlin paraphrases this line as "when you're called out to deal with minor disturbances and
swagger around as you do in barracks" (654). Aldershot was an important military training center
in Surrey.

An' you'll lick the bloomin' boots of 'im that's got it.
Now in Injia's[5] sunny clime,
Where I used to spend my time
A-servin' of 'Er Majesty the Queen,
Of all them black-faced crew   10
The finest man I knew
Was our regimental *bhisti*,[6] Gunga Din.
    He was "Din! Din! Din!
      'You limpin' lump o' brick-dust, Gunga Din!
    'Hi! *slippy hitherao!*[7]   15
      'Water, get it! *Panee lao!*[8]
    'You squidgy-nosed old idol, Gunga Din."

The uniform 'e wore
Was nothin' much before,
An' rather less than 'arf o' that be'ind,   20
For a twisty piece o' rag
An' a goatskin water-bag
Was all the field-equipment 'e could find.
When the sweatin' troop-train lay
In a sidin' through the day,   25
Where the 'eat would make your bloomin' eyebrows crawl,
We shouted "Harry By!"[9]
Till our throats were bricky-dry,
Then we wopped 'im 'cause 'e couldn't serve us all.
It was "Din! Din! Din!   30
    'You 'eathen, where the mischief 'ave you been?
    You put some *juldee*[10] in it
    'Or I'll *marrow*[11] you this minute
    'If you don't fill up my helmet, Gunga Din."

'E would dot an' carry one[12]   35
Till the longest day was done;
An' 'e didn't seem to know the use o' fear.

---

5. Injia: India.
6. Water carrier. [RK]
7. Come here. [RK]
8. Bring water swiftly. [RK]
9. Mr. Atkins's equivalent for 'O brother.' [RK]
10. Be quick. [RK]
11. Hit you. [RK]
12. Karlin paraphrases this figure of speech as "carry on with his duties (bringing water to one man after another)" (654).

If we charged or broke or cut,[13]
You could bet your bloomin' nut,
'E'd be waitin' fifty paces right flank rear.   40
With 'is mussick[14] on 'is back,
'E would skip with our attack,
An' watch us till the bugles made 'Retire,'
An' for all 'is dirty 'ide
'E was white, clear white, inside   45
When 'e went to tend the wounded under fire!
    It was "Din! Din! Din!'
    With the bullets kickin' dust-spots on the green.
    When the cartridges ran out,
    You could 'ear the front-files shout,   50
    'Hi! ammunition-mules an' Gunga Din!"

I sha'n't forgit the night
When I dropped be'ind the fight
With a bullet where my belt-plate should 'a' been.
I was chokin' mad with thirst,   55
An' the man that spied me first
Was our good old grinnin,' gruntin' Gunga Din.
'E lifted up my 'ead,
An' he plugged me where I bled,
An' 'e guv me 'arf-a-pint o' water—green: 60
It was crawlin' and it stunk,
But of all the drinks I've drunk,
I'm gratefullest to one from Gunga Din.
    It was "Din! Din! Din!
    "Ere's a beggar with a bullet through 'is spleen;   65
    "E's chawin' up the ground,
    'An' 'e's kickin' all around:
    'For Gawd's sake git the water, Gunga Din!'

'E carried me away
To where a *dooli*[15] lay,   70
An' a bullet come an' drilled the beggar clean.
'E put me safe inside,
An' just before 'e died,
"I 'ope you liked your drink," sez Gunga Din.

---

13. Broke or cut: to break ranks or to cut and run.
14. Water-skin. [RK]
15. Bamboo stretcher. [RK]

So I'll meet 'im later on   75
In the place where 'e is gone—
Where it's always double drill and no canteen;
'E'll be squattin' on the coals
Givin' drink to poor damned souls,
An' I'll get a swig in hell from Gunga Din.   80
    Yes, Din! Din! Din!
    You Lazarushian-leather[16] Gunga Din!
    Tho' I've belted you an' flayed you,
    By the livin' Gawd that made you,
    You're a better man than I am, Gunga Din!   85

The Sons of the Widow

'Ave you 'eard o' the Widow at Windsor[17]
    With a hairy[18] gold crown on 'er 'ead?
She 'as ships on the foam—she 'as millions at 'ome,
    An' she pays us poor beggars in red.
        (Ow, poor beggars in red!)   5
There's 'er nick on the cavalry 'orses,
    There's 'er mark on the medical stores—
An' 'er troopers you'll find with a fair wind be'ind
    That takes us to various wars.
        (Poor beggars!—barbarious wars!)   10
    Then 'ere's to the Widow at Windsor,
        An' 'ere's to the stores an' the guns,
    The men an' the 'orses what makes up the forces
        O' Missis Victorier's sons.
        (Poor beggars! Victorier's sons!)   15

---

16. Lazarushian-leather: Karlin supposes that since *lazarus* is equivalent to *leprous,* the intention here may be "beggarly-looking (with skin like dirty leather)" (654). According to Representative Poetry Online, C. M. C. Fawcett wrote that "My ancestors the Lazarus family had a furniture company in Calcutta India . . . called C Lazarus and Co. They were well respected in the community and produced extremely fine furniture which was used in decorating of many Durber palaces. They were also friends of Kipling's. The leather which they produced was called Lazarushian leather" (http://rpo.library.utoronto.ca/poem/3381.html).

17. The Widow at Windsor: Queen Victoria.

18. Hairy: splendid, famous (Partridge, Eric and Jacqueline Simpson, *The Routledge Dictionary of Historical Slang.* [London: Routledge & Kegan Paul, 1973], 416).

Walk wide o' the Widow at Windsor,
 For 'alf o' Creation she owns:
We 'ave bought 'er the same with the sword an' the flame,
 An' we've salted it down with our bones.
  (Poor beggars!—it's blue with our bones!)   20
Hands off o' the sons o' the Widow,[19]
 Hands off o' the goods in 'er shop,
For the Kings must come down an' the Emperors frown
 When the Widow at Windsor says "Stop!"
  (Poor beggars!—we're sent to say "Stop!")   25
   Then 'ere's to the Lodge[20] o' the Widow,
    From the Pole to the Tropics it runs—
   To the Lodge that we tile[21] with the rank an' the file,
    An' open in form with the guns.[22]
   (Poor beggars!—it's always them guns!)   30

We 'ave 'eard o' the Widow at Windsor,
 It's safest to let 'er alone:
For 'er sentries we stand by the sea an' the land
 Wherever the bugles are blown.
  (Poor beggars!—an' don't we get blown!)   35
Take 'old o' the Wings o' the Mornin,'
 An' flop round the earth till you're dead;
But you won't get away from the tune that they play
 To the bloomin' old rag over'head.
  (Poor beggars!—it's 'ot over'ead!)   40
   Then 'ere's to the sons o' the Widow,
    Wherever, 'owever they roam.
   'Ere's all they desire, an' if they require
    A speedy return to their 'ome.
   (Poor beggars!—they'll never see 'ome.) 45

---

19. According to Karlin (653), Freemasons referred to themselves as "Sons of the Widow,"
alluding to 1 Kings 7:14, which describes the craftsman Hiram, whose mother was a widow.
 20. Lodge: the term for an organization of Freemasons, as well as the location where they meet.
 21. According to Karlin (653), "to 'tile' a Lodge is to protect it from intruders; the 'tiler' or
'tyler,' also known as the 'Outer Guard' is an official stationed outside the entrance to the Lodge."
 22. Open in form: traditionally, a Masonic Lodge is opened through a formal ritual in which
questions are asked and answered, and prayers and invocations made (Karlin, 558).

The Last Suttee

Not many years ago a King died in one of
the Rajpoot States. His wives, disregarding
the orders of the English against Suttee,
would have broken out of the palace had not
the gates been barred. But one of them,
disguised as the King's favourite dancing-
girl, passed through the line of guards and
reached the pyre. There, her courage fail-
ing, she prayed her cousin, a baron of the
court, to kill her. This he did, not knowing
who she was.

Udai Chand lay sick to death
   In his hold by Gungra hill.
All night we heard the death-gongs ring
For the soul of the dying Rajpoot King,[23]
All night beat up from the women's wing   5
   A cry that we could not still.

All night the barons came and went,
   The lords of the outer guard:
All night the cressets glimmered pale
On Ulwar[24] sabre and Tonk jezail,[25]   10
Mewar headstall and Marwar mail,[26]
   That clinked in the palace yard.

In the Golden room on the palace roof
   All night he fought for air:
And there was sobbing behind the screen,   15
Rustle and whisper of women unseen,
And the hungry eyes of the Boondi[27] Queen
   On the death she might not share.

---

    23. Rajpoot (Rajput) King: one of the warrior kings who controlled princely states in the
northwest of India, in present-day Rajasthan.
    24. A long curved sword. [RK]
    25. Jezail: a heavy Afghan rifle.
    26. Ulwar (also Alwar), Mewar, and Marwar: these were all princely states controlled by Rajput
kings; Tonk: a Muslim-held princely state (Smith, *Geography of British India*).
    27. Boondi (Bundi): a Rajput princely state.

He passed at dawn—the death-fire leaped
    From ridge to river-head, 20
From the Malwa plains to the Abu scars:
And wail upon wail went up to the stars
Behind the grim zenana-bars,[28]
    When they knew that the King was dead.

The dumb priest knelt to tie his mouth 25
    And robe him for the pyre.
The Boondi Queen beneath us cried:
"See, now, that we die as our mothers died
"In the bridal-bed by our master's side!
    "Out, women!—to the fire!" 30

We drove the great gates home apace:
    White hands were on the sill:
But ere the rush of the unseen feet
Had reached the turn to the open street,
The bars shot down, the guard-drum beat— 35
    We held the dovecot[29] still.

A face looked down in the gathering day,
    And laughing spoke from the wall:
"Ohé,[30] they mourn here: let me by—
"Azizun,[31] the Lucknow[32] nautch-girl,[33] I! 40
"When the house is rotten, the rats must fly,
    "And I seek another thrall.

"For I ruled the King as ne'er did Queen,—
    "To-night the Queens rule me!
"Guard them safely, but let me go, 45
"Or ever they pay the debt they owe
"In scourge and torture!" She leaped below,
    And the grim guard watched her flee.

---

28. Bars of the women's quarters. [RK]

29. Dovecot (dovecote): a structure in which doves or pigeons are kept; figuratively referring to the zenana.

30. Ohé: Oh (Hindi).

31. Azizun: a woman's name.

32. Lucknow: a city in the Awadh region, which is located in the northeast of India (the Rajput states were located in the northwest).

33. Nautch-girl: dancing girl.

They knew that the King had spent his soul
On a North-bred dancing-girl: 50
That he prayed to a flat-nosed Lucknow god,
And kissed the ground where her feet had trod,
And doomed to death at her drunken nod,
    And swore by her lightest curl.

We bore the King to his fathers' place,   55
    Where the tombs of the Sun-born[34] stand:
Where the grey apes swing, and the peacocks preen
On fretted pillar and jewelled screen,
And the wild boar couch in the house of the Queen
    On the drift of the desert sand.   60

The herald read his titles forth,
    We set the logs aglow:
"Friend of the English, free from fear,
"Baron of Luni[35] to Jeysulmeer,[36]
"Lord of the Desert of Bikaneer,[37]   65
    "King of the Jungle,—go!"

All night the red flame stabbed the sky
    With wavering wind-tossed spears:
And out of a shattered temple crept
A woman who veiled her head and wept,   70
And called on the King—but the great King slept,
    And turned not for her tears.

Small thought had he to mark the strife—
    Cold fear with hot desire—
When thrice she leaped from the leaping flame,   75
And thrice she beat her breast for shame,
And thrice like a wounded dove she came
    And moaned about the fire.

One watched, a bow-shot from the blaze,
    The silent streets between,   80

---

34. Sun-born: belonging the Suryavansha, or Sun dynasty. The Rajput kings belonged to different clans, each of which claimed patrilineage from one of the Hindu dynasties.

35. Luni: a river in present-day Rajasthan.

36. Jeysulmeer (Jaisalmer): the main city of a Rajput princely state.

37. Bikaneer (Bikaner): a Rajput princely state.

Who had stood by the King in sport and fray,
To blade in ambush or boar at bay,
And he was a baron old and grey,
    And kin to the Boondi Queen.

He said: "O shameless, put aside   85
    "The veil upon thy brow!
"Who held the King and all his land
"To the wanton will of a harlot's hand!
"Will the white ash rise from the blistered brand?
    "Stoop down, and call him now!"   90

Then she: "By the faith of my tarnished soul,
    "All things I did not well,
"I had hoped to clear ere the fire died,
"And lay me down by my master's side
"To rule in Heaven his only bride,   95
    "While the others howl in Hell.

"But I have felt the fire's breath,
    "And hard it is to die!
"Yet if I may pray a Rajpoot lord
"To sully the steel of a Thakur's[38] sword   100
"With base-born blood of a trade abhorred,"—
    And the Thakur answered, "Ay."

He drew and struck: the straight blade drank
    The life beneath the breast.
"I had looked for the Queen to face the flame,   105
"But the harlot dies for the Rajpoot dame—
"Sister of mine, pass, free from shame,
    "Pass with thy King to rest!"

The black log crashed above the white:
    The little flames and lean,   110
Red as slaughter and blue as steel,
That whistled and fluttered from head to heel,
Leaped up anew, for they found their meal
    On the heart of—the Boondi Queen!

---

38. Thakur: a respectful term for addressing a Rajput noble (*Hobson-Jobson*).

The Lament of the Border Cattle Thief

O Woe is me for the merry life
    I led beyond the Bar,
And a treble woe for my winsome wife
    That weeps at Shalimar.[39]

They have taken away my long jezail,   5
    My shield and sabre fine,
And heaved me into the Central Jail
    For lifting of the kine.

The steer may low within the byre,[40]
    The Jut[41] may tend his grain,   10
But there'll be neither loot nor fire
    Till I come back again.

And God have mercy on the Jut
    When once my fetters fall,
And Heaven defend the farmer's hut   15
    When I am loosed from thrall.

It's woe to bend the stubborn back
    Above the grinching quern,[42]
It's woe to hear the leg-bar clack
    And jingle when I turn!   20

But for the sorrow and the shame,
    The brand on me and mine,
I'll pay you back in leaping flame
    And loss of the butchered kine.

For every cow I spared before   25
    In charity set free,
If I may reach my hold once more
    I'll reive[43] an honest three!

---

39. Shalimar: gardens in Lahore built by the Mughal emperor Shāh Jāhan.
40. Kine: cattle, penned within a byre or barn.
41. Jut (Jat): a people in the Punjabi region who were known for being farmers.
42. Quern: a stone that grinds grain into flour.
43. Reive: rob, carry off.

For every time I raised the low
    That scared the dusty plain,
By sword and cord, by torch and tow
    I'll light the land with twain!   30

Ride hard, ride hard to Abazai,
    Young *Sahib*[44] with the yellow hair—
Lie close, lie close as khuttucks[45] lie,   35
    Fat herds below Bonair![46]

The one I'll shoot at twilight-tide,
    At dawn I'll drive the other;
The black shall mourn for hoof and hide.
    The white man for his brother!   40

'Tis war, red war, I'll give you then,
    War till my sinews fail;
For the wrong you have done to a chief of men
    And a thief of the Zukka Kheyl.[47]

And if I fall to your hand afresh   45
    I give you leave for the sin,
That you cram my throat with the foul pig's flesh,
    And swing me in the skin!

Recessional

God of our fathers, known of old,
Lord of our far-flung battle-line,
Beneath whose awful Hand we hold
Dominion over palm and pine
Lord God of Hosts be with us yet,   5
Lest we forget—lest we forget!
The tumult and the shouting dies;
The Captains and the Kings depart:

---

44. "Sir" or "Master." [RK]

45. Khuttucks: one of the clans whose members were recruited for the Corps of Guides, a regiment of the British army that was tasked with defending the frontier.

46. Bonair: the Buner Valley in what is now the Northwest Frontier Provinces of Pakistan.

47. Zukka Kheyl (Zakka Khel): a clan from what is the present-day Bazar Valley in Pakistan.

Still stands Thine ancient sacrifice,
An humble and a contrite heart.   10
Lord God of Hosts, be with us yet,
Lest we forget—lest we forget!
Far-called, our navies melt away;
On dune and headland sinks the fire:
Lo, all our pomp of yesterday   15
Is one with Nineveh and Tyre![48]
Judge of the Nations, spare us yet,
Lest we forget—lest we forget!
If, drunk with sight of power, we loose
Wild tongues that have not Thee in awe,   20
Such boastings as the Gentiles use,
Or lesser breeds without the Law
Lord God of Hosts, be with us yet,
Lest we forget—lest we forget!
For heathen heart that puts her trust   25
In reeking tube and iron shard,
All valiant dust that builds on dust,
And guarding, calls not Thee to guard,
For frantic boast and foolish word
Thy mercy on Thy People, Lord!   30

---

48. Nineveh and Tyre: the capital cities of the ancient Assyrian and Phoenician empires, re-
spectively. Both empires declined after their capital cities fell to enemy siege. Both cities are
prophesied against in the Old Testament for their excessive pride; see, for example, Ezekiel 28 and
the book of Nahum.

Manmohan Ghose

ONE MIGHT view Manmohan Ghose's early childhood as the converse of Rudyard Kipling's. Whereas Kipling was reared in his early years by an Indian ayah speaking Hindustani in preference to English, Ghose (1869–1924) was cared for by an English governess. Thus, unlike Kipling, Ghose experienced his first language as English. Ghose's immersion in the English language was the result of his father's great admiration for European learning. It may also have been the indirect result of his mother's mental illness.

Ghose's parents were distinguished members of the reformist religious movement, the Brahmo Samaj. His father, Krishna Dhan Ghose, had joined the Bengal Medical Service after a medical education in Scotland, and his mother, Swarnalata Basu, was the daughter of Rajnarayan Basu, a poet and historian of Bengali literature. Most biographical accounts suggest that after her marriage, Swarnalata suffered from mental illness and, when unwell, abused her children. Apparently to put distance between them and their mother as well as to facilitate his children's English education, Krishna Dhan Ghose sent his three eldest sons to an English-medium school run by the nuns of the Loreto convent in Darjeeling. Manmohan was then eight years old. Two years later, the family visited Britain, and the brothers were left in Manchester to study in the home of the Reverend William Drewett, a kindhearted Congregational minister. Manmohan discovered a lifelong passion for the classics at the Manchester grammar school.

By 1884, Manmohan was enrolled at St. Paul's School in London, where he met Laurence Binyon, with whom he formed a crucial friendship based on their mutual interests in poetry and art. After winning a scholarship to Christ Church, Oxford, in 1887, Manmohan found himself in straitened circumstances and barely able to remain enrolled. He spent time in London, where he built upon his Oxford acquaintances and became associated with Oscar Wilde and with various fin-de-siècle poets.

In 1890, Ghose, Binyon, and two other young poets brought out a joint volume entitled *Primavera*, with a lovely cover by Selwyn Image (a poet and designer already important in the Arts and Crafts movement). Binyon later recalled that the volume was "received with the indulgence often accorded to such youthful efforts, and was soon in a second edition" (*Songs of Love and Death*, 12). *Primavera* was favorably reviewed by Oscar Wilde in the *Pall Mall Gazette* and by John Addington

Symonds in *The Academy*. Subsequently, Ghose became a member of the Rhymer's Club, the association of poets begun by W. B. Yeats and Ernest Rhys. Ghose's work, however, was not represented in their collections, as the poets themselves had to bear the expenses of publication. As he struggled in London, Ghose attempted writing fiction, encouraged by Oscar Wilde, who offered to assist him in publishing his work. But Ghose felt, on the one hand, that he needed a sense of vernacular Bangla (which he set about learning) and, on the other, that his incipient work of fiction was not a success. During these years, Ghose spent holidays in Wales, perhaps thinking (as Matthew Arnold and Ghose's contemporary Sarojini Naidu did) that the "Celtic" spirit of Wales would form an antidote to late-nineteenth-century earnestness. In any case, these holidays gave rise to several of Ghose's love poems, addressed to a real or fictional person who seems to be nearly indistinguishable from nature itself.

In 1893, Ghose's life took an unexpected turn. While Manmohan was still seeking employment in England, his father died of a sudden heart attack after hearing a false report that one of his sons had drowned en route home to India. Ghose returned to India, where he began a long career in education, working in various colleges and, for a time, as an inspector of country schools. He ended his professional life as a professor at Presidency College in Calcutta, where he was widely regarded as a fine teacher of poetry. In 1908, at the persuasion of Laurence Binyon, Ghose published a chapbook of lyrics.

Though his work as a teacher and school inspector was exhausting, the circumstances of Manmohan's personal life were more challenging, owing to the political activities of his brothers. While Manmohan concentrated on the pleasures of Greek and English poetry, for he was a fine classicist, two of his brothers, Aravinda and Barindra Kumar, became increasingly engaged in revolutionary activity in support of Indian independence. They began a revolutionary association and conducted what was essentially a bomb-making enterprise and training school in the family garden. Manmohan, as a result, fell under suspicion.

In 1908, Barindra and Aravinda were arrested in what became known as the Alipore Bomb Case; after a year in prison, Aravinda was acquitted, but Barindra was convicted with a capital sentence that was later reduced to exile for life to the Andaman Islands. (Barindra was released in the general pardon of 1920.) During his imprisonment, Aravinda had begun to gravitate away from politics and toward religious activity. When a few months after his release it became clear that he might again be liable to prosecution in British India, he moved to Chandernagore and then to French-controlled Pondicherry. There he built an ashram and engaged in spiritual writing, eventually becoming famous as the poet and guru Sri Aurobindo. Manmohan continued to teach in Calcutta, though he was watched closely by the British authorities. As a result, in 1914, he was forced to abandon work on his epic poem, *Perseus*, after a threatened arrest. His daughters, in an attempt to prevent his imprisonment, went to Ghose's friend, the jurist

C. R. Das. Das intervened and persuaded the British authorities that Manmohan harbored no revolutionary plans. Das, as a compromise, gave his word that Manmohan would neither continue writing nor publish his epic, which the British feared might be understood as political allegory. According to his daughter Lotika Ghose, her father "sacrificed his life's work" rather than "dishonour the word given by his friend on his behalf" (Collected Poems, 2:ix). At his death, manuscript copies of six of twelve projected books of this magnum opus remained, comprising more than 7,500 lines of blank verse. Subsequently, they moldered in the Calcutta University Library and were never published in their entirety.

During his years in Calcutta, a second source of concern for Manmohan was the lingering illness of his wife, who became paralyzed with what Ghose described as "a strange and mysterious nervous malady with complete loss of speech and the use of her right limbs . . . combined with psychical and hysteric symptoms, and aversion to all food" (letter to Binyon, quoted in Collected Poems, 2:xiii). His wife's illness and Manmohan's preoccupation with nursing her, coupled with his financial and perhaps emotional need to protect himself against political suspicion, led to Manmohan's increasing isolation in Calcutta. In a poignant letter to Binyon, he wrote, "With English people in India there can only be a nodding acquaintance or official connection and with Indians my purely English bringing up and breeding puts me out of harmony: denationalized, that is their word for me" (Collected Poems, 2:xiii). Despite these obstacles, Manmohan continued to write. His most affecting poems are a series written after his wife's death, which are comparable in intensity if not always in technique to Thomas Hardy's late Poems of 1912–13. Unlike Hardy, Manmohan did not live to complete revisions of these poems and see them through the press.

In 1923, Ghose planned his retirement and booked passage for a long-anticipated trip to England with his daughters, but three weeks before their planned departure, he died suddenly on January 4, 1924. He left behind manuscript poetry that was eventually published by Laurence Binyon in Songs of Love and Death (1926) and by his daughter in four of five projected volumes of Collected Poems.

Sources

Manmohan Ghose, with Laurence Binyon, Stephen Phillips, and Arthur Cripps, Primavera (Oxford: B. H. Blackwell, 1890); Ghose, Love Songs and Elegies, Elkin Mathew's Shilling Garland no. 9 (London: Elkin Mathews, 1898); Ghose, Songs of Love and Death, ed. Laurence Binyon (Oxford: Blackwell, 1926). See also Ghose, Collected Poems, 4 vols., ed. Lotika Ghose (Calcutta: University of Calcutta, 1970).

from *Primavera*

'Tis my twentieth year: dim, now, youth stretches behind me;
Breaking fresh at my feet, lies, like an ocean, the world.
And despised seem, now, those quiet fields I have travell'd:
Eager to thee I turn, Life, and thy visions of joy.
Fame I see, with her wreath, far off approaching to crown me;   5
Love, whose starry eyes fever my heart with desire:
And impassion'd I yearn for the future, all unconscious,
Ah, poor dreamer! what ills life in its circle enfolds.
Not more restless the boy, whose eager, confident bosom
The wide, unknown sea fills with a hunger to roam.   10
Often beside the surge of the desolate ocean he paces;
Ingrate, dreams on a sky brighter, serener than his.
Passionate soul! light holds he a mother's tearful entreaties,
Lightly leaves he behind all the sad faces of home;
Never again, perchance, to behold them; lost in the tempest,   15
Or on some tropic shore dying in fever and pain!

Myvanwy

Spring, that in greenest shade, all wet, unguessed by any,
    Hidest some flower, to sway for the cool showery breeze,
    Now that Myvanwy's face the great thronged city sees,
Hast thou a blossom yet more fresh and rainy?

Ocean-cave, that never through dimmest water dayward   5
    Thy bright pearl sufferest, where sea-weed forests keep
    Safe from the diver's hand the radiance of the deep,
How shall I keep her heart so wild and wayward?

Unrebuked as the breeze, so joyous is she, a creature
    So like the wild, free things of the pure forest, a part   10
    Of mountain and fern, that I tremble to think her heart
Into green leaves should glide and be lost in Nature.

O so beautiful in her every step and motion,
    Surely the earth must feel and quiver at her tread!
    And O, the grace of her hand, the poise of her head!   15
Surely the air must know it and thrill with emotion.

Out in the garish noon she walks, and such light presses
    On my faint heart, that I scarce for gazing see!
    Lost in the black shadow of my love's jealousy,
I grudge her cheek to the sun, her hair to the breezes.   20

Street, all thronged with eyes, ah! look not so at Myvanwy!
    Life, that streamest on so various and bright,
    Cease, for thou wooest, but canst not win her sight!
World, she must not be thine, forget thy envy!

Yet O, so bright and so white is she, and I so lowly,   25
    Green Spring, I fear, or the world may steal her yet.
    Would that I knew her heart, what pansy or violet
'Tis that its working rules, to what snowdrops holy!

Peace, poor heart, torment not thyself with vain endeavour.
    Dost thou not know her heart? So warm and so proud, 'twould break,   30
    The hand that confides in hers a moment to forsake!
Once what Myvanwy loves, she loves for ever!

Myvanwy in the Woods

        Virgin darkness, wet and deep,
    Where dwells but April, dwells but sleep,
            What presence clear,
            Like a beam has entered here?
            What loved footsteps, that the trees   5
            Freshen the soliloquies,
    Birds break into louder lays,
            All fair nature's heart runs wild
            To remember her sweet child?
    In the wood Myvanwy strays.   10

            O what gladness thrills her through
    Her wayward darling back to woo
            From life again,
    Thought and passion, stir and men!
            Clasp her now from that great lure,   15
            O sweet nature, clasp her sure!
    Where no alien eye perceives,

Lead her; where dim brooks have birth,
Fill her with the smell of earth,
Sheet her in a thousand leaves!   20

Bloom in foliage like the flowers,
Myvanwy; to that world of ours,
        Of throng and street,
How strayed in your vernal feet?
        There, where not a daisy smiles,   25
        There, where green earth's pale exiles
Toil and toil and never cease!
        Who is this? the passer said;
        Rustic grass was in your tread,
In your laughter the wild breeze.   30

Ah! no gift of heath to city,
It was love led you, love and pity,
        To my sad heart,
Child, your rapture to impart.
        Me, fast-bound like wintry earth,   35
        Your intoxicating mirth
Loosed, and rained delightful showers,
        Showed me where their song birds borrow,—
        All the uselessness of sorrow,
All the joy of April flowers.   40

Joseph Furtado

J OSEPH FURTADO (1872–1947) was born and raised in the multicultural and multilingual town of Pilerne in Goa. After attending school there for a few years, Furtado left the school system to be educated at home. Besides learning Portuguese and Marathi, Furtado also learned to speak English, an unusual skill for most boys in Pilerne. He later said that he learned English to further his career and in the belief that if his writings stood any chance of success, they stood "that chance with the enlightened speakers of that noble tongue" (preface, *Poems*). Furtado finished his schooling in Bombay and went on to work for the Great Indian Peninsular Railway at Jubbulpore, progressing to the role of draftsman.

As is evident from his 1901 volume of English verse, he also spent some time in Calcutta, where he began his career as a poet. The excerpts here, in keeping with the period covered by this anthology, are from his 1901 book, though his later work was published to a wider audience. A prolific writer, Furtado had produced at least four books by 1927, when he returned to Goa from Bombay. His first book published from Goa, *My Country Charms,* was not well received, and he did not publish much, if anything, for nine years following. However, his collections of poetry *Lays of Goa* and *The Goan Fiddler* caught the eye of Sir Edmund Gosse, who had introduced Sarojini Naidu to the British public. Furtado's *Goan Fiddler* was published in England in 1927. *The Desterrado* (The Exile) appeared in London. In 1938, Furtado published two further books: *Golden Goa!* a work of historical fiction, and a book of poems titled *Songs of Exile.* His final book, *Selected Poems,* appeared in 1942. He has been credited by the *Oxford English Dictionary* as the person who coined the word "Goan." He was one of the first writers to incorporate Goan English dialect into his poems, as can be seen in his work featuring local Goan characters. Furtado returned to Bombay toward the end of his life and died there in 1947.

Sources

Joseph Furtado, *Poems* (Calcutta: Thacker, Spink, 1901). See also http://www.himalmag
.com/The-Goan-fiddler_nw2951.html and http://www.mail-archive.com/goanet@lists
.goanet.org/msg45868.html.

Homesick

To the banks of the Hooghly, so sacred in th' eyes
Of all Ind, where the "City of Palaces" stands,
To a spot which its fairest prospect commands,
Have I come all forlorn, as sad yearnings arise
In my bosom and bitterly trouble my mind—   5
Yearnings wild for my country and home far away—
To see if aught in that city's fair sights I can find
To stifle those feelings as well as I may.
Rightly "City of Palaces" called, for so high,
So stately and fair, are thy domes, and replete   10
With all art can embellish and wealth can supply,
As becometh an opulent empire's chief seat:
Which, glimmering now in the sun's parting beams
Appears like a beautiful vision in dreams!
Not so proud are the scenes in my country I see,   15
Yet they, they are a thousand times dearer to me.
For a mortal here runs but a feverish race
Through vices and follies and vanities base;
Where pleasure, as false as the harlot's false smiles,
But poisons the victim whose hour it beguiles;   20
Where wealth, to few minions of fortune confined,
But mocks at the poverty thinning mankind,
While dooming a million of wretches to sigh—
Of diseases and hunger a thousand to die!
And though vessels by hundreds now gaudily ride   25
On the river, all laden with goods and with gold,
And a million people are pressing each side
With bustle and clamour,—lo! Numbers untold
Shall be suddenly dead ere the morning arise,
As a direful scourge is there raging within,   30
And its homes are now rent with wild wailings and cries—
For the Lord, He is wreaking His wrath on our sin!
Oh! I shudder to dwell on the fate of this land,
Of this empire so wide and so rich and so fair.
If the Mighty extend not His merciful hand,   35
All its fields shall lie waste, and, abandoned and bare,
All its harbours and towns—when a decade hath fled—
And the half of the thrice hundred millions be dead,
With a silent voice moaning in air, "Spare, Lord, spare!"

Oh! I shudder to think—for this moment my breath   40
May have drawn in the venomous microbes of death.
On my homeward return I may stagger and fall
Of a sudden—neglected, unpitied by all;
And, remote from my home and all dearest I hold.
The heart of the patriot for e'er may be cold,   45
Now so warm with the love of his country and lute,
And the tongue of the minstrel for ever be mute!

Yet a country there lies, which the sea-waters lave—
By a saint[1] it is guarded—from pestilence free;
The land where the mango and cocoanut wave—   50
My own native land, fairest isle of the sea!
And now summer is coming, the season of joy,
When Love does not tarry and maidens feel coy;
For the bridegrooms will go to their homes with the ring,[2]
And the birds they will merrily, merrily sing   55
'Mid the fruits that are ripe on the trees: to be heard,
At the window the bulbul will come, and the bird
Of tiny dark wings but snowy-white breast—
The bonny blithe birdie that sings without rest—
It will come to my garden to build up its nest;   60
And remind the lone fair, in the balcony near,
Of her love far away, who presented them grain
While hearing enraptured their musical strain,
And wring from the lady a sigh and a tear!

Oh to be once again in the land of my birth,   65
To awake with the dawn to the herald's cry,
And greet from the hill the sun gilding the earth
To the welcoming hymn of the lark in the sky;
Then to wander till eve o'er the fields that I love;
Then to glory of sunset to watch from the lea;   70
Then to gaze at the stars in the heavens above,
And be lulled to sweet sleep by the roar of the sea!—
Oh! to share these delights for a month or a day,
I would turn from the gift of yon sceptre and sway![3]

---

1. St. Francis Xavier, Apostle to the Indies. [JF]
2. Some of the conditions mentioned in this passage are peculiar to Gôa. [JF]
3. The viceregal palace is supposed to be within view of the author. [JF]

O my country! thou land of my birth and my sires,   75
Source of joy and the centre of all my desires!
Oh! remembering thee, with such raptures I dwell
On thy thousand sweet charms, and I love thee so well,
That my love and my raptures no language could tell!
What other can vie with thy green cashew hill,   80
With thy mineral springs and thy fish-teeming rills,
With thy picturesque groves and thy rice-waving plains,
With thy palm-covered shores and magnificent fanes?
And yet, O my country so fair! art thou blest?
Alas! great are the evils thy children molest!   85

Rise, my countrymen, rise to the bard's earnest cry!
And march to his lyre, for the moment is nigh
When the Genius of Goa shall vanquish its foes,
And triumphantly seize on the trophies it owes.
Let nothing—till Heaven your labours should crown—   90
Let not shame of your birth, let not Fortune's grim frown,
Or the taunt of the foemen—discourage your hearts,
For yours—yours are the laurels in Science and Arts.
But forget not, forsake not your country and home,
Whate'er heights ye may climb, whate'er lands ye may roam.   95
And shame on the coward his land or his birth
Who disclaims,—he's the meanest of wretches on earth:
He shall own to his sorrow, but own it too late—
When disowned by his sons—leave the wretch to his fate.
Rise, my countrymen! oceans between ye may roll;   100
Though sundered by oceans, be joined in the soul,
Like sons of one mother—rise ye then all:
Rise, my brothers, oh rise to the minstrel's loud call!
And march ye this forward for life's noblest end:
With virtue for weapon and god for your friend,   105
And the weal of your country for e'er in your eyes,
Be courage your watch-word and glory your prize!

The moon hath arisen! with radiance mild
It shines o'er the town with its million abed,—
The bride with her bridegroom, the mother with child,   110
The lord in his mansion, the swain in his shed:
Each asleep in the home of his pride or his choice,
All reposing from toil and from trouble and care;
And unbroken the silence is, save by the voice

Of one pouring his bitter laments to the air, 115
A lone exile, and victim to sorrow and pain,
Who pines for his country and home—but in vain!
Hark! the clock—it is twelve—I must homewards retreat,
To a home where no children await by the fire,
Nor a wife, nor a comrade, my entrance to greet,— 120
But retreat to a garret, alone with my lyre!
Good-night, my sweet country: may angels descend
With blessings for ever thy sons to befriend;
And, whatever the lot to me Heaven decree,
E'er my prayers shall rise for the welfare of thee. 125
Good-night, my dear country, my heart's best delight;
Good-night, my dear brothers,—sweet country, good-night!

Aurobindo Ghose

~) (~

A MYSTIC SEER and guru, an Edwardian aesthetic poet, a fire-breathing revolutionary—one could describe Aurobindo Ghose (1872–1950) in these contradictory ways. Or one could parcel out such descriptions, assigning them respectively to Aurobindo and to his brothers Manmohan and Barindra Kumar. All three achieved fame, or at least notoriety, in turn-of-the-century Bengal. Manmohan became a respected poet and teacher; Barindra Kumar became a revolutionary and convicted terrorist; and Aurobindo, finally, became best known as a religious teacher, espousing human evolution toward the divine and forms of yogic practice designed to facilitate unity with the transcendent.

Born Aravinda Ackroyd Ghose in Calcutta to Krishna Dhan Ghose, a medical officer in the civil service, and Swarnalata Basu, the daughter of a distinguished poet and historian of Bengali literature, Aurobindo was soon sent, with his two brothers, to an English-medium school in Darjeeling. Although Aurobindo was only four years old, his father, by later accounts, evidently wished to separate the children from their mother, who was subject to bouts of mental illness during which she abused the children.

Two years later, in 1879, the family traveled to England. There Swarnalata gave birth to her fifth child, Barindra Kumar, who along with his sister (born in 1877) returned to India, while the three older boys remained in Manchester, in the home of the clergyman William Drewett, who treated the boys well and prepared them for competitive schools. Both Manmohan and Aurobindo won scholarships to St. Paul's School in London, and both went on to study at university, with Aurobindo winning a senior classical scholarship to King's College, Cambridge. At Cambridge, Aurobindo continued to excel, earning a first class in the classical tripos at the end of his second year. He left Cambridge without a degree at this point, largely because his father had destined him for the Indian Civil Service and he was to sit for the ICS examination. Aurobindo duly passed the examination, though perhaps demonstrating his ambivalence toward a career in the Civil Service by his poor performance. At this point, only the ICS riding examination remained between him and what his father judged to be a good posting in India, but he failed a first attempt, failed to show up to a second examination, and when offered yet a third opportunity did not respond to the examiner's requests and even lied about his absences. Despite special pleading from his English friends, the ICS administration felt obliged to fail him, notwithstanding his obvious brilliance at St. Paul's and at Cambridge. His biographer, Peter Heehs, argues that while we cannot know precisely how clearly Aurobindo planned this failure, it relieved him of a burden he did not wish to take up; Aurobindo wrote in later years that he could not reject the Civil Service outright because of his obligation to his father but was "greatly relieved and overjoyed" by the ICS failure (Heehs, 32). Indeed, Heehs shows that Aurobindo's failure in the ICS was owing to what amounted to a personal and generational shift between his father's views and his own.

Aurobindo's political views had already led him to conclude that he could do little to improve the lot of his countrymen from within the government. With the assistance of British friends, accordingly, he found employment with the maharaja of Baroda. There he served as the maharaja's private secretary and taught in the college. Living in Baroda for thirteen years, he studied Sanskrit and Indian vernacular languages and wrote a great deal of poetry. As a "princely state," Baroda was not under direct British rule, and it served as Aurobindo's introduction to India. His circumstances differed markedly, then, from those of his brother Manmohan, who felt himself isolated in Calcutta as an Anglicized Indian, fully accepted neither by Indians nor by the British. As the nationalist movement increased in intensity and the partition of Bengal in 1905 gave rise to strong opposition, Aurobindo resigned his position, moving in 1906 to Calcutta, where he edited the English language newspaper *Bande-Mataram*. Aurobindo and his brother Barindra began organizing secret societies in Bengal, bent on radical opposition to the British raj. Aurobindo was prosecuted for and acquitted of sedition charges in 1907 but was arrested along with Barindra Kumar and others in 1908 on charges stemming from an unsuccessful attempt to assassinate a British judge who had handed down harsh sentences to nationalist activists. The plot went awry; the bomb intended for the judge's carriage landed instead in another, killing two British women. In the subsequent trial which became known as the Alipore bomb case, Aurobindo was acquitted, but his brother was convicted and sentenced finally to transportation for life to the Andaman Islands. Aurobindo continued his nationalist activities but, when told in 1910 that he was again about to be arrested on sedition charges, fled to Chandernagore and thence to Pondicherry, the capital of French India.

Although he had married a child bride, Mrinalini Bose, in 1901, they spent little time together and had no children. Aurobindo spent the rest of his life in Pondicherry, never sending for his hopeful wife. Instead he devoted himself to building an ashram, to writing, and to the practice of yoga. He wrote voluminously—letters, philosophical treatises, poems, and what is perhaps the longest epic in English, a poem titled *Savitri*. His collected works run to more than thirty volumes, including *The Life Divine*, *The Synthesis of Yoga*, and *The Future Poetry*. Despite his nationalist agenda and his emphasis on yogic practice, Aurobindo continued throughout his life to write poems in English. Many of his shorter poems written in Pondicherry constituted experiments in quantitative meter, much influenced by his early study of the Greek classics.

The poems presented here come from Aurobindo's early English verse; they were first printed privately in Baroda in 1895 in a volume titled *Songs to Myrtilla* and were reprinted under the same title in 1923 in Calcutta. They reveal two of Aurobindo's principal concerns during his years in Baroda—his enthusiasm for Indian vernacular languages and his growing nationalist convictions. His poems to Michael Madhusudan Dutt (whose work appears in this volume) and to Bankim Chandra Chattopadhyay [Chatterji] celebrate their achievements as makers of literary Bangla. His poems and elegies for Ireland and for Charles Stewart Parnell, disgraced leader of the Irish Land League and the Home Rule Party, reveal his profound sense of the connections between Irish nationalism and Indian nationalism. These poems stand in contrast to Aurobindo's later religious poetry in their concreteness and in their political rhetoric. At the same time, they reveal how thoroughly his European classical education shaped his imagination, for they continually draw comparisons between Greek history and tropes and the poet's current situation.

In the envoi to *Songs to Myrtilla*, the poet turns from the "Hellenic Muse" to Sarasvatī, the Indian muse. He bids farewell to his completed verses with these words:

> For in Sicilian olive-groves no more
> Or seldom must my footprints now be seen,
> Nor tread Athenian lanes, nor yet explore
> Parnassus or thy voiceful shores, O Hippocrene.
> Me from her lotus heaven Saraswati
> Has called to regions of eternal snow
> And Ganges pacing to the southern sea,
> Ganges upon whose shores the flowers of Eden blow.

> (*Songs*, [1923], 57)

Very much like Sir William Jones pairing Hindu and European deities, Aurobindo matches Parnassas and its Castalian spring with the Himalayas and the Ganges River. Yet the Ganges as it paces to the "southern sea," or the Bay of Bengal, still flows, watering the flowers of the poet's Eden.

Sources

Aurobindo Ghose, *Songs to Myrtilla* (Baroda: privately printed, 1895); repr. (Calcutta: Sarat Chandra Guha, 1923). See also Peter Heehs, *The Lives of Sri Aurobindo* (New York: Columbia University Press, 2008).

O Coil, Coil

O coil,[1] honied envoy of the spring,
Cease thy too happy voice, grief's record, cease:
For I recall that day of vernal trees,
The soft asoca's[2] bloom, the laden winds
And green felicity of leaves, the hush,   5
The sense of nature living in the woods.
Only the river rippled, only hummed
The languid murmuring bee, far-borne and slow,

Emparadised in odours, only used
The ringdove[3] his divine, heart-moving speech;   10
But sweetest to my pleased and singing heart
Thy voice, O coil, in the peepel tree.[4]

O me! for pleasure turned to bitterest tears!
O me! for the swift joy, too great to live,
That only bloomed one hour! O wondrous day,   15
That crowned the bliss of those delicious years.

The vernal radiance of my lover's lips
Was shut like a red rose upon my mouth,
His voice was richer than the murmuring leaves,
His love around me than the summer air.   20

Five hours entangled in the coil's cry
Lay my beloved twixt my happy breasts.
O voice of tears! O sweetness uttering death!
O lost ere yet that happy cry was still!

O tireless voice of spring! Again I lie   25
In odorous gloom of trees; unseen and near
The windlark gurgles in the golden leaves,
The woodworm spins in shrillness on the bough:

---

1. Coil: the Indian Cuckoo, often invoked in poetry.
2. The ashoke or ashoka tree, sometimes called the sita-ashoke, is a small evergreen tree with fragrant red flowers. Ashoka, in Sanskrit, literally translates as "sorrowless." In the *Rāmāyaṇa*, Rama searches for his kidnapped wife, Sita, and appeals to the plants and animals of the forest to help him, calling on the ashoka tree for aid. Meanwhile, Sita, in the garden of her captor, Rāvaṇa, sinks down beneath an ashoka tree as she weeps.
3. Ringdove: a European pigeon, sometimes mentioned in British poetry.
4. Peepel (peepul): the sacred fig or bodhi tree.

Thou by the waters wailing to thy love,
O chocrobacque![5] Have comfort, since to thee   30
The dawn brings sweetest recompense of tears
And she thou lovest hears thy pain. But I
Am desolate in the heart of fruitful months,
Am widowed in the sight of happy things,
Uttering my moan to the unhoused winds,   35
O coil, coil, to the winds and thee.

Charles Stewart Parnell

1891

O pale and guiding light, now star unsphered,[6]
Deliverer lately hailed, since by our lords
Most feared, most hated, hated because feared,
Who smot'st them with an edge surpassing swords!
Thou too wert then a child of tragic earth,   5
Since vainly filled thy luminous doom of birth.

---

5. In his translation of the play *Vikramorvasie*, Aurobindo mentions the legend of the *chocrobacque*,
a "wild-drake" who believed he had lost his mate:

Thou, wild-drake, when thy love,
Her body hidden by a lotus-leaf,
Lurks near thee in the pool, deemest her far
And wailest musically to the flowers
A wild deep dirge. Such is thy conjugal
Yearning, thy terror such of even a little
Division from her nearness.

Excerpted from the Sri Aurobindo Ashram's
collection of online texts,
at http://www.sriaurobindoashram.com

6. Charles Stewart Parnell (1846–1891) was an Irish nationalist who led the fight for home
rule. He was an elected member of the British parliament and the leader of the Irish Parliamentary
Party (previously known as the Home Rule Party). He also founded the Irish National League,
which replaced the defeated Irish National Land League and expanded its mission to include home
rule as well as economic reforms. It is difficult to overstate Parnell's importance as a political figure
in nineteenth-century Ireland; he is sometimes referred to as Ireland's "uncrowned king."

Hic Jacet

Patriots, behold your guerdon.[7] This man found
Erin,[8] his mother, bleeding, chastised, bound,
Naked to imputation, poor, denied,
While alien masters held her house of pride.
And now behold her! Terrible and fair   5
With the eternal ivy in her hair,
Armed with the clamorous thunder, how she stands
Like Pallas' self the Gorgon[9] in her hands.
True that her puissance will be easily past,
The vision ended; she herself has cast   10
Her fate behind her: yet the work not vain
Since that which once has been may be again,
And she this image yet recover, fired
With godlike workings, brain and hands inspired,
So stand, the blush of battle on her cheek,   15
Voice made omnipotent, deeds that loudly speak,
Like some dread Sphinx, half patent to the eye,
Half veiled in formidable secrecy
And he who raised her from her forlorn life
Loosening the fountains of that mighty strife,   20
Where sits he? On what high, foreshadowing throne
Guarded by grateful hearts? Beneath this stone
He lies: this guerdon only Ireland gave,
A broken heart and an unhonoured grave.[10]

---

7. Hic Jacet (Latin): "here lies." The poem addresses Parnell at his grave; he was buried in
Glasnevin cemetery. Guerdon: reward.

8. Erin: Ireland.

9. The Greeks had multiple, conflicting myths about the Gorgons. In the Attic tradition, re-
counted in Euripides' *Ion*, the Gorgons were monsters created by Gaia to fight with the Titans
against the gods, but Athena (Pallas) slew one of the Gorgons and wore this monster's head on her
aegis, or breastplate.

10. Aurobindo is referencing Parnell's disgrace. In 1880, Parnell began an affair with Kather-
ine (Kitty) O'Shea, and despite the fact that she was married, their liaison continued for years. In
1889, Mrs. O'Shea's husband filed for a divorce, and the trial brought her relationship with Par-
nell to national attention, causing him to alienate Liberals in England who had supported home
rule. In June 1891, he and Katherine were married, and many Irish supporters of his own party,
whose Catholic sensibilities were no doubt offended, turned against him. On October 6, 1891,
when Parnell died, he was in poor health and at the head of a deeply fractured party.

Bunkim Chandra Chatterji

How hast thou lost, O month of honey and flowers,
The voice that was thy soul![11] Creative showers,
The cuckoo's daylong cry and moan of bees,
Zephyrs and streams and tender-blossoming trees
And murmuring laughter and heart-easing tears   5
And tender thoughts and great and the compeers
Of lily and jasmine and melodious birds,
All these thy children into lovely words
He changed at will and made soul-moving books
From hearts of men and women's honied looks.   10
O master of delicious words! the bloom
Of chompuk[12] and the breath of king-perfume
Have made each musical sentence with the noise
Of women's ornaments and sweet household joys
And laughter tender as the voice of leaves   15
Playing with vernal winds. The eye receives
That reads these lines an image of delight,
A world with shapes of spring and summer, noon and night;
All nature in a page, no pleasing show
But men more real than the friends we know.   20
O plains, O hills, O rivers of sweet Bengal,
O land of love and flowers, the spring-bird's call
And southern wind are sweet among your trees:
Your poet's words are sweeter far than these.
Your heart was this man's heart. Subtly he knew   25
The beauty and divinity in you.
His nature kingly was and as a god
In large serenity and light he trod
His daily way, yet beauty, like soft flowers
Wreathing a hero's sword, ruled all his hours.   30
Thus moving in these iron times and drear,

---

11. Bunkim Chandra Chatterji (Bankim Chandra Chattopadhyay) (1838–1894), Bengal's first
major novelist, was also a poet and a journalist. He famously authored the poem "Vande Mataram,"
which became India's national anthem, and he is credited with creating Bangla as a literary
language.

12. Chompuk (chumpuk): "A highly ornamental and sacred tree (*Micheliachampaca*, L., also
M. Rheedii), a kind of magnolia, whose odorous yellow blossoms are much prized by Hindus, offered
at shrines, and rubbed on the body at marriages, &c. H. *champak*, Skt. *champaka*" (*Hobson-Jobson*).

Barren of bliss and robbed of golden cheer,
He sowed the desert with ruddy-hearted rose,
The sweetest voice that ever spoke in prose.

Madhusudan Dutt

Poet, who first with skill inspired did teach
Greatness to our divine Bengali speech,—
Divine, but rather with delightful moan
Spring's golden mother makes when twin-alone
She lies with golden Love and heaven's birds   5
Call hymeneal with enchanting words
Over their passionate faces, rather these
Than with the calm and grandiose melodies
(Such calm as consciousness of godhead owns)
The high gods speak upon their ivory thrones   10
Sitting in council high,—till taught by thee
Fragrance and noise of the world-shaking sea.
Thus do they praise thee who amazed espy
Thy winged epic and hear the arrows cry
And journeyings of alarmed gods; and due   15
The praise, since with great verse and numbers new
Thou mad'st her godlike who was only fair.
And yet my heart more perfectly ensnare
Thy soft impassionated flutes and more thy Muse
To wander in the honied months doth choose   20
Than courts of kings, with Sita in the grove
Of happy blossoms, (O musical voice of love
Murmuring sweet words with sweeter sobs between!)
With Shoorpa in the Vindhyan[13] forests green
Laying her wonderful heart upon the sod   25

---

13. Surpanakha (also Soorphanaka or Shurpanakha) is a demoness, and Rāvaṇa's sister in the *Rāmāyaṇa*. A widow, she meets Rama while he is searching for his wife in the Vindhyan forests, and she falls immediately in love with him, hoping to marry first him, then his brother Lakshman. When she threatens to eat Sita to make Rama available, Lakshman cuts off her nose. According to Paula Richman, Sita and Surpanakha can be taken as feminine archetypes that are ubiquitous in mythology: "Sita is good, pure, light, auspicious, and subordinate, whereas Surpanakha is evil, impure, dark, inauspicious, and insubordinate" (*Many Ramayanas*, Berkeley: University of California Press, 1991, 83).

Made holy by the well-loved feet that trod
Its vocal shades; and more unearthly bright
Thy jeweled songs made of relucent light
Wherein the birds of spring and summer and all flowers
And murmuring waters flow, her widowed hours   30
Making melodious who divinely loved.
No human hands such notes ambrosial moved;
These accents are not of the imperfect earth;
Rather the god was voiceful in their birth,
The god himself of the enchanting flute,   35
The god himself took up thy pen and wrote.

Sarojini Naidu

S AROJINI NAIDU'S encounter with the English language is perhaps the most curious of any Indian poet's. In a letter to Arthur Symons—her British friend and poetic mentor—Naidu (1879–1949) recounted her childhood obstinacy. Her siblings, she said, were taught English at an early age. "I," she writes, "was stubborn and refused to speak it. So one day when I was nine years old my father punished me—the only time I was ever punished—by shutting me in a room alone for a whole day. I came out of it a full-blown linguist. I have never spoken any other language to him, or to my mother, who always speaks to me in Hindustani" (*Golden Threshold*, 11). This story, though surely apocryphal in its details, betrays the kind of stubborn resolution that characterized the young Sarojini's study, her voyage to England, her marriage, and even her later political career. From the room where she resolved to speak English to the prisons she endured years later during the movement for Indian independence, Sarojini's path was her own.

Born to a Bengali Brahmin family living in Hyderabad, Sarojini Chattopadhyay had an unconventional upbringing. Her parents were members of the Brahmo Samaj, the religious offshoot of Hinduism that both influenced and in some ways resembled Unitarianism. Her father, Agorenath, received his medical education in Aberdeen and found employment at the court of the nizam of Hyderabad. At the nizam's request, Agorenath established a school, and his home became the meeting place of an extraordinarily cosmopolitan group of intellectuals and poets. Aghorenath Chattopadhyay was noted for his work in education and social reform, his love of literature, and a strong religious (perhaps mystical) streak that resulted in a dedication to alchemy. Rabindranath Tagore affectionately satirized him in his story "The Hungry Stones." Sarojini's mother, Barada Sundari Devi, studied in a Brahmo school for women while her husband studied in Scotland; a singer and storyteller, she wrote many lovely Bengali lyrics that Sarojini fondly recalled in her correspondence with Symons. The family was freethinking, breathing art and politics together. Sarojini's seven siblings were a talented lot as well— her brother Virendranath became an internationally known revolutionary later forced to live abroad; a sister, Mrinalini, studied at Cambridge and became the principal of a girls' college in Lahore; her youngest brother, Harindranath, became a poet, actor, dramatist, and member of Parliament; and her youngest sister married a trade unionist and was active in the independence movement.

The youthful Sarojini was an intellectual and poetic prodigy. At the age of twelve, she passed the Madras University matriculation examination. In her early teens, she composed long poems, a volume of which her father published. She fell in love at about fourteen with her father's colleague Govindarajulu Naidu—unsuitable in her parents' eyes because of his caste and age and because he was not Bengali. Partly to separate the two, Sarojini's father persuaded the nizam to offer her a scholarship to Cambridge. She left for London at age sixteen and subsequently studied at Girton College, Cambridge, though without taking a degree. During her three years in England, Sarojini spent much of her time moving in literary circles. Edmund Gosse, a promoter of Toru Dutt's poetry, and his family befriended her. She also became close friends with Arthur Symons, the Decadent poet and critic, which led her into the same orbit as the Rhymer's Club, a group including W. B. Yeats, Ernest Rhys, and Lionel Johnson, as well as Symons. In a fictional autobiography, written while she was on a European trip about this time, Sarojini described her alter ego, Sunalini, this way: "Unlike the girls of her own nation, she had been brought up in an atmosphere of large unconvention and culture and absolute freedom of thought and action; her education had been based, chiefly on European models, and yet she was totally unlike any European girl: she was not a type. She was a personality" ("Sunalini," 9). Sarojini's letters to Symons testify to the accuracy of this portrait, for she was both brilliant and in many ways unconventional. Symons published one of her poems, "Indian Dancers," in his short-lived but influential magazine, *The Savoy*.

In 1898 Sarojini returned to India following a difficult but passionate epistolary courtship with the man her father had sent her to England to forget, Govindarajulu Naidu. Possibly playing a part in her decision was the fact that Edmund Gosse advised her to write on Indian subjects rather than following too closely the conventions of fin-de-siècle poetics. Sarojini married Naidu in 1898, under the provisions of Act III of 1872 that allowed civil marriages. Their wedding was, in its time, quite outside the usual norms because it crossed the cultural borders of caste and language. Sarojini had four children in rapid succession between 1901 and 1904. In 1905, Symons persuaded her to bring out a book of poetry. As a result, *The Golden Threshold* was published in London to positive reviews, followed in the next decade by two other collections, *The Bird of Time: Songs of Life, Death and the Spring* and *The Broken Wing: Songs of Love, Death and Destiny, 1915–1916*.

Makarand Paranjape's editions of letters and of selected poetry and prose provide a full sense of Sarojini's achievement in multiple spheres; Paranjape argues that Sarojini's accomplishments as a political orator exceed the importance of her verse. Indeed, from about 1914 until her death in 1949, two years after independence, Sarojini Naidu was known for her political activism and for her oratorical skills, including the recitation of poems. Her political mentor, Gopal Krishna Gokhale, had urged her to engage in nationalist activity, and subsequently she became close friends with Gandhi and Nehru. She became a leader in the Indian National Congress, eventually becoming the first Indian woman to serve as its president. She worked at the same time for the rights of women and lower-caste men. As a native of Hyderabad with many Muslim friends, as a poet fluent in Urdu, and as a student of Persian, she was always a strong supporter of Hindu-Muslim accord. She counted M. A. Jinnah, leader of the Muslim League, among her friends. Her activities on behalf of Indian independence led to more than one arrest, but she persisted. Naidu accompanied Gandhi on the Salt March and, as a national leader, joined the round-table conference in London in 1931. After independence, she became governor of the United Provinces, dying in office two years later.

Naidu's poems can be read in the context of late English romanticism but also in the context of Indian nationalism. She organized her poems, especially those collected in *The Broken Wing*, on an implicit principle of communal harmony, making a place for all of India's religions within its ambit. While her lasting reputation rests on her political activity, her poetry reveals a passionate and fiercely independent mind.

Sources

Sarojini Naidu, *The Golden Threshold* (London: William Heinemann; New York: John Lane, 1905); Naidu, *The Bird of Time: Songs of Life, Death and the Spring* (London: William Heinemann; New York: John Lane, 1912); and Naidu, *The Broken Wing: Songs of Love, Death and Destiny, 1915–1916* (London: William Heinemann; New York: John Lane, 1917). See also Naidu, *Selected Letters*, ed. Makarand Paranjape (New Delhi: Kali for Women, 1996); Naidu, *Selected Poetry and Prose*, ed. Makarand Paranjape (New Delhi: Indus, 1993); and Naidu, "Sunalini," ms. EUR.A.95, British Library.

Humayun to Zobeida

(From the Urdu)

You flaunt your beauty in the rose, your glory in the dawn,
Your sweetness in the nightingale, your whiteness in the swan.

You haunt my waking like a dream, my slumber like a moon,
Pervade me like a musky scent, possess me like a tune.

Yet, when I crave of you, my sweet, one tender moment's grace,   5
You cry, *"I sit behind the veil, I cannot show my face."*

Shall any foolish veil divide my longing from my bliss?
Shall any fragile curtain hide your beauty from my kiss?

What war is this of *Thee* and Me? Give o'er the wanton strife,
You are the heart within my heart, the life within my life.   10

Indian Dancers

Eyes ravished with rapture, celestially panting,
    what passionate bosoms aflaming with
    fire[1]

Drink deep of the hush of the hyacinth
    heavens that glimmer around them in   5
    fountains of light;
O wild and entrancing the strain of keen music
    that cleaveth the stars like a wail of
    desire,
And beautiful dancers with houri-like faces   10
    bewitch the voluptuous watches of
    night.

The scents of red roses and sandalwood flutter
    and die in the maze of their gem-tangled
    hair,   15
And smiles are entwining like magical ser-
    pents the poppies of lips that are opiate
    sweet;
Their glittering garments of purple are burn-
    ing like tremulous dawns in the quiver-   20
    ing air,
And exquisite, subtle and slow are the tinkle
    and tread of their rhythmical, slumber-
    soft feet.

Now silent, now singing and swaying and swing-   25
    ing, like blossoms that bend to the
    breezes or showers,

---

1. The text here follows the lineation in *The Golden Threshold*, which appears to have been designed
to mimic the motions of dancers and to create a patterned appearance on the page as each wrapped
line was justified, creating an intricate rhythm to the reading.

Now wantonly winding, they flash, now they
        falter, and, lingering, languish in radiant
        choir;   30
Their jewel-girt arms and warm, wavering, lily-
        long fingers enchant through melodious
        hours,
Eyes ravished with rapture, celestially pant-
        ing, what passionate bosoms aflaming   35
        with fire!

Awake!

To Mohamed Ali Jinnah

Waken, O mother! thy children implore thee,[2]
Who kneel in thy presence to serve and adore thee!
The night is aflush with a dream of the morrow,
Why still dost thou sleep in thy bondage of sorrow?
Awaken and sever the woes that enthrall us,   5
And hallow our hands for the triumphs that call us!

Are we not thine, O Belov'd, to inherit
The manifold pride and power of thy spirit?
Ne'er shall we fail thee, forsake thee or falter,
Whose hearts are thy home and thy shield and thine altar.   10
Lo! we would thrill the high stars with thy story,
And set thee again in the forefront of glory.

Hindus: Mother! the flowers of our worship have crowned thee!

Parsees: Mother! the flame of our hope shall surround thee!

Mussulmans: Mother! the sword of our love shall defend thee!   15

Christians: Mother! the song of our faith shall attend thee!

All Creeds: Shall not our dauntless devotion avail thee?
                  Hearken! O queen and O goddess, we hail thee!

---

2. Recited at the Indian National Congress, 1915. [SN]
Naidu attached the note number to the title.

The Royal Tombs of Golconda

I muse among these silent fanes[3]
Whose spacious darkness guards your dust;
Around me sleep the hoary plains
That hold your ancient wars in trust.
I pause, my dreaming spirit hears,   5
Across the wind's unquiet tides,
The glimmering music of your spears,
The laughter of your royal brides.

In vain, O Kings, doth time aspire
To make your names oblivion's sport,   10
While yonder hill wears like a tiar[4]
The ruined grandeur of your fort.

Though centuries falter and decline,
Your proven strongholds shall remain
Embodied memories of your line,   15
Incarnate legends of your reign.

O Queens, in vain old Fate decreed
Your flower-like bodies to the tomb;
Death is in truth the vital seed
Of your imperishable bloom   20
Each new-born year the bulbuls sing
Their songs of your renascent loves;
Your beauty wakens with the spring
To kindle these pomegranate groves.

3. Golconda is a ruined fort, once the capital of the Qutb Shahi kingdom, located a few miles west of Hyderabad (now in Andra Pradesh). In the sixteenth and seventeenth centuries, the kingdom was famous for its wealth, particularly its diamonds. Golconda was conquered by the Mughal emperor Aurengzeb in 1687. The fort at Golconda in the hills west of Hyderabad has remained a popular destination for tourists; its ruins became a frequent subject for poets. Naidu's two poems on Golconda reflect her growing politicization; this first poem, "The Royal Tombs" (published in 1905), celebrates the ancient glory of Sarojini's birthplace but does not evoke an explicitly political reading. "At Twilight," published seven years later, in contrast touches both personal and political notes.

4. Tiar: tiara or crown.

from *"The Temple"*

The Offering

Were beauty mine, Beloved, I would bring it[5]
Like a rare blossom to Love's glowing shrine;
Were dear youth mine, Beloved, I would fling it
Like a rich pearl into Love's lustrous wine.

Were greatness mine, Beloved, I would offer   5
Such radiant gifts of glory and of fame,
Like camphor and like curds to pour and proffer
Before Love's bright and sacrificial flame.

But I have naught save my heart's deathless passion
That craves no recompense divinely sweet,   10
Content to wait in proud and lowly fashion,
And kiss the shadow of Love's passing feet.

The Menace of Love

How long, O Love, shall ruthless pride avail you[6]
Or wisdom shield you with her gracious wing,
When the sharp winds of memory shall assail you
In all the poignant malice of the spring?

All the sealed anguish of my blood shall taunt you   5
In the rich menace of red-flowering trees;
The yearning sorrow of my voice shall haunt you
In the low wailing of the midnight seas.

The tumult of your own wild heart shall smite you
With strong and sleepless pinions of desire,   10
The subtle hunger in your veins shall bite you
With swift and unrelenting fangs of fire.

---

5. This is the initial poem of Naidu's long sequence, "The Temple," which is subdivided into three parts: "The Gate of Delight," "The Path of Tears," and "The Sanctuary." The sequence traces the vicissitudes of a tempestuous love affair. This poem and the next slightly extend the temporal bounds of this anthology but are included to give a sense of the poet's most compelling work.

6. "The Menace of Love" appeared as the third poem of the second section, "The Path of Tears," of "The Temple."

When youth and spring and passion shall betray you
And mock your proud rebellion with defeat,
God knows, O Love, if I shall save or slay you   15
As you lie spent and broken at my feet!

At Twilight

On the way to Golconda

Weary, I sought kind Death among the rills[7]
That drink of purple twilight where the plain
Broods in the shadow of untroubled hills:
I cried, "High dreams and hope and love are vain,
Absolve my spirit of its poignant ills,   5
And cleanse me from the bondage of my pain!

"Shall hope prevail where clamorous hate is rife,
Shall sweet love prosper or high dreams find place
Amid the tumult of reverberant strife
'Twixt ancient creeds, 'twixt race and ancient race,   10
That mars the grave, glad purposes of life,
Leaving no refuge save thy succouring face?"

          ·   ·   ·   ·   ·

E'en as I spake, a mournful wind drew near,
Heavy with scent of drooping roses shed,
And incense scattered from the passing bier   15
Of some loved woman canopied in red,
Borne with slow chant and swift-remembering tear,
To the blind, ultimate silence of the dead

          ·   ·   ·   ·   ·

O lost, O quenched in unawakening sleep
The glory of her dear, reluctant eyes!   20
O hushed the eager feet that knew the steep
And intricate ways of ecstasy and sighs!
And dumb with alien slumber, dim and deep,
The living heart that was love's paradise!

          ·   ·   ·   ·   ·

---

7. "At Twilight" was published in *The Bird of Time* (1912) and alludes to the communal strife and
disagreements that marked the nationalist movement. The ellipses are the poet's own.

Quick with the sense of joys she hath foregone,   25
Returned my soul to beckoning joys that wait,
Laughter of children and the lyric dawn,
And love's delight, profound and passionate,
Winged dreams that blow their golden clarion,
And hope that conquers immemorial hate.   30

Comic and Satiric Poets of the Long Nineteenth Century

Quiz

Referring to *The Grand Master; or, Adventures of Qui Hi in Hindostan: A Hudibrastic Poem in Eight Cantos by Quiz*, the 1862 printing of the *Bookseller's Catalogue* declares, "The intention of this work was to hold up to opprobrium the Marquis of Hastings, who was Governor-General of India, and also Commander-in-Chief, from Oct. 1813 to Jan. 1823. It was probably written by W.H. Ireland." The author is now more widely believed to have been William Combe, a British satirical poet (1741–June 19, 1823). This attribution may also be flawed, for Combe appears to have never lived in India, and the poem attributed to him has a fluent command of Indian argot. Combe, however, did work in partnership with Thomas Rowlandson, a British caricaturist, on most of his books, and Rowlandson was clearly responsible for the highly amusing illustrations that accompanied *The Grand Master. Qui hi,* translated as "Is anybody there?" was the common term for servant and was used by Indians to mockingly refer to the British.

Sources

[William Combe.] *The Grand Master; or, Adventures of Qui Hi in Hindostan: A Hudibrastic Poem in Eight Cantos by Quiz* (London: Thomas Tegg, 1816). See also Willis and Sotheran, *A Catalogue of Upwards of Fifty Thousand Volumes of Ancient and Modern Books: English and Foreign, in All Classes of Literature and the Fine Arts Including Rare and Curious Books* (London: Willis and Sotheran, 1862).

from *The Grand Master*

Now, with ambitious hopes elated,
Our youth has been initiated
To all *his honors,* in a word,
Assumes the gorget, sash and sword,
Whether adorn'd with cat[1] or lion,   5
Or *plain* G.R. we can't rely on;
Our information only goes
To shew the *colour* of his cloths;
'Twas *red,* of course, this information,
Convinces you he serv'd *the nation,*   10
Whether a company or king,
The muse will not pretend to sing:
The reader may, if he's inclin'd,
Make him serve *which* he has a mind,
And he's at liberty to *guess,*   15
Of what description was his dress;
'Tis certain that his *facings* bore
The designation of his corps;
But whether black, or *white* or blue,
Is nothing now to me or you;   20
Or whether a mistake[2] he made
By accident, and *for them* paid;
For sometimes it may be aver'd,
That *subs* pay *only* with their word.
(If an apology's of use)   25
Necessity has some excuse,
For sad experience often shews
That poverty can truth oppose,
And subalterns, like others, find
Justice is rightly painted *blind.*   30
Dame fortune frequently bestows
On vice her wealth, on merit blows;
For, after many "a hair bread'th scape,"
Troubles and wants in evr'y shape,

---

1. A well-*known crest;* but so miserably executed by the Indian artists, that it bears *more* resemblance to a *rampant cat,* than a rampant lion; which gives a subject for ridicule to some *wags* in the King's service. [Quiz]

2. *Quiz* says mistake here. He repeats it; because he is perfectly aware that the most honourable young men in the army of India are placed under such pecuniary embarrassments, that they are *obliged to promise,* without the hope of performing that promise. [Quiz]

Here and in other notes, Quiz speaks in the editorial third person.

He sees, with an indignant frown,   35
His *airy* castles tumbling down;
All his fair claims are soon forgot—
Mendacity must be his lot:
He scorns to act an *abject* part,
And droops beneath a broken heart.   40
Too well the Indian *subs.* can *feel*
The truth of what I here reveal;
How often, with a doleful face,
They pay for breakfast with their *lace:*[3]
They find the *tenure* of a sword,   45
Can scarcely bread and cheese afford,
While, *'tis a fact,* tho' strange to tell,
Riches attend the paltry quill.[4]
Civilian luxury attends
The powerful interest of friends,   50
While *merit's* claim is scarcely heard,
Neglect its whole and sole reward:
But now the chearful smile of peace,
Has lighten'd every Briton's face;
Now that John Bull with beef and beer,   55
Treats as a friend poor old *Monsieur,*
Nor casts a surly look from Dover,
Defying Monsieur to come over,
But lands him from the very boat,
Where he had vow'd to cut his throat;   60
With *Boney's* fate John's anger ends,
And *Boney's* foes and now his friends.
Russians and Prussians, Swedes, and Poles,
Among his friends he now enrolls,
And Giles, with open mouth and hat off,   65
Takes every one for Marshal Platoff;
And this John Bull at once forgets,

---

3. The Indian army is magnificently dressed; indeed, rather too much so, for the scanty pay of an ensign—130 rupees a month. Some of those young gentlemen, from the loads of lace with which their jackets are covered, appear, at a distance, not unlike a *sideboard* of plate: they, consequently, very often have more silver on their jackets than in their pockets; and an old jacket is a *valuable* commodity. [Quiz]

Here and in the preceding lines, Quiz laments the plight of ensigns or subs. (subalterns).

4. Pro bono publico.—I shall just observe, that ensigns have remained for seven years on their paltry allowance; while a young gentleman, who comes out a writer, or kind of clerk, has been almost immediately put in a situation of no trouble, and in the possession of an allowance of one thousand or two thousand rupees a month!!! The latter description of people generally return to England with a fortune. [Quiz]

Twenty years taxes, war, and debts.
Now with the bravery in view
Of Briton's sons at Waterloo,   70
Surely the public are inclin'd,[5]
To bear our Indian troops in mind,
And pay some mark of approbation,
To soldiers on a foreign station;
If then a compliment they'll pay,   75
The muse will shew the proper way;—
Send out fair Justice to Bengal,—
If she be found at Leadenhall;
Or with her we might chance to grapple,
Somewhere about *St. Stephen's* chapel;   80
Let her prepare her *"cut and thrust"*[6]
Take out the gaps, wipe off the rust,
Then if she likes, without a doubt,
Some noxious animals she'll rout:
Let her prepare her weights and scales,   85
(Her balance *very often* fails;)
And thus equip'd, I here aver,
The *Hindoos* tribe would worship her:
Her voyage over you would ask,
"What then would be the lady's task?"   90
And thus I simply answer you—
"Let her give ev'ry man his due."
Let her expose the asses' ears,
Of all the group—Judges or Peers;
Let her, in just consideration,   95
Alter the people's situation;
Let her examine, and she'll find,
That certain people are inclin'd
To give rewards where *none*[7] are due,
Unto a servile, stupid crew.   100

---

5. *Quiz* thinks he has asked very little for the army, by noticing the very great distinction between the civil and military servants of the Company; and he trusts his request may be granted, to have the officers' allowances, particularly the junior part, a little better arranged. [Quiz]

6. All my readers know what a cut-and-thrust sword is. *Justice* is said to carry one. Whether it is of this description, or the King's order, I cannot say; but either will answer the purpose,—He thinks the idea as requisite as it is original, of polishing the sword, and taking out the *gaps*. [Quiz]

7. Every one knows about the annual distribution of gold medals, and *thousands* of rupees, at Calcutta *college!!!* while the distributor, and, of course, *judge*, cannot understand a syllable that is *said*; but concludes, that the youth who *talks most* is most learned. [Quiz]

Sir Charles D'Oyly

Charles D'Oyly (1781–1845) was a civil servant, a painter, and an amateur poet. He held posts in Dhaka, in Patna, and finally as a senior member of the East India Company's Board of Customs, Salt, and Opium. After his retirement in 1838, he lived the remainder of his life in Italy. He became a baronet on the death of his father. His paintings and sketches of Dhaka and of Indian characters and landscapes were much reproduced, as was his one long comic poem, *Tom Raw the Griffin*. D'Oyly's conceit, the misadventures of a young man new to India—a "griffin," in company slang—was not new. Both *The Grand Master; or, Adventures of Qui Hi* and James Atkinson's "City of Palaces" employ the same conceit. But the poem achieved considerable popularity and remained continuously in print in India throughout most of the nineteenth century.

Source

Charles D'Oyly, *Tom Raw, the Griffin: A Burlesque Poem in Twelve Cantos, Illustrated by Twenty-five Engravings, Descriptive of the Adventures of a Cadet in the East India Company's Service* (London: R. Ackermann, 1828).

from *Tom Raw, the Griffin, Canto I*

I.

When poets write, they usually invoke
Apollo or the Muses to their aid,
Making a cruel rumpus to provoke
The deities, as patrons of their trade:
We hear their calls—but not the answers made;   5
We read of frenzied eyes, from earth to heaven
Most frantically rolling, see the head
Thumped for ideas sublime, from morn to even,
And minds with intellectual labours heaving.

II.

Whether a mode so generally followed   10
Is of much use, we can't pretend to say;
Or, whether strains be—Clio'd or Apollo'd,
More glibly run, than when self-tuned they stray,
Is problematical;—but, as our lay
Will do quite well, we question not, without 'em,   15
We'll not contend for one celestial ray
To gild our visions (having cause to doubt 'em),
But soberly proceed, not caring aught about 'em.

III.

Th' adventures of a Griffin bid our lyre
Awaken all its powers; but then some readers   20
A sort of explanation may require
Of what a Griffin is—or they'll not heed us,
In this our great essay; which doubtings lead us
(Shielding ourselves from hypercritic claws,)
To tell the honest truth, which this indeed is,—   25
The Griffin which our lofty poem draws
Is—not chimerical, but—man with all his flaws.

IV.

Our Griffin is an inexperienced youth,
A raw, bewildered boy, who seeks his fortune
In Asiatic climes, unfledged, in truth,   30
But told the fickle goddess to importune,
Lacking the means at home:—One of a boon
She showered on his parents, in the shape
Of an o'erbrimming family, whose spoon
Is not half large enough for mouths that gape   35
With hunger unrequited, northward of the Cape.

V.

The colonies and foreign governments
Are famous drains for pride and poverty;
For gentlemen deficient in their rents,
Always on India turn a longing eye.   40
They talk in England of a precious tree,
That, but to shake, brings down its fruit,—(pagodas)
And fancy every one's rapacity
May be indulged, with just as great a load as
Would satisfy Pindarries—(those well-known marauders).   45

VI.

Of money-making, in the glorious East,
Such and a thousand other odd conceits,
(By rich returning Nabobs sore increased),
Fill the parental mind with feverish heats:
Golconda's mine the golden dream completes,   50
With all the sparkling gems of Samarcand,
Letters are written—double, treble sheets.
To various sharers of the eastern fund.
Alias—proprietors of India stock in Lond':

VII.

'On, we'd have added, but 'twould spoil the metre,   55
And we've no leisure to consult the rhyming
Dictionary, to make the sense completer;
Besides, abbreviations there's no crime in,
When fancy might supply the "on" to chime in:
But to return—and even the Directors,   60
Whether they're out of court, or—at the time—in,
Are sorely harassed by these place expectors,
And, turning a deaf ear, must turn rejectors.

VIII.

If writerships are got, they're thought a prize
Equal to twenty thousand pounds at Bish's,   65
Cadetships, now, as times are sorry, rise
In value, satisfying mod'rate wishes;
Assistant surgeonships the Scotchman fishes
Successfully enough, too—fra' the North;
And, as the court's supplied with various dishes,   70
From turtle-soup, to oatcakes and sheep's broth,
Of hungry applicants they have their money's worth.[1]

IX.

Tis time, however, now, to introduce
The hero of our tale;—his nomenclature
Has puzzled us extremely, but we choose   75
Tom Raw, as applicable to his nature.
Some critics may object, but we so hate your
Romantic designations, that we rest
Contented with our choice.—In face and stature
He was not an Apollo—nor the best-   80
Looking young man I've seen, transported from the West:

X.

But well enough—a round, unmeaning face,
Snub nose, and dumpy form, complexion ruddy,
Limbs quite devoid of elegance and grace,
And then his small gray eyes were something muddy: 85
But, notwithstanding this, the little blood, he
Had germs intuitive of foppishness.
Had he but found the means its points to study:
Books and arithmetic caused him distress,
Orthography and writing, not a jot the less.   90

---

1. The poet alludes to the directors of the East India Company, who at this time still had pa-
tronage appointments to what became the Civil Service (writerships) and to the Indian Army (ca-
detships) and the medical corps (whose doctors were often trained at the superior medical schools
in Scotland—hence dining on oatcakes).

XI.

Who knows not Welch and Stalker's magazine
To fit out boys, on India's voyage going,
Where every thing is furnished them, we ween,
Without a thought on what they want bestowing?
Here Tom was introduced, and they're so knowing,   95
That, at a glance, his youthful form they fit,
(With every due allowance for his growing).
And, as he's military, add a spit,
A regulation sword,—of his trade, emblem fit.

XII.

In short, there nought was left him to desire,   100
From coarse check shirts and trowsers, while at sea.
To landing suits, which gentlemen require
To visit Governors, or C. in C.
And, thus equipped, there was no more to be
Arranged, but cramming him and all his luggage   105
On board a small free trader instantly,
Where, when arrived, he popped into a snug cage
Of only six by four—but not without much tuggage.

Pips

The anonymous volume *Lyrics and Lays* by Pips has been attributed to William Henry Abbott Jr. by Samuel Halkett and John Laing in their *Dictionary of Anonymous and Pseudonymous Publications in the English Language* but has also been attributed to Frederick F. Wyman. It was first published in Calcutta in 1867 by Wyman Brothers.

Source

Pips [William Henry Abbott, Jr.? or Frederick F. Wyman?]. *Lyrics and Lays* (Calcutta: Wyman Brothers, 1867).

The Chee-Chee Ball

The Chee-Chees held high festival in old Domingo's Hall,[1]
And I was there, tho' I was not invited to the ball;
But they received me kindly, all owing, as I trust
To my appearance proving me one of the "upper crust"

And merrily I passed the time, although 'twas somewhat slow—   5
I danced like mad each polka, with lots of heel and toe:
For Chee-Chees think that polkas are very like Scotch reels,
And that to dance them properly you must kick up your heels.

And there was one, a petite belle, a modest little girl.
Her hair was twisted down her cheeks in many a spiral curl;   10
Her teeth were polish'd ivory, her eyes were very bright,
And the little thing look'd blacker from being dress'd in white.

And ever as I saw this girl I mark'd a little man
Whom lovingly she ogled behind her pretty fan:
They always danced together, or, as far as I could see,   15
When they couldn't dance together they stood up vis-à-vis.

'Twas clear they were affianced, that very happy pair.
They seem'd to think themselves to be the only couple there;
And so they whiled away the time till dinner was announced—
Oh! how quickly at that word all through the doorway bounced.   20

Alas! for some poor hungry ones the supper-room was small,
And the company was numerous, it couldn't hold them all;
So while the few and lucky ones were eating stews and grills
The others kept their hunger down with polkas and quadrilles.

---

1. "Chee-Chee ball": chaperoned parties hosted by the directors of the Female Orphan Asylum in Calcutta, at which girls of mixed ethnicity were presented to prospective suitors. *Hobson-Jobson* defines "Chee-Chee" thus: "A disparaging term applied to half-castes or Eurasians (q.v.) (corresponding to the Lip-lap of the Dutch in Java) and also to their manner of speech. The word is said to be taken from chī (Fie!), a common native (S. Indian) interjection of remonstrance or reproof, supposed to be much used by the class in question. The term is, however, perhaps also a kind of onomatopœia, indicating the mincing pronunciation which often characterises them (see below). It should, however, be added that there are many well-educated East Indians who are quite free from this mincing accent."

Now while the supper disappear'd, I sought for fresher air.   25
My nose 'mid Kentish hop-grounds rear'd is not the nose to bear
The scent of oil of cocoanut with that of bad perfume
And the odour of hot dishes in a densely crowded room.

And while I stroll'd alone outside I started at the sound
Of whispering voices near me—I turn'd and gazed around;   30
Yes, there they were, that happy pair, their steps they slowly traced.
Her arm was on his shoulder, and his was round her waist;

And, wandering by thus lovingly, their words fell on my ear,—
For he had slightly raised his voice, not thinking I was near.
And the very moon looked clearer, and brighter shone each star,—   35
As the little man imploringly said "Betsy, bolo hah!"[2]

I turn'd and quickly left the spot, I did not like to stay.
To be, as I must else have been, in those two lovers' way;
(To spoil such sport has ever been from my intention far)
And as I walked away I heard her gently murmur "Hah."   40

The dance was o'er; before I left, I found myself once more
Close to that happy Chee-Chee pair outside Domingo's door;
What pass'd between them I can't say, but those who wish to know
May judge from what I heard, which was "Our ekto kissee do."

---

2. Bolo: literally, "speak." By implication here, the suitor means, "Whisper sweet nothings in
my ear."

A. D. C.

Best Man and Chief-Mourner
"Last season the female European attendant
of a certain noble lady, but just out from
England, became the wife of a confidential
clerk in a Government Office here; she was
much respected by her mistress, who was
herself in the Church the day she was mar-
ried, and generously presented her with
handsome presents; at the request of her
mistress, she was honored by being given
away by the principal A. D. C. This year an
equal degree of kindly feeling had been
manifested towards the lady's maid; in less
than ten months she became a bride, a
mother and a corpse. The A. D. C. again
attended to do honor, but this time it was at
the funeral."

—*Englishman's letter from Simla, 8th July.*

Après Hemans

In the snowy Himalayas
    Voices were heard in prayer,
'Twas a happy marriage rite.
And every eye was bright,
    And an A. D. C. was there![3]   5

For a "noble Lady's" maid,
    Far from her native land,
To a "confidential clerk"
    Was giving heart and hand.

And the "noble lady" vow'd   10
    That the rite should honor'd be
By the presence of herself
    And a lordly A. D. C.!!

In the snowy Himalayas
    Voices were raised in prayer.   15

---

3. A.D.C.: aide-de-camp, an important post usually as right-hand man to a high government
official. Pip mocks the British tendency to venerate rank.

And 'twas a glorious sight
That happy marriage rite
  For an A. D. C. was there!!

But a year had not pass'd o'er
  The head of that young bride   20
Ere she became a mother,
  Then sicken'd, pined, and died.

The "noble lady" grieved for
  Her sad untimely end,
And to the lowly burial   25
  Her A. D. C. did send!!

In the snowy Himalayas
  Voices were heard in prayer,
'Twas a solemn funeral rite,
But a most imposing sight   30
  For an A. D. C. was there!!

Then let her calmly rest
  Where the snow-clad pine-trees wave,
For a lordly A. D. C.
  Attended at her grave!   35

When A. D. C.s thus follow
  The lowly to their rest
Oh! 'twould be wickedness to doubt
  The burial must be blessed.

Then, husband, do not mourn her,   40
  That young and loving wife,
For surely she was honor'd
  In death as when in life.

In the snowy Himalayas
  Voices were heard in prayer,   45
'Twas a solemn funeral rite
But a most imposing sight
  For an A. D. C. was there!!

Aliph Cheem [Walter Yeldham]

Walter Yeldham (b. 1837) served in India in the 18th Royal Hussars. He was also the author of *Basil Ormond and Christabel's Love* (London, Calcutta, and Bombay: Thacker, 1878), comprising two serious domestic narratives set in Britain. His *Lays of Ind,* satiric and humorous verse on Indian subjects, was printed in numerous nineteenth-century editions and is still popular.

Source

Walter Yeldham, *Lays of Ind* (Bombay: Thacker, Spink and Co., 1883).

The Sensitive Fakeer

On the bank of a river in Hindostan—
    The "Bagh-o-Bahar" relates—
Lived a very hairy and holy man,
    Who cured the sick at his gates.
He would shut himself up for the space of a year,   5
    And study the state of his soul,
And only on Sheevrat[1] days would appear
    And make the sufferers whole.
Then at dawn he would plunge in the river, and swim
    Like a fish with sportive mind,   10
While the fishes would wonder much at him,
    With his long hair streaming behind.
When of this diversion he'd had enough,
    To a shallow part he came,
And smeared some ashes and oily stuff   15
    All over his skinny frame.
Then full in the reverend gaze of all
    Who were huddling there for the cure,
He made what we will his toilet call—
    It was rather light, to be sure.   20
On a shoulder he laid a towel spare—
    It was all the linen he'd got—
Next shook the wet from his matted hair,

---

1. Sheevrat: Shivaratri, religious festival celebrating the dance in which Shiva destroys the universe; it also marks the god's marriage to Pārvāti. The fakir those who seek his aid on this and other Shaivite holy days.

And twisted it up in a knot.
Then stood on the steps, and cleansed his feet 25
    From the river's clinging ooze.
Then twiddled and made his whiskers neat,
    And shuffled into his shoes.
Some spots, of the size of fourpenny coins,
    On his forehead he made with clay; 30
Then fastened a string about his loins—
    And, lo! he was dressed for the day.
In another minute or so his prayers,
    With mysterious signs, were done;
And then he slowly ascended the stairs, 35
    And the doctoring begun.
He took from his nose a jewelled pen,
    And wrote a prescription clear,
For every one of the women and men
    And children pressing near. 40
Now, on one occasion a patient came
    With something wrong in his head.
The Fakeer's eyes burst into a flame.
    "'Tis a Kunkhujoora!" he said.
"A worm that preys on the human brain— 45
    Cerebral maggot, no doubt.
The horrible thing is there, 'tis plain.
    Young man, we must cut him out!"
So he took the youth, and his friend as well,
    While the rest remained spell-bound, 50
To his operating-chamber, a cell
    In a rock, deep underground.
Then he seized an instrument, sharply steeled,
    With a semicircular shank,
And a pivot, such as carpenters wield 55
    In boring a hole in a plank.
And he bored away at the patient's head,
    Till he drilled right into the brain.
"Behold the Kunkhujoora!" he said.
    "He never will vex you again!" 60
Then he grasped his pincers to pull it out;
    But the friend in amazement cried,
"O holy Fakeer, what are you about?
    You'll be drawing the brain beside!
The animal lies on the topmost fold, 65
    Curled up, and sticking like glue;

And if you pull him, he'll only hold
    The tighter, and drag it too.
Just heat the pincers a minute or so,
    And apply to the creature's back;   70
No injury then to the brain you'll do,
    And the worm will out in a crack."
The holy one pitched away pincers and shoes,
    And hurried forth into the air,
And, twining his long locks into a noose,   75
    Straight hanged himself in his hair.
Of the fate of the youth, by the "Bagh-o-Bahar"
    No information's supplied;
But perhaps it would hardly be going too far
    To conclude that "the beggar died."   80
The story's a story, and that is all,
    But a truth is underlaid:
Woe to the wretched people who call
    A native quack to their aid!
And pity it is that all the clan,   85
    Whom their countrymen well can spare,
Don't follow the line of this sensitive man,
    And hang themselves in their hair!

Cardozo the Half-Caste

Emanuel Cardozo kept a beer store in Madras;
He sold it casked and bottled, and he sold it by the glass;
He also sold tinned sausages, and hams, and marmalade;
Moreover turned an honest penny in the blacking trade.

In course of time he gave to his transactions wider scope,—   5
He dealt in hair-pins, calico, in crockery and soap,
In boots and shoes, in hats and gloves, in walking-sticks, and socks,
And, later on, he blossomed into chandeliers and clocks.

His shop, in fact, in Blacktown soon the leading shop became,
You'd hardly fail to purchase there a thing that you could name.   10
To it, alike to buy or lounge, the world Madrassee went,
And sleek Cardozo bowed and smiled, and made his cent, per cent.

And straightway he invested in a big barouche and pair,
And in the "People's Park" at even ate the dusty air.
He was a sight to see, as with his sisters three he sat;   15
And oh, his native coachman! oh, the breeches, boots, and hat!

'Tis time, perhaps, I should essay to give a sketch of him.
Black eyes and hair, white gleaming teeth, black whiskers curled and trim,
A cunning smile, a shiny tile, a frock coat tight and spruce,
And hue of cheeks like blood contending hard with walnut juice.   20

His sisters three were decked in silks most gorgeous to behold:
The blaze of colour almost made you blink, as by they rolled.
Great lustrous eyes, and shadowy brows, black crimpy piles of hair.
Complexions—well, you scarce could tell for powder, I declare.

Three times the gaudy equipage would circle round the band,   25
Then, where the crush was thickest, would draw up and take its stand;
While on the cushioned seat Cardozo'd loll and look about,
And think, "You English lady swells, some day I'll pay you out!

"You buy my goods, you paupers proud, and when I send my bill,
You call it impudence, and say you'll settle when you will;   30
You bate my price and beat me down, and, now you're cantering past,
You turn your heads away, and say, 'Cardozo, the Half-Caste.'

"Half-caste, indeed! I've blood in me that you'd be glad to own.
Cardozo's deeds in Seville are of course to you unknown.
The sunny South has giv'n an olive tinge to all my race.   35
You think all men are half-caste who have olive in the face.

"You scorn the colour of my cheeks, but, if I'm rightly told,
You'd not object so strongly to the colour of my gold.
I see around me even here what the rupee can do,
And one of these fine days, my dears, I'll marry one of you!"   40

Time passed. Cardozo richer grew, and one succeeding May
He took a passage, first-class, P. and O.,[2] and sailed away.
He kissed his sisters, saying he'd be quickly back again.
Somehow he didn't book himself for any port in *Spain!*

---

2. P. and O.: Peninsular and Oriental Steam Navigation Company.

He booked him for Southampton. I suppose he didn't care   45
For his grand Seville connections, with their stiff patrician air.
One's kin are often chilly, when one's been an exile long.
He thought h'd like a spree in London, and its giddy throng.

He *had* a spree in London. *"De"* Cardozo sounded fair;
And gold will buy a deal within a mile of Leicester Square.   50
He did the theatres, music halls, the Crystal Palace—oh!
At sight of the Alhambra[3] how his Spanish blood would glow!

He also did the Park, and,—yes, why should I blush to say?
To drawing-rooms in Eaton Square he managed an *entree.*
A *"De"* 's a *"De,"* and gold is gold, and his he freely spent,   55
And people didn't ask him for the proofs of his descent.

His "type" was so "Castilian," and his manners were "so nice."
His olive hue was "charming"; no one thought of liquorice;
His accent was "so taking," and his singing was "so sweet,"
To hear him talk of Anglo-Indians really was a treat!   60

One lovely widow nearly fell a victim to his wiles,
His Spanish blood, his gleaming teeth, his presents, and his smiles;
He actually meant to pop the question, when, alas!
She said she had a brother in a regiment at *Madras!*

That lady, I need hardly say, was left a widow still.   65
Next day he summoned up "mine host," and paid his little bill,
And, thinking it were prudent to levant to pastures new,
He went to Southsea, there to try what Spanish blood would do.

Extremely well it did indeed in that amphibious town—
The "merchant prince from India" decidedly went down: 70
At yachting parties, picnics, at the Rink, upon the pier,
To see the ladies smile at him was exquisitely queer.

It chanced a country parson—Smith—was lodging in the place,
And Smith a daughter Fanny had, with a seraphic face.
Cardozo met her picnicing, and Cupid's little dart   75
Forthwith made deadly practice at Cardozo's Spanish heart.

---

3. The Alhambra proper is the famed Moorish palace in Granada, but here the name indicates
a music hall.